The Kiss of Death

The Kiss of Death

Chagas' Disease in the Americas

Joseph William Bastien

THE UNIVERSITY OF UTAH PRESS

SALT LAKE CITY

LIBRARY OF CONGRESS CATALOGING-IN-PUBLICATION DATA

Bastien, Joseph William, 1935–
    The kiss of death : Chagas' disease in the Americas / Joseph
William Bastien.
    p.   cm.
    Includes bibliographical references and index.
    ISBN 0-87480-559-7 (alk. paper)
        1. Chagas' disease—Bolivia—Epidemiology.   2. Chagas'
disease—Latin America—Epidemiology.   3. Chagas' disease—Social aspects—Bolivia.   4. Chagas' disease—Social
aspects—Latin America.   5. Chagas' disease—Bolivia—
Prevention.   6. Chagas' disease—Latin America—Prevention.   7. Housing and health—Bolivia.   8. Housing and
health—Latin America.   9. Public health surveillance—
Bolivia.   10. Public health surveillance—Latin America.
I. Title.
RA644.C26B37   1998
614.5'33—dc21   98-18279

For my father

WILLIAM JOSEPH BASTIEN
1887–1964

who spent the twilight of his life
crippled in bed with a chronic disease
that is now curable.

He and those with Chagas' disease
are the inspiration of this book.

Contents

Acknowledgments

I am deeply indebted to the following people and institutions. George Stewart of the University of Texas at Arlington taught me epidemiology, parasitology, and immunology. He contributed greatly to this book. Dorothy Ahlstrom, Linda Gregg, Lori Lee, Kathy Rowe, Jane Nicol, Brad Watson, and Sharon Young helped in the preparation of this manuscript. Librarians John Dillard and Trudy de Goede of the University of Texas at Arlington, Karen Harken of the University of Texas Southwestern Medical Center, and Regina Lee at the University of North Texas Health Science Center endlessly pursued articles and obscure references. The University of Texas at Arlington gave me sabbatical leave to prepare this manuscript and also provided funding through a research grant for summer research. The Wenner-Gren Fund also provided me with funding to do research in Bolivia. The Fulbright-Hayes Foundation provided me with support for three months in Bolivia as a scholar/researcher in residence.

Andy Arata and Robert J. Tonn of Vector Biology and Control Project in Arlington, Virginia, provided me with my first information about Chagas' disease when I assisted them in planning the Bolivian Chagas Control Project. Joel Kuritsky of the Centers for Disease Control in Atlanta, Georgia, invited me to Bolivia to study Chagas' disease and greatly assisted me. More than anyone, Kuritsky recognized the problem of Chagas' disease in Bolivia and coordinated experts to help prevent the spread of this disease. These experts included Stephen Ault, Ralph Bryan, Fanor Balderrama, Hernan Bermudez, Jesse Hobbs, Robert Klein, and Rodrigo Zeledón. These scientists also helped me with information about vector control.

I am especially grateful to Ruth Sensano, director of the Cardenal Maurer (CM) project in Sucre. Sensano shared with me the planning and design of her successful Chagas' control project in the Department of Chuquisaca. She also invited me to accompany Abraham Jemio Alarico and Ariel Sempertegui on an evaluation study of communities where Proyecto Britanico Cardenal Maurer (PBCM) had constructed houses. Alarico, an epidemiologist from the *Ministerio de Prevision Social y Salud Pública* (MPSSP), and Sempertegui, a health worker from the *Programa de Coordinación de Supervivencia Infantil Organizaciones Privadas Voluntarias* (PROCOSI), an organization of nongovernmental projects that receives money from USAID and contributes to PBCM, instructed me about *vinchucas,* Chagas' control, insecticides, and peasant behavior. Sempertegui also gave me a copy of his organization's evaluation study. Dr. Mario Torres assisted me with his vast clinical knowledge of chronic Chagas' colonopathy.

Fanor Balderrama and Hernan Bermúdez directed the Bolivian Secretariat of Health/Community and Child Health Project (SOH/CCH) Chagas' control projects in the Cochabamba Valley of Bolivia. They assisted me by providing literature and allowing me to visit the community of Aramasi. Simon Delgadillo and Feliciano Rodríguez, community leaders of Aramasi, assisted me in this evaluation. In the Department of Tarija, Dr. Roberto Márquez showed me the results of a Chagas' control project that he had directed under the Bolivian Secretariat of Health. Dr. Ciro Figaroa provided me with his research findings on the parasite and vector. Robert Tonn and Buzz McHenry allowed me to visit Las Lajas, where SOH/CCH was sponsoring a housing project.

The French/Bolivian Institute for High Altitude Biology (IBBA) conducts parasitological studies concerning Chagas' disease. I spent many days talking with them and am indebted to the following scientists for increasing my knowledge of *Trypanosoma cruzi* and *Triatoma infestans:* S.F. Breniere, C. Camacho, R. Carrasco, M. Tibayrenc, P. Braquemond, H. Miguez, L. Echalar, S. Revollo, T. Ampuero, and J.P. Dedet.

Dr. Gerardo Antezana, director of Chagas' Research Institute in Sucre, shared with me his research on chronic chagasic cardiopathology. Staff of the Gastroinstestinal Institute in Sucre also shared hospital records with me concerning cases of chronic esophageal and colon Chagas.

José Beltrán informed me about and allowed me to participate in the Tarija Chagas' control project. He also illustrated how education about Chagas' disease should be done. Community health workers Edwin Ayala and Lourdes Elizabeth Anyazgo instructed me about their work in Chagas' control. Ronald Gutiérrez informed me about the political economy of Chagas' control.

Jaime Zalles provided me with names of medicinal plants and natural remedies used in the treatment of Chagas' disease. Oscar Velasco, M.D., contributed significantly to Chapter 10 and also instructed me concerning the integration of ethnomedicine and biomedicine. Dr. Oscar Velasco also shared with me his knowledge of Chagas' disease among patients of the Department of Potosí, and he introduced me to the cultural context model of health projects discussed in this book. Dr. Evaristo Mayda explained to me how Quechua *curanderos* deal with Chagas' disease, and he let me observe a system of integrating biomedicine and ethnomedicine in the treatment of this disease in the valley of Cochabamba. Dr. Mayda also contributed to the design of a culture context model for health care. Antonio Prieto provided economic solutions to productivity problems in rural Bolivia. Dr. Coco Velasco assisted me throughout with his insights and encouragement. David Ratermann provided me with information about economic and social problems in Bolivia. Roberto Melegrano presented alternative housing designs. Javier Albo, Jose Juan Alva, and Silverio Gonzales assisted in the anthropological and social analysis.

Paul Regalsky of CENDA and Kevin Healey of the Interamerican Foundation provided me with assistance for two summers. Wenner-Gren, Fulbright-Hayes, the National Institute of Health, Texas Christian University, the University of Texas, the United States Agency for International Development, and the Interamerican Foundation provided me with funding for this research.

Dr. Pedro Jáuregui Tapia allowed me to visit his patients with chronic Chagas' disease and explained to me their medical histories. Dr. Johnny Mendez instructed me about megacolon symptoms of Chagas' disease and how it can be treated; he also provided epidemiological information for the Department of Chuquisaca. Dr. Ben Termini, cardiologist in Arlington, Texas, provided me with information about heart disease, and he sponsored a research assistant for this project. Manfred Reinecke, chemist at Texas Christian University, Bill Mahler, botanist at Southern Methodist University, and William Richardson, pathologist at the University of California at Riverside, assisted in the molecular analyses of plants being used to treat Chagas' disease; and, through a collaborative research grant with them, I was able to conduct fieldwork in Bolivia for five consecutive summers.

John Donahue and Chris Greenway reviewed the manuscript and provided excellent suggestions to improve it. I am especially grateful to Jeffrey Grathwohl, director of The University of Utah Press. Finally, John V. Murra, Leighton Hazzlehurst, Frank Young, and David Davidson, my professors at Cornell University during graduate studies, instructed me in research.

I thank you.

Introduction

Trypanosoma cruzi is as potentially destructive to human beings as is a nuclear bomb, yet it is so minuscule that it largely goes unnoticed. *Trypanosoma cruzi* (*T. cruzi*) causes what is known as American trypanosomiasis, or Chagas' disease. The first time that I saw *T. cruzi* was June 6, 1991, in Cochabamba, Bolivia. I recorded the following notes:

> Yesterday, I saw *T. cruzi* under the electronic microscope. They clustered together, like strands of tangled wool, and were wiggling violently, like so many minuscule hydra monsters, trying to break free with their tentacles and attack you. One broke free and swam toward me....
>
> Hernan Bermudez, laboratory technician, then looked into the microscope and exclaimed *"El Asesino!"* ["The Assassin!"]. I felt thrilled to be face to face with the parasite that was infecting millions of people in Latin America, that has spread so rapidly throughout Latin America, and that can multiply to millions of offspring in the human body.

The sighting of *T. cruzi* did not generate hatred but awe and respect. It began a lasting relationship.

T. cruzi infects 18 million people in Latin America and is the major public health problem for development in Latin America, because it debilitates and kills adults during their prime of life (World Health Organization 1985, 1991, 1994, 1996). The Pan American Health Organization has identified Chagas' disease as the most important parasitic disease in Latin America and the major cause of myocardial illness (PAHO 1984). This flagellate protozoan parasite travels to humans through the bite of triatomine bugs—a particular order of sucking insects—entering neuron tissues of the heart and other organs and causing irreversible cardiac and gastrointestinal tract lesions in 30 to 40 percent of the cases. *T. cruzi* migrates by means of infected bugs, animals, humans, blood transfusions, and organ transplants. Currently, there is no cure for the chronic stage of Chagas' disease, but *T. cruzi* can be controlled through improved housing and hygiene. Named after Carlos Chagas, who discovered *T. cruzi* in Brazil in 1909, Chagas' disease has spread throughout Latin America and the Southwestern United States (see Figure 1).

This book concerns Chagas' disease in Bolivia, where infection rates are higher than in any other Latin American country (SOH/CCH 1994). It shows how human beings have created environmental and social contexts for the spread of Chagas' disease and addresses such questions as these: Can humans be

Figure 1. Geographic distribution of Chagas' disease in Latin America. Although it is still difficult to form an accurate picture of the geographic distribution and prevalence of Chagas' disease, among an estimated total population in the endemic countries of 360 million people (excluding Mexico and Nicaragua, for which adequate data are not available), at least 90 million persons (25 percent) are at risk of infection, and from 16 to 18 million people are infected. (World Health Organization 1991:27). (See Appendices 6 and 7.)

as effective in eliminating such diseases as they are in promulgating them? What are successful prevention projects and what are not? What factors are necessary to design a successful intervention project? Further, it shows how Andeans have culturally adapted to the spread of the disease and illustrates why understanding cultural belief systems is critical to the success of prevention programs.

Surprisingly, many Bolivians are unaware of Chagas' disease and rarely suspect it as the cause of death. They attribute its symptoms to other causes such as heart disease, volvulus, improper foods, and fatigue. While it is unnecessary that most individuals understand Chagas' disease from a biomedical perspective, health educators need to translate scientific information about the disease into culturally appropriate categories that are sensitive to indigenous values, traditions, and motivations. To do this, health educators need to integrate the biomedical knowledge of Chagas' disease with the ethnomedical practices of Andeans.

Chagas' disease has received little attention and funding of research, treatment, and prevention measures, perhaps because of who gets it—poor, illiterate, indigenous Andean peasants. This lack of attention is also a result of the disease's latent periods in the human body (see Figure 8). Frequently, *T. cruzi* lies dormant for years until manifesting itself in the critically debilitating chronic state. Peasants seldom connect bites from *vinchuca* bugs to heart disease, so the disease spread by the bite goes undetected at early, treatable stages.

Chagas' latent states and mobility relate it to other slow-acting killers—other epidemics and diseases that cross boundaries. Infected insects, humans, and animals allow *T. cruzi* to travel swiftly and to enter homes unannounced to its hosts. In this, Chagas' disease shares certain features with other diseases, such as AIDS. It is environmentally driven, as is AIDS. Similar "new" diseases have emerged from the savannas of eastern Bolivia (Hemorrhagic Fever), the rainforests of northern Zaire (Ebola virus), a Navajo reservation in the Four Corners region of the western United States (Hantavirus), and the urban poverty of the south Bronx (see Garret 1994). Yet, Chagas' disease is ancient. In this case, it is a parasitic disease encouraged by environmental changes that bring *T. cruzi, vinchucas,* and humans into close contact. Humans destroy natural animal hosts for this parasite and habitats for its vector bug. As a result, parasite and vector have moved to humans. Parallels also can be found with Lyme disease. Suburban housing developments encroach on forest areas where humans come into contact with rodents, especially white-footed deer mice. These rodents host Ixodid ticks, vectors of *Borrelia burgdorferi,* a spirochete that causes Lyme disease (see Spielman et al. 1985; Burgdorfer et al. 1985).

Our awakening to these disease agents is a challenge of the coming millennium. To catch a glimpse of diseases to come, this book details an epidemic battle in Bolivia, a seemingly remote country, and shows how to win it. It provides suggestions for community members, health workers, and social scientists on how to stop Chagas' disease. It is also important to examine factors of the disease's spread in Bolivia to prevent this from happening elsewhere.

Andeans have excellent ways of dealing with native diseases, but they also need anthropologists with cultural sensitivity and doctors with biomedical expertise to help them adapt to potential epidemics. These epidemics are in part phenomena of the late twentieth century. They are aided by overpopulation, massive migrations, urbanization, widespread impoverishment, destruction of the rainforests, and erosion of valuable soil, among other factors. Curtailing Chagas' disease calls for public policy changes to stop the above practices, to increase research and international assistance, and to recognize and utilize indigenous medical systems in its control.

To what extent does a personal agenda interfere with objective research? It is difficult for medical anthropologists to espouse scientific positivism when they are studying traditional medical systems based on premises other than positivism, such as divination, spirits, balances, social relationships, and cultural continuity. Often there are no ways to prove why things work in a culture; the fact can only be noted that they do. Consequently, analyses and interpretations of medical anthropologists are personal and to some degree subjective.

What gives credibility to anthropologists' interpretations is their fieldwork and their data. The following explains some of the reasons why I argue throughout this book for an understanding of Andean ethnomedicine and a culturally sensitive approach to Chagas' control in Bolivia. This book results from thirty-four years of experience, research, and fieldwork in Bolivia, beginning in 1963 when I first arrived as a Maryknoll priest and worked for six years among the Aymaras of the Altiplano (a plateau 12,500 feet high). I learned the Aymara and Spanish languages. After certain misgivings about missionization, I left the priesthood in 1969 and studied anthropology and the Quechua language at Cornell University to learn about Andean culture. In 1971 I married Judy Wagner and we returned to Bolivia to live with the Kallawaya people, only this time to participate in their rituals and to study how Andean religion has enabled these people to adapt to sickness. Their rituals were symbolic and spiritual processes of dealing with Western diseases (typhoid fever, septicemia, and heart disease) and cultural illnesses (*chullpa usu, liquichado, cólico miserere*), to name a few. This resulted in my first book, *Mountain of the Condor: Metaphor and Ritual in an Andean Ayllu* (Bastien 1978). I had become aware of the importance of Andean rituals in the society's health maintenance and that the biology of disease is perceived differently by these people.

I next studied Kallawaya herbalists to learn about their uses of medicinal plants and how these could be used with biomedicine. Kallawayas employ about a thousand medicinal plants and are renowned throughout Argentina, Bolivia, Peru, and Chile as very skilled herbalists. This research resulted in *Healers of the Andes: Kallawaya Herbalists and Their Medicinal Plants* (Bastien 1987). I published an herbal manual in Spanish for peasants that was used for training community health workers in the Department of Oruro, Bolivia (Bastien 1983). I returned to Bolivia almost every year to do research.[1]

By 1980, I again felt the missionary's impulse, not to evangelize but to argue for the inclusion of Andean traditional medicine, especially herbal medicines, rituals, and *curanderos,* into national and international health programs. I became an advisor to the National Secretariat of Health and the United States Agency of International Development on the integration of ethnomedicine and community health workers into primary health care programs.[2]

A more recent endeavor to integrate both types of medicine has been my collaborative research with chemists and pathologists in the testing of Kallawaya-Bolivian medicinal plants for curing AIDS, cancer, Chagas' disease, and tuberculosis. The results are significant, with certain plants being protease inhibitors for AIDS, and others curing cancer and tuberculosis (Bastien et al. 1990, 1994, 1996). Kallawaya plant medicines also show promise as cures for Chagas' disease. Scientists at the University of Antofagasta, Chile, are examining these plants.

Bolivian and international health personnel are beginning to integrate ethnomedicine and biomedicine in Bolivia, as I discuss in *Drum and Stethoscope: Integrating Ethnomedicine and Biomedicine in Bolivia* (Bastien 1992). Doctors, nurses, and project workers work with shamans, midwives, and community health workers in joint clinics. Associations of community health workers, midwives, and herbalists negotiate with doctors and nurses. The National Secretariat of Health coordinates both types of medicine, including providing staffed positions in ethnomedicine. State-run pharmacies stock and sell herbal medicines. This recognition and respect of Andean traditional medicine is encouraging; however, the current hegemony of biomedical medicine, propelled by pharmaceutical and insurance companies, medical associations, and privatization, essentially pits capitalist entrepreneurs against ethnic *curanderos* and shamans in what becomes for the latter a losing battle.

Kiss of Death's call for activism is unusual in a scholarly text, but I feel it is appropriate if it helps lead to the creation of prevention programs. Western medical ethics has come to address the manner of distributing resources that affect the maintenance or restoration of health as a moral problem (see Lieban 1990:227). The pattern of allocating resources basic to health and survival raises serious ethical issues in light of the principle of distributive justice, defined as "the justified distribution of benefits and burdens in society" (Beauchamp and Childress 1983:184). Does distribution of resources for combatting Chagas' disease involve a conflict between the perceived higher valuation of certain communities over others, males over females, adults over children, and wealthier countries over poorer countries?

Because Chagas' control projects are expensive and involve only a small percentage of communities in Bolivia, an evaluation of their effectiveness as pilot projects is important. For this reason, I concentrate on two pilot projects in the Departments of Chuquisaca and Tarija. The Proyecto Británico-Cardenal Mauer (PBCM) project in the Department of Chuquisaca was considered a successful Chagas' control project in 1991 by the National Chagas' Control Committee, which recommended it as a model for other projects throughout Bolivia. It provided a primary health care infrastructure into which Chagas' control was included. Ruth Sensano organized this infrastructure. The Tarija project stands out for its education of the local populace about Chagas' disease. José Beltran is the leading educator in this project. Sensano and Beltran are highlighted in these projects because they illustrate what individual Bolivians are doing. These projects serve to help create an improved model that reaches more people more economically and within the cultural context of the community.

I observed other projects, which were heavily funded, hastily done, and had limited effect on Chagas' control. These projects concentrated on new houses and insecticides, measures that are not affordable and sustainable over time. Insecticides have become too expensive for most communities without government subsidies, which have been discontinued. The pilot nature of these projects failed because they never presented a model to follow. This book assesses the justice of the allocation of health resources in regard to Chagas' disease. Moreover, it suggests alternative solutions to the problem of providing more people with the means to prevent Chagas' disease.

Personal Awareness of Chagas' Disease

Chagas' disease first became a major health concern in Bolivia in 1991. Until then, it had been a "silent killer" of millions of Bolivians. After twenty years of fieldwork, I first learned about the disease in 1984 when a doctor/epidemiologist and I were visiting Cocapata, a Quechua community, located between snow-crested mountains to the west and the Amazon to the east. We lodged in a peasant's hut of adobe and thatch and slept on llama skins covering the dirt floor. Even though insects bit me, I slept through the night. As the sun came through the tiny window, I arose and asked my companion how he slept.

"I didn't sleep at all," he replied. When I asked why, he continued. "I refused to sleep. I chased *vinchucas* from my body. I didn't want them to bite me!" When I asked what *vinchucas* were, he told me that they cause Chagas' disease. He was not afraid of malaria and syphilis, but he dreaded Chagas' disease. He explained what this disease was, and, for the first time in my life, I questioned the potential price of a good night's sleep. Having lived years in peasants' huts, I realized that I had long been at risk and wondered why no one had advised me about Chagas' disease. Even today, Chagas' disease remains unknown to many educated people and doctors throughout the world. Tropical diseases in impoverished countries receive little recognition and research, primarily because biomedical technology and pharmaceutical companies concentrate on wealthier clientele in temperate zones of industrial countries. The doctor's final comments were, "Chagas' disease is a poverty-driven disease."

Once I began looking for Chagas' disease, I found it throughout Bolivia. When I was researching Kallawaya herbalists outside of Charazani, Bolivia, they reported increased *mal de corazon* (heart problems) and *muerto subito* (sudden death) among their peasants, which seemed strange to them. Andeans living at high altitudes are noted for their strong hearts as well as increased lung capacity. Acute respiratory diseases are major diseases in higher altitudes. Peasants complained of fatigue, somewhat unusual for people accustomed to working above 9,750 feet (3,000 m.). I suspected that Kallawayas were dying of Chagas' disease, and, not surprisingly, as I later learned, the Kallawaya region is an endemic area of Chagas' disease.

When I interviewed Kallawaya herbalists about local diseases and plant uses, I found no direct references to Chagas' disease. This is not unusual, however, because the symptoms of Chagas' disease are varied and diffuse. I suspected that they were treating the disease's symptoms, such as fevers, intestinal disorders, and heart problems. One local herbalist, Florentino Alvarez, taught me herbal curing (see Bastien 1987a:9–10). When I met him in 1979 he was paralyzed from a stroke and hardly able to walk and talk. I massaged his legs, gave him vitamins, and helped him along with crutches. As he slowly recovered, he showed me some plants and explained how they were used. Florentino Alvarez died in 1981, of unknown causes, perhaps from Chagas' disease.

The full impact of Chagas' disease struck me in November 1990 when I attended a planning session for Chagas' control in Bolivia. Earlier that year, Paul Hartenberger of the United States Agency for International Development (USAID) and Joel Kuritsky of the Centers for Disease Control (CDC) asked Robert Gelbard, U.S. ambassador to Bolivia, to request monies from President George Bush for prevention of Chagas' disease in Bolivia. Although the Ministry of Health in Bolivia had been granted $20 million for a child survival program from 1989 to 1994, no monies had been allocated for Chagas' control. Gelbard asked the newly inaugurated president of Bolivia, Jaime Paz Zamora, to request monies from President Bush when he visited the White House later that year. Bush granted one million dollars to immediately begin a Chagas' campaign in Bolivia. Later, several million more dollars were added to fund the SOH/CCH Chagas' control pilot projects.

Kuritsky convened world experts on Chagas' disease to meet in La Paz, Bolivia, in November 1990 to design a Chagas' program. He invited me to assist in regard to cultural and social aspects of Chagas' disease and prevention. After five days of participation in these meetings, I learned about the disease's epidemic proportions, problems in prevention, and complex nature. Philip Marsden shared with me details of how he had stopped its spread in parts of Brazil. Andy Arata and Bob Tonn of Vector Biology and Control Project (VBC) convinced me that vector control of Chagas' disease is possible with insecticides and the improvement of houses. Hartenberger, Kuritsky, and Charles Lewellyn led a group of Bolivian epidemiologists, public health workers, and social scientists into accepting the challenge to eradicate Chagas' disease in Bolivia. War had been declared against the disease, and control of Chagas' disease was made an important component of the USAID Child Survival Program in Bolivia (CCH), which had a joint program with *Secretariat Nacional de Salud* (SNS) (see SOH/CCH 1994).[3] We left the workshop with T-shirts and buttons emblazoned with the crossed-circle stamping out an ugly *vinchuca* bug.

I returned to Bolivia during the summers of 1992, 1994, 1995, and 1997 to observe projects of SOH/CCH that included building new houses and improving hygiene as ways to prevent Chagas' disease. Their success was limited to the degree that they used education, community participation, cultural sensitivity, and employment of native economic systems. More than 3,000 houses were built by project monies and peasant labor. I observed, however, that building new houses was not economically feasible for the majority of Bolivians, and that people generally were not practicing housing hygiene. As one example, in Aramasi, Department of Cochabamba, peasants resisted improving their houses because they thought that once the houses were improved they would be taken from them. This problem could be confronted by the education and preparation of community members. Another concern was that it is easier to kill bugs with insecticides (the technological quick fix) than to get peasants to maintain their houses and practice housing hygiene. This problem required being culturally and socially sensitive towards peasants, educating them to participate wholeheartedly in Chagas' control, and assisting them in the maintenance of this control. Pro-Habitat of Bolivia designed posters and videos towards these ends. This book presents some of these successful strategies to prevent Chagas' disease.

Review of the Literature

This book contributes to scholarly research by being the only text in English that covers Chagas' disease in a comprehensive manner. Other monographs concentrate on specific issues; for example, *Control of Chagas'*

Disease, published in 1991 by the World Health Organization, contains information on epidemiology and vector control. An evaluation study, *Chagas Disease in Bolivia: The Work of the SOH/CCH Chagas Control Pilot Program,* 1994, describes the results of housing improvement by the national control program in Bolivia.

A landmark study in Spanish, *La Casa Enferma: Sociología de la Enfermedad de Chagas* by Roberto Briceño-León, 1990, centers upon understanding social processes and human behavior that bring into contact humans, triatomine vectors, *T. cruzi,* and Chagas' disease. Briceño's book provides an analysis of a housing improvement project in Venezuela that served as a guide for the Bolivian control project.

Chagas' Disease and the Nervous System, published by the Pan American Health Organization in 1994, covers the pathogenesis of Chagas' disease and supports the theory that morbidity in Chagas' disease results from misdirected effects of the humoral and cellular immune responses in infected patients, induced by a breakdown of self-tolerance. The involvement of autoimmune mechanisms in the pathogenesis of Chagas' disease compares it in some ways with AIDS; hopefully, more research on the role of the immune system in both diseases will provide some solutions.

Kiss of Death incorporates findings from these books into an interdisciplinary study that looks at the broader picture of the relationship of Bolivians to this disease. It highlights how they culturally adapt to the disease. As one illustration, when I questioned herbalists about Chagas' disease, many had not heard about it. They complained about *vinchucas* biting them at night but had no idea that these trumpet-nosed blood-sucking bugs were bearers of a deadly parasite. However, some herbalists recommended burning eucalyptus leaves to drive out *vinchucas.* This and other ways that natives have adapted to disease constitute important knowledge. *Kiss of Death* provides this information.

As an anthropologist, I have learned to deal with the unusual and threatening in a way that is understandable; this is my perspective throughout the book, one that tries to make the scientific knowledge understandable and the human suffering bearable and redeemable. One premise of this book is that it is necessary to relate the microbiology of Chagas' disease to environmental, economic, political, social, and cultural factors in order to prevent Chagas' disease. There is no quick fix, such as spraying with insecticides or employing vaccinations. The challenge of Chagas' disease requires an interdisciplinary approach, discussed in the concluding chapter.

Frequently, I have been told by doctors that the disease is not a problem in the United States because it does not appear in clinical records. It may well be, however, that Chagas' disease is more prevalent in America than clinical records show, because doctors are not looking for it. "If you are in America and hear hoof beats, you don't look for zebras," one doctor told me. However, parasites and bugs are able to travel from one continent to the other much faster than zebras. Also, diagnostic tests for Chagas' disease are rarely called for in the United States, if they are available at all, although ELISA tests are used to detect Chagas' antibodies throughout Bolivia.

The first indigenous case of Chagas' disease reported in the United States was a ten-month-old white female child from Corpus Christi, Texas, on July 28, 1954 (Woody and Woody 1955). The disease had spread through triatomine bugs and opossums. This case shows that *Trypanosoma cruzi*, naturally occurring in animals and triatomine bugs in this area, are infective for humans, and it implies that unrecognized cases are probably present in the area. Since the mid-1970s, large numbers of immigrants have entered the United States from regions in Latin America where Chagas' disease is common (Ciesielski et al. 1993, Kirchhoff et al. 1987). Epidemiological evidence suggests that many of these people are infected with Chagas' disease (Kirchhoff 1993). Because Chagas' heart disease is frequently overlooked, Hagar and Rahimtoola (1991) studied the records of forty-two patients with Chagas' heart disease seen at one southern California institution since 1974. Eighteen out of twenty-five patients treated for presumed coronary artery disease or dilated cardiomyopathy had gone for as long as 108 months before the diagnosis of Chagas' disease was considered. Chagas' heart disease is not rare in the United States among persons from endemic areas but still may be underdiagnosed. Chagas' disease has also spread to the United States through blood transfusions from Latin American donors with this disease (Kirchhoff 1989; Schmuñis 1985, 1991, 1994).

The medical profession is slowly becoming aware of Chagas' disease, but, as it first did for AIDS, sees it as restricted to certain social groups and areas. At a recent national conference for tropical medicine in New Orleans, experts were warned of the increase of Chagas' disease in the United States and provided with a course on the disease to review for their certification exams. This book contributes to this growing awareness by providing a unique holistic perspective of Chagas' disease and by calling attention to the seriousness of the Chagas' epidemic in Bolivia and Latin America. The perspective is structural and views the elements of Chagas' disease within a contextual relationship rather than exclusively focusing on some aspect. However, there are focused perspectives within the chapters. Accounts of a number of interesting individuals tell something important about Chagas' disease. The disease is viewed from their perspective—how they experience, interpret, prevent, and treat it. This book interrelates microbiology and medicine with social, economic, and environmental factors to show how Chagas' disease can be prevented.

This book also views Chagas' disease as related to the political economy. This interdisciplinary view relates economics to biology, culture, community ecology, and politics. It is essential to adopt a broad perspective that includes many factors before attempting preventative actions.

Another focus is upon housing, where parasites, insects, and humans interrelate. Houses are centers of peasants' land, livestock, and base economy. Negative factors affecting the household are migration, abandonment, and loss of land. Houses are cultural institutions, symbols and refuges from the outside. Houses also are containers of parasites, insects, animals, and people. This book concerns the anthropology of the house.

Even though this book deals with houses infested with parasites and insects, one cannot help but think of the homes of the "homeless"—shacks, bridges, cars, tents, and streets—which shelter the mass of generally shifting populations in Bosnia, Ruwanda, the United States, Latin America, and elsewhere. It is hoped that readers of this book will become more active in support of building homes for the homeless and in protecting the wild homes of animals, insects, and plants while supporting the treatment of people sick with Chagas' disease.

From the Microscope to the Telescope

The viewpoint of the chapters is similar to an optical device that begins as a microscope and ends as a telescope, going from the infinitesimal parasite to humans, communities, nations, and continents. The world of microbiology is an amazing universe continually being newly discovered. Chapter 1, Discovering Chagas' Disease, reveals the medical history of this disease. Chapter 2, An Early Andean Disease, contains its history in the Andes. Chapter 3, *Jampiris* and *Yachajs:* Andean Ethnomedicine, looks at how Bolivian *curanderos* treat its symptoms. Chapter 4, The Crawling Epidemic: Epidemiology, deals with infestation by *vinchucas,* means of infection, and the extent of the epidemic. In Chapter 5, *Cólico miserere:* Enlarged Colon, and Chapter 6, Bertha: *Mal de Corazon,* one reads about the illness in its chronic stages of megacolon and heart disease. This is presented through the lives of people from two Bolivian families.

Reversing the microscope into a telescope to examine the environment relating to Chagas' disease, Chapter 7, Cultural and Political Economy of Infested Houses, deals with the relationship of cultural and political-economic factors in bringing into physical proximity parasites, vectors, and hosts.

What can be done to prevent Chagas' disease is considered in the last chapters. Housing improvement projects are described in Chapter 8, *Pachamama* Snatched Her: Getting Involved, and Chapter 9, Sharing Ideas. Chapter 10, A Culture Context Model, presents a model for future health projects. The concluding chapter, Solutions, contains answers to punctuated approaches, economic causes, and environmental issues precipitating Chagas' disease. Humans have created the social and environmental context for the spread of this debilitating disease, and it is to be hoped that they can be as successful in eliminating such diseases as they are in proliferating them.

This book includes appendices to learn more about biomedical aspects of Chagas' disease. These appendices provide information in the forms of tables and charts concerning the vector species and hosts of *T. cruzi* in the Americas. It includes a discussion of the strains of *T. cruzi*, vaccine development, and an important section of the immune response, coauthored with the noted parasitologist Dr. George Stewart.

The perspective of *Kiss of Death: Challenging Chagas' Disease* is to look at the relationship of many factors, almost as if one were looking at it from a galactic point of view, with the details of the puzzle examined in Bolivia, a small country with a small population (seven million people) and a high rate of Chagas' disease, a variety of climatic and geographic features—tropical forests, high plateaus, and still higher mountains—containing varied ethnic groups, social classes, and economic systems. Bolivia gives us the gift of the dervish in *A Thousand and One Nights* who claimed the power of seeing all the world at once, or that of Jorge Luis Borges's Aleph, the diameter of which "was only two or three centimeters, but the whole of space was in it, without sacrifice of scale" (Borges 1977:625, Fernández-Armesto 1995:19).

Reading about Chagas' disease in Bolivia gives a perspective for understanding this disease throughout Latin America and for predicting what might happen in the United States and Europe, where it is spreading. Chagas' disease is the space in which are encapsulated minutely infinite forces and from which we might get a broader perspective of the universe.

CHAPTER ONE

Discovering Chagas' Disease

In 1909 Carlos Chagas discovered American trypanosomiasis by intuition, induction, scientific method, hard work, genius, and a pinch of luck.[1] Carlos Chagas represents a rare example of a medical scientist who described a disease after having found its causative agent, *T. cruzi*, in the intestines of triatomine insects. He observed its pathogenicity to mammals, located its domestic and wild reservoirs, and then went on to find infected humans. He finally documented its acute and chronic phases. Chagas ranks with the greatest scientists of the twentieth century; Chagas' disease remains a scourge of this century and a battle of the next.

Chagas' discovery coincided with conquests of the Amazon. It was a time when symbiotic microorganisms, living in animal reservoirs within the Amazon, became pathogenic for invading settlers. Such is now the case for Bolivians with Chagas' disease.

As a budding parasitologist in that discipline's age of discovery, Carlos Chagas realized that microbiology could reveal the causes of tropical diseases. The microscope was to biology what the telescope was to astronomy. Within a generation, scientists had discovered the world of microbiology and shattered many age-old aetiologies: Robert Koch discovered the tuberculin bacterium in 1882 and liberated tuberculosis from its association with consumption, vapors, and "bad air." Louis Pasteur isolated the rabies virus and produced an attenuated strain or vaccine in 1884. Pasteur disproved the notion that the disease resulted from nervous trauma allegedly suffered by sexually frustrated dogs (rabid men were said to be priapic and sexually insatiable) (Geison 1995:179; Kete 1988). D.D. Cunningham described leishmania organisms found in skin lesions in India in 1885; F. Schaudinn depicted trophozoites and cysts of *Entamoeba histolytica* (amoebic dysentery) in 1903 (dying at thirty-five as a result of his self-experimentation). R.M. Forde showed that *Trypanosoma brucei gambiense* caused sleeping sickness in 1902, providing a pathogenic agent rather than African laziness as its cause. The microscope did for the minuscule world what the telescope did for the universe: it changed beliefs in origins of disease and cosmic phenomena. The sequel to these discoveries, however, is that tropical diseases remain as prevalent as ever. The impoverished tropics aren't considered profitable enough for the investment of wide-scale remedies. The spectacular research mentioned above was primarily for the health of colonialists and workers in industrial expansion.

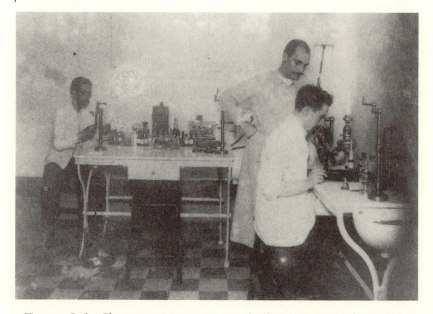

Figure 2. Carlos Chagas examining parasites under the microscope at the Oswaldo Cruz Institute in Rio de Janeiro, where he studied in 1902. (Photo from Renato Clark Bacellar, *Brazil's Contribution to Tropical Medicine and Malaria*, Rio de Janeiro, 1963)

Carlos Justiniano Ribeiro Chagas was born on July 9, 1879, in the small town of Oliveira, Minas Gerais, Brazil, of Portuguese farmers who were descendants of immigrants who had come to Brazil in the late seventeenth century (Lewinsohn 1981). His upper-class parents owned a small coffee plantation with a modest income. When he was four, his father died, and his mother, a strong-willed farmer, raised him and three younger children. She tried to persuade him to become a mining engineer, but he refused and instead chose medical school, being swayed by a physician uncle who convinced him that for Brazil to develop industrially it was necessary to rid the country of endemic diseases. (Many European ships refused to dock in Brazilian ports because of fear of contracting yellow fever, smallpox, bubonic plague, and syphilis).

Carlos Chagas studied at the Oswaldo Cruz Institute in 1902, where he wrote his M.D. thesis on the "Hematological Aspects of Malaria" (1903) under the leading Brazilian parasitologist, Oswaldo Cruz. Cruz tackled the task of ridding Rio de Janeiro of yellow fever by the systematic combat of the mosquito vector and the isolation of victims in special hospitals. He also provided vaccinations against the plague and smallpox. Eradication of vectors and mass vaccinations were revolutionary measures at this time. Many diseases were thought to be caused by vapors emanating from the hot and humid earth, such as *mal de aire* ("evil from the air") or malaria. Cruz was successful fighting yellow fever in Rio, and similar methods also decreased the disease in Panama for the building of the canal. However, Cruz's fight against mosquitos in Brazil continued for years.

When Cruz invited Chagas to work on malaria research, Chagas refused, saying that he was not cut out to do research and preferred to practice family medicine. Chagas worked in a hospital at Jurujuba from 1903 until 1905, where he introduced antipest serotherapy, which Cruz had modified from that introduced by Louis Pasteur in France around 1890. Pasteur led the way in germ therapy in opposition to theories of spontaneous generation as principles of life and causes of diseases (see Geison 1995). Following Pasteur's and Cruz's assumptions that negative organic elements fermented positive organic elements, Chagas first prepared an antipestic serum, then cut into a patient's swollen glands and inserted this serum to destroy the *"peste"* (see Chagas Filho 1993). Chagas was a very innovative and experimental doctor who looked for answers in practice rather than in the laboratory.

Malaria Closes Brazilian Ports

On March 30, 1905, the Santos Dock Company of Santos, near Sâo Paulo, Brazil, hired Carlos Chagas to combat malaria. Its workers were so weakened by fever that they could not complete the port of Santos, the most important in Brazil. Carlos Chagas accepted the challenge to do fieldwork ("*trabalhar no campo*") and to observe firsthand malaria within its natural and social environment. Chagas used his first paycheck to buy a microscope; he then had the only tool needed to examine the microcosm.

Carlos Chagas' earlier studies of malaria and later studies of Chagas' disease stimulated new concepts of these diseases that incorporated parasitology, entomology, and human physiology while studying relationships of parasites, vectors, and hosts. Vectors are carriers, usually arthropods or insects, that transmit causative organisms of disease, parasites, from infected to noninfected individuals. A parasite usually goes through one or more stages in its life cycle within the vector. The host is the organism in which parasites obtain nourishment and reproduce. Knowledge of the parasitic cycles enhances our understanding of tropical diseases and their relationship to the environment.

Carlos Chagas disagreed with the then-current practices of pouring toxic substances on lakes, reservoirs, and stagnant water to eliminate malaria. Doctors had used this method in Panama and Cuba under the assumptions of marasmus theory that attributed malaria to vapors. Chagas recognized that the use of smoke, toxic substances, and the drainage of swamps were ineffective remedies because they destroyed only the larvae of the mosquito. He also objected that such methods destroyed fish and reptiles and could never be applied to all the ponds, lakes, and waterholes in the tropics.

Because mosquito larvae are not infected with parasites, Carlos Chagas' strategy against malaria in 1905 was to attack the adult vectors by preventing uninfected (also sometimes called sterile) mosquitos from coming into contact with infected humans and infected mosquitos from coming into contact with healthy humans (Chagas 1935). Chagas observed that after mosquito vectors acquire their fill of blood, they lose the ability to take off in flight and can hardly fly over the walls and furniture of a house to begin digestion of the ingested blood (Chagas Filho 1993:78). He advocated closing off houses with doors and screens and disinfecting houses by burning pyrethrum from chrysanthemum flowers, which kills mosquitos in flight.

Realizing the futility of trying to destroy mosquitos, Chagas devised ways to prevent mosquitos from coming into contact with malaria patients. He found that mosquitos ingest most parasites during the erythrocytic cycle, when merozoites abundantly attack the red blood cells. The erythrocytic cycle corresponds to parasitemia, characterized by high fever, which naturally attracts mosquitos. He advocated that these patients be quarantined in closed-off areas with walls, screens, ceilings, and caulked joints, as distant as possible from mosquitos. Moreover, Chagas treated patients with quinine to reduce fever and destroy parasites. Quinine is an Andean medicinal remedy for malarial fever from the bark of the *Chinchona calasaya* tree. Kallawaya herbalists have used it for centuries and brought it to workers of the Panama Canal (see Bastien 1987a).

Chagas devised a threefold program in Santos which became a protocol for malaria campaigns in other regions of Brazil by 1917. The approach consisted of 1) administration of quinine in dosages of 50 centigrams every three days, 2) isolation of patients from mosquitos in infirmaries with fine metal screens and continual treatment with quinine of other malarial patients in the region, and 3) periodic and systematic disinfecting of domiciles with pyrethrum. Chagas further contributed to malariology by describing the edematous form of Quartan fever (attacks occurring every fourth day), the bone-marrow lesions of malaria, and the description of the disease as a domiciliary infection, rarely contracted outdoors (Lewinsohn 1981:452).

Carlos Chagas succeeded against malaria primarily because he did fieldwork, observed the disease in its environment, and addressed the problem in a scientific and therapeutic way. He also worked with patients, parasites, and insects in epidemic settings to get an enlarged perspective of the disease. On returning to Rio from Santos, Chagas went to work on malaria control for the

Xerem River dam and had similar success. In 1906 he became an associate of the Oswaldo Cruz Institute in Rio de Janeiro.

Railroad Stop at Lassance

At about the same time, Europeans and Brazilians intruded into the forests of Brazil to build a railroad connecting Rio de Janeiro with the northern city of Belem, near the mouth of the Amazon River. Indians, animals, insects, and parasites resisted the invaders, causing a standstill in Lassance, located on the banks of the São Francisco River in Minas Gerais. Rail workers from Asia and Europe and slaves from Africa died by the thousands. In 1908, *Estrada de Ferro Central do Brasil* (the Central Railroad of Brazil) invited Carlos Chagas to come to Lassance.

Thirty-one years old, Carlos left his wife in Juiz de Fora, her native village, in December 1908. He traveled by train for twenty-four hours to Lassance, the end of the rail. Named after a French railroad engineer, Lassance had 1,500 people. African, Chinese, Irish, and Portuguese railroad workers lived in mobile encampments of boxcars fitted with bunks. Chagas was given one boxcar to serve as clinic, dormitory, and laboratory.

Lassance also had comfortable ranch homes and townhouses for the long-established Portuguese settlers—merchants, farmers, and ranchers—who considered themselves a class apart. Socially positioned between the upper-class denizens and lower-class migrants were itinerant cowboys. The cowboys fought with each other and looked down upon the immigrants. The immigrants in particular suffered from the parasitic diseases of the tropics. They had not developed partial immunity, and many died from acute infections of parasitic diseases. (Partial immunity occurs when someone is already infected with parasites and *usually* will not suffer another acute attack because the parasites partially protect the host; this is the case with Chagas' disease.)

Chagas had to treat the ailments of the people of Lassance. Parallel to the tracks lay the main street, Avenue Alfonso Pena, where the merchants, landowners, and authorities lived in townhouses, enclaves shut off from the bustle and dust of the street. Farther down were the infamously named streets, including Street of the Knife and Street of the Shot, all noted for their brothels, bars, and fights. Along these streets, merchants catered to the Brazilian cowboys, mixed breeds of blacks, Indians, and Portuguese, who herded cattle through Lassance while on the way to slaughterhouses in the southern cities of Curvelo and Belo Horizonte.

Carlos Chagas described Lassance years later to his son Carlos Chagas Filho (1988):

> The village resembled the many movie versions of the settlement of the American West. The boisterous visitors considered me an "officer." For

several months none of those wounded during brawling (I could hear the shots in the distance) would come to the hospital I directed. After awhile, they came to me, and I treated their injuries.

Chagas treated the railroad workers so they could lay tracks. He treated them with arsenic for syphilis and quinine for malaria; he also advocated burning chrysanthemum to keep down the mosquitos. He employed a railroad car as a hospital and conducted research using another railway car as laboratory, clinic, and bedroom.

As Chagas treated the injured and diseased, he noticed that some symptoms were not from malaria. Like clockwork, the malarial parasite sporulates periodically with accompanying parasitemia (alternating chills and fevers). Latin Americans still refer to malaria as either *M. quotidian* (*P. vivax* causes paroxysms every twenty-four hours), *M. tertian* (*P. falciparium* causes paroxysms every forty-eight hours), and *M. quartan* (*P. malariae* causes paroxysms every four days). Chronic malaria also results in splenomegaly (enlargement of the spleen). Unlike malaria with its violent attacks, some Lassance patients suffered arrhythmias and other cardiac disorders which resulted in a sudden and nonviolent death.

At first, Chagas figured it was *morbus gallicus* (French disease), as syphilis was popularly called in Brazil, and treated the patients with arsenic. He wrote (Chagas Filho 1993:81):

> Faced with an unknown disease, one usually thinks of syphilis, especially for railroad workers, undernourished, ravaged by malaria, victims of *morbus gallicus,* which usually accompanies those laying iron tracks. A population complaining about irregular heartbeats and atypical arrhythmias, indications of cardiac insufficiencies, and frequently leading to sudden death...inexplicable!

Barbeiros/Vinchucas: Triatoma infestans

A clue was provided by an engineer who showed Carlos an arthropod insect known as a *barbeiro* or *vinchuca* (*Triatoma infestans*) that infested the barracks and sucked blood from the workers during the night. The workers complained that *barbeiros* bit them nocturnally, drew blood, and caused painful welts. The engineer inquired whether *barbeiros* as well as anopheles mosquitos spread malaria, and Chagas knew that anopheles mosquitos transmitted plasmodium parasites whose sexual reproductive cycle was limited to the gut of the mosquito. "Knowing the domiciliary habits of the insect, and its abundance in all the human habitations of the region," Chagas (1922) wrote, "we immediately stayed on, interested in finding out the exact biology of the *barbeiro,* and the transmission of some parasite to man or to another vertebrate."

Figure 3. Triatoma infestans.

Barbeiros have six strong legs, an inch-long body covered with fragile, transparent wings, bulbous eyes, and a proboscis nested under its body that can extend downward to ingest blood from mammals, including humans. Brazilians call these triatomine insects *barbeiros,* from the Portuguese word for barber, indicating that these insects cut like a barber—referring not to the fact that barbers accidentally cut the face with razors but that they also practice bloodletting, done at the time for medical purposes. *Barbeiros* are scientifically classified as *Triatoma infestans* (see Figure 3).

Carlos Chagas observed that *barbeiros* are sensitive to light and during the day hide in cracks and crevices of walls and ceilings where they rest, copulate, and lay eggs, which are tiny, white, and ball-shaped. *Barbeiros* are considered vampire bugs; they become active at night, descend from nests, are drawn to warmth, and draw blood from animals and humans. Faces are attractive targets that *barbeiros* pierce with their needle-sharp proboscises. They inject anesthetic and anticoagulant fluids that enable them to leisurely ingest blood from unwary and tired victims. Sleepers sometimes awake and smash the *barbeiros,* exploding the blood on their bodies or other surfaces as the bugs sluggishly return to their nests. They are superb crawlers and can attack victims by crawling beneath mosquito netting or from inside mattresses.

People also refer to *barbeiros* (or *vinchucas*) as "kissing bugs" because of their predilection for the face. Chagas called the resulting chagoma (carbuncle sore) from a bite beneath the eye *Signo de Romaña* and pointed this out as an important diagnostic indicator of acute Chagas', discussed more in Chapter 4 (see Figure 4).

Barbeiros (*vinchucas*) are triatomines, with more than 100 species that are vectors of *Trypanosoma cruzi. Triatoma infestans* is the most widespread and effective species vector of *T. cruzi* in Bolivia, and Bolivians refer to it as *vin-*

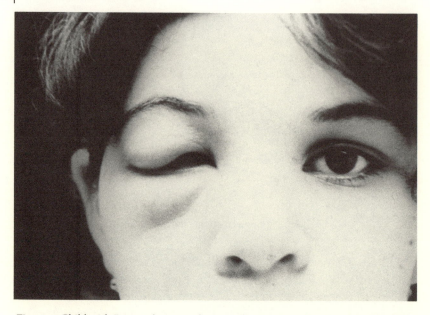

Figure 4. Child with Romaña's sign, a chagoma that occurs at the site of the bite from the *vinchuca* bug. This occurs during the acute phase in about one-fourth of those infected with *T. cruzi*. (Photograph from the Pan American Health Organization)

chuca. Sometimes classified as reduviid bugs, *barbeiros* do not have the painful bite of other reduviids. *Barbeiros* have injector-needlelike snouts or noses that fold back under their bodies and protrude down, like half-opened jackknives, to pierce the victim's skin. They can engorge more blood than their body weight, and when they defecate they can leave small blotches of tobaccolike stains on the skin. They need blood meals, one for each of five instar (life) stages, in which they transform from barely the size of a flea to that of a small cockroach. At the final, adult stage, they grow wings, copulate, lay eggs, and die. Rather simple in their needs, triatomine insects need only a place to hide during the day and mammals to feed on during the night. (See Chapter 4 and appendices for more on triatomines).

Lassance was infested with *barbeiros* because of its impoverished socioeconomic conditions and human intrusion into nearby forests. Triatomines were driven from their native habitats as railroads expanded. Crawling aboard railway cars, *barbeiros* followed westward expansion across Brazil. Many houses for humans were made of thatched roofs and adobe walls, with cracks, crevices, and cornices providing nesting sites for *barbeiros.* Carlos Chagas recognized the impact poverty has upon the spread of insects, parasites, and disease, something Walter Reed also had observed in regard to malaria.

Years earlier, Charles Darwin had also been fascinated by *vinchucas,* and it could be wondered if Darwin's fascination augmented Chagas' curiosity about these bugs. Both shared essential ingredients of successful fieldworkers, curiosity about certain creatures and how they relate to other creatures. It is likely that Carlos Chagas, like most classically trained biologists at the time, had read about *vinchuca* bugs in the *Diary of the Beagle*, written by Darwin on March 26, 1835:

> We crossed the river of Luxan (Andean region of Mendoza)....At night I experienced an attack, & it deserves no less a name, of the Benchuca, the great black bug of the Pampas. It is most disgusting to feel soft wingless insects, about an inch long, crawling over ones body; before sucking they are quite thin, but afterwards round & bloated with blood, & in this state they are easily squashed. They are found in the Northern part of Chili & in Peru: one which I caught at Iquiqui was very empty; being placed on the table & though surrounded by people, if a finger was presented, its sucker was withdrawn, & the bold insect began to draw blood. It was curious to watch the change in size of the insects body in less than ten minutes. There was no pain felt.—This one meal kept the insect fat for four months; In a fortnight, however, it was ready, if allowed, to suck more blood. (Darwin, in Keynes 1988:315)

Several years later, Darwin wrote in his zoology notebook at Edinburgh (1837–1839) a partial description of *vinchucas* in French, which I translate: "*Vinchucas* or *Benchucas*. The individual wings can be (four) five lines [*lignes*] long and they fly." Darwin had found this quote from an earlier description by the naturalist Azara (1809, I:208–9): "*La vinchuca* [is] very annoying for those who travel from Mendoza to Buenos Aires....It is a beetle or scarab, whose body is oval and very flat, and who becomes fat like a grain of raisin, from the blood which he sucks. This insect only comes out at night. The individual wings can be five lines [lignes] and they fly, at least the large ones."[2] He was referring to the fact that *vinchucas* grow wings only at the adult, or fifth instar, stage.

Darwin's Disease

Experimentally, Darwin allowed *vinchucas* to draw blood from his finger and marveled at the dexterity of their proboscises. Some scholars have interpreted this to suggest that he became infected with *T. cruzi*, which would explain his semidebilitated state five years after the *Beagle* landed.[3] Several weeks after being bitten, Darwin wrote in his diary for April 9, 1835: "From this day till I reached Valparaiso, I was not very well & saw nothing & admired nothing" (Keynes 1988:323). Darwin reached Valparaiso on April 17. The incubation period corresponds to the lead time for acute Chagas' disease, but nine days is relatively short for its duration.

A second indication is that several years after the *vinchuca* bite Darwin began suffering a complex of symptoms from an undiagnosed chronic illness. Chagas' disease gradually develops into a chronic phase, what has been called an intricate lifelong minuet that is danced by the parasite and the host's immune system (Goldstein 1989). This could explain Darwin's illness: nonspecific symptoms of increased parasitemia such as malaise, fever, fatigue, and decreased energy when the immune system was down. Advancing age, periodic illnesses, psychological stress, and exhaustion could certainly have weakened Darwin's immune system, which was necessary to keep *T. cruzi* at bay.

At the age of thirty-three, Darwin's period of great physical activity was over. Darwin logs continual, nagging complaints in his diaries from 1839 until his death in 1882 that indicate a persistent and not readily diagnosed problem:

the smallest exertion is most irksome...periodic vomiting....I was almost quite broken down, head swimmy, hands trembling and never a week without violent vomiting...very weak...only able to tolerate short walks...headaches...fatigued...oppressed...flatulence...prolonged spells of daily vomiting of "acid & slime," fright...sinking sensation...trembling...shivering...and fatigue. (Darwin, in Goldstein 1989)

These symptoms waxed and waned throughout Darwin's life and greatly curtailed his professional activities, travels, and social life. In 1882 Darwin developed myocardial degeneration which progressed to angina pectoris; he died that year.

Some facts, however, work against the idea that Darwin died from Chagas' disease. Darwin's illness in many ways is not characteristic of Chagas' disease. Darwin never mentioned the first signs of the acute phase, development of a chagoma, a rash consisting of tiny red spots, fever, and spleen and heart problems. However, the majority of afflicted adults (60 to 70 percent) do *not* suffer symptoms of the acute phase. Ignorance of this factor remains a problem because many infected individuals with chronic Chagas' disease claim they are not infected since they did not suffer symptoms of the acute phase. Chagas' disease is frequently asymptomatic until years after the initial infection. The observation that Darwin reported no high fever is not sufficient in itself to rule out Chagas' disease.

Exhibiting limited knowledge, Browne (1995:280) refers to Chagas' disease as a South American sleeping sickness, with the implication that because Darwin did not suffer a fever typical of African sleeping sickness he did not have Chagas' disease. American trypanosomiasis (Chagas' disease) and African trypanosomiasis (African sleeping sickness) are both caused by *trypanosome* parasites: one by *Salivaria,* which lives in the saliva of its vector insect, and the other by *Sterecoria,* which lives in the feces of its vector insect. The difference between these parasites is that African trypanosomes remain in the blood and cause recurring fevers that exhaust the immune system; in contrast, American trypanosomes enter the neuron cells and frequently do not trigger immediate action of the immune system. American trypanosomes also reenter the blood.

Although Darwin's symptoms did not indicate heart disease until he was seventy-one, a relatively long life for the nineteenth century, he could have suffered subtler degrees of myocardial dysfunction, associated with *T. cruzi*, causing many of the complaints listed in his correspondence (see Adler 1959; Medawar 1964; Goldstein 1989). This debate has brought attention to Chagas' disease, sometimes referred to as Darwin's disease, and its diffuse nature and complex symptoms. Some hope that Darwin's body will be exhumed and its tissues examined for *T. cruzi*.

Discovering the Parasite

Darwin studied evolution from simple to complex creatures; Chagas studied how simple organisms destroy complex organisms. Chagas examined *barbeiros* which he collected. In sunlight he dried them and dissected their intestines, eventually finding some flagellates inside the lower intestines (see Figure 5).

Flagellates are protozoa, unicellular creatures that usually reproduce asexually and have flagella, or hairlike whips, propelling or pulling them. There are about 66,000 documented species of protozoa, with about half being represented in fossils; of the living species, about 10,000 are parasitic (Katz, Despommier, and Gwadz 1989). Unlike most of the helminths (worms), parasitic protozoa reproduce within the host to produce hundreds of thousands of individuals within a few days. They can pose major problems to human existence, causing malaria, giardia, vaginitis, amoebic dysentery, *Toxoplasma gondii*, African sleeping sickness, leishmaniasis, and pneumonia, among other ailments.

Chagas observed the newly found flagellates with the microscope, making fixed and stained microscope preparations, hoping to recognize the species or be able to characterize it as a new one. He observed that the parasite possessed a different morphological aspect than *Trypanosoma minasensi*, already recognized in Brazil, although it was a trypanosome, characterized by the undulating membrane, the large size of its basal body, or centriole, an organelle for cell division, and its undulating flagellum.

Chagas correctly identified the flagellated protozoan as a member of the family of *trypanosomidae*, but he believed it to be a previously undescribed genus and species. He named it *Schizotrypanum cruzi:* "in tribute to the master, Oswaldo Cruz, to whom I owe everything in my scientific career, and who guided me in these studies toward wide horizons, an adviser at any moment, a

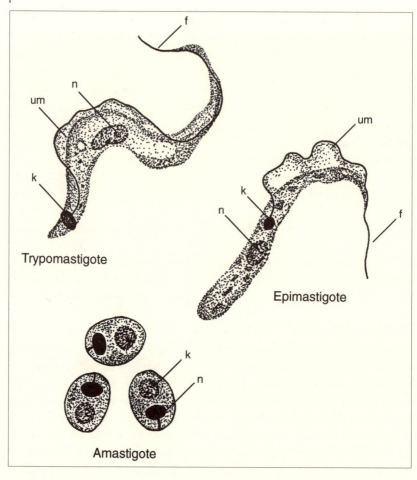

Figure 5. Forms of *T. cruzi*: n = nucleus, k = kinetoplast, um = undulating membrane, f = flagellum. (See Appendix 1.)

spirit of light and kindness, always quick in giving me the benefits of his knowledge and protecting me in the greatness of his affection" (in Kean 1977). (Oswaldo Cruz would also be memorialized by the founding of the *Instituto Oswaldo Cruz,* a world-renowned research center of tropical diseases in Brazil.) *Schizotrypanum cruzi* was later reclassified as *Trypanosoma cruzi* because it fits better into the genus of trypanosomes (see Chagas Filho 1993:85).

Once Chagas had found *T. cruzi,* he still wasn't sure that this parasite inhabited humans or other mammals, or that it caused the "strange disease." Countless parasites are beneficial to humans; it was even possible that *T. cruzi* curtailed the reproduction of *vinchucas.* Hypothetically, Carlos Chagas reasoned that his *Schizotrypanum cruzi* was either natural to *barbeiros,* creating no sickness, or that the flagellates found in the gut of *barbeiros* represented one stage of a transforming parasite that passed over to mammals and caused the reported symptoms in Lassance. Consequently, he examined tissues of animals and humans who had died from this "strange disease" to see if they were infected with *T. cruzi.*

Another clue for Chagas was that *Trypanosoma cruzi* resembles *Trypanosoma brucei gambiense,* a flagellate protozoan that lives in the blood of cattle and humans, causing African sleeping sickness. Uninfected tsetse flies bite cattle and humans infected with *T. b. gambiense,* which are frequently asleep during the middle of the day (hence the origin of the disease's name) and ingest the parasite. The parasite transforms into a metacyclic trypanosome in the saliva of the fly; from there it moves on to another host. Using plasmodia and trypanosoma parasites as models, Chagas suspected that *T. cruzi* had a similar cycle between *barbeiros* and mammals, causing yet another disease within them. He suspected that because *T. cruzi* was found in the rear gut of *barbeiros,* it was passed through the insect's fecal matter to humans after the insect bit and then defecated near the wound. The parasite then entered through the bite wound.

In April 1908 Chagas spent the night in a house where he found a sickly cat, which he examined, finding *T. cruzi.* Two weeks later, he again visited the same house to treat a three-year-old child, Rita, feverishly ill. He found a large swarm of insects biting the inhabitants, including Rita, who had been healthy during his earlier visit. After he examined her blood, he found "the existence of flagellates," as Chagas (1922) described it, "in good number and the fixing and staining of blood films made it possible to characterize the parasite's morphology and to identify it with *Trypanosoma cruzi.*"

Rita had a fever of 40°C (105°F) for two weeks. Her spleen and liver were enlarged and her lymph nodes were swollen. Most noticeable to Chagas was a generalized infiltration, more pronounced in the face, and which did not show the characteristics of renal edema but rather of myxedema. Carlos Chagas (1911) found this last symptom to be one of the most characteristic forms of the acute stage of the disease; it revealed some functional alteration of the thyroid gland, perhaps affected by the pathogenic action of the parasite.

Three days later, Rita died from parasitemia caused by *T. cruzi.* Today, some ninety years after Rita's death, seven children die each day from the acute phase of Chagas' disease in Bolivia (Ault et al. 1992:9). Carlos Chagas also treated another patient in 1908, a woman named Bernice, who died in 1989 still harboring the parasite but with no evidence of pathology (Carlos Chagas Filho 1993).

The pathology of Chagas' disease varies from a mild and inapparent infec-

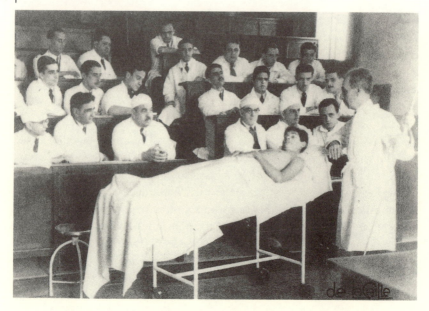

Figure 6. Carlos Chagas lecturing to doctors about Chagas' disease.
(Photo from Renato Clark Bacellar, *Brazil's Contribution to Tropical Medicine and Malaria*, Rio de Janeiro, 1963)

tion as was found in Bernice, who outlived Carlos Chagas by twenty-seven years, to Rita, the three-year-old girl who died from a virulent acute infection. Because its pathology varies so widely, the diagnosis of Chagas' disease from symptoms is difficult.

Animal studies were needed by Chagas to claim that *Trypanosoma cruzi* was the pathogenetic agent causing the fever and heart diseases. Even though the parasite had been found in insects and in a human, evidence was still lacking that it created the observed symptoms. Chagas sent some *barbeiros* infected with *Trypanosoma cruzi* to Cruz in Rio. Cruz injected the bugs' intestinal contents into three uninfected callithrix monkeys. When the monkeys started dying some days later, Cruz cabled Chagas to come to Rio to see the results.

The journey from Lassance was a grueling twenty-four-hour trip, with two train changes and long waits. Chagas and Cruz knew that this discovery would place them, the Institute Oswaldo Cruz, and Brazil in the forefront of tropical medicine throughout the world. Cruz met Chagas at the railroad station and took him directly to the laboratory, where the mammalian pathogenicity of the flagellate was confirmed.

Carlos Chagas and Oswaldo Cruz later proved that *T. cruzi* passes from *Triatoma infestans* through fecal matter when these bugs defecate near the bite

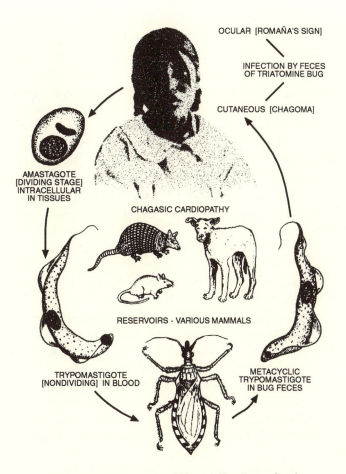

Figure 7. Parasitic cycle of *T. cruzi*. (See Appendix 1.)

site. *T. cruzi* then enters through the skin or bite site into the human's blood and nerve cells. The parasitic cycle of this disease included *T. cruzi* as the pathogenic agent, which was transmitted by triatomine insects through their fecal matter to mammalian hosts (animals and humans). People become infected with *T. cruzi* by indirect contamination through the fecal matter of *vinchucas* and by direct transmission through blood or cells at birth and in blood transfusions and organ transplants. *Vinchucas* are directly infected with *T. cruzi* through their ingestion of the blood of infected animals and humans. *T. cruzi* transforms and reproduces in the vector and the host, both being necessary for its survival (see Figure 7).

Progression of Chagas' Disease

Carlos Chagas discovered the symptoms and progression of Chagas' disease. Figure 8 illustrates how Chagas' disease progresses, which is a complex and in part unresolved issue. Primary Chagas' disease refers to the acute infection stage, which may not be clinically apparent, with about 25 percent of infected patients indicating it (see Appendix 9). If apparent, it is characterized by inflammation that may include fever, general malaise, swelling and soreness of the lymph nodes and spleen, and by *Signo de Romaña*, severe swelling around the eye. People die or suffer permanent damage during the acute phase; those who survive have classic chronic or tertiary Chagas' disease.

Infected victims pass into early latent Chagas', which is asymptomatic. Latent Chagas' offers several possibilities: 1) the infection is arrested at this stage, 2) it develops later to late latent Chagas' with minor clinical findings, or 3) it develops into classic chronic (tertiary) Chagas' disease. Those with minor clinical findings progress to either early latent arrested (secondary) Chagas' or classic chronic (tertiary) Chagas'.

A certain number of patients live out their lives in the early latent arrested phase, with no noticeable symptoms, except perhaps fatigue. As mentioned, one acute patient of Carlos Chagas in 1909, Bernice, lived past the age of seventy and was checked annually, with no symptoms of the disease ever being manifested (Lewinsohn 1979:519). However, in many instances, the disease culminates with classic chronic symptoms of tertiary Chagas'—heart disease and enlarged colon and esophagus—which if untreated result in death. There is no known cure for the chronic phase.

Chagas' disease is closely related to the immune system. Its progression varies greatly with the immunocompetence of each individual. Bolivians suffer so greatly from it in part because many are malnourished and infected with other diseases (see Appendix 11).

At the Brazilian National Academy of Medicine's session on April 22, 1909, Oswaldo Cruz read Chagas' work entitled "A New Human Trypanosomiasis." Cruz referred to the new disease as American trypanosomiasis to distinguish it from African trypanosomiasis, but American trypanosomiasis was soon known as Chagas' disease (Kean 1977). Shortly after the reading of the paper, Cruz and a group of distinguished physicians traveled to Lassance to visit Chagas at work. Miguel Couto described the visit:

Carlos Chagas was waiting for us with his museum of laboratory items. Examination between cover-glass and slide revealed the rarities—several dozen patients of all ages, some idiots, others paralytics, others heart cases, thyroids, myxedemics and asthenics. Microscopes were scattered all over the tables showing trypanosomes in movement, or pathological anatomic lesions. In the cases were animals experimentally infected and jars full of

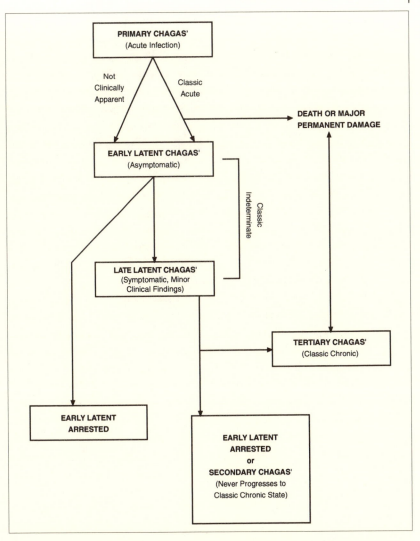

Figure 8. Progression of Chagas' disease. (From Jared Goldstein, "Darwin, Chagas', Mind, and Body," *Perspectives in Biology and Medicine* 32, no. 4([1989]:595.)

triatomines in all stages of development. Every item of this demonstration was carefully examined by us. The doctors gathered there, undisputable authorities in their fields…had nothing to deny or add to the analysis of the symptoms or their interpretations.…On that day it was up to me to give a name to those traditional diseases of the Minas backlands, which were now unified as one disease with cause and development clearly established. To name it after only one of its symptoms would be to limit its description, and to name it for all its symptoms would be impossible....And so, at dinner, while toasting Carlos Chagas, I...chosen because of my age, standing with Oswaldo Cruz on my right and surrounded by the men most representative of Brazilian medicine of that era, with gravity equal to a liturgical act in our religion, such as a baptism, gave the name of Chagas' Disease to that illness...in the name of the entire delegation (Couto, in Kean 1977).

Carlos Chagas died in 1933 of angina pectoris as he was looking through a microscope into the universe of parasites. A year before his death, he optimistically spoke to a class of graduating physicians: "Gentlemen, the practical applications of hygiene and tropical medicine have destroyed the prejudice of a fatal climate; the scientific methods are prevailing against the sickness of the tropics" (Kean 1977). On a less optimistic occasion, he remarked, "This is a beautiful land, with its tremendous variety of vegetation. Nature made animal and vegetable life stronger and thus created conditions which bring sickness and death to the men who live here" (Chagas Filho 1993).

Since Carlos Chagas' amazingly rapid discovery of it in 1909, research concerning this disease has been slow. After Chagas discovered *Trypanosoma cruzi*, the disease was not described until ten years later and was not recognized as a serious health problem in Brazil for another forty years. Other countries of Latin America have been even slower in recognizing the problem, with Bolivia beginning in 1991. The first and only drugs—nifurtimox and benznidazole—for treatment did not appear until 1970 and then met with only partial success. Discovering disease is only a short first step toward treating and preventing it.

CHAPTER TWO

Early Andean Disease

The earliest indications of Chagas' disease in the Andes are found among mummies dated as living at A.D. 400. Anthropologists Roth-hammer, Allison, Nuñez, Standen, and Arriaza (1985) recently discovered the ancient mummies of twenty-two Andeans in Quebrada de Tarapacá, Chile. The mummies were 1,500 years old and belonged to an extinct culture, called the Wankari. Eleven of the bodies had greatly enlarged hearts, colons, or esophagi. One forty-five-year-old male had both an enlarged colon and heart. Another twenty-five-year-old male had an enlarged colon and esophagus. Three forty-five-year-old males had enlarged colons, and a three-year-old boy had an enlarged heart and colon. Four women had enlarged colons.

What caused the enlarged organs in half of these bodies? Scientists considered various explanations. Cardiomegaly, enlarged heart, sometimes results from atrophied heart muscles caused by degenerative diseases associated with aging. This could explain the older victims of ages forty to forty-five but not the enlarged heart of the child. The average life span of the people was around thirty-five years at this time.

Megasyndromes appeared in all cases. Enlargement of the colon was explainable by fermentation of food, creating gas and causing intestinal walls to expand, a condition found in unembalmed corpses in warmer climates. The climate of Quebrada de Tarapacá in the northern highlands of Chile is frigid because of its high altitude. The nerves of the intestinal walls were severely atrophied, perhaps resulting from a long-term disease condition.

Another possibility was that the corpses could have suffered severe gastritis and flatulence from spoiled lima beans shortly before death. After the petrified contents (coprolites) of the colons were examined, scientists found carob-tree sheaths (*Prosopis juliflora*) but no lima beans (*Phaseolus lunatus*). It is possible that the victims may have eaten the carob sheaths as medicine. The impacted bowels indicated long-term constipation, usually caused by the inability of the colon's sphincter muscles to contract, expand, and dispel the feces. Degenerated neuron cells of the sphincter muscles can cause this as well as enlarged hearts and esophagi.

The anthropologists inquired about modern Andeans from this region to see if they suffered from similar symptoms, and, not surprisingly, many peasants suffered these symptoms. Among modern Andeans 90 percent of individuals with megacolon and 100 percent of those with megacolon and megaesophagus are tested seropositive for Chagas' disease (Atias 1980). Degeneration of neuron tissues of the heart, esophagus, and colon are common to patients with chronic Chagas' disease. The exhumed Wankari Andeans likely died from Chagas' disease, which was quite likely as debilitating and as deadly a disease then as it is now, 1,500 years later.

Long-Term Adaptation of *T. cruzi*

Modern Andeans, however, from this region suffer milder forms of Chagas' disease than those living in lower regions. This indicates long-term adaptation of early Andeans at Quebrada de Tarapacá. Clinical surveys of chronic Chagas' patients indicate that in the lower Andean region of northern Chile the infection rate is low and great evidence of cardiac involvement is detected by electrocardiograms (Arribada et al. 1990). In the higher Andean region of Quebrada de Tarapacá a very high infection rate is detected, but cardiac involvement is lower than that of the lower region (Apt et al. 1987). This indicates the importance of altitudinal factors on the *T. cruzi* infection causing cardiac involvement (Villarroel et al. 1991). The more benign character of Chagas' disease detected in higher altitudes of Chile is significant because it may relate to the ancient adaptation of the parasite to the human host in the Andean highlands of Quebrada de Tarapacá (González et al. 1995:126; Neghme 1982).

It is possible that the varying severities of Chagas' disease may be due to different strains of *T. cruzi* circulating in each area. Such *T. cruzi* strains display unique characteristics. Individual *T. cruzi* strains and geographic distribution of different strains and their source (sylvatic or domestic) play a role in the wide variety of clinical signs encountered in Chagas' disease (Rassi 1977). Nevertheless, early adaptation of *T. cruzi* to humans in the southern Andean highlands likely explains the more benign character of Chagas' disease found there today (González et al. 1995: 132–33) (see Appendix 2: Strains of *T. cruzi*).

Enlarged Colons in Bolivia: A Case of *Empacho*

In Bolivia in 1992 I observed similar megasyndromes among Quechua peasants in the village of Choromoro, about seventy-five miles east of Sucre, Bolivia. One woman suffered an enormously enlarged heart (five times its normal size) and had died shortly before I arrived. A man named Jacinto had an enlarged intestine about the size of a basketball (see Figure 9). Jacinto hadn't gone to the toilet for half a year and was dying. Jacinto said that he had *empacho,* a culturally defined illness that includes constipation. *Empacho* has accompanying emotions of sadness, lethargy, and embarrassment. Even though his constipation sounded like it could relate to the anthropologists' fermented-bean theory, Jacinto understood his body better than did physical anthropologists.

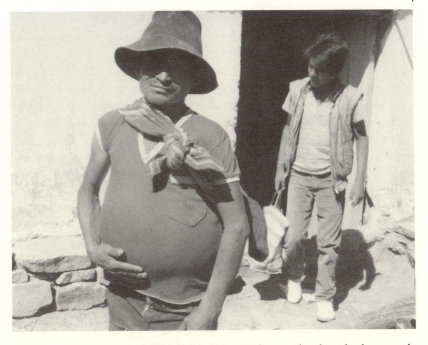

Figure 9. Peasant from the Department of Sucre, Bolivia, with enlarged colon caused by chronic Chagas' disease. He had not defecated for five months because *T. cruzi* parasites had destroyed his colon muscles. Surgeons eventually removed the damaged colon and a colestomy was performed. (Photograph by staff of Proyecto Británico Cardenal Maurer)

Curanderos explain that *empacho* is caused by the accumulation of poison-ous fluids excreted by the distillation process of the inner organs. Jacinto's *chuyma* (inner organs: from heart to lower bowels) were *usu* (unable to con-centrate and dispel fluids). Andeans such as Jacinto understand the human body as a hydraulic system with a muscular-skeletal framework and conduits through which air, blood, feces, milk, phlegm, semen, sweat, and urine flow in centrifugal and centripetal motion (Bastien 1985). To Jacinto, his body was un-able to exchange foods and fluids by means of ingestion and expulsion. He needed to expel toxic substances by increasing the centrifugal motion of his blood, diagnosed as cold and wet.

After many herbal and ritual treatments, Jacinto's *empacho* persisted. His stomach grew to the size of that of a pregnant woman. He stopped eating and stayed home. Fearing he would die from *empacho,* as others have, relatives transported him by truck to the hospital in Sucre, the *Instituto de Gastroen-terología Boliviano Japonés.* Surgeons there removed a large part of his lower colon, stitched him up, and loaded him back on the truck to Choromoro. Jacinto appreciated the "patch up," as he put it, but believed that the *empacho* would return, as it had for previous victims in Choromoro. "You always die from it, my uncle and mother did," he said.

I traveled from Choromoro to Sucre, where I talked with a resident surgeon who had operated on Jacinto, and I explained that *Trypanosoma cruzi* was the cause of Jacinto's *empacho*. After initial infection, metacyclic trypomastigote forms of *T. cruzi* rapidly travel from the blood to neuron cells of the heart, colon, and esophagus (see Figure 5). There the trypomastigotes encyst, reproduce, and produce amastigotes. These amastigotes change into trypomastigotes and then reenter the blood to be picked up by *vinchuca* bugs. Encysted amastigotes live within these basically hollow organs, which they eventually destroy. They denervate muscles of the intraneural nervous plexus.

Particular zydomes (strains) of the parasite show a preference for particular organs. *T. cruzi* zydomes in the geographical Department of Sucre seem to prefer the colon. *T. cruzi*, although once considered as a single pathogenic factor in Chagas' disease, is further differentiated into some 100 strains in Bolivia alone, each with its unique genetic structure and destructive capabilities (see Appendix 2: Strains of *T. cruzi*).

The Spread of Chagas' Disease in the Andes

The spread of Chagas' disease throughout the Andes is related to environmental and social factors that bring together *T. cruzi, Triatoma infestans,* and humans. *Vinchucas* (*Triatoma infestans*) probably transmitted *T. cruzi* to humans as early as 6,000 years ago when early Andeans occupied caves and rock shelters in the central Andes around Pampa de Junin (Wheeler, Pires-Ferreira, and Kailicke 1976).

Another possibility is that early Andeans acquired Chagas' disease by ingesting raw infected meat of alpacas, llamas, guanacos, guinea pigs, cavy, and deer. These animals *probably* hosted *T. infestans* before the Pleistocene epoch and have been found in early Andean archaeological sites (Neghme 1982, Dauelsberg 1983).

The cohabitation of *vinchucas, T. cruzi,* and humans probably started during the third millennium B.C., a preceramic period, when Andeans began living in settled agricultural communities in permanent dwellings of stone or structures of adobe walls with straw roofs (Nuñez 1983). One such community, at La Galgada, Peru, has recently been excavated (Grieder et al. 1988). These early Andeans cultivated squash, gourds, guava, *lúcuma*, lima beans, and avocado using irrigation canals. They lived in scattered clusters of small houses, carrying out ceremonies in various chambers which permitted seating only around a circle with a fire in the center. They made cloth with harness looms.

By the second millennium B.C., the people at La Galgada were trading for shells from as far off as Ecuador. They lived in hereditary kin groups. The spread of Chagas' disease probably was precipitated in such settlements by the proximity of humans and animals (especially guinea pigs) in houses and villages where insect vectors could easily feed, rapidly passing parasites from infected to uninfected mammals. Infected Andeans spread the parasite from village to village in their travels with alpacas and llamas, also carrying parasites and insects in their cargo.

The Wankaris of Tarapacá descended from nomadic hunters and gatherers who had migrated 3,000 years ago from the shores of Lake Poopó in the southern highlands of the Andean mountains across the Atacama desert into the Quebrada de Tarapacá (Nuñez 1982). For thousands of years they foraged and hunted within the southern Andes. They fished and gathered mollusks, berries, nuts, and carrion meat. They lived in caves where they built fires, cooked meat, and told stories. These caves were also inhabited by bears, rats, cavies, viscacha, bats, and triatomine insects.

Around the beginning of the first millennium B.C., Wankaris had changed their nomadic and foraging lifestyle to become semisedentary farmers, herders, and gatherers (Wheeler, Pires-Ferreira, and Kailicke 1976). The Quebrada de Tarapacá provided a more habitable place to settle down, with a warmer climate and lower altitude, 3,737 feet (1,100 m.), than the frigid climate and higher altitudes of the mountains around Lake Poopó at 11,700 feet (3,600 m.).

Also by this time, it is thought that *vinchucas* inhabited human houses as their primary environment in agroceramic centers of Argentina, southern Peru, and eastern and central Bolivia (notably in Cochabamba, an epicenter from where they evolved from sylvatic, or forest, to domiciliary environments, a fact indicated by the presence of both types there today). Domiciliary preferences of *vinchucas* enabled them to rapidly reproduce and infect animals and humans, resulting in widespread endemic Chagas' disease. Vinchucas becoming domiciliary was about as devastating to Andeans' health as the domestication of alpacas and llamas was to improving their lives. *Vinchucas* traveled and lived with their herds, spreading *T. cruzi* up and down the Andes and well into the Amazon.

Certain environmental factors contributed then, as they do now, to triatomines adapting from sylvatic to domestic habitats: the increased size and growth of villages encroached upon their forest habitats and diminished the number of sylvatic mammals from which they could ingest blood meals, while domiciliary environments with humans and animals crowded together provided increased feeding and nesting opportunities for *vinchucas.*

Human migrants are important vectors of ecological exchange. Humans tend to dominate any environment in which they are a part, and colonists are a decisive element in any biological conquest. Because the constantly migrating early Andeans were subject to changing environments, they were less able to dominate these environments, in part because diseases spread faster than they could adapt to them. Early Andeans then, and migrating peasants today, transverse a range of microbes, as also was illustrated in the previous chapter when railroad expansion into tropical forests of Brazil brought a disproportionate amount of disease to the workers.

Even though *Triatoma infestans* inhabited houses in the Andes for thousands of years and symptoms of Chagas' disease were found among the Wankaris, *T. cruzi* is first found within an Inca mummy of the central Andes dated around 1400 B.C. (Fornaciari et al. 1992). In 1992, paleopathologists from the University of Pisa examined the mummy of a twenty-year-old woman from Cuzco, ancient capital of the Inca empire from 1275 to 1532, kept at the National Museum of Anthropology and Ethnology in Florence. The mummy sits in a crouched position, wrapped in coils of a basket, with her face protruding through the top. Mummification was customary for Incas until the conquest of Peru in 1532, after which missionaries prohibited it, considering it ancestor worship. The mummified Inca's heart, esophagus, and colon were abnormally enlarged, suggesting a megavisceral syndrome similar to that of the Wankari mummies.

Paleopathologists examined the mummy's tissues by means of electronomicroscopy and immunohistochemistry and discovered round nests of amastigotes of *Trypanosoma cruzi* within the myocardium and esophagus. Their conclusions were written in *The Lancet,* January 11, 1992: "The macroscopic, historical, immunohistochemical, and ultrastructural findings in this Peruvian mummy constitute an ancient case of chronic Chagas' disease. This is the first direct demonstration of this disease, and agent causing it in South America during the Inca empire immediately before the Spanish conquest of that continent."

Discoveries at Lassance, Quebrada de Tarapacá, and Cuzco fill in some of the early history of Chagas' disease in the Andes, but there remains a large void. Archaeologists, physical anthropologists, parasitologists, and paleopathologists have contributed to our knowledge of Chagas' disease, and further interdisciplinary research is relevant to understanding Chagas' disease.

Inca Expansion and the Spread of Chagas' Disease

Medical anthropologists can interpret how sociocultural factors contribute to the parasitic cycle of Chagas' disease. Inca civilization illustrates this. Often compared to the Romans, Incas are famous for their conquests, empire building, architecture, and treatment of diseases (see Lumbreras 1974, Rowe 1946, and Zuidema 1964). These achievements influenced the transmission of *T. cruzi* and the treatment of its syndromes. The Inca empire extended from Chile to Ecuador, and from the Pacific Ocean into the Amazon. An extensive road network was established between colonies. During the empire's height in the fifteenth century several hundred ethnic groups and thousands of communities exchanged resources, ranging from parrots of the Amazon in Ecuador, Peru, and Bolivia to salt from the high Atacama desert in Argentina and Chile.

When Incas expanded their empire from Cuzco to Bolivia, Chile, and Ecuador, *T. infestans* rapidly spread to communities across the Andes, providing an example of biotic exchange following "civilizing" forces. *T. infestans* became a commensal species (such as mice), living in close proximity to humans. Houses provided proximity to animals and humans and a protected habitat from the cold. Unknowingly, Incas transported *vinchucas* in llama caravans throughout the empire.

During the expansionist fifteenth century in Incaic America, Pacha Kuteq Inca Yupanki, the ninth king, conquered the Chanka, a powerful neighboring kingdom, and his son, Tupac Inca Yupanki, extended the empire from the Mapuche line in central Chile to Quito, Ecuador, as well as westward to the coast and eastward to the Amazon. The Inca empire was named Tawantinsuyo for four triangulated sections that were formed with the bases of the triangle at Cuzco, the apexes extending to the four directions: two long-sided isosceles triangles pointing north and south, and short-sided triangles pointing east and west.

The Inca present a unique example of how a mountain civilization was able to incorporate many ecological zones and cultures within a continent. During the Incario there was a massive exchange of people, cultures, resources, animals, plants, insects, and parasites. Only within the last twenty years has there been a comparable ethnic and biotic exchange within the Andes.

The Andes are characterized by their verticality—as one travels up a mountain, the width of the ecological band decreases. Climbing an Andean mountain, one finds tropical leafy plants, monkeys, and parrots in the lower valleys; corn, vegetables, and fruits on the lower slopes, potatoes, oca, and barley on the central slopes; alpacas, llamas, and bunch grass on the higher slopes; and mossy and furry plants on the tundra near the summit. Andean communities live, farm, and herd in these zones. They then exchange resources with others, often relatives, from communities at another level. For example, highland Aymara herders raise alpacas and llamas at 15,000 feet whose meat they exchange to Quechua farmers at lower levels who raise potatoes, and to other farmers at still lower levels who grow corn.

The Incas moved *mitmakuna,* colonists, from each of the several hundred ethnic groups to different regions of the Andes as well as to different elevations. These colonists expanded the groups' access to products throughout the Andes. The Incas profited politically by being able to better control each group, now weakened at home by the exportation of members and by the settlement within the ethnic group of Inca administrators. The ethnic groups were not entirely unhappy, however, because *mitmakuna* opened up the possibility of exchanging resources with many different regions. The Incas demanded portions of all produce for the state, to be stored in warehouses and used in times of famine and war. An elaborate system of roads, runners (*chasquis*), *quipus* (knotted cords used to keep records), warehouses, and military posts linked the communities with the capital, Cuzco, and each other.

Chagas' disease increased with this exchange of people and resources that had previously been restricted to smaller levels of the region. The Incas brought herbalists and ritualists to Cuzco from the Lake Titicaca region for medicinal purposes. Especially recognized, the Kallawayas, now located in Province Bautista Saavedra, Charazani, Bolivia, carried the chair of the Inca king and practiced herbal medicine in Cuzco and other parts of the Incario (Bastien 1987a, Oblitas Poblete 1968, 1969, 1978). (Kallawaya treatments for Chagas' disease are discussed in the next chapter.)

Inca Housing and Settlement

Architecture and housing affected the infestation of *vinchucas* in Cuzco. Inca rulers divided Cuzco into two parts, called upper and lower Cuzco; each was further divided into clans of pure-blood Incas, half-breed people, and foreigners (see Zuidema 1964). The clans were matrilineal, with matrilateral cross-cousin marriages between the clans. Clustered gatherings of houses and their inhabitants provided *T. infestans* (harboring *T. cruzi*) ample opportunities to hide and feed.

The imperial city of Cuzco provided many havens for insects. Imperial houses and temples were built of tightly fit dressed stone. Mortar and plaster were little used, providing openings at cornices and foundations for *vinchucas* to enter. Roofs consisted of wood—primarily thatch—preferred sites for *T. infestans* to nest. Houses in the suburbs were constructed of field stone, clay, or adobe. They were rectangular with gabled and thatched roofs. The rooms were built around a courtyard where animals were kept. The proximity of animals to sleeping quarters facilitates the transmission of *T. cruzi* from infected animals to humans through the bite of *vinchucas*.

Spanish Conquest and *Vinchucas*

The sequel to the Inca empire was the Spanish conquest in 1532, partially facilitated by civil war and diseases. As Tupac Yupanki lay dying in Quito about 1527, he was informed of white-skinned people with hair on their faces and shining clothes riding on big animals, they having appeared around Panama. Tupac Yupanki established a dual government. One ruler, Atawallpa, wanted total control, attacked the other, and imprisoned him after five years of civil war. Francisco Pizarro met Atawallpa on the plains of Cajamarca in 1532, slaughtered thousands of Incas, held Atawallpa ransom for gold payments from Cuzco, and then beheaded him after receiving the shipment of gold.

It is not certain to what extent Chagas' disease debilitated the Incas, but from the evidence of this disease among Inca mummies one can assume that at least some Incas suffered from chronic Chagas' disease. Chronic Chagas' disease is considered by some to be the greatest hindrance to development in Latin America today.

After the Spanish conquest of the Incas, Andeans were weakened with diseases of Old World origin (see Dobyns 1963). Smallpox, measles, malaria, yellow fever, bubonic plague, and undoubtedly several other diseases were unknown in the pre-Columbian New World (Ashburn 1947; Crosby 1976). Andeans were especially stricken by smallpox, which was accompanied by respiratory ailments, possibly measles and tuberculosis. These diseases are considered virgin-soil epidemics because Andeans had no previous contact with them and were immunologically almost defenseless.

An epidemic of the 1520s in Peru was caused by either measles or smallpox. Smallpox is the prime suspect. It was a major blow to the Inca empire because it killed Wayna Capac, the Inca emperor, and as many as one-half of the population (Crosby 1972:52). "When Wayna Capac died," wrote Cieza de León (1959), "the mourning was such that the lamentation and shrieks rose to the skies, causing the birds to fall to the ground. The news traveled far and wide, and nowhere did it not evoke great sorrow." Conquistador Pedro Pizarro (1921) recorded that had "Wayna Capac been alive when we Spaniards entered this land, it would have been impossible for us to win it, for he was much beloved by all his vassals." Andeans of the Inca empire told Pedro Pizarro that they had no acquaintance with smallpox in pre-Columbian times (see Crosby 1972:62, note 38). Smallpox is only one of the epidemics that decimated Andean populations. The pre-Columbian population for the central Andes has been estimated at 6 million inhabitants; by 1650 the population had decreased to 1.5 million (see Dobyns 1966:397–98).

Conquest also brought drastic social changes, one being that Andeans were expected to exchange resources, silver, and gold with Spain. Many of the ties across the Andes were diminished as others were created from the mountains to the coast and across the Atlantic. During colonial and post-colonial times, large cities were established along the Pacific and Atlantic coasts of South America. Trade routes were established between coastal ports and interior cities. A major route was established between the oceans from Lima, through

Cuzco, across the central Andes to La Paz, to the mines of Potosí and Sucre, and down across Argentina to Buenos Aires. Infected *vinchucas,* animals, and humans traveled this and other routes until all the countries of Latin America had Chagas' disease.

Vinchucas had become a nuisance in Chile in the 1800s. The following is a translation of Rodolfo Amando Phillippi's *Viaje al Desierto de Atacama hecho por orden del Gobierno de Chile en el verano 1853:*

> Fleas and lice are not found in Atacama, and the natives assure me that these animals die whenever they are introduced by chance. Instead of these, the houses abound with *vinchucas.* It is a species of flying bug with very large legs; its length is 11 lineas, but it is very slender, of dark color. They rarely fly, and during the day they principally hide in the thatch of the roof where they descend at night to feed themselves on human blood. Their bite does not cause pain, but sensitive people develop boils that become inflamed for several days, accompanied by a species of fever. If a *vinchuca* is squashed, it leaves a very black mark that never can be removed. One morning, I counted in my bed forty-one *vinchucas* between large and small. They appear to belong to various distinct species, and there are some rare ones in the middle of the desert (Amando Phillippi 1860:54).

This account indicates that *vinchucas* continued to infest houses in the nineteenth century. The author also makes the point that *vinchucas* colonize areas not frequented much by other insects; he also emphasizes the insects' abundance.

Conclusion

An important factor in the spread of Chagas' disease was the political economy of colonization, accompanied by impoverishment of people, destruction of land, and attempts to replace Andean culture with European and American culture. It is no wonder that Andeans still refer to foreigners as "*vinchucas.*"

Andean Indians celebrated the quincentennial of Columbus's discovery of America with sorrow because of their perceived destruction of the New World. Some Bolivians designed a flag for the occasion. Written on this flag, which symbolizes a pan-Andean nativistic movement, is the word "*Pachacutej*" ("reversed time") and "500 years." An Aymara leader explained its significance: "For five hundred years we have suffered diseases, poverty, and destruction of land which started with the Conquest. Now, we have to travel five hundred years back to return to what has been taken away by others." Bolivians of all classes are working towards restoring the values, beliefs, and practices inherent in Andean culture. One finding of this book is the importance of renewing certain Andean traditional patterns to help prevent Chagas' disease. These patterns involve environmental factors that impinge upon housing, herding, and farming, and that in turn are related to parasites, insects, mammals, and humans. Restoration of cultural values can help Bolivians get rid of the *"vinchucas."*

CHAPTER THREE

Jampiris and *Yachajs:* Andean Ethnomedicine

Kallawaya herbalists have dealt with the symptoms of Chagas' disease for many years. Kallawaya herbalists and diviners practiced as early as the Wankaris and Incas, with a healing tradition that dates back to A.D. 500. Even today, these diviners and traveling herbalists are recognized for their curing techniques in Argentina, Bolivia, Chile, and Peru (see Bastien 1987a). Kallawayas live in the Province of Bautista Saavedra in northwestern Bolivia near the Peruvian border. Approximately 120 herbalists (*jampiris*) and sixty diviners (*yachajs*) continue to practice the rituals and herbal healing that have been passed down by their ancestors for over a thousand years.

Andeans have effectively adapted to Chagas' disease for thousands of years, illustrating that traditional medical systems can work independently of biomedical systems, and perhaps even more efficiently and economically, and that it is not necessary that Andeans understand Chagas' disease in terms of Western biomedicine. Conversely, Americans rarely understand how Kallawaya medicine operates. Medical systems are peculiar to different cultures, as they function within environmental and sociocultural parameters. Kallawaya *curanderos,* for instance, provide valuable lessons about the relationship of disease to environment. They symbolically express that Chagas' disease spreads through deforestation, impoverishment, and urbanization bringing *T. cruzi*, *vinchucas,* animals, and humans into proximity. Chagas' disease results from this disorder and must be washed away in the river. These ancient medicine men drive home the lesson of an uncared-for earth.

Misfortune Ritual: Dispelling Chagas' Disease

The following "misfortune ritual" of a Kallawaya *warmi yachaj* (woman diviner) illustrates how ailments of Chagas' disease can be seen to reflect the forces of nature. It is derived from contemporary research of rituals among the Kallawayas from 1963 to the present (see Bastien 1978, 1987a, 1992). Pseudonyms are used and the account is narrated in the first person. The patient's name is Tika, "flower" in Quechua. Tika tells about her ailments:

> *Chuyma usu* [heart disease], I asked for a *yachajs* [soothsayer] to read the coca leaves and the bowels of a *cuy* [guinea pig] to see why my *ajayu* [spiritual fluid] and *vira* [fat: material energy] do not flow back and forth between the earth. Why my *chuyma* [heart] gets bigger and bigger....
>
> The *yachaj* spoke with *Pachamama* [Mother Earth], who said that my

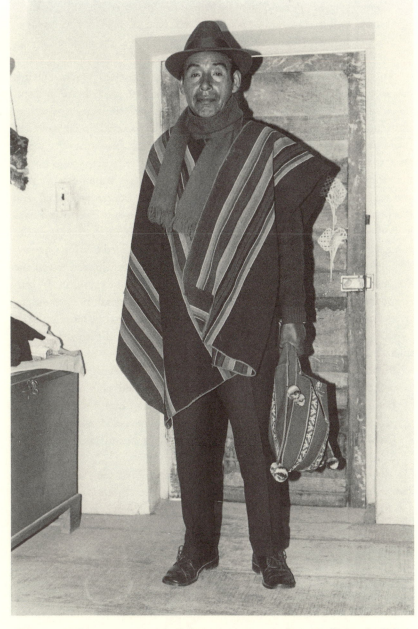

Figure 10. Kallawaya *jampiri* or herbal curer. Approximately 120 Kallawaya herbalists
live in the Department of Bautista Saavedra, Bolivia. They travel throughout Andean
countries treating people with Chagas' disease and other illnesses. They practice a
thousand-year-old tradition and use over one thousand plants.
(Photograph by Joseph W. Bastien)

chuyma contains fluids that must flow down the river like my *yawar* [blood] used to flow. *Yawar, ajayu,* and *vira* have stopped. I must call a *Jampiri* [herbalist] and a *Warmi Yachajs* to perform a *sajjra mesa* [misfortune ritual] to the *mayu* [river].

Tuta Korota, a *warmi yachaj,* was called to perform a *sajjra mesa.* The first part of the ritual was performed in the cooking room of Tika's house to dispel the misfortune with the wind; the second part was performed near the river to wash the misfortune away. A woman performs sickness rituals to the wind and river due to her structural position in a society in which she marries and moves away from her matrilineage but in which her daughters marry and return to their mother's land. She links the generations in marriage in a movement away and yet continuous. According to age-old traditions, women are linked with misfortunes, both causing as well as removing them. So, too, rivers wash away misfortunes but also restore. Rivers form the boundaries of the land. The configuration of Cuzco as the body of a puma was defined by rivers flowing through the capital of the Incas (Rowe 1967). Rivers are also seen to traverse the heavens and netherworld. The Milky Way is believed to connect the stars across the sky. Concomitantly, it is believed that underneath the ground are rivers along which the dead travel on their return to the earth (Bastien 1978).

Tuta Korota arrived at Tika's house on a Friday night, shortly before midnight. Tika described it:

> Tuta Korota sat in the eastern corner facing west, I sat with my mother and sisters around her. We placed cloth, potatoes, oca, and coca leaves in a bundle, *tawichu,* a woman like us. Tuta Korota was a wizard of the wind also. She purified us with incense and asked permission of the wind [*Wayra*] to perform the ritual by throwing *aqha* [*chicha*/corn beer] into the air so that *Wayra* could carry it "to where *Wayra* blows."

Wayra had supposedly brought *chuyma usu* to Tika, and, in retaliation, Tuta Korota poured another cup of *chicha* for the community wind. She passed this cup over Tika's and her matrilineal relatives' heads and went into the courtyard to throw it into the wind. This toast was to ensure that the wind of those who cursed Tika would be destroyed.

Wayra has two aspects: it serves as a metaphorical vehicle for cursing people, and it also brings the rain clouds to wash away sickness—to remove the *chijekuna* (invisible troublesome substances) within Tika and to dispose of them within the river. The wind's two climatic properties parallel the river's two relationships to the mountain as both erosive and cyclical. As Andean etiology parallels telluric forces of nature, so too Andean ethnomedicine symbolically serves these forces (see Bastien 1978, 1985, 1987a, 1992). Tika continued:

> Tuta Korota laid a *wayllasa* [ritual cloth] between us. She laid a rat at the head of *wayllasa* and sorted out twenty wads of dark llama wool. *Mamay*

[my mother] brought coca leaves from *Cabildo* [shrine of patio] and *Capilla* [Chapel]. Tuta Korota put slivers of llama fat on the coca, saying, "Here's some food for the rats and mice." Tuta Korota also served daisies, seeds, herb clumps, and moss. The wads were wrapped to the rat's back and two wads were given to each of us. Tuta Korota rubbed me with the wads, demanding, *"Chijekuna purijchej! Chijekuna purijchej! Chijekuna purijchej!"* [Be gone!]....

Tika traveled with Tuta Korota and her relatives to the river to wash themselves and to expel the inner fluids contaminating her. Tuta Korota dispelled Tika's misfortunes [*chijekuna*] into the river to be washed away, as Tika narrated it:

> ...I put one wad in my sandal and the other inside my headband. We filed out the front gate into the mud and rain. Everyone carried a large pack of dirty clothes to wash in the river. We stumbled along in the dark. *Tatay* [my father] led. Tuta Korota followed. She was old but kept up with us.
>
> ...we arrived at the Kunochayuh River and climbed another steep path up the mountain. Tatay showed me a cave alongside the river. "This goes to the *Uma Pacha* [place of origin and return]" he explained. "It is where we feed our ancestors."
>
> ...Tatay built a small fire inside the cave. Tuta Korota placed one wad in each of my hands. I prayed to *Mayu* and asked her to remove the *chijekuna* within my *chuyma*. I knelt facing the river's descent. Tuta Korota threw the yolk and white from a duck egg into the water, and then she removed the black wads from my headband and sandal. She broke wool threads around my right and left hands and right and left feet. She put the black wads into an old coca cloth with guinea pigs, rat, coca quids, and ashes. Everyone looked away, as Tuta Korota flung the cloth into the river, saying, "Puriychej chijekuna! Puriychej chijekuna! Puriychej chijekuna" ["Begone Invisible substance!"]

As is the case in other Andean misfortune rituals, the participants entered the icy waters to cleanse their bodies and then returned home. Tuta Korota revealed that sickness was related to corporeal, social, and geographical entities and that the human body in its constitution and dissolution is related to similar factors within the environment. In a sense, every symbol in the ritual suggested returning the misfortune to its place in nature. In a symbolic way, this could be seen as the desired return of *vinchucas* and *T.cruzi* to their forest environments.

The misfortune ritual is far removed from the microscopic view of the disease of the paleopathologists who examined Tika's Inca ancestors. The former found wind, river, and earth; the latter found nests of amastigotes of *Trypanosoma cruzi* within human tissue. Neither perspective presents an entirely complete picture of Chagas' disease. Andean ritual symbolically and spiritually adds to microbiology by metaphorically reversing the microscope and seeing the broader context.

Interpreting Symptoms and Locating Causality

Jampiris and *yachajs* symbolically interpret symptoms of Chagas' disease and refer to natural deities that have hidden power over our bodies (an apt image for *T. cruzi*). They rarely refer to disease entities, instead referring mostly to symptoms, which they reinterpret for specific purposes such as to perform a ritual, redress a conflict, or produce a male offspring. Chagas' disease lends itself to multiple interpretations because of its unclear and varied symptomology, being difficult to diagnose even clinically without laboratory tests by doctors.

After the Bolivian national Chagas' campaign began in 1991, educational programs educated the rural peasantry concerning the danger of Chagas' disease and its parasitic cycle relating to *vinchuca* bugs. Reeducation campaigns strongly push for the destruction of *vinchucas* by insecticides and housing improvement. Problems exist. Although not publicly endorsed, the insecticide DDT is used. Housing improvement generally is too expensive for poor peasants. Motivation also is low because the relationship of parasites to vectors and hosts is incomprehensible to many peasants, who find it difficult to connect Chagas' disease to a bug bite years before. (On the other hand, malaria offers little problem in that regard, with its rapid attacks following infection.)

A concern of biomedical ethics is to what degree Western scientists should impose their medical paradigms upon natives and disrupt their cultural systems of dealing with infirmities. Western scientists claim a privileged sense of truth in regard to health questions, but Andeans prefer not to see Chagas' disease in terms of "biological warfare" or "us versus them." In the rich biota of the Andes and Amazon, insects play a vital role, and, as any *camba* (lowlander) will tell you, "the ant is the king of the jungle, and one has to respect them and learn to live with them."

Jampiris and *yachajs* are little concerned with clinical definitions of Chagas' disease, fearing that such classifications relegate the discourse to doctors. They recognize the loss of their patients to medical doctors, and only rarely do doctors refer patients to *curanderos*. Moreover, *Jampiris* and *yachajs* fear that doctors could prohibit their practices. *Jampiris* and *yachajs* also do not refer patients with Chagas' disease to doctors, because doctors and drugs are expensive and they cannot cure Chagas' chronic forms. Doctors, however, can learn from *jampiris* and *yachajs* how to better diagnose the symptoms of Chagas' disease, something which has potential for the disease's prevention (see Chapter 10).

Jampiris and *yachajs* always consult coca leaves to interpret the symptoms of

Chagas' disease. Some examples of how *jampiris* and *yachajs* interpret the symptoms of Chagas' disease follow. An enlarged heart is particularly meaningful to them as *chuyma usu* (heart sickness), possibly caused by a death, unrequited love, slapping a mother-in-law, or indigestion. Kallawaya diviners throw and "read" coca leaves to uncover hidden causes for *chuyma usu*. A simple parasitic explanation does not satisfy Andeans' desires for semiotically rich interpretations of ailments. Inability to swallow might refer to fears and anxieties over some bad deed or, as a worse scenario, that the sufferer told a devastating tale. For typhoid fever, as another example, the coca leaves once read that I was the cause because I had given sugar to a neighbor who was an enemy of the family with whom I lived (Bastien 1978).

Empacho has all sorts of possible explanations connected to cutting oneself off from the nutritive fluids or sustenance of the environment. It is corrected by sharing a meal with the earth shrines—for example, burning coca, llama fat, and guinea-pig blood in the sacred sites that are spread throughout the ayllu (community). The symptoms of Chagas' disease, diffuse as they are, are read much as one would play a hand of cards—that is, according to what is needed at the time.

Kallawaya herbalists recommend enemas and purgatives to cure *empacho, fievre,* and *chuyma usu,* which are symptoms of Chagas' disease but which they understand as a malfunctioning of the body's hydraulic system rather than the intrusion of a parasite. Kallawayas conceptualize the body as a skeletal-muscular framework with openings, conduits, and processing organs. Fluids enter and are processed into other fluids. Poisons that develop from distillation must be periodically eliminated before they attain toxic levels. Illness is caused by obstructed tubes and accumulated fluids, gas, urine, feces, mucus, and sweat. Therapeutically, Kallawayas employ enemas, emetics, and sweat baths to cleanse the body of these fluids.

According to their ethnophysiology, megasyndromes of the esophagus, colon, and heart are interpreted by Bolivian peasants as caused by the accumulation of fluids and need to cured by emetics and purges. Megasyndromes are interpreted as the congestion of distillation processes of the *chuyma*—the internal organs. Frequently, the only complaint of peasants stricken with *T. cruzi* is *chuyma usu,* "my heart is sick," quite literally, "I have a congested heart" (as well as other internal organs). The widespread practice of emetics and purges in Andean medicine for the last thousand years results from dealing with the congestions of Chagas' disease (heart, colon, and esophageal blockages). For this reason, peasants most readily associate Chagas' disease with *empacho*— meaning their bodily fluids no longer circulate from within the body to the outside but are locked into a centripetal movement. In educating Andeans about Chagas' disease, a comparison can be made with the parasitic relation-

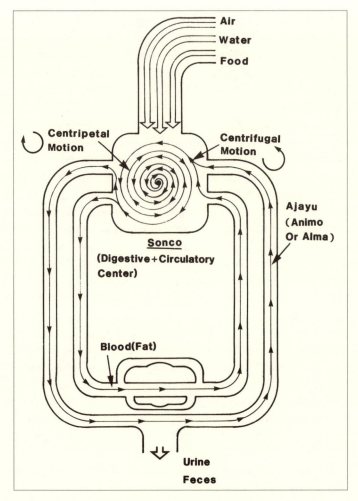

Figure 11. Kallawaya ethnophysiology.

ship of *T. cruzi* to triatomines, animals, and humans in that this microorganism flows in and out of the body in what could be called centripetal and centrifugal motion.

Traditional Herbal Cures

For the treatment of constipation and accompanying gastric pain, such as caused by megacolon of Chagas' disease, or even for congestive heart failure, Kallawayas used *guayusa* and *sayre* with an enema syringe to purge the patients. Tobacco is a particularly favored Andean remedy of long usage; it was widely used as a purgative and narcotic in pre-Columbian times.

Two species of tobacco, *Nicotiana tabacum* and *rustica* (*sayre*), were sources of narcotics in the Americas during the Incario (Elferink 1983; Schultes 1967, 1972). Nicotine was absorbed through the membranes of both the nose and anus by means of sniffing or the insertion of wild tobacco.

Guayusa and *sayre* were used by Kallawayas as early as A.D. 400, as indicated by a herbalist's tomb found near Charazani that contained snuff trays and tubes for nasal inhalation, a gourd container for a powder, leaves from *Ilex guayusa* (Loes.), enema syringes, and a trephined and artificially deformed skull (Wassén 1972). Their purpose can only be guessed at: were they for medicine, stimulants, beverages, or ritual paraphernalia? The leaves are rich in caffeine, and *guayusa* was, and still is, used as a stimulant beverage in South America; for example, the people of Pasto, Colombia, still drink it. During the seventeenth century and after, the Jivaros of Rio Marañon drank it daily to stay awake, particularly when they feared attack by enemies (Patiño 1968). The Maynas of Peru and the Pinches of the Rio Pastaza region in Ecuador and Peru drank it for stomach disorders.

The ancient Kallawaya medicine man was equipped with enema syringes which were buried with him. One was made from a reed about 14 cm long, with a dried bulb of intestines tied to the tube with a cotton thread. Similar instruments appear in the Ollacha Valley of Bolivia, where Quechua Indians use them for enema syringes. The Jivaros of the Amazona region use similar syringes and prepare enemas from plants to purify the stomachs of male children. Andean diviners sometimes received enemas with narcotic fluids to enhance their spiritual powers (Tschudi 1918). The use of enemas during the Incario was important for warriors, who received douches before battle to become strong in battle (Guaman Poma 1944). Shortly after the Conquest, the medicinal qualities of *sayre* became known in Spain, where it was called a "holy weed" (Garcilaso de la Vega 1963).

Even today, Kallawayas claim that wild tobacco is an effective vermifuge and parasiticide. The Andean pharmacopeia featured potent parasiticides and vermifuges because of selective aspects or uses of certain plants able to kill predatory organisms. Kallawayas sometimes sniff tobacco leaves to induce sneezing for congestion and blockage of body parts. Air is understandably considered a vital fluid that must flow in and out of the nostrils; mucus must therefore be eliminated. Sniffing tobacco and *guayusa* not only cleanses these passageways by causing sneezing, tobacco also stimulates the cardiovascular system when nicotine enters the bloodstream. Thus some of the debilitating effects of chronic Chagas' disease are meliorated.

Andeans conceptualize breath, *samay*, as a life force animating them and as a fluid element joining them with other vitalizing principles of the environment. Shortness of breath due to cardiac irregularities deeply puzzles Andeans, who feel that their lifeline with the natural world around them is cut off. The blockages of the esophagus, heart, and colon inherent in Chagas' disease further turn the hydraulic processes inward in a damming effect of centripetal movement. The health of Andeans is believed by them to be a continual exchange of fluids with animals and plants, because they breathe the same air. For example, Kallawaya diviners communicate symbolically with the earth by blowing on their ritual offerings, which are then burned inside the earth shrines. Symbolically, breathing in and out is the means by which Kallawayas become united with their animals, land, and plants. Among a different ethnic group of ritualists, the people of Ausangate in southern Peru call their shamans *samayuh runa*, "people possessing breath" (Jorge Flores, in Custred 1979). These shamans commune with the hill spirits by taking deep breaths. Breathing in is the way knowledge and power are received from the spirit, and breathing out in ritual context is the way they place themselves in the offering made to the earth.

Within the first millennium, humoral theories in Europe, Asia, and Africa held similar assumptions that the body's physiology is a distillation process in which productive fluids are distilled from primary fluids of food, air, and liquids, and toxic fluids are eliminated in sweat, urine, and feces. These humoral theories, especially the Hippocratic-Galenic ones, assumed that the humors (blood, phlegm, black bile, and yellow bile) were regulated according to principles of balance.

Kallawayas echoed European humoral theory in regard to *fievre* (fever), and they still treat acute cases of Chagas' disease with cooling remedies. Andeans are primarily concerned with balancing the hot with the cold in dealing with *fievre*, rather than recognizing the fact that it could refer to parasitemia (parasites in the blood) and distinguishing acute phases of malaria, Chagas' disease, and leishmaniasis. They refuse to bathe someone with a high fever in alcohol, which for them is classified as a hot remedy and should never be used to treat a hot disease (*fievre*). Because chagasic parasitemia is deadly for infants, health workers need to recommend a therapy that Andeans classify as cool, such as chamomile teas and baths (however, this varies with the region).

Andean humoral theory differs from Hippocratic-Galenic theory in that health is seen not as a balance of humors but a processional motion of concentration and dispersal of the humors (air, blood, and fat) (see Bastien 1985, 1987a). Health is the maintenance of this centripetal and centrifugal motion, and sickness is associated with either loss of fluids or the inability to dispel fluids. Andean pharmacopeia is complete with herbal matés (teas) ingested to increase fluids, and enemas and purges to expel fluids. Incidences of chagasic congestion of the colon, esophagus, and heart provide a physiologically based etiology corresponding to Andean ethnophysiology. This explains why traditional healers use purges and enemas to relieve the megasyndromes of Chagas' disease. It also provides some insights into their curing rituals.

Kallawaya herbalists employ concepts of hydraulics and centripetal and centrifugal motion in regard to the empirical use of medicinal plants. They attribute problems to the accumulation of fluids within the central organs. Herbalists determine hydraulic forces by taking the pulse. One elderly herbalist, Juan Wilka, classifies bloods as strong, weak, frightened, and exhausted. In one instance, he diagnosed the pulse of a patient as weak because a landslide had thinned her blood with water. He suggested that she receive new blood by transfusion. Kallawaya herbalists refer to the qualities of blood according to four symbols: hot, cold, wet, and dry. These qualities refer to the blood being too fast (hot), too slow (cold), too thick (wet), and too thin (dry). Herbalists diagnose these qualities by reading the pulse. Sometimes they combine qualities: hot and wet blood is associated with energetic people and refers to fast-moving blood with much fat. Herbalists frequently associate symptoms of Chagas' disease, especially *empacho,* with a pulse that is cold and wet. This implies that primary and secondary body fluids have accumulated and are unable to flow properly—there is need for strong emetics and purgatives.

An Herbal Cure?

Bolivian herbal doctor Nicolás Carrasco claims to have cured patients of Chagas' disease with an herbal remedy called "Regenerator" (Zalles 1996). This discovery shows how the path to medical cures sometimes begins in ethnomedicine. Carrasco was born in Sucre in 1902 and lived to the age of ninety. He studied medicine at the Universidad Mayor de San Francisco Xavier in Sucre and received his medical degree in 1927. He received a doctorate in medicine in Ecuador for his studies concerning the use of aralan in the treatment of cancer. He received recognition from the mayor of Cochabamba in 1983 for his medical discoveries.

Bolivian doctors disregarded his discoveries, and Carrasco wrote of "an environment of incomprehension" among them to his findings. Carrasco practiced both biomedicine and ethnomedicine. He was a *mestizo* who basically adopted European clothing and spoke Spanish, although he spoke and thought more like a Quechua Indian. He identified closely with native *curanderos* and treated all classes, peasants, *cholos,* and *mestizos.* (Bolivia has a highly stratified class system, which at the time separated ethnomedicine from biomedicine along class lines.) On weekends he traveled to native communities to search for cures. He asked *yachajs* and *jampiris* for herbal remedies to test on his patients.

While he was in the Caranavi region of the Yungas (the eastern lower slopes of the Andes, noted for coca production), he learned from *jampiris* about the medicinal qualities of a resin from the fruit of the Rotan palm tree (*Calamus drago*), called *Sangre de Drago* (Blood of the Dragon). *Sangre de Drago* has a dark red color, hence its name, and contains many active ingredients, including draconine and benzoic acid, therapeutically used for their astringent and hemostatic properties (Carrasco 1984:8). There is considerable debate about the remedy and its components. Manuel de Luca, famous Kallawaya herbalist of La Paz, identified *Sangre de Drago* as *Croton roborensis* HBK and said that it should be used sparingly to treat Chagas' disease, because it destroys red blood cells. He claimed it improves the immune system. Other herbalists refer to it as *Sillu supay* (Devil's Seat), *Kuru kuru*, and *Llausa mora*, and frequently employ palm leaves to bathe someone suffering from *susto* (soul loss), a frequent symptom of depression or fatigue related to Chagas' disease. The plant's seeds are toasted, crushed, put into a small glass of pisco liquor, and drunk daily. This purges the body of toxic fluids, changing cold and wet blood into hot and dry. According to their ethnophysiology, it accelerates the centrifugal forces in the body (see Figure 11). The seeds can be crushed, making a salve that relieves rheumatism. Active ingredients of fresh seeds are acetic acid (like vinegar), butyric acid (like arnica oil), glyceride (like soap), and croton oil (castor oil), forming a powerful purgative.[1]

Combining ethnomedicine with biomedicine, Carrasco refined the herbal remedy for Chagas' disease and reworked the ingredients of *Sangre de Drago* until he had concocted a "secret" recipe, which he called "Regenerator." He tested it on his patients, injecting it into their muscles and observing its effects on arthritis, cancer, and Chagas' disease.

Bolivian herbalists develop their skills by learning from other herbalists and through practice. When they treat a disease with an experimental herb, they give the patient small doses to observe its effects over several weeks. If a patient dies in treatment, they are held responsible. Bolivians practice retributive justice, and an herbalist may be killed by relatives of the deceased. Herbalists generally refuse to treat anyone they are unsure of curing; and this apparently works to the disadvantage of terminally ill patients. In instances of those chronically ill with Chagas' disease, however, herbalists and victims are concerned less with its potential fatality than they are with the victim being unable to work. Illness for Andeans is basically a condition when they cannot work, and Western biomedicine's definition of illness does not apply with Bolivian peasants who have tuberculosis and Chagas' disease.

At first, Carrasco claimed that Regenerator cured several illnesses, as suggested by the following remark from a doctor: "If Carrasco was a serious scientist, he would only investigate cancer, but he indiscriminately injects *Regenerator* into patients of all diseases" (Zalles 1996). Oblivious to biomedical ethics, they blamed him not for experimenting on humans but for not focusing on cancer, a disease of upper-class Bolivians. They begrudgingly admitted that Carrasco was a "scientist of sorts" and that *Regenerator* had therapeutic potential.[2]

In spite of the medical doctors' criticism, Carrasco continued to experiment on patients. Bolivians frequented his clinic in large numbers, forming lines into the streets to receive Regenerator. Carrasco published his results in 1984: "*Regenerator* serves as a muscle regenerator and a proven parasiticide for *Plasmodium vivax* (malaria) and *T. cruzi.*"

The success of Regenerator became internationally known, and at least one Japanese scientist visited Carrasco to learn about it. For years, Carrasco had kept the formula secret, but with the possibility of fame and fortune, he gave the formula to this person. The Japanese man patented it, produced it, and profited. He didn't pay Carrasco.[3] Carrasco took his claim to the Bolivian court. After three years of litigation, however, he died and the case was discontinued.

The validity of Carrasco's claims for Regenerator is found in case studies. Carrasco records thirty-eight patients cured of Chagas' disease with Regenerator (Carrasco Capriles 1984). He lists the patients' names and the results of laboratory tests for *T. cruzi* at the first and final analyses, with dates and name of the testing laboratory.[4] He daily injected one-half cubic centimeter of a synthesized form of Regenerator mixed with Vitamin K (10 mg) and a liver extract into the patient's muscles (Carrasco 1984:72). Treatments were conducted daily from one month to under three years, or until the patient was cured, although it is doubtful whether Bolivian patients followed this strict regime.

Analyzing thirty-three records (five were incomplete), I found that fourteen (42 percent) of the patients were cured over a short period of from one to six months; fifteen (45 percent) of the patients were cured over a longer period of from seven to thirteen months; and four patients (12 percent) were cured over a long period of from fourteen to thirty-four months. The average cure was nine months (somewhat similar to a treatment plan of nifurtimox and benznidazole. An equal number of men and women were treated, indicating some equality in regard to infection and to treatment. Generally speaking, adult males in Bolivia have a higher incidence of Chagas' disease and prefer doctors, whereas women prefer herbalists and diviners.

Carrasco claimed that patients with heart blockage were cured with Regenerator, being able to work even at strenuous jobs without cardiac fatigue. "Various of my patients had cardiac lesions, alterations of the nervous system and disturbances of digestive tubes, which had been determined by medical specialists, who deemed organ damage irreversible," Carrasco (1984:49) wrote, "but fortunately I managed to cure many of these, or at least to avoid greater deterioration with my therapy." Carrasco concluded that Chagas' disease can be cured with Regenerator, which lyses, or gradually destroys, *T. cruzi*, and that it is more effective and has fewer side effects than do nifurtimox and benznidazole.

Carrasco made his case from clinical records and laboratory results. One concern with the results of the final analysis for each patient is that the majority of tests (thirty-five) were direct examinations of the blood, and *T. cruzi* is not easily found in the blood, being predominantly intracellular. Three tests were indirect (detection of antibodies to *T. cruzi*) immunofluorescent tests, similar to the ELISA test used for AIDS. Not used by Carrasco, xenodiagnosis is where uninfected *vinchucas* are allowed to bite the patient for thirty minutes under the armpit, and their fecal matter is observed thirty days later to see if it contains *T. cruzi*. All these tests are commonly used in Bolivia for Chagas' disease. It is possible that some patients with positive results from the Carrasco study still harbor *T. cruzi* but in lesser numbers than previously found. Even this would indicate some effectiveness of Regenerator. However, recent studies indicate that Chagas' disease can manifest itself clinically even though parasites have been eliminated, because of misdirection of the human immune system (see Appendix II: Immune Response).

Therapy for Chagas' disease comes in varying degrees—from controlling the parasite population in the body to completely eliminating it. Jaime Zalles, in an interview on 11 May 1997, said that *Sangre de Drago* (*Croton roborensis* HBK) is an effective treatment for Chagas' disease, not in the refined form of Regenerator, but in a pattern of administering four drops daily for four days, then rest for four days, then the resumption of the drops for another four days—all for the length of six months. It should not be used for anemic patients, however, because it decreases red blood cells in the body.

Sangre de Drago is sold in small bottles by herbal vendors throughout Bolivia for ten pesos in Bolivian money (U.S. two dollars), and it is purchased by Bolivians for Chagas' disease. Patients claim that it cures them, although it more probably relieves the disease's symptoms; but its properties as a parasiticide have yet to be verified by laboratory tests.

Jaime Zalles treats chagasic heart disease with three flowers of *retama* (*Spartum junceum*) in maté (steeped in hot water), with two leaves of *cedrón* (*Lippia triphylla* Kunth). Ingredients serve as a tranquilizer for heart attacks. *Toronjil* (*Melissa officinalis* L.) is also used for heart problems.

Zalles treats chagasic constipation by placing clay on the stomach, then providing a drink of papaya juice (including the fruit's skin) and flax seeds (*Linum usitatissimum*). Zalles' wife, Negrita, recommends castor oil. Herbalists often have patients with sore throats from Chagas' disease gargle with warm coca water. These remedies can relieve the symptoms of Chagas' disease, allowing patients to return to work. Restoration to complete health is an im-

Figure 12. Jaime Zalles talking to a herbal vendor in Tarija, Bolivia, about the use of Sangre de Drago for curing Chagas' disease. Zalles is Bolivia's foremost expert in the use of medicinal plants for medicines and has written herbal manuals for Bolivians in Spanish, Aymara, Quechua, and Guarani languages. (Photograph by Joseph W. Bastien)

possible dream for many peasants who lack the resources to pay for cures. They adapt through the use of household remedies, herbs, and rituals, which provide some level of relief and renewal. Until the problem is addressed by wealthier nations, the simple products of Mother Earth (*Pachamama*) remain their primary resource.

More successfully, native plants provide insecticides for eliminating *vinchucas:* compounds including *ruda* (rue, *Ruta chalapensis*), *ajenjo* (absinthe, *Artemisia absinthum*), *andres waylla* (*Cestrum mathewsi*), and *jaya pichana* (*Schurria octoarustica*) are experimentally proven insecticides. Bolivians have learned this and use large quantities of these plants. They cut them into small pieces, smash them, and boil them in water. This is then mixed with dirt and used to fill holes in the adobe. Another method used is to pound small rocks into the holes of the adobe. Plaster is mixed with coca, an excellent insecticide, and fleshy parts of prickly pear cactus (*Penca de Tuna* or *Opuntia ficus indica*) to form a glue that helps the plaster stick to the adobe. A compound called *el paraiso,* made from *muña* (*Satureja boliviana*), is used to kill potato worms and has been suggested for *vinchucas*. Peasants also use spiders and *carpinteros* (small household lizards) to rid their houses of *vinchucas*. The plant *floripondio*

(*Datura sanguinea*) gives off a nightly fragrance that discourages vinchucas from entering the houses around which it is planted.[5] Eucalyptus leaves burned inside the house at evening have a similar effect. These native remedies and insecticides are all relatively safe and environmentally sound, something that cannot be said for pharmaceutical drugs and commercial insecticides.

Scientists in Cochabamba are investigating native plants for use in insecticides against *vinchucas*.[6] They are presently using an organic phosphorus, Deltametrina (Pirotroides), a French product from a piretro plant. It is biodegradable, inexpensive, and protects an area from six months to a year. Only 25 milligrams per square meter are used for *vinchucas*. It is toxic for larger animals only in greater quantities. Deltametrina costs ten dollars a liter, while Petramina costs $1,200 a liter. One problem, however, is the availability of Deltametrina.

Chilean scientists have been testing Kallawaya medicinal plants for the treatment of Chagas' disease. Initial findings have been very encouraging in that several of the plants appear to work towards the cure of Chagas' disease. Herbalists in Bolivia regularly use plant extracts with indole alkaloids, which suggests the possibility of medicinal effectiveness without excessive toxicity (Bastien 1987a; Cavin and Rodríguez 1982). Various tropical plant species used by tribal groups contain beta-Carboline alkaloids (Allen and Holmstedt 1980). Scientists at the University of California, Irvine, tested these alkaloids and found them to reduce population growth of *T. cruzi* epimastigote forms (Cavin, Krassner, and Rodríguez 1987). Native herbalists can be of help in identifying potentially effective drugs from natural sources. Using native lore can reduce the number of empirical tests often conducted on natural plant products. Plant products provide an alternative to toxic synthetic drugs and indicate potentially active structures for chemists interested in synthetic molecular modifications. This research, along with that of Carrasco, strongly points to the possibilities of dealing with Chagas' disease by the use of medicinal plants.

The connection is interesting between herbalists' treatment of Chagas' disease through the use of castor oil as a purgative for *empacho* and *susto* and Carrasco's concoction of the shrub's agents into an injectable solution, Regenerator. Native herbalists have an entirely different ethnophysiology of how the symptoms of Chagas' disease are cured by purgatives, yet it was their use of this substance for that disease that led Carrasco to further refine it for biomedical purposes. As another example, peasants chew coca leaves after eating potatoes, which they say is necessary to balance the hot with the cold. Chewing coca leaves regulates carbohydrate metabolism. It frequently happens that folk beliefs, rituals, and home remedies reveal effective treatments for Chagas' disease. Andeans follow these native systems of medicine because at least to some degree they work. Doctors and scientists exclusively advocate biomedicine. A wiser path would appear to be to integrate ethnomedicine with biomedicine for the prevention and treatment of Chagas' disease.

Parasiticides: Nifurtimox and Benznidazole

Andean traditional medicine provides treatments for Chagas' disease as well as insecticides that may even be better than the present products produced by pharmaceutical and chemical companies. Western biomedicine does not have an effective cure for chronic Chagas' disease. Presently, the two prescription drugs used for treating Chagas' disease are nifurtimox (produced by Bayer, recently discontinued) and benznidazole (Roche), used for acute and chronic phases (see Appendix 13). Bolivians find both costly, unsatisfactory, and painful, and many prefer to go to native herbalists for cures. Neither drug is available in the United States, except through special permission from the Centers for Disease Control in Atlanta. No drug is registered for use to help prevent Chagas' disease.

Nifurtimox and benznidazole are used in short-term cases, but their efficacy varies in different geographical areas, probably as a consequence of variation of parasitic strains. Many patients object to taking large doses of these drugs over a long period of time (as long as one year).[7] Patients can also suffer serious side effects, including anorexia, vomiting, skin allergies, and various neurological disorders, which may be a consequence of damage to their tissues (Urbina et al. 1996). Bolivians also realize that the pharmaceutical cure is only temporary if they live in chagasic areas, as it is likely they will be reinfected with *T. cruzi*. One advantage of actually harboring *T. cruzi* is that it provides partial immunity from suffering another acute attack.

The complexity of Chagas' disease has been addressed by Andean culture in a number of ways. Andeans deal with the symptoms of Chagas' disease through rituals, community concern, and herbal medicines. *Yachajs* and *yatiris* have combined forces with doctors to combat or adapt to *T. cruzi*. They appear to have dealt with Chagas' disease as adequately as has biomedicine. Even if this is not so, its possibility necessitates much closer examination of ethnomedical systems for solutions to endemic diseases throughout the world. Andean rituals also provide a great service to medical science by indicating the interrelatedness of Chagas' disease to the environment, showing how the human body is related to the earth and its organisms in reciprocal ways.

CHAPTER FOUR

The Crawling Epidemic: Epidemiology

One of my first encounters with kissing bugs, *vinchucas,* was in the airport in Cochabamba, Bolivia, where I went to meet Benjamin Menesis, who had arrived from Sucre and was carrying a suitcase with over 1,000 specimens of the insect. Menesis was a technician for the *Proyecto Británico Cardenal Maurer* (PBCM), which was conducting a *vinchuca*-eradication program in the Department of Chuquisaca, Bolivia. An important part of this program at the University in Cochabamba was to determine the rate that *vinchuca* bugs became infected.

Staff had collected *vinchucas* from houses in Chuquisaca with flypaper and by means of a contest among schoolchildren to see who could bring the most *vinchucas* to school. Pupils thus realized how infested their homes were and received a lesson on Chagas' disease. The director of PBCM, Ruth Sensano, stored the *vinchucas* in an ice chest. They became active in the dark box, being nocturnal creatures, and began a scratching sound clearly audible to anyone within twenty feet. When the box was opened and a lit flashlight placed inside, the vinchucas quieted down due to their photosensitive nature.

Menesis hand-carried the freezer box onto the airplane in Sucre, refusing to put it in the hold where the cold might kill the *vinchucas.* He carried a radio to drown out chirping in flight with some loud music. Airport surveillance questioned Menesis about the chest, and he told them that he was carrying medical samples. Ruth Sensano convinced the inspector that Menesis needed to get the contents of the box to Cochabamba as quickly as possible for medical reasons. Menesis arrived without mishap in Cochabamba an hour later, and we joked about what could have happened if the box had come open inside the airplane and 1,000 *vinchucas* were released, with over half of them carrying *T. cruzi.*

The *vinchuca* species most largely responsible for chagasic transmission in Bolivia is *Triatoma infestans,* which is relatively non-aggressive and whose bite is more annoying than it is painful. Consequently, Bolivians do not refer to the insects as "assassin bugs," as they are called in the U.S., but as *"vinchucas,"* from the Quechua word *huinchicuy,* which means something that falls rapidly, because they glide down from the rafters, and as "kissing bugs," because they prefer to suck blood from the face—often from the lips and from near the eyes. Although *Triatoma infestans* has thus avoided the name "assassin bug" for the more benign name "kissing bug," there is the subtle irony that the "kiss" of the bug can lead to death.

Epidemiology of Chagas' Disease in Bolivia

In Bolivia, estimates are that one in five (1.5 million people) of the total population (7.3 million) have Chagas' disease, and that half the population live in endemic areas of the disease (SOH/CCH 1994; see Figure 13). An earlier epidemiological survey of Chagas' disease was carried out in 1978 in Pongo, a village situated eleven miles from Santa Cruz, capital of the tropical oriental plains (De Muynck et al. 1978). Researchers examined the infection rate of houses by triatomines; the infection rate of the triatomines by *T. cruzi;* the infection rate of human, canine, and feline populations; cardiac and digestive morbidity; and the construction of houses. Some 26 percent of the houses were infested with *T. infestans,* 53 percent of the humans were found infected with *T. cruzi;* and 23 percent of the dogs and 7 percent of the cats were also infected. Some 7 percent of those older than five years showed electrocardiogram signs compatible with chagasic myocardiopathy, and 2 percent had an elevated risk for sudden death as a consequence of their chagasic heart disease. More recent studies have found similar results throughout many rural areas in Bolivia (Valencia 1990a, 1990b; see Appendix 5).

The incidence of disease is highest in rural areas, where 42 percent of the people live and where poverty, lack of education, and poor housing facilitate infestation by *vinchucas.* The average rural income per year is $580, the illiteracy rate is 50 percent, and the fertility index is 6.1 per mother (1992 census). Forty to eighty percent of rural people are infected with *T. cruzi,* and 38–78 percent of the homes are infested with *T. infestans.* Over 30 percent of the insect vectors captured in and around rural houses are infected with *T. cruzi.* These areas are generally those lived in by the indigenous population (60 percent of the population) and to a lesser extent by the *mestizo* population (25 percent) and those of European descent (15 percent). Some ethnic communities are seriously debilitated by Chagas' disease, and their survival and well-being can be seen as a race against *T. cruzi.*

Cardiac morbidity due to chronic Chagas' disease is high in rural communities of Bolivia. According to one study in a community in the central Andes, sixty-nine of 104 persons (66 percent) tested positive to *T. cruzi* by two serological methods (Weinke et al. 1988). Twenty-one of the sixty-nine people (30 percent) showed modest and severe cardiac abnormalities. This community had a high percentage (56 percent) of houses infested with *Triatoma infestans* infected with *T. cruzi.* Epidemiologically, there was a significant relationship between substandard housing, infested houses, and cardiac morbidity.

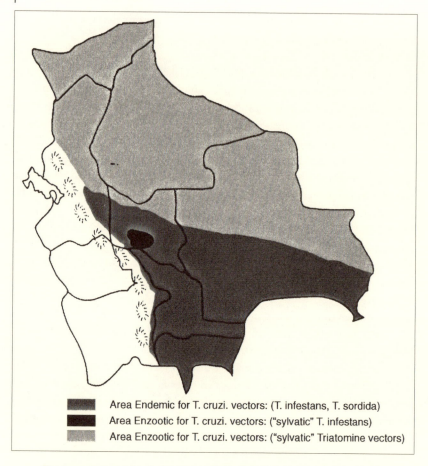

Area Endemic for T. cruzi. vectors: (T. infestans, T. sordida)
Area Enzootic for T. cruzi. vectors: ("sylvatic" T. infestans)
Area Enzootic for T. cruzi. vectors: ("sylvatic" Triatomine vectors)

Figure 13. Areas endemic for *T. cruzi* in Bolivia. (See Appendices 5 and 7.)

Seven children in Bolivia die each day from the acute phase of Chagas' disease, which leads to meningoencephalitis (Ault et al. 1992:9). Estimates throughout Latin America are that 10 percent of children with acute infection die from the disease (Manson-Bahr and Bell 1987:80). Treatment of acute Chagas' disease is important to lessen the severity of symptoms and prevent death. Chemotherapy has decreased the mortality rate from about 50 percent in 1900 to 10 percent currently (see Appendix 13).

The majority of new infections of Chagas' disease are found in children from only a few weeks of age to two years of age. Bolivian children are more vulnerable than adults to acute forms because they have developing immune systems and often have other diseases and are malnourished. The immaturity of the immune system in the fetus and the child partially explains the appearance of cerebral involvement of the disease almost exclusively at these times (Moya 1994).[1]

With adults, the acute phase occurs in roughly 25 percent of people infected with *T. cruzi*, and a much lower percentage of that number die than among infants. The lesser occurrence of the acute phase in adults presents a problem for those treating the disease in that the victims are frequently unaware of having Chagas' disease and go untreated until the incurable chronic phase, when the symptoms frequently are not attributed to *T. cruzi*. Thus the age of the victim is important in the epidemiology and treatment of Chagas' disease (WHO 1991:2).

Some generalized symptoms of the acute phase are fever, enlarged liver and spleen, generalized edema, and swollen lymph nodes (WHO 1991). Symptoms can be sudden and dramatic, as a person may suffer from moment to moment with fever, chills, coughing, diarrhea, dysphagia, tachycardia, headaches, excitation, muscle pains, lack of appetite, neuropsychological alternations, exanthematous rash, and general malaise (Borda 1981; Chagas 1911; Katz, Despommier, and Gwadz 1989; Köberle 1968). Fevers range from 99.5 to 102.2 degrees Fahrenheit; temperatures above 104 degrees are rare and not indicative of the severity of infection. The fever may be continuous or recurrent, lasting four to five weeks and then falling gradually towards the normal range. Infants under one year of age frequently have higher temperatures and suffer symptoms of meningeal irritations (rigidness of neck and spinal column), convulsions, ocular seizures, stupor, and coma, which often lead to death. Coughing is caused by bronchial irritation associated with abundant mucus secretion. Diarrhea is frequent, very obstinate, and cannot be explained either by bacterial or by parasitic intestinal infections (see Appendix 9).

One common symptom of acute Chagas' disease is development of a chagoma, which is a local inflammatory swelling, like a large, hard boil, found frequently below the eye as well as elsewhere on the body, that lasts for weeks (Manson-Bahr and Bell 1987:80). Chagomas differ from the local swelling and edema that follow a bug bite, which resolves quickly. Chagomas result from local inflammatory swelling caused by amastigotes multiplying in fat cells. When the chagoma occurs near the eye, the eyelids become filled with liquid and one eye often becomes inflamed, which is called Romaña's sign (see Figure 4). Carlos Chagas considered Romaña's sign the hallmark symptom of Chagas' disease; however, this is misleading, because it is present only in one-fourth of all acute phases, and only 25 percent of infected people suffer the acute phase. For every one hundred persons infected with *T. cruzi*, only six manifest Romaña's sign. Some Bolivians think they are not infected with *T. cruzi* because they can't recall having a swollen eye. Others attribute Romaña's sign to conjunctivitis due to the dusty regions of Bolivia and seldom report it to doctors. They should be advised that if the swollen eye continues for longer than a week they should consult a doctor.

Children also suffer painful subcutaneous nodules (lipochagomas) on the body. The chagoma stage is followed by fever and the appearance of trypanosomes in the blood about fourteen days after infection. Amastigotes remain in the lymph glands, causing generalized pathology in lymphatic tissue (see Figures 15 and 16). A rash may appear on the chest or abdomen, with precise red spots the size of pinheads. These spots are painless and disappear after ten days. Acute patients may suffer more serious pathologies of enlarged colon, spleen, or liver, irregular heartbeat, and cardiac deficiency and failure. It is important to recognize that there is no clearly defined set of symptoms that characterizes either acute or chronic Chagas' disease and that many of the above symptoms can refer to other diseases. Clinical diagnosis of Chagas' disease is difficult without testing for the parasite, and frequently it goes undetected in Bolivia.

Treatment of Chagas' Disease

Dr. Ciro Figaroa, a medical doctor in Tarija, Bolivia, administers the following dosages of nifurtimox for acute Chagas' disease: for children, 15 to 20 milligrams per kilo of weight in four doses per day for 90 days; for adults, 8 to 10 milligrams per kilo of weight for 120 days. Figaroa claims that he has cured Chagas' disease in the acute phase but is unable to do this once patients have passed the acute stage. In Sucre, doctors recommend Radanil (Roche's benznidazole product) in the following dosage: 7 milligrams per kilo of weight three times a day for four weeks. The cost for Radanil for an average-size adult for one month is $340 Bolivian (or U.S. $70), a month's wage for the average Bolivian.

An advantage of the acute phase of Chagas' disease is that its symptoms signal a point when it can be treated. Asymptomatic patients may realize they are infected only at the chronic stage, when cardiac and gastrointestinal damage is pronounced. There currently is no adequate treatment for the chronic phase (for future possibilities see Urbina et al. 1996). Since the trypanocidal drugs currently available are effective during the acute period of the disease, it is important to diagnose earlier infections as well as to distinguish recent infections from older infections. New tools for the serodiagnosis of Chagas' disease have proven to have great diagnostic potential in distinguishing different stages of the disease (see Frasch and Reyes 1990: 137–41).

Chemotherapy treatment of the disease is not completely satisfactory for reasons already discussed in Chapter 3. Nifurtimox and benznidazole have serious adverse effects and yet do not destroy all the parasites, which soon repopulate the body. Their therapeutic efficacy depends upon variations in parasite virulence and variations in the human response to infection as they relate to a particular chemotherapeutic strategy.

In Bolivia and other Andean countries, the inadequacy of chemotherapy is related to the fact that trypanosomiasis generally is a disease of rural subsistence farmers in developing areas. Here, medical service is usually inadequate because of the inequitable distribution of health resources in favor of urban centers. To be useful in this environment, a drug must be inexpensive, have a long shelf-life without refrigeration, and be able to be administered by paramedics orally without side effects.[2]

Infestation with *T. infestans*

A major reason for the spread of Chagas' disease throughout Bolivia and Latin America is the domestication of *T. infestans* (see Appendices 5 and 6). In endemic areas of the disease in Bolivia, *T. infestans* has invaded domestic areas to a staggering degree. The percentages of infestation for houses in the departments of Bolivia are as follows: Cochabamba, 38.2 percent; Chuquisaca, 78.4 percent; Tarija, 78.2 percent; La Paz, 42.2 percent; Potosí, 62.5 percent; and Santa Cruz, 96.5 percent (SOH/CCH 1994:20; Valencia 1990a:44). Thus, 70 percent of houses in the most populated departments of Bolivia are infested with *T. infestans*.

Once they are inside domestic areas, triatomines hide in a variety of places. Of 1,090 *vinchucas* gathered from 191 houses, 529 were in the walls, 46 in the roof, 48 in the beds, 324 in the peridomicile area, and 143 in surrounding corrals (Valencia 1990a:42–65). All *vinchucas* were identified as *T. infestans*: 581 (53 percent) were nymphs and 509 (47 percent) were adults. The infestation rate for homes in the study area was 92 percent (Valencia 1990a:44).

The medium index of *vinchucas* with *T. cruzi* parasites was 31 percent, with the index reaching as high as 53 percent in one community (Valencia 1990a: 44). Some 46 percent of the infected *vinchucas* were found in dormitories, which indicates that they transmit *T. cruzi* best among sleeping humans. Infection rates within the nymph stages was 25 percent; within the adult stage it was 37 percent. The vector was infected incrementally with *T. cruzi* from its initial nymph stages to adult stages.[3]

T. infestans is accountable for 97 percent of the cases of Chagas' disease in Bolivia; twelve other species account for the remaining 3 percent. The most prominent of these species are *T. guasyana*, *T. melanocephala*, *T. oswaldoi*, and *T. venosa*, which are primarily sylvatic, prey on wild animals, and spread Chagas' disease among such animals. This becomes another threat to the threatened and depleted species of wild animals in the Andes and Amazon. Large numbers of *Triatoma infestans* and lesser numbers of *Triatoma sordida* are found in every department of Bolivia except Oruro, which is located at an elevation of 3,500 meters.

Triatoma infestans usually inhabits areas at elevations from 1,100 to 11,200 feet (330 to 3,450 m.) above sea level; nevertheless, it has been found at higher elevations, such as Llallagua, Potosí, at 13,300 feet (4,100 m.) (Borda 1981:16). Sylvatic triatomine vectors of *T. cruzi* are primarily found within forested areas of the departments of Beni, Pando, and Santa Cruz and within the Yungas area of the Department of La Paz. Sylvatic triatomines spread Chagas' disease more in animals than in humans within the departments of Santa Cruz, Beni, and Pando, although they do infect some forest dwellers.

Although *T. infestans* are found throughout Bolivia, the insects prefer warm and humid conditions, being found more in the lower elevations and warmer climates of the central regions and the lowlands rather than in the highlands such as La Paz and the Altiplano. Chagas' disease occurs primarily in the valleys, plains, and forests lying between elevations of 1,000 to 11,400 feet (300 and 3,500 m.) above sea level. Roughly 84 percent of Bolivian territory lies within this zone. Some 47 percent of Bolivia's populace reside in endemic areas of the disease, thereby placing approximately 3 million people at risk for Chagas' disease. Many more Bolivians are also at risk because of possible infection through blood transfusions in non-endemic urban areas (Ault 1992, Schmuñis 1991, Valencia 1990a).

Rates of household infestation of *T. infestans* are higher in rural and peri-urban areas of Bolivia; but urban infestation has increased significantly with increased urban migration and rapid transportation between rural and urban areas. Infestation rates presently are 70–100 percent for rural areas, 40–60 percent for peri-urban areas, and 20–40 percent for urban areas (SOH/CCH 1994). A general average is that 50 percent of *vinchucas* found anywhere in Bolivia are infected with *T. cruzi* parasites. This percentage increases proportionally as more people become infected with these parasites and pass them on to uninfected *vinchucas*. In endemic areas, *T. cruzi* passes rapidly from sick persons to healthy persons, because *vinchucas* prey on different people, many of them sleeping together, until virtually all the hosts are infected with Chagas' disease.

Adaptation of Bolivians and Bugs
The spread of *T. cruzi* throughout Bolivia is accomplished by certain selective and adaptive mechanisms of *vinchucas*. A combination of nocturnal predation, crawling and gliding, and transformation through nymph stages, means that there are bugs with different sizes, air and land mobility, and the cover of darkness in which to hide, move, and draw blood from humans, easily targeting those sleeping in run-down adobe houses with thatched roofs.

Vinchucas are sensitive to light, and, at the laboratory for *Proyecto Chagas* at the National University at Cochabamba, biologist J. Delgado keeps them in loosely covered jars during the day. As he explained to me, "as long as there's light in the room, they stay as still as sleeping sloths." Reaching into the jar

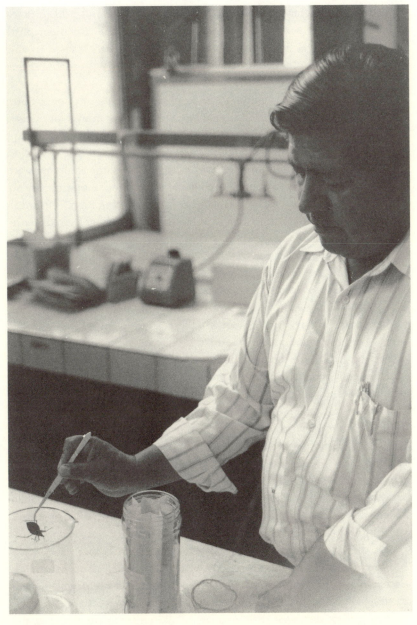

Figure 14 . Laboratory assistant at Chagas Project at the Universidad San Simon in Cochabamba holding a *vinchuca* bug that will be used to diagnose victims of Chagas' disease. Uninfected *vinchucas* are placed under the armpit for thirty minutes to draw blood; thirty days later their feces are examined for *T. cruzi*. This diagnostic test is called xenodiagnosis and is commonly used throughout Bolivia to determine parasite population and zydomenes. Indirect ELISA tests are frequently used first to determine antibodies to *T. cruzi*. (Photograph by Joseph W. Bastien)

with pinchers, he grabbed a *vinchuca* around the thorax and held it. It remained motionless, occasionally wiggling its antennae, while I photographed it (see Figure 14). He then replaced the *vinchuca* in a tightly covered jar and draped a dark cloth over its top and sides; within seconds you could hear this *vinchuca* moving about inside the jar.

When *vinchucas* are caught in the light of day, they appear to be friendly domesticated bugs, neither biting, kicking, or trying to get away. Not surprisingly, many Bolivian children play with them. Boys race the bugs, and some put them in girls' lunch boxes. Girls gather their rice-shaped eggs in tiny wicker baskets, pretending they are chicken eggs. Even some adults consider the insects' eggs to be good omens predicting fertility or a bountiful harvest. They are referred to as "harbingers of good luck," "kissing bugs," "friends," and "toys." Their perceived personalities disassociate these bugs from their disease-carrying capability.

Attitudes about *vinchucas* were revealed in the following conversation I had with Sarah Arredondo outside of Tarija, Bolivia, in 1997 (see Figure 15). Sarah was seven years old at the time and had been bitten while she was sleeping by a *vinchuca,* which her mother removed from under her nightie. Her mother squashed it against the floor and blood squeezed out. Sarah said that she didn't mind *vinchucas* and was unaware that they caused sickness. Sarah wants to be a hairdresser because she likes to dress up dolls. She coyly expressed herself, slightly twisting her head to purse her lips to hide shyness, which eventually turned into a smile. She then told me how her ducks ate *vinchucas.* Sarah's mother hated *vinchucas* and had grown up in a house filled with them. She said that they were inside the house and that she had removed unnecessary items from the sleeping areas, but that they needed to plaster the walls. She feared that Sarah had Chagas' disease and asked me to examine the wound from the bite. I explained that I couldn't tell by looking at the wound, and informed her to watch for a high fever; if that occurred, she should take Sarah to a doctor for testing and treatment. Talking with a child bitten by a *vinchuca* whose future as a hairdresser was threatened by a parasite made the statistics of Chagas' disease more meaningful and alarming to me.

Public health educators, in efforts to dispel friendly attitudes towards *vinchucas,* in a rather bizarre fashion have sponsored contests for schoolchildren to see who could bring the most bugs to school (somewhat akin to a campaign to collect discarded drug needles). Children captured *vinchucas,* put them in matchboxes, and brought them to the school, where they were later examined for *T. cruzi* infection. Obviously, this technique encouraged children to handle *vinchucas* despite the fact that contamination is the major route of infection and thus this campaign put them at risk. Posters and videos are a

Figure 15. Sarah Arredondo showing where she had been bitten by a *vinchuca* and possibly infected with Chagas' disease. Several thousand children die each year in Bolivia from acute Chagas' disease. (Photograph by Joseph W. Bastien)

much safer pedagogical method to educate Bolivians about *vinchucas* as vectors of Chagas' disease.

The insect world fascinates children in part perhaps because tiny creatures are more proportionate to their size. José Beltrán, health educator, observed that children are much quicker than adults to learn about the different species of *vinchucas,* many of which are beneficial. Many Bolivian children also love to see parasites through microscopes and learn about Chagas' disease.

On the other hand, Quechua peasants in Choromoro hate *vinchucas* because they suffer from their annoying bites at night. These peasants in the Department of Chuquisaca, Bolivia, are accustomed to having *vinchucas* in their beds, with sometimes as many as thirty to forty housed within their mattresses. One complained, "All night we are taking off their heads and destroying them. We have to sleep outside the huts to escape them. Sometimes we don't sleep all night because we have to kill *vinchucas,* and when they bite us, we scratch it."

Some Bolivians are allergic to *vinchuca* bites, which then result in festering sores (see Figure 16). Others vigorously scratch the itching bite, opening the skin and rubbing infected fecal matter into the wound. *T. cruzi* travel to the opening or are aided when the victim scratches the wound, frequently damaging the skin or pushing the parasites into the wound.

Vinchucas are not fast-flying insects like mosquitoes or flies; they only glide by means of poorly developed wings. The wings of triatomines move slowly and arduously and can barely, if at all, lift them upward, unless they are first descending from a perch. Brazilian scientists photographed the flight of these bugs with a low-light-sensitive camera. Triatomines take off from window ledges and ceilings and descend, riding air waves back and forth in large sweeping movements until they alight on their victims. Although they prefer to stay in one house, they can glide up to 1,000 meters, enabling them to travel from house to house in search of blood meals. Radar-like detectors, the two long antennae on their heads, are sensitive to carbon dioxide respiration and guide the triatomines to the exposed and heat-emitting areas of warm-blooded animals.

Compensating for being poor flyers, *vinchucas* are excellent crawlers, with six long and strong legs. After a blood meal, *vinchucas* return to their nests, literally like tankers, trailing blood and fecal matter across bedding, tables, floors, walls, and ceilings. Their tracks contaminate food and clothing, as does their fecal matter dropped from the ceiling.

As ugly as these trailing streaks are, they do provide warning signs to wary travelers wishing to spend the night in some unfamiliar room. Wary Bolivians check rooms thoroughly with flashlights and ask if and when the house and rooms have been sprayed for *vinchucas.* Tiny white eggs and brown blotches on the walls provide evidence that the guest will not spend the night alone. Nor does mosquito netting provide protection against the bugs' instar stages,

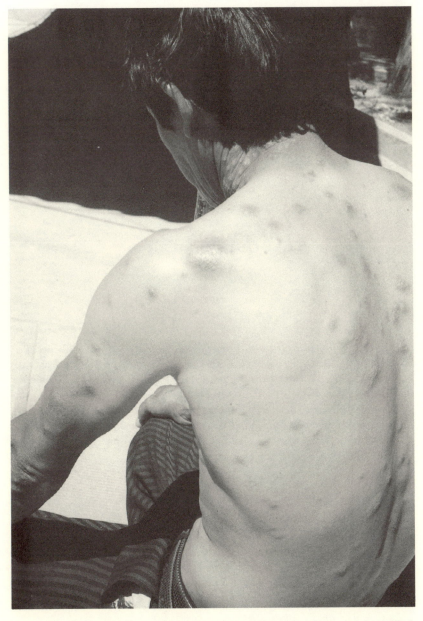

Figure 16. Infected bites from *Triatoma infestans (vinchucas)*. (Photograph by staff of Proyecto Cardenal Maurer)

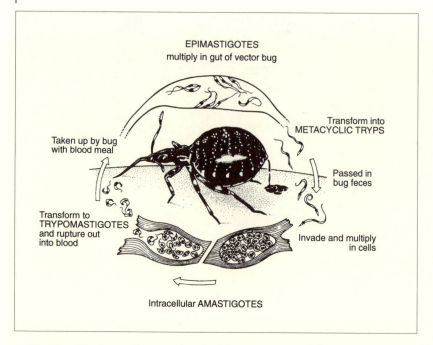

EPIMASTIGOTES
multiply in gut of vector bug

Transform into
METACYCLIC TRYPS

Taken up by bug
with blood meal

Passed in
bug feces

Transform to
TRYPOMASTIGOTES
and rupture out
into blood

Invade and multiply
in cells

Intracellular AMASTIGOTES

Figure 17. *Vinchuca* and stages of *T. cruzi*. Vinchucas (*Triatoma infestans*) deposit metacyclic trypomastigotes in their feces that are infective to humans (as well as other mammals) and temporarily enter the blood. They enter tissues where they become amastigotes, then divide into other amastigotes and short, stumpy trypomastigotes that reenter the blood. These trypomastigotes are ingested by uninfected and infected *vinchucas,* where they transform into epimastigotes and then metacylic trypomastigotes. (From Franklin Neva and Harold Brown, *Basic Clinical Parasitology*, p. 66) (See Appendix 1.)

which are the size of fleas, from crawling underneath the netting. *Vinchucas* can live and reproduce for weeks with one blood meal; they remain content until their energy runs low, at which time they begin to look for another blood meal.

Contamination through the Feces

Contamination through the bugs' feces is the major mechanism by which *T. cruzi* passes from *vinchucas* to humans. *T. cruzi* transforms from a trypomastigote to an epimastigote to a metacyclic trypomastigote inside *vinchucas* (see Figure 17). When infected *vinchucas* take a blood meal, they usually defecate and deposit a metacyclic trypomastigote, which is found in the insect's intestines, onto the victim's skin. Metacyclic trypanosomes (tryps) travel from the feces and enter through the bite site, the eye, or other abraded skin. People often scratch the wound and rub parasites into the skin. Meta-cyclic tryps circulate for a short while in the blood, then enter neuron cells and become encysted as amastigotes. Amastigotes reproduce tryps that enter the blood, where they can be picked up by a *vinchuca* during its blood meal. (Be-cause *T. cruzi* is such an infectious parasite, some laboratories in the United States do not experiment with it).

Not all species defecate at the same rate: *Rhodnius prolixus* and *Panstrongy-lus megistus* defecate at a great rate, while *Triatoma infestans* defecates at only 30 percent of that rate, and *Triatoma sordida* at only 10 percent (Calvo et al. 1978:70–81). Those species that defecate closest to the injection wound are the most infectious; consequently, *T. infestans* is most dangerous to humans and most adaptive for *T. cruzi*, being a very effective vector in transmitting this par-asite to hosts. The longer *T. cruzi* is outside the vector and host, the more vul-nerable it is to being lysed, or disintegrating. Children are easily contaminated with the feces of *vinchucas*. Babies and infants spend considerable time within and around the house, sometimes with little clothing, and they are defenseless victims for *vinchucas* to feed upon.

Infection through Blood Transfusions

Blood transfusion is the second most important mechanism of transmission of Chagas' disease. Blood transfusions have enabled *T. cruzi* to travel beyond tropical and semitropical zones, where it was environmentally limited by the fact that its triatomine vectors needed the warmth and humid-ity of these areas. This makes Chagas' disease a worldwide problem, because Latin American countries have been major exporters of blood, as well as or-gans, through the years (Moraes-Souza et al. 1995; WHO 1990, 1991; Docampo et al 1988). In Brazil alone, 10,000 to 20,000 cases of Chagas' disease occur yearly because of infections through transfusions (Dias and Brener 1984).[4] Bo-livia has a high rate of infected blood. The National Secretariat of Health esti-mated that in 1988 there were five new cases of Chagas' disease each day (Bryan and Tonn 1990:15). In seven capital departments of Bolivia, 1,298 sera samples from blood banks were examined for *T. cruzi* (Carrasco et al. 1990). Percent-ages of infected blood reached 28 percent, with the following distribution: Santa Cruz (at an elevation of 430 m), 51 percent; Tarija (1,951 m), 45 percent; Sucre (2,750 m), 39 percent; Cochabamba (2,570 m), 28 percent; Potosí (4,060 m), 28 percent; Oruro (3,706 m), 6 percent; and La Paz (3,640 m), 4.9 percent. Other studies for contaminated blood range from 56 percent to 70 percent contamination (Valencia 1990a, Bryan and Tonn 1990) to a less alarming 8 per-cent (Schmuñis 1991). High percentages of infected blood are found in rural migrants and low-income donors who live in infested dwellings and need money.

Measures to decrease contaminated blood include the screening of donors and the lysing of *T. cruzi* with gentian violet, a trypanocide (Moraes-Souza et al. 1995; see Appendix 13: Chemotherapy). Blood needs to be stored with gentian violet for twenty-four hours at 4° C for the substance to destroy *T. cruzi* (Nussenzweig et al. 1953, Schmuñis 1991). Gentian violet gives blood a deep violet coloration, and its side effects are unclear.

Bolivians generally have not adopted these screening measures. Blood is rarely stored in Bolivia, except for export. People receive transfusions directly from someone for about twenty dollars or they purchase a blood bag for five dollars and then have someone fill it for a fee (J. Méndez, interview 5/6/97). Bolivians often refuse transfusions of violet blood, and serological and clinical examinations are expensive.

Fortunately, only 14 to 18 percent of people who receive a transfusion of infected blood develop Chagas' disease. The following factors are important: the quantity of infected blood received in one or a series of transfusions, the general state of the person's health, and the immunocompetence of the person (Toro Wayar, interview 6/20/91). Patients receiving multiple transfusions are at high risk, and many patients are immunosuppressed from sickness. People at risk are generally from the poorer classes; wealthy patients usually go to private clinics which have access to blood banks. However, there are not many wealthy people in Bolivia; only 2,000 Bolivians receive annual salaries of more than U.S. $10,000 (*Presencia*, May 11, 1997).

Chagas' disease is no longer restricted to Latin America. Immigrants from El Salvador and Nicaragua in Washington, D.C., have tested positive for *T. cruzi* infection. In 1985, estimates were that 100,000 individuals living in the United States were infected with *T. cruzi* (Kirchhoff, Gam, and Gillian 1987). I now estimate that number to be more than one million people because of increased immigration from Latin America, increased travel back and forth between countries in Latin America, increased numbers of blood transfusions and organ transplants, and transmission of the disease through birth.[5]

Transmission through Birth

T. cruzi can travel through the placenta, birth canal, and maternal milk. Infected mothers pass Chagas' disease to their children, but in lesser percentages than might be expected. Some unknown immunologic process often protects the infant (Calvo et al. 1978:80). In general, the incidence of congenital *T. cruzi* transmission is under 10 percent, although this rate is much higher in endemic areas such as Bolivia (Muñoz and Acevedo 1994). In Punata, Bolivia, the mortality rate for children infected congenitally was 47 percent (SOH/ CCH 1994). Rates of congenital transmission have increased over the years (Azogue, La Fuente, and Darras 1985:176).[6]

In Bolivia, congenital transmission rates were 7 percent in La Paz and 43 percent in Cochabamba (Brénière et al. 1983). Antibodies were detected in the serum of the mother and in the umbilical cord, with the concentration and quality of the antibodies similar. In Santa Cruz, Bolivia, 329 newborn babies were examined from 1979 to 1980; *T. cruzi* was found in twenty-five cases (Azogue, La Fuente, and Darras 1985:176–80).[7] Some 51 percent of the mothers and 13 percent of the infants tested positive for Chagas' disease. Twenty-one (80 percent) of the infected infants weighed less than 2,500 grams (5.5 pounds). It is not clear whether nutrition is an independent or dependent variable; that is, whether the immune system of nutritionally healthy babies resists Chagas' disease or whether babies infected with Chagas' disease lose weight. Also, not one case was found before the sixth month of gestation. Although the mother is infected from conception, transmission of *T. cruzi* from her to the fetus takes time.[8]

The delayed infection of fetuses raises the possibility of treating infected mothers during pregnancy to reduce transmission of the disease to the fetus. The high toxicity levels of nifurtimox and benznidazole used pose serious threats to unborn infants. Moreover, congenitally infected fetuses have been delivered from mothers both positive and negative for parasitemia, and infants have been born uninfected from pregnant women with acute infections and positive parasitemia. Intrauterine *T. cruzi* infection can cause abortions and premature births (WHO 1991:5).

Mechanisms of transmission of the disease from mother to fetus have not been determined. Possibilities include through the extra-embryonic membranes by diffusion of the parasites, or through progressive migration of the parasite throughout the stroma of the umbilical cord towards the blood vessels, provoking fetal infection by way of the blood (Azogue, La Fuente, and Darras 1985:180).[9]

The chances of getting Chagas' disease from contaminated blood in Bolivia are higher (14 to 18 percent) than they are of contracting the disease by being born from a Bolivian mother infected with *T. cruzi* (5 to 10 percent). Even though these percentages vary greatly and are in part guess-estimates, the figures are perplexing in that rates of infected blood and infected mothers are roughly the same—from 40 to 50 percent. One explanation for the lower rates of congenitally transmitted disease is that it is difficult to diagnose, especially in endemic areas, unless the tests are conducted at birth, since the possibility also exists of infection, or reinfection, by the vector (Muñoz and Acevedo 1994). Secondly, parasites are difficult to detect in the placenta, and, even if they are present, they may not infect the fetus (Thiermann et al. 1985; Muñoz 1990).

Significantly, Chagas' disease in newborns correlates highly with low weight: in one study, 13 percent of babies weighing less than 2,500 grams (5.5 pounds) were infected with Chagas' disease in Bolivia (Azogue, La Fuente, and Darras 1985:176–80). Prenatal and postnatal nutrition helps babies resist *T. cruzi*.

Oral and Organ Transmission

Some less-frequent forms of transmission are by direct ingestion, organ transplant, and skin contact with infected material (Bittencourt 1975; Katz, Despommier, and Gwadz 1989; Schofield, Apt, and Miles 1982). Oral transmission to humans is not well documented, although it is easy to infect animals by this route (Marsden 1967).[10] Because *vinchucas* defecate in domiciliary and peridomiciliary areas, the possibility of contamination through contact with the insect's feces and subsequent ingestion of the parasite exists but is not likely.

Three microepidemics in Brazil are attributed to oral transmission (Nery-Guimaraes et al. 1968). Schoolchildren became infected with *T. cruzi* from drinking contaminated milk in Estrella, Rio Grande do Sul, Brazil, an area where triatomines were not found (Calvo et al. 1978:80). The milk had been transported from an endemic area.

In an agricultural school in Rio Grande do Sul, seventeen people were infected and six died from *T. cruzi* transmitted through food contaminated with opossum urine infected with *T. cruzi*. The initial misdiagnosis of the illness and the patients' treatment with steroids aggravated the infection (Di Primio 1971). Trypanosomes can be found in the saliva and urine of animals suffering from acute parasitemia. This constitutes an infective risk for humans working with these animals (Marsden and Hagstrom 1968).

A third instance was in Belem, Para, Brazil, at the mouth of the Amazon, where human Chagas' disease is rare (Lainson et al. 1979) because only sylvatic species of bugs in this area are known to be infected. It is possible that an infected bug entered the house and fell in a cold soup customarily prepared (Lainson et al. 1980) and infected it with *T. cruzi*. Because contamination is the major route of transmission, many other possibilities exist for humans coming in contact with *T. cruzi* through *vinchuca* feces falling from the ceiling, getting into clothing, and being deposited on tools, among other things. As already mentioned, the periodic washing of the body and clothes is important in combatting the disease, as are good house hygienic practices.

Animals can transmit *T. cruzi* to humans by licking their skin, and nursing mothers can pass it on to their babies in lactation, possibly through the milk but more likely through sores or inflammations on the breast (Carrasco and Antezana 1991). The parasite's presence in maternal milk has been confirmed by Medina (1983), but the incidence of transmission by this route has not been reported, probably due to the problem of differentiating it from congenital transmission (Moya 1994).

Transmission by breast-feeding appears to be highly unlikely, and infected mothers need not restrict breast-feeding their infants (WHO 1991:33). This conclusion was based on a systematic parasitological study of 100 milk, or colostrum, samples from seventy-eight mothers with chronic Chagas' disease in Bahia, Brazil. Even though five mothers had detectable parasitemia, all samples were negative (Bittencourt et al. 1988). In another study in Córdoba, Argentina, and Santa Cruz, Bolivia, ninety-seven children (100 percent of the sample) born free of the infection from infected mothers and subsequently breast-fed tested serologically negative (WHO 1991:33).

Organ transplants from infected donors is an increasing route of *T. cruzi* transmission for recipients in the United States and Europe. There is an increasing number of organs being sold through the "black market" to patients in the United States from Latin American countries. Americans also travel to clinics in Latin America for organ transplants. Kidney transplants have been shown to be a source of *T. cruzi* infection, and organ recipients have developed acute episodes of Chagas' disease (Chocair et al. 1981). In certain transplants, fatality has been attributed to donated organs infected with *T. cruzi*, because recipients are under immunosuppressive therapy (WHO 1991:34). Conversely, Chagas' disease patients who receive organ transplants can suffer exacerbation of the infection when given immunosuppressive treatment (Leiguarda et al. 1990).

Laboratories treat *T. cruzi* with respect. It is the most infectious of the human blood protozoa. By 1976 more than fifty lab technicians had been infected with Chagas' disease; they suffered meningoencephalitis and megasyndromes (Marsden 1976). Since this time, technicians have learned how to better handle high-risk organisms, but certain research hospitals still refuse to do research on *T. cruzi* because of its risk factor. Laboratory infections are usually due to punctures with infected needles, contact with contaminated materials, breathing *T. cruzi* cultures while pipetting, and splashing *T. cruzi* suspensions on the conjunctivae. Measures for prevention and control are outlined in WHO (1991).

Laboratories in Bolivia present great risks for contracting Chagas' disease because of their often rudimentary facilities, inadequately trained staff, and insufficient funds to provide protective measures. The exception is the *Instituto Boliviano de Biología de Altura* (IBBA), located in La Paz and affiliated with the Pasteur Institute in Paris. Eminent French and Bolivian scientists direct this research laboratory and have done leading work on parasitology. Other, much less developed, laboratories are under control of the Secretaria Nacional de Salud and are funded with minimal budgets. Nonetheless, technicians make do. One technician observed that he was not worried about Chagas' disease, being already infected—which perhaps is the case for many Bolivian researchers.

Epidemiological Reflections

T. cruzi is a silent traveler through *vinchucas* that has infected 1.5 million people in Bolivia and some 17 million more in other Latin American countries (see Appendix 6). *T. cruzi* infects people through contamination, blood transfusions, and congenital infection. *Vinchucas, T. infestans,* have adopted domestic and peridomestic habitats, finding run-down houses crowded with people and animals very suitable for shelter and food. *Vinchucas* follow migrants and animals to the cities. For the prevention as well as the treatment of Chagas' disease, the chain of life-stages of the parasite needs to be broken at some point. The possibilities include the elimination of triatomine insects, which is highly unlikely in certain places; prevention of transmission through the bite of the triatomines by means of improved housing, which is presently being done but is very costly; and through vaccinations to block some transformation of epimastigotes to metacyclic trypomastigotes to amastigotes to blood-form trypomastigotes, which is discussed in Appendix 3: Immunization Against *T. cruzi.*

Even though measures are taken to destroy *vinchucas* and purify blood banks, the congenital transmission of Chagas' disease will still occur in Bolivia due to the large percentage—50 percent—of women who are infected with *T. cruzi* transmitting the parasite during pregnancy. The incidence of congenital transmission of Chagas' disease is 10 percent in Bolivia, which is double that found in Argentina and Brazil, but this may be due to the fact that the latter two countries did not consider newborns in their counts. Preventative measures that relate to early detection of the infection and the subsequent treatment of newborns are required.

T. cruzi can travel in blood and organs to infect people in nonendemic regions. It travels with women as they migrate from rural to urban areas and from Bolivia to other countries of the world, and it is passed along to their children, usually for two generations. The transmission of *T. cruzi* is no longer limited to Latin America and the environments of its primary vectors, triatomines. It is becoming a worldwide problem. The silent traveler has arrived on distant shores.

CHAPTER 5

Cólico miserere: Enlarged Colon

Chagas' disease is an elusive target for medical practitioners. It has a diffuse symptomology, if any, until the classic chronic stage, and its clinical symptoms could result from a number of other diseases and causes. It cannot be cured in its advanced stages. It is an autoimmune disease. Moreover, in Bolivia and most other places, Chagas' disease is not well known and patients are rarely tested for it. Biomedical and ethnomedical practitioners treat its symptoms with a combination of home remedies, herbs, surgical practices, and rituals. Cultural and social interpretations of its symptoms sometimes delay medical treatment, but they help Bolivians understand in meaningful terms the suffering it causes. These interpretations can also be used to educate Bolivians about Chagas' disease.

Juana

Juana is a Quechua-speaking peasant of the Calcha ethnic group in the north of Potosí. She and several other members of her family became sick with Chagas' disease. Doctors Oscar Velasco and Francisco Delgadillo treated them and reported on how Juana experienced this disease and how she was treated. Velasco and Delgadillo are skilled in using ethnomedicine in conjunction with biomedicine. They do not subordinate one to the other, but respect each as distinct practices that converge towards a common goal of the patient's health.

The Department of Potosí is situated in southwest Bolivia, between 18 and 23 degrees latitude and 65 and 69 degrees longitude. It is the fourth largest department in Bolivia and has 300,000 inhabitants living in a variety of ecological zones that range from 3,900 meters (13,000 feet) above sea level, where there is sparse vegetation, scarce rain, and permafrost, to valleys that range from 2,800 to 3,000 meters (9,200 to 9,850 feet) above sea level, where a moderate climate and fertile soil provide many agricultural products and where the majority of the population lives. The lower valleys constitute 38 percent of the territory; its natives speak Quechua and some Spanish. Other local ethnic groups are the Chichas, Chara, Calchas, and Yuras. Despite concerted European culture incursions, these groups have maintained traditional Andean cultures, especially the Calchas and Yuras, who are noted for their ethnocentrism.

Throughout her youth, Juana lived in this temperate valley climate, noted for its vast production of fruits and vegetables. Her parents worked as peasants

| 65

Figure 18. Bolivian doctors Oscar Velasco (pictured here) and Francisco Delgadillo work with a patient (Juana C.). Velasco and Delgadillo are skilled in using ethnomedicine with biomedicine as parallel sciences in treating Chagas' disease. (Photograph by Joseph W. Bastien)

for vast Spanish estates. During the colonial epoch, Spanish conquistadors and farmers entered these valleys to produce food and materials for the mines of Potosí, situated in a higher and drier zone. Spanish families and religious congregations divided the territory as they established *adelantamietos* (frontier posts), missions, and parishes. Farmers produced apples, apricots, figs, grapes, and vegetables, primarily to suit Spanish tastes.

When Juana was fifteen, the Calchas elected her to be trained as a *Responsable Popular de Salud* (community health worker—CHW) for their community (see Bastien 1990a for discussion of community health workers). Juana quickly learned how to provide basic medical treatment, give advice on health matters, refer cases to primary-health posts, and collect health data about the people in her community. She also educated Calchas about the care of infants, maternal care, family planning, and how to build a smokeless oven (*horno loreno*). Juana worked without wages for seven years as a CHW and was so successful that she received financial support to study as an *Auxiliar de Enfermería* (auxiliary nurse) in Sucre.

Auxiliary nurses constitute the principal biomedical personnel throughout rural Bolivia. Doctors staff the hospitals in the municipalities and are required to do a year of practice in rural areas (*año de provincia*). Many do this grudgingly, making little effort to speak native languages and even less effort to understand Andean culture. Juana excelled in the six-month course and became the first native nurse among the Calchas, receiving a monthly salary of fifty dollars in 1985. She worked in a *Posta Sanitaria* (health post), where she vaccinated people, attended birth deliveries, and administered medicines and first aid. She educated Calchas in their native language about their health.

Juana became the pride of her family and community, having established herself as the local link between ethnomedicine and biomedicine. She was commended by the *Secretaria Nacional de Salud* for her work in rural Bolivia. She remained poor, as was her family, but they loved one another and were happy.

The ecology of these Bolivian valleys had changed drastically since the Conquest due to vast deforestation to provide timbers for the mines of Potosí and also to the erosive action of rivers, which during the rainy season carry topsoil from plantations and peasant farm plots to lower regions. Especially devastating, floods and droughts of the 1980s, followed by economic hyperinflation, increased impoverishment and migration among the Calchas and others within these valleys.

These factors also made these valleys endemic areas for Chagas' disease, with *vinchucas* inhabiting every community and infecting more than half the population with *T. cruzi*. People became accustomed to *vinchucas,* which many say are harmless and don't bite. Others believe that their bite is only a minor irritation. The fact that the bugs' bite causes death is foreign to their natural view of more gentle balance and reciprocity. Juana and others have been unaware of the biomedical realities of Chagas' disease.

As a nurse, Juana dealt with the following cultural illnesses in Calcha: *las cámaras* (diarrhea), *la congestión* (acute respiratory infections), *las fiebres* (fevers), *las flegmasías* (inflammation), *orejo* and *susto* (soul loss, depression), *tabardillo* (typhus), *las tercianas* (three-day fever), and *cólico miserere* (deadly colic). The Calchas attribute these illnesses to a combination of cultural and biomedical factors: *las cámaras* is due to imbalance of the hot and cold foods and unhygienic conditions; *las tercianas* to bad humors (*mal de aire,* or malaria), *susto* to social concerns and the loss of fluids; *la congestion* to the concentration of fluids in the body and respiratory infections. As discussed in Chapter 3, Andean ethnophysiology adheres to a topographic-hydraulic model of the body combined with some aspects of a European humoral theory (balancing the hot and cold and the wet and dry) adapted from the teachings of Spanish missionaries (see Figure 11). Early missionaries taught humoral theory in medical schools throughout Latin America (see Foster 1978, 1987).

Cólico miserere approximates the megacolon symptom of Chagas' disease but also refers to *vólvulo* (volvulus), which is the twisting of the bowel upon itself, and to ileus, which is blockage, both causing obstruction.[1] People of Potosí especially fear this cultural and symptom complex, which cannot be cured and causes death. Far from being caused by a parasite, *cólico miserere* is thought to be caused by the consumption of either very fresh or left-over foods that produce gas and swell the stomach. If the person cannot *ventosear* (break wind) or *zurrar* (have a bowel movement) to dispel the *cuezcos* (cooked things), the stomach is thought to swell more and more until it shuts off the heart and the person dies. Potosiños say that "eating pork and drinking cold water brings *cólico miserere,* and if someone does this, don't ask why they died." Eating fresh foods without "hot" foods also causes *cólico miserere;* thus, eating cooked potatoes (a cold food because it grows in the ground) and not chewing coca leaves (a hot food) might cause *cólico miserere.* Rarely do Potosiños violate these dietary practices, which effectively serve as preventative medicine.

All classes of Potosiños and ethnic groups suffer from *cólico miserere.* Unusually fat people are prone to *cólico miserere.* Signs of the oncoming illness are choking, fainting, and indigestion. They are called *"personas estreñidas"* (constipated, up-tight, and niggardly people), having a stomach that holds things in rather than in a more open exchange with the outside environment.

Juana was frequently called to assist births in neighboring villages and could be away for days at a time. One time, on her return, her mother, Doña Isica, complained that she was *"muy esteñida"* (very constipated) and had been unable to go to the toilet for four days. Juana gave her an herbal laxative that relieved her. A month later, Doña Isica again became constipated, and her husband, Don Yupay, took her to a famous *curandera* of Chalca, Doña Fonseca, who was ninety years old. Yupay also brought along coca leaves and a large white guinea pig that belonged to Isica. Fonseca greeted them with coca leaves and soon began divining by means of coca leaves and the guinea pig. Fonseca marked the leaves with neat bite marks to designate wind, road, water, and *ajayu* (spirit). For more than an hour, Fonseca debated with Yupay and Isica the cause of the constipation. Fonseca then dug her fingers into the belly of the guinea pig, laying bare its intestines, which were bloated with grain. She whispered slowly that Isica was cold in the stomach, most certainly because she had eaten pork and that she had been taken by a *mal viento* (bad wind). *Wayra* is the wind deity that brings the rains and droughts, as well as good and evil.

Isica and Yupay feared Fonseca's diagnosis of *cólico miserere* with its fatalistic implication, so they asked the *curandera* to *pichar* (sweep) the *sajjra wayra* (troublesome wind) away from her stomach by means of a *picharada* ritual. Fonseca mixed fat from a black hen with copal and hediondilla (*Cestrum matthewsii* Dun). She stroked Isica's stomach in a dispelling motion, praying in Quechua, *Sajjra Wayra, purijchej* ("Be gone, troublesome wind!"). Fonseca left later that evening to deposit the ritual items with money attached at the crossroads so that someone else would find it and carry the evil to their house.

Isica improved, and the family resumed its daily activities. Towards the end of that year, Jovita, a thirteen-year-old sister of Juana, began complaining of chest pains and such fatigue that she felt like falling asleep even while herding goats. Juana examined her and found nothing abnormal. She gave her injections of vitamin B, saying that this would give her energy. Her grandmother said that Jovita was losing too much blood through menstruation and recommended that she drink fresh blood from a freshly sacrificed hen. These folk remedies were unsuccessful, however, and Jovita had to work sitting down. She complained that her legs were so weak that she couldn't walk, and she lost her breath at the least exertion. She also still had pains in her chest.

Juana reported Jovita's symptoms to the doctor at the regional hospital, who diagnosed the malady as nervousness and prescribed tranquilizers. He also said that she probably had some irritation in the liver or lungs that was causing the pain. He prescribed an injection of magnesium sulfate.

In September, a few months later, a child arrived at the house to inform Isica that Jovita had passed out while harvesting corn. Isica found the girl lying in the *chacra* (field). Jovita was trying to vomit and was gasping for breath. She felt very dizzy. Isica gave her chamomile and rose-hip tea, wrapped her in a blanket, and carried her home. After remaining in bed for two days, Jovita again felt *"completo"* (normal).

Around Carnival of the following year, Juana's family celebrated the coming of Lent. They danced, drank, and ate for three days. A week later, Isica complained again that she had been unable to defecate for four days. Juana and Jovita rubbed her stomach with chicken fat and herbs, as the *curandera* had recommended. They gave her tea as a purgative.

Two nights later, Isica became very vexed. At first, it seemed like indigestion; she complained about a severe stomachache. Towards morning, Juana massaged her mother with a solution made from burro dung and boiled *hediondilla*. Isica got worse and her stomach enlarged. By sunrise, Isica suffered intense pain and could barely breathe. Her stomach was pushing against her heart.

Juana called a nurse from the neighboring health post, who diagnosed it as *vólvulo*. She prescribed an enema but they couldn't insert it. In desperation, Juana and her father transported Isica in the back of a truck to the hospital in Potosí. The truck traveled for five hours along winding and bumpy roads that agitated the bloated stomach. Isica screamed in pain.

In late afternoon Isica arrived at the public hospital. A doctor said that he needed to operate and wasn't sure what might happen. Juana said that they didn't want an operation, only some medication to relieve the pain. The doctor then told them to leave and asked the orderly to remove them from the hospital. His parting comments were: "These peasants wait until the last moment to bring their relatives to the hospital,…they expect miracles,…if the patient dies, they blame the doctor!" His remarks hurt Juana, who understood Spanish and had served the medical profession freely for five years.[2]

Feeling ashamed and rejected, Juana and Yupay transported Isica to a private clinic. An attending nurse explained that Isica's lower intestines had become so knotted that she could not pass gas and other matter. She needed to be operated upon to remove the knot or she would die. Juana's father agreed and paid the U.S. equivalent of $200 to have the doctor proceed.

When the surgeon had finished, he said that he had removed part of the lower colon, which was damaged. He showed them a small hole on Isica's left side, a temporary anus (colostomy) to be used until the intestine healed. In several months, he would tie the separated intestines together and Isica could defecate normally.

They were horrified. Yupay told the surgeon that he had said nothing about making such a hole. They argued, but it was too late; the situation could not be remedied. When Isica realized she had a colostomy, matters became worse. A foul odor came from the bandages, and she asked what caused this. Juana explained what happened. Isica said that they should have let her die. Isica refused to cooperate with the nurses when they tried to help her. They tried to instruct her to use a plastic bag to collect the excrement, but she refused.

Juana returned to her community several days later to plant the crops and take care of the cows and chickens. Villagers were coming in and out of her house, and a neighbor told her in tears that her sister Jovita had died that morning. The night before her sister had complained that the pain had returned to her chest. They had found her dead in her *chacra,* the field she owned and worked and in which she had her earth shrine. "At least," as Isica said, "she died with *Pachamama.*"

After burying her sister, Juana visited her mother in the clinic and told her about the death of her youngest daughter. Isica remained silent for a long while and then screamed, "Why do we have to suffer so much?" The doctor arrived to comfort them. He then told Juana that Jovita likely had died from Chagas' disease and that Isica was also suffering from it. He suggested that all members of the family be tested for it.

Some time after, Juana, Isica, Yupay, and Ramon, the youngest son, were tested for Chagas' disease. Juana, Isica, and Yupay were found to be infected; Ramon was not infected. Juana has a damaged heart muscle and a slightly enlarged lower intestine. Yupay has severely dilated intestines that are developing into *cólico miserere.* The doctor prescribed nifurtimox for Juana and Yupay to curtail their infection. However, they discontinued chemotherapy because they were unable to pay the necessary $200 a month, roughly equivalent to half a year's earnings, for nifurtimox.

Dr. Oscar Velasco recently spoke with Juana at a conference for auxiliary nurses in Potosí. She still does not believe that *vinchucas* contributed to the death of her sister and to other illnesses. She said that peasants had always lived in houses with *vinchucas* and that they never got sick from their bites; and it is true that in the past *vinchucas* were not infected with *T. cruzi* to the extent that they are today. When Dr. Velasco asked her if she had ever seen *vinchucas* suck blood from humans, she said that *vinchucas* suck blood from animals but not from humans. Certain nongovernmental agencies have participated in housing-improvement projects to combat *vinchucas* in Calcha, but she admits that no one in her community pays much attention to their advice.

Of major concern to doctors in Bolivia is that peasants see little connection between severe constipation and possible *T. cruzi* infection. Constipation is associated with the eating of improper and unbalanced foods, and people with megacolon are said to have died from *"dolor de barriga"* (stomachache), *"se ha hinchado la barriga"* (swollen stomach), or *"me ha dolido mucho y no he podido hacer qaqa"* (severe stomachache accompanied by the inability to defecate). These frequently reported symptoms all can be attributable to *T. cruzi* parasites, although many Bolivians think they are caused by failing to maintain a balance of the hot and cold and wet and dry principles they associate with natural foods and other objects.

As mentioned before (see Figure 11), a native Andean understands his/her body as the center of a distillation process that takes in fluids (air, water, food) and processes them into useful fluids (milk, semen, blood, and fat) and toxic fluids (feces, urine, and sweat) that need to be eliminated. The circulation of fluids is believed to be a process of centripetal (fluids concentrating in distillation) and centrifugal (fluids going to the peripheral) motions. Volvulus, *empacho*, is understood as the stopping of the centripetal movement. This has cultural significance in that Andeans thus suffering are unable to connect with the blood and fat outside their bodies—the energy and life forces of nature.

Chagasic Colonopathy

Chagasic colonopathy has two progressive stages (Köberle 1968: 95). The first stage features no dilatation of the colon but includes disturbances of the motility of the large intestines, as Isica first suffered. Usual complaints are abdominal distention caused by gas (meteorism), irregularity of peristalsis, and difficulties in defecation. Similar symptomology is also found in the elderly and is attributed to the physiological diminution of ganglion cells in the colon with the increase of age. In similar fashion, Chagas' disease diminishes ganglion cells in the colon. If *T. cruzi* reduce the ganglion cells below a critical limit of 55 percent, dilatation and hypertrophy of the colon begin. The mechanisms of destruction of the nervous intramural plexus are still not clear, but there is strong experimental data indicating that it is related to cell-mediated immunity.[3]

As happened with Isica, this destruction normally leads to the second stage, megacolon, which Andeans usually attribute to entangled colon (*vólvulo*). Its major symptoms are an enlarged colon and the inability to defecate. Peasants sometimes have not defecated for from two to six months before they die (see Figure 9).

In megacolon, amastigote forms of *T. cruzi* encyst within the muscles of the colon. These amastigotes form psuedocysts which burst within the muscle and cause damage to the nerve ganglia within the myenteric plexus. Another possibility is that ganglia present *T. cruzi* antigen markers on their surfaces that become targets for attack by the immune system—sort of self attacking self—and are then destroyed. Without proper innervation of the smooth muscles of the gastrointestinal tract, peristalsis diminishes and, in an attempt to compensate, the muscle layers enlarge (hypertrophy). It is not the hypertrophy of the muscles that causes the most dramatic enlargement of the colon, it is the loss of rigidity provided by the muscle layers. The circular and longitudinal muscles give the gastrointestinal tract its shape, a boundary. Once the muscles hypertrophy and begin to lose their functional capability, the intestine begins to lose its form. Food taken in through the mouth can remain in the gut (gastroin-

Figure 19. Dr. Johnny Méndez is a surgeon at the Instituto de Gastroenterología Boliviana Japones in Sucre, Department of Chuquisaca. Méndez specializes in operating on patients with megacolon, a common chronic symptom of Chagas' disease. (Photograph by Joseph W. Bastien)

testinal tract) for great periods of time, due to lack of peristalsis. As the gut fills up, the intestine expands to hold the contents, having lost its rigidity. Atonic constipation develops and parts of the bowel can become necrous and die. As the disease develops, the entire gastrointestinal tract can be affected—hence, the term megacolon.

In the Department of Chuquisaca, Bolivia, approximately 40 percent of patients' gastrointestinal problems are attributed to Chagas' disease. Both forms of chagasic colonopathy are found in the Department of Chuquisaca. In contrast, none of the patients in Viacha on the Altiplano, outside of La Paz, suffering from *vólvulo* had Chagas' disease.[4] This complicates the problem, in that entangled colon (*vólvulo*) caused by altitudinal and genetic factors is found in Andean communities along with chagasic colonopathy. Only recently have biomedical personnel begun to distinguish between entangled colon (*vólvulo*) and chagasic colonopathy. Some Bolivian doctors dispute the high reported percentages of Chagas' disease and attribute its pathology to altitudinal factors, genetics, and tangled colon (*vólvulo*) caused by improper diets.

Dr. Johnny Méndez Acuña is a surgeon at the Instituto de Gastroenterología Boliviano Japones in Sucre, Department of Chuquisaca. Méndez attributes toxins produced by *T. cruzi* as the cause of pathogenesis, a slightly dated theory for which there is less proof than for that of the antigenic mimicry hypothesis theory (Van Voorhis et al. 1991), discussed in Appendix 11. Méndez specializes in operating on patients with megacolon, and he presents a surgeon's view of the situation:

T. cruzi prefers to settle in the large intestines. The problem resulting is dolicomegacolon [large and wide colon]. It starts as retractile mesenteritis, an inflammation and drawing back of the mesentery. The mesentery contains fibers and vessels that support the intestines as well as pass the various nutrients to it. Toxins also affect the muscular walls of the intestines so that they become large and extended. When the intestines become large and wide, they are less able to contract and pass the digested food along, eventually causing aperistalsis. Gases accumulate. There is a problem of impacted bowels and inability to defecate.

Toxins eventually destroy the supporting wall of the mesentery that provides blood to the intestines. When the large intestine becomes too enlarged, it breaks loose from the mesentery and spins around, forming a volvulus, a twisting of the intestine upon itself that causes obstruction. Many Bolivians suffer from volvulus. This is deadly because the stomach becomes extremely enlarged, the person is unable to pass gas and fecal matter, and blood cannot reach the stomach. All patients with volvulus at our hospital have tested positive for Chagas' disease. These patients have decreased nerve plexus of the colon.

We perform about fifteen operations a year for volvulus. Called the operation of Hartmann, it is a sigmoidectomy where we remove the engorged section of the intestines, disconnecting the intestines from the anus. The patient goes to the bathroom using a tube outside of the body. In six months, we perform an operation of reconversion, to connect the intestines with the rectum. (Méndez Acuña 6/24/91).

As Méndez indicated, for chagasic megacolon surgical repair is needed to remove part of the bowel.[5] Unfortunately, many Bolivians die from severe constipation because they go undiagnosed or are unable to pay for an operation. Others would rather die than undergo an operation and deal with the inconvenience associated with ileostomy, such as Isica illustrated. Ileostomy presents an extremely complicated technological situation for subsistence peasants.

A useful new technique for the treatment of chagasic megacolon is restorative proctocolectomy, practiced in Brazil (MacSweeny, Shankar, and Theodorous 1995:479). A twenty-two-year-old woman was suffering from chronic constipation with overall malaise. Despite regular treatment with laxatives, she became worse. Finally her abdomen was opened and surgically examined. Surgeons found the entire colon grossly dilated, with small perforations of the transverse colon and ischemic caecum. They excised part of the colon (colectomy) and created a surgical passage through the abdominal wall into the ileum so that fecal matter drained into a bag worn on the abdomen (ileostomy). She wished to avoid permanent ileostomy, so they removed the anus and created a J-pouch with a covering-loop ileostomy followed by closure of the ileostomy. Restorative proctocolectomy produced good results in her case in that she subsequently has had four bowel actions per day and full control of continence.

Esophageal Problems

Another gastrointestinal complication found in the Department of Chuquisaca, Bolivia, in chagasic patients is achalasia of the esophagus, or the nonrelaxation of the lower esophageal sphincter (see Marcondes de Rezende and Ostermayer 1994:151–58). Motility of the esophagus is altered in chagasic patients throughout Latin America, and there is no agreement on the prevalence of either megaesophagus or megacolon.[6] The function of the esophagus is to contract and expand so as to push food through the throat to the stomach. A variety of explanations are found for intrinsic denervated esophagus that produces loss of peristalsis, so that the esophagus does not dilate and food cannot pass through it (Marcondes de Rezende and Luquetti 1994). The upper part of the esophagus enlarges, and patients have difficulty swallowing (dysphagia), at times being unable to swallow liquids.[7] Chagasic patients in Santa Cruz often gloss over the fact that they are suffering from dysphagia by a stereotypical answer to the physician's inquiry. Many respond: "But, Doctor, who doesn't have difficulty when eating cold rice?"

Very significantly, patients with megaesophagus have lost more than 95 percent of the ganglion cells of the myenteric plexuses (Köberle 1968:91).[8] Temporary stagnation or retention of food stretches the esophagus, causing distention of the muscle fibers, which leads to hypertrophy of the muscle, causing more powerful contractions and making still more difficult the passage of food.

In Sucre, chagasic megaesophagus is commonly found. Resulting serious side effects among patients who are unable to swallow for several days include starvation and malnourishment.[9] Sufferers regurgitate food and water into the bronchial tubes and lungs, either choking or becoming further infected with respiratory diseases. Again, this is particularly deadly in high-altitude regions, which have markedly lower oxygen levels and a higher prevalence of respiratory pathogens.

Many Bolivians adapt to chagasic esophageal problems by consuming liquids whenever they are able to do so. Herbalists recommend teas from coca leaves to relax the throat and relieve the soreness. Peasants frequently chew coca leaves to achieve the same effects. Coca leaves have fourteen alkaloids, some of which are activated only through hydrolysis—that is, released by saliva or water (Bastien 1987a:57; Martin 1970:422; Duke, Aulik, and Plowman 1975). Bolivian doctors generally recommend bland semi-solid foods, especially cooked Andean cereals of quinua and cañiwa, warmed to body temperature so that the esophagus will drain by force of gravity; but this is often ineffective. The solution has been to surgically cut the esophageal muscle. Doctors in Sucre performed about twenty such operations in eleven years; but this figure doesn't indicate the actual number of achalasia patients who are unable to afford an operation, fear such procedures, or remain unaware of the option. Doctors at the Gastro-Intestinal Hospital in Sucre use the Heller technique modified by Pinotti. Originally, Heller cut the restricted area, but this did not produce effective results. Pinotti modified the procedure by only removing a narrow strip of muscle lengthwise along the constricted region. The resulting outcome of these operations has been satisfactory (Méndez Acuña, interview 6/24/91).

Bolivians rarely attribute difficulty swallowing to infection of *T. cruzi.* They explain choking and regurgitating as emotional states caused by disproportion of the certain humors or to the fact that they have not balanced their meals with wet and dry substances. This results in inadequate proportions of phlegm to aid in swallowing. They also relate certain emotions to these humors; so that, for example, someone with excessive bile is said to be angry and consequently has insufficient phlegm to swallow. As another explanation, they see the accumulation of fluids as a malfunctioning of the tubes relating to distillation processes of the body that work in centripetal and centrifugal motions.

An Afterthought

Juana's history demonstrates both the hubris and humility that can be associated with Chagas' disease and other diseases that at first appear so clinically self-evident to scientists. When serious scholars begin to examine disease pathogens, they often discover that the world of microbiology can be immersed in environmental, social, and cultural systems. For years Andeans have suffered from *cólico miserere* and *vólvulo,* which they have understood according to their ethnophysiology. When modern science explains this away in terms of bugs and parasites, there often persists continued adherence to what they have believed. A crucial insight can be gained when *cólico miserere* is seen not only as an entity with a cause but as a sign or symbol of some disequilibrium, imbalance, social infraction, or spiritual chaos. This sign is written upon the human body in painful and contorted ways. To remove part of a bodily tube or insert another orifice while detaching another can be seen to sacrilegiously deform a body that is imaged after the land, with fluids entering, concentrating, and dispersing. The hubris of the scientists who imagine that their uncovering of clinical facts will save people from disease is often turned to humility. And Juana, recognizing that she, her sister, and her mother had been bitten by infected *vinchucas,* still reverted to folk beliefs surrounding *cólico miserere.* She recognizes, as do most other Andean peasants, that biomedical science is only as valuable as its capacity to eradicate disease and heal the sick; within her family, it is not a social and economic reality.

On the side of doctors and biomedical science, there is no clear agreement either—certain doctors are hesitant to accept that the high incidence of gastrointestinal problems in some communities is related to chagasic colonopathy; other doctors contend that *T. cruzi* is the exclusive cause of volvulus in other communities. Scientists are slow to believe that Chagas' disease exists in higher altitudes, such as the Altiplano, where it is too cold for *vinchucas,* so they attribute gastrointestinal symptoms to other factors. Yet, evidence shows that Chagas' disease is found in higher regions, and its present spread includes many new regions. The rule should be that when some of the above symptoms appear in Bolivia, a largely endemic zone of the disease, patients should be tested for Chagas' disease.

CHAPTER SIX

Bertha: *Mal de Corazon*

Bertha (a pseudonym) is a resident of La Paz, Bolivia, who suffers chronic heart ailments from Chagas' disease. Bertha's medical history provides insights into the natural history of Chagas' disease. As a child in the 1930s, Bertha was bitten by *vinchuca* bugs and infected with *Trypanosoma cruzi* in Tupiza, a small rural village in Bolivia. Later, as a mother with four daughters, she moved to La Paz after being abandoned by her husband. She made a meager living sewing for wealthy people. Late in 1974 she suffered heart disease and was diagnosed with Chagas' disease. Presently, at age sixty-one, Bertha still sews dresses but also receives additional income from her married daughters.

Bertha is a small slender lady with sparkling dark brown eyes. She speaks Spanish, dresses in western-style clothes, and is of the *mestizo* class, in contrast to the *cholo* class, those who maintain Aymara and Quechua identity. Bertha narrated the following account to Dr. Pedro Jáuregui, her personal physician, on July 22, 1991, illustrating the effects of chronic Chagas' disease.

I was raised in a community of Tupiza, a valley of Potosí. We always traveled to the country. In the village the *vinchucas* entered the houses. I didn't know anything about them when I was a child. *Vinchucas* were an inch long with wings, some were brown, brown-black, and they usually bit us. They laid their eggs, and we played with their eggs. At night without electricity we could feel them, we would pull off their heads. This was the way to kill them.

At other times I awoke with eyes swollen, then I put a little tea water and some leaves over the swelling. It was not a large swelling.

We didn't have fear of them. As a child, I played with them, putting their eggs in a basket as if they were chicken eggs. I didn't know that this bug was dangerous. We had sheep, chickens, and corrals where *vinchucas* would dig their nests. Another insect was *chinchina*. There were both types of insects because we lived in the valley. My father was an administrator in a mine so he traveled frequently. I think that *vinchucas (barbeiros)* inhabited most of the houses.

I left Tupisa when I was twenty years old and moved to La Paz. And until the age of forty-four I was a healthy person, going up and down the hills. I had no idea that I was sick with Chagas' disease until 1974 when I felt fatigue, although before [that time] I had some allergies when I ate lentils. I began to get a swollen throat and spit blood. I didn't know what it was. I didn't feel anything for forty years. I didn't have any idea that this was caused by *vinchucas*. I would get tired, fatigued, and experienced dizziness and many fainting [spells] around 1974. I was without a husband and when I knit alone, I experienced fainting. My daughter who slept at my feet felt that I was trying to kick her. This fainting continued for a year, and the next year I had more severe fainting, and the next year I was found laying in my room with another stroke after I had arose to get a drink of water.

After my children found me, they insisted that I see a doctor. Dr. Jáuregui hospitalized me. He felt my pulse which was very low. He suspected Chagas' disease and had me undergo a test [xenodiagnosis] where they determined it was Chagas' disease with the same bites of [uninfected] *vinchucas*. I could feel the bites, and after they itched and burned a bit.

Only then did I learn about Chagas' disease that was caused by *vinchucas*. I thought my sickness was from overwork and problems with work (Bertha interview 7/22/91).

After Bertha was hospitalized, Dr. Jáuregui examined her and found a low pulse. An electrocardiogram indicated that she was suffering from arrhythmia (irregular heartbeats) and bradycardia (slow heartbeats). X-rays indicated a normal-sized heart, not one enlarged as in cardiomegaly. Jáuregui suspected that trypanosomes had affected the nervous system of the heart and that Bertha had developed a heart block, a potentially fatal complication. He believed that a heart block is more deadly than cardiomegaly, a more frequent cardiac form caused by lesions.

Heart block occurs when there is blockage in the conduction system of the heart. The sinoatrial (SA) node is a small control center near the top of the heart that emits signals to the atrioventricular (AV) node, which regulates heartbeats. It is similar to the electrical control harness in an automobile that regulates electricity to the horn, lights, and radio. If one of these wires is cut, for example, then the horn will not work. In Chagas' disease, heart block occurs when there are lesions in the conduction system causing the heart's beats to be slow.

Because Bertha grew up in an endemic chagasic area, Jáuregui suspected that *T. cruzi* were weakening her heart, and he used xenodiagnosis to determine if *T. cruzi* could be found in her blood. For Bertha's exam, forty uninfected *vinchucas* were divided into two small jars. The jars were placed underneath Bertha's arms so that the bugs could draw her blood. This continued for one-half hour, until all the bugs had ingested from 7 to 8 milliliters of blood. Bertha later complained about the bites and itching, and, when her daughter was later suspected of having Chagas' disease, Bertha discouraged her from this exam. Results for Bertha tested positive, so Jáuregui began treating her with benznidazole, diuretics, and tranquilizers.

By 1980 Bertha's heart rhythm had worsened, so Jáuregui implanted a pacemaker that same year, which was replaced in 1991. The pacemaker regulated her heartbeat and the fainting spells diminished, so Bertha was able to resume her work as a seamstress, although she suffered from minor fatigue when she climbed the streets of La Paz at 12,000 feet.

Most likely as a result of congenital infection, two of Bertha's daughters also have heart problems. The eldest daughter, now thirty-eight, was born with heart trouble and suffers continual fatigue. After Bertha learned that Chagas' disease was congenitally transmitted, she encouraged her daughter to undergo xenodiagnosis. Dreading being bitten by *vinchucas,* the daughter refused testing. She is afraid because the bites are irritating; alternative serological tests, such as ELISA Immunosorbent, are available in La Paz and are painless except for the drawing of blood. The second daughter has tachycardia and was tested by xenodiagnosis, with negative results (see Appendix 12).

Dr. Jáuregui has treated the symptoms of many patients suffering from heart diseases caused by chronic Chagas' disease in the Thorax Hospital in La Paz. This hospital was built earlier this century and features high ceilings, tile floors, and tall steel beds, reminiscent of the nineteenth century when some diseases were believed to be caused by emanations from the earth—miasma theory. Jáuregui has claimed no cures for chronic Chagas' disease and only treats its symptoms, as in the case of Bertha. As Jáuregui described it in an interview on July 19, 1991:

> *T. cruzi* are *muy listo* ("shrewd critters")! They circulate in the blood as little as possible, only to be transmitted. They inhabit cells of heart and intestines, vital areas where, to kill them, you have to destroy the organs. All I can do is help patients live a little longer by treating their symptoms. There is no cure for chronic Chagas' disease.

Bertha's case history is illustrative of that of many Bolivians who suffer cardiac problems from chronic Chagas' disease. Ventricular tachycardia frequently occurs among patients of La Paz such as Bertha and is perhaps related to hypoxia (low oxygen) stress. La Paz is situated on slopes with elevations ranging from 11,000 to 12,000 feet. Infected chagasic patients continually climb up and down those slopes in the course of daily life, and for those with heart disease this is difficult and dangerous. Andeans are traditionally renowned for their strong hearts, extra lung capacity, and numerous red blood cells.

Until the recent epidemic of Chagas' disease in Bolivia, heart disease was not considered the killer there that it is in the United States. However, with the increasing number of chronic chagasic patients, recent Bolivian studies indicate increasing electrocardiographic abnormalities characteristic of Chagas' disease–related heart disease. Jáuregui and Casanovas (1987:30–33) observed a total of 4,108 patients throughout Bolivia and found 853 (20.8 percent) with cardiac abnormalities, out of which 436 (10.6 percent) were infected with Chagas' disease. Pless and colleagues (1992) did a clinicoepidemiological study in the remote rural village of Tabacal in southcentral Cochabamba, Bolivia. They examined 153 out of 160 villagers for signs of Chagas' disease and found that 116 people (76 percent) tested positive. The people infected with *T. cruzi* were 3.5 times more likely than uninfected people to have signs and symptoms of heart failure and nine times more likely to have electrocardiogram (ECG) abnormalities. Some 33 percent of ECG conduction defects occurred in adults over thirty-five years of age. Tabacal is similar to hundreds of other villages in southcentral Bolivia, which suggests that heart disease could be a major public health problem in this area (Pless et al. 1992, Weinke et al. 1988; see Appendix 10: Chronic Heart Disease).

Altitude appears to affect the manifestations of chronic chagasic heart disease. The lower levels of oxygen characteristic of high altitudes (hypoxia) place additional stress on chronic chagasic patients emigrating from lower to higher regions of the Andes. Patients with heart disease in La Paz are at greater risk of mortality than those at lower levels. The aerobic effect of living at high altitude, which traditionally endows Andeans with strong hearts, is counterproductive to individuals suffering with hearts afflicted with *T. cruzi*.

Therapeutically, patients with chronic Chagas' disease stand a better chance of living longer at lower altitudes if they can avoid *vinchuca* bites, which intensify parasitic infestation of the victim's body; furthermore, *Trypanosoma cruzi* has different strains, or zymodemes, which hypothetically possess different clinical manifestations (see Appendix 2: Strains of *Trypanosoma cruzi*). One advantage, already discussed, is that the victim is not likely to suffer another acute phase, which often is deadly.

Dr. Toro Wayar has studied and treated patients with chagasic heart disease in Sucre, Department of Chuquisaca, Bolivia, where he practices as a cardiologist and is director of the Centro de Investigación y Diagnóstico de la Enfermedad de Chagas-Sucre.[1] The Department of Chuquisaca is heavily infested with triatomine bugs and has a high number of infected chagasic patients. For eight years, Dr. Wayar and his staff have performed clinical and electrocardiographic studies of patients either diagnosed with or suspected of having Chagas' disease. The following are excepts from an interview with Dr. Wayar on June 20, 1991:

> The majority of our patients have positive serological indicators that they are infected with Chagas' disease but totally lack clinical indicators by radiology or electrocardiography. We refer to these patients as *infectados*

chagasicos [people infected with Chagas' disease]. They become aware of being infected when they are examined for other reasons or they realize they have lived in endemic chagasic areas and want to see if they are infected.

A minority have clinical symptoms discovered in the cardiovascular system. They could have alterations determined by x-ray in the size of the heart or alterations in the heart rhythm determined by electrocardiogram. Concerning alterations of the heart size, when trypanosomes settle in the heart, they could affect all heart muscles, causing chronic inflammation of the myocardium [myocarditis]. The heart becomes structurally disorganized in all the muscular fibers; it increases in size and presents different degrees of malfunctioning, depending upon the grade of increase, which can be anywhere from two to three times its normal size. But this is infrequent because the person seldom survives to this stage.

The more common type of alteration is found when trypanosomes damage the electrical system of conduction of the heart, which controls the number and intensity of heart beats. Trypanosomes could alter any sector and cause many variations in the form of arrhythmias. This is a characteristic particular to chronic chagasic patients. Arrhythmias range from very light to very severe, which can cause sudden death (*muerto subito*). Treatment for these patients is limited to resolving cardiac problems, with rather unsuccessful treatments for ridding patients of trypanosomes. (Toro Wayar, interview 6/20/91.)

Dr. Wayar questioned the fact that trypanicides were able to rid chagasic patients of trypanosomes, and there is considerable debate concerning this. Even if the patient can be rid of *T. cruzi,* that would not eliminate the immunological consequences of the original infection (see Appendix 11: Immune Response).

An important conclusion of Toro Wayar is that electrocardiographic abnormalities were found in lower percentages than was commonly thought. He attributed this to strains of *T. cruzi* infecting the colons of patients rather than their hearts. Wayar's conclusion supports the adaptive ability of *T. cruzi* strains to select intracellular locations that promote their reproductive process. As in La Paz, heart disease is especially lethal in Sucre because of hypoxia, and it is only natural that strains of parasites that reside in the colon have a longer time to reproduce than those in the heart, which die off with their hosts.

Apparently this reasoning runs counter to the findings of Jáuregui and Casanovas (1987:30–33), who reported a higher incidence of heart disease in mesothermic regions than was typically found in tropic zones. It does suggest that many chronic chagasic patients with heart problems in La Paz were infected at lower altitudes and later moved to La Paz. The resulting hypoxic stress then interacted with chagasic heart disease to produce ECG abnormalities.

As already mentioned, natives of higher altitudes have developed physiologically to hypoxia and have well-adapted cardiovascular systems to deal with the resulting low-oxygen stress. Conversely, peasants migrating from the lowlands to higher altitudes lack these adaptive features and, if they become infected with Chagas' disease, they are at greater risk for heart problems because they are unaccustomed to hypoxic stress, which interacts synergistically with chronic myocarditis. One advantage these migrant lowlanders have in living in La Paz is the decreased possibility of reinfection with additional parasites or new strains brought about by *vinchuca* bites. Thus, verticality, or people living at different altitudes in Bolivia, adds additional complexity to chronic Chagas' disease in this country.

Although cardiopathy is frequently associated with chronic Chagas' disease in Bolivia, this disease also manifests itself in other organs of the body, possibly as a function of strain diversity within *T. cruzi*—the organisms adapting to host physiology and hypoxic stress. As living organisms, *T. cruzi* and humans establish parasitic relationships that dynamically vary with environmental stresses. By the time the patient is chronically ill, these parasites have become established in human organs, where they have had ample time to reproduce. It is often environmental stresses, such as moving to higher altitudes, or compromised immune systems that eventually destroy the host.

Chronic heart disease is treated symptomatically, with emphasis placed on the cardiovascular aspects. Bolivian doctors also recommend benznidazole or nifurtimox to prevent the spread of parasites from tissue to tissue, but these trypanocides are questionable with regard to their effectiveness against intracellular parasites in the amastigote form (Gutteridge 1982, 1985; Brener 1975, 1979; see also Appendix 13: Chemotherapy).

The Burden of a Weakened Heart in the Andes

Very few Bolivians with chagasic heart disease (.01 percent) are as fortunate as Bertha in being able to have pacemakers installed and to be treated by an expert doctor. Acquired in her infancy, Chagas' disease has left Bertha with irreversible heart damage: arrhythmia (irregular heartbeats) and bradycardia (slow heartbeats), which could lead to heart failure or sudden death without the help of a pacemaker. Many Bolivians have no medical insurance. Pacemaker implantation costs about U.S. $3,000 per person in Bolivia, prohibitively expensive where the average income is U.S. $580 per person per year. No drug exists to reverse these patients' chronic condition, because of the immunological consequences of the original infection. Many victims are farm or mine workers who are unqualified to find lighter jobs. They have little alternative but to continue work and face the daily prospect of their hearts failing to pump enough blood through their bodies to keep them alive. Chagas' disease can seem especially cruel to these workers: when they are supposed to be at the strongest phase of their lives and most able to support young children, they are debilitated and unable to work as hard.

The socioeconomic impact of the disease during the chronic stage is high, as data from Bolivia show: about 25 percent of the infected population (1,500,000 people) will develop severe cardiac and digestive lesions such as cardiac arrhythmia (215,000) and megaesophagus and megacolon (150,000; see Valencia, Jemio, and Aguilar 1989).[2] In 1992, the indirect costs of lost production in Bolivia due to Chagas' disease morbidity and mortality amounted to $100 million, and the direct cost for Chagas' disease treatment reached $20 million (SOH/CCH 1994). The collective biomedical cost for pacemakers and corrective surgery at $3,000 per person would run about $1 billion—astronomically unfeasible in Bolivia as well as in other Andean countries. Put another way, this is enough for the improvement or construction of a million rural dwellings at a minimum estimated cost for each of U.S. $1,000. Data from Brazil are equally grim, with 45,000 cases of cardiac arrhythmia and 30,000 cases of megaesophagus and megacolon estimated annually, with the collective cost at about U.S. $225 million per year (Special Programmes 1991 Report).

In the Andes, chronic Chagas' disease debilitates Andeans who have evolved with strong hearts adapted to the low oxygen of higher altitudes. Highland Andeans have an extra pint of blood in their bodies and larger lungs to accommodate the 20 to 30 percent less oxygen at levels between 9,000 and 16,000 feet. Climbing up and down hills and mountains, Andeans have enjoyed the aerobic effect that daily exercise provides runners. Chagas' disease has not been particularly prevalent at higher altitudes because *vinchucas* prefer warmer and more humid climates. However, this has drastically changed with the massive migration of infected Bolivians and *vinchucas* to practically every site in the Andes. Because of layoffs in the mines, droughts, floods, and increased cocaine production, peasants seasonally travel to endemic areas, where some become infected with *T. cruzi* and bring it and *vinchucas* to other regions. Lowland peoples have also spread this disease to highland Andeans through blood transfusions.

Pathology of Chronic Disease

Chronic manifestations usually take three forms—in order of prevalence: cardiac, colonic, and esophageal—and more than half of the patients with Chagas' disease reveal abnormal electrocardiograms. Up to 30 percent of people with the indeterminate or inapparent form of the infection suffer from cardiac, digestive, or neurological damage ten to twenty years after having contracted the disease, while the remainder never exhibit any manifest organ involvement (WHO 1991; see Figure 8). Symptoms of chagasic heart disease progress from barely decipherable indicators, such as fever, anemia, and hypertension, to serious pathologies.[3] Cardiomegaly results in the heart enlarging five or six times its normal size; but it is not found in all chronic patients, such as Bertha, whose symptoms of Chagas' disease were expressed by ventricular arrhythmias, which frequently cause death sooner than does cardiomegaly.[4] Heart disease illustrates how widespread the damage of Chagas's disease can be and how difficult it is to diagnose this disease by means of only a specific set of symptoms.

The pathology of the chronic stage of Chagas' disease is related to denervation within the nervous system of the colonized organ (Brener 1994). Degeneration of neurons in the heart's parasympathetic ganglia is common in chagasic patients with heart ailments. With megacolon and megaesophagus, lesions of the colon and esophagus are caused by destruction of nerve cells. These lesions are jointly caused by the parasite (intracellular invasion of the trypomastigotes, encystation of amastigotes, and bursting of cells) and by the autoimmune response of the host. Increasing evidence indicates that the pathogenesis of Chagas' disease is related to the parasite's ability to manipulate the host's immune system.[5] It has been found that people die from chronic manifestations in which lesions are left from *T. cruzi* but the parasite is not present, perhaps being lysed at an earlier stage. This has led scientists to suspect that the traces or lesions left from the parasite mimic human antigens. The immune system mistakes these human cells as epitopes from *T. cruzi* and attacks them (discussed in Appendix 11). This is similar to rheumatic fever, where people die from the disease long after the pathogen has been removed.

During the acute phase, inflammation, fevers, and cell damage are related to overactivity of the lymphocytes (see Appendix 9). This polyclonal stimulation is triggered by macrophages devouring trypomastigotes. Results include violent onslaughts on the parasites that drive them into central nervous system cells, lysing cells encapsulated with parasites that release toxins into the body, ineffective destruction of antigens, and eventual weakening of immune response. In short, damage from acute Chagas' disease is more a result of overactivity of the immune system than damage due directly to *T. cruzi*.

The cardiopathy of chronic Chagas' disease is an issue of considerable debate, with several lines of evidence to account for, including the inability to consistently find parasites in damaged areas (Torres 1930). The passive transfer of heart lesions by CD4+ T cells from *T. cruzi*-infected mice to uninfected mice indicates that inflammatory heart lesions could be of an autoimmune nature (Andrade 1958, Ribeiro-dos-Santos et al. 1992). (In simpler terms, the T cells from infected mice were encoded with self-destructive tendencies, and when these T cells were placed in uninfected mice, they caused damage as if the sterile mice had the parasites.)

Referred to as the antigenic mimicry hypothesis, lymphocytes in the heart recognize and mount delayed-type hypersensitivity responses toward a tissue-specific heart component bearing structural similarities to a given *T. cruzi* antigen.[6] A recent study indicates that heart-tissue destruction in chronic Chagas' disease may be caused by autoimmune recognition of heart tissue by a mononuclear cell infiltrate decades after *T. cruzi* infection (Cunha-Neto et al. 1995). Indirect evidence suggests that there are antigenic cross-reactions between *T. cruzi* and heart tissue. Myosin heavy chain (myosin HC) is the most abundant heart protein—50 percent of total protein by weight—and is recognized in heart-specific autoimmunity in rheumatic heart disease (Neu, Beisel, et al. 1987). Research indicates the involvement of cross-reactions between cardiac myosin and a recombinant *T. cruzi* protein (B13) as targets for attack by the victim's T cells (Cunha-Neto et al. 1995).[7]

The immune response is also impaired in the chronic stage of Chagas' disease (see Appendix 11: Immune Response). An improper response of the cellular immune system results in tissue damage, which might lead to the autoimmune cardiac and neural damage of chronic *T. cruzi* infection (Botasso et al. 1994). *Trypanosoma cruzi* infection impairs immunity to many antigens and mitogens.[8] Chagasic patients have a reduced cellular immune response to common mycobacteria antigens, such as those of tuberculosis and leprosy (Bottasso et al. 1994).[9] *T. cruzi* causes loss of the TH1 response to mycobacterial antigens.

HIV patients are also unresponsive to mycobacterial antigens (Khoo et al. 1993). The progression from HIV seropositivity to AIDS is accompanied by a shift in T-helper (TH) cells from TH1 to TH2 and selective loss of the response to mycobacterial antigens. Significantly, chagasic patients are predisposed to the establishment of HIV infection and its rapid progression to AIDS (Botasso et al. 1994).

In conclusion, the rapid spread and progression of HIV infection in Latin America is related to the frequency of infection of Chagas' disease. The rapid spread and progression of tuberculosis and other acute respiratory infections in Bolivia is also related to Chagas' disease. Bolivian public policy makers often object to the fact that AIDS and tuberculosis take medical priority to Chagas' disease, when the fact is that Chagas' disease is also related to the epidemiology of other diseases by the nature of the autoimmune response to it that predisposes its victims to these diseases.

Reflections on the Epidemiology of the Immune System

The following reflections are intuitive considerations of the above findings. AIDS and Chagas' disease have contributed greatly to our knowledge of the immune system and immunopathology. In Western allopathic medicine, diseases are caused by viruses, bacteria, and parasites; the cure is to rid oneself of the organism. The miracle drugs of the twentieth century have been the antibiotics, which are very successful for lysing bacterial infections but less so for viruses, and they are ineffective for parasites. Trypanicides were developed to lyse trypanosomes of *T. cruzi,* but they have met with less than satisfactory results.

By the turn of the millennium, super-bacteria, viruses, and parasites have emerged unscathed by antibiotics. Simple principles of natural selection explain this: antibiotics essentially select individuals of the species that are resistant to the drugs; when they reproduce, they pass on these selective features to their offspring. The unwarranted use of antibiotics in Western culture has led to their increasing ineffectiveness and to the evolution of super-pathogens. This unwarranted use has also led to humans being less dependent upon their immune systems.

With Chagas' disease and AIDS, researchers have learned much more about the human immune system and how this system is responsible for illnesses. We are also learning how to live with immune-driven diseases—diabetes, rheumatism, AIDS, and Chagas' disease—and how to build up the immune system by alternative methods of therapy, including dieting, meditation, ritual, and use of herbal medicines. The paradigm of health is changing from that of allopathic medicine, where we lyse the causal agent, to one of immunopathic medicine.

Immunopathic medicine includes figuring out ways to build up our immune system and to help it deal with the realities of our bodies and the organisms within them. Health is learning how to live with what you have. This alternative way of health is not very attractive for those who want the technical quick cure of a drug or vaccine to destroy the pathogen; but, as we have seen, this does not work with Chagas' disease, among others.

CHAPTER SEVEN
Culture and Political Economy of Homes

The condition of houses is a major factor in the spread of Chagas' disease. Bolivian houses have become habitats for triatomine vectors of *Trypanosoma cruzi* (see Appendix 5: Housing Infestation in Bolivia). Thatched roofs, cracked walls, and scattered domestic belongings provide nesting sites and hiding places for *vinchucas* in Bolivian houses. Peasants do not place their clothes in closets but rather beneath beds, in bundles, and in corners. Triatomines nest within mattresses, newspapers, and behind objects hung on walls. Peasants also frequently store wood and crops inside their houses.

House Tour with an Entomologist

Juan Mamani lives with his wife and six children in an adobe house, roughly about the size of a single-car garage in the United States. The adobe walls are unplastered and cracked. Entering the wooden-framed doorway, one sees openings between the frame and the walls. The dirt floor is smoothly packed but covered with stacks of corn, potatoes, rice, and dried beans in one corner. A small earthen stove without a chimney is nestled in another corner with pots and pans surrounding it. The room smells of smoke and cooking. The ceiling is black from the soot of smoke. The building has a thatched roof, which forms the ceiling, and from crossbeams hang clothes, baskets, and several drums. Wooden beds with straw mattresses lie along each wall. Juan and his wife sleep in one bed, their children in the others. Beneath the beds lie shoes, clothes, boxes of valuables, and costumes for fiestas. A table with wooden chairs is in the center of the room. A small window provides a little light inside the cool, damp, and dark room. The house is basically a place to eat, sleep, and store things. Several guinea pigs scatter across the room, foraging on leftover food lying on the floor; others peek out from underneath the beds. A dog lies next to a bed, and one of four cats of the household sleeps on the window ledge. Eight humans and thirteen other mammals sleep in this room.

Along with the entomologists, we use a flashlight to search for *vinchucas*—kissing bugs. On the wall are telltale signs—brownish streaks—indicating *vinchucas* have taken blood meals and defecated as they crawled up the wall. There also are several splotches of dried blood remaining where Juan swatted *vinchucas*. The inside of the house becomes more and more disgusting to us as we shine the flashlight into cracks and see hundreds of *vinchuca* eggs, like rice being stored inside the walls. After we lift up pictures on the wall, a large *vinchuca* sits paralyzed by the light. Kissing bugs lie hidden in the clothes hanging from the rafters and underneath the bed. Several bugs are hidden underneath the gunnysacks filled with food. Within half an hour, we find about twenty-five bugs. However, this cursory investigation exposes only the tip of the iceberg—a thorough investigation of the Mamani household would reveal hundreds of *vinchucas.*

With reason, social scientists have described the Mamani household as a "sick house," *Casa Enferma,* the title of Briseño-León's study of Chagas' disease in Venezuela. Social scientists often use similar terms to describe unhygienic houses in cities. When urban renewals are promoted to improve housing, these houses often are classified as "run-down housing." In Bolivia, political economists envision the country as developing through ecotourism and becoming a transportation link between neighboring countries; so many believe it is necessary to cover up certain places. For example, houses were painted along one street when the Pope visited Bolivia in 1987. Altruistic and political considerations frequently concentrate on the house as a focal point of disease rather than considering it as a family and cultural institution.

The House—A Vertical Entity

Gaston Bachelard writes in *The Poetics of Space:* "A house is imagined as a vertical being. It rises upward. It is a concentrated being. It appeals to our consciousness of centrality." People never forget the house where they were born and raised. When they return to the hometown of their youth, they often visit this house, perhaps walking through it or at least driving by it. It is imbued with values which remain after the house is gone. The family home is a cherished image in society.

If within their home their fathers and mothers worked producing something, which in turn was stored in the basement of the house, the home also is remembered as a place of sustenance and supply. It evokes memories of banquets in the living room and parties in the yard. A certain room, for example, evokes scenes for me where my grandmother was laid out for burial. A home constitutes a body of images that give us proofs or illusions of stability.

The house is a familial and cultural institution that deserves understanding and respect from anyone attempting to improve it. Even though some houses are environments conducive to sickness, they are endowed with sacred, social, and economic meanings.

For Andean peasants, the house is the coming together of the vertical and the horizontal. Andeans frequently relate their homes to gender relationships and to land and body concepts. The Kallawayas of Bolivia understand their homes according to a mountain-body metaphor (see Bastien 1978). If they take care of the mountain and feed its earth shrines, corresponding geographically to parts of their body, then their homes, households, and bodies will be synchronized and they will be healthy. Health is the metaphorical synchronization of the house, household, and environment. These relationships are symbolically expressed in elaborate rituals which can also be used to explain the relationship of the vector, host, and parasites in Chagas' disease.

The Aymaras of Qaqachaka, Bolivia, for example, think of their houses as the cosmos and cosmogony (Arnold 1992). Qaqachaka is located in valleys of the Altiplano, Department of Oruro. When a house is being constructed, the Aymaras sprinkle the foundation and walls with blood and sing about it as *nido del cóndor y el halcón* ("nest of the condor and hawk") and *la madre nido* ("mother nest"). The rooms of the house are symbolically associated with the woman and uxorlocal residence. The house is an entity within a system of parallel descent, and the feminine spirit of the house is what unites theoretically incompatible dualities, such as matrilineal and patrilineal descent, filiation and residence, and hypergamy and hypogamy, as Lévi-Strauss (1979) writes.

In Qaqachaka, the floor plan and arrangement of buildings within the patio are carefully arranged to synchronize with certain cosmological axes in order to connect the house with cosmic centers, such as those of the Incas, and ground the household firmly within cultural traditions. Each step of construction is preceded by a *challa*, a ritual sprinkling of blood, accompanied by prayers. "By analogy," Arnold (1992:54) writes, "in the construction of the house, the sprinkling of animal blood provides power to the house as the mother nest to stand erect for generations and to maintain its honor." The people of Qaqachaka say that the walls are made to stand with blood of the female. The roof is understood as the masculine zone and is related to the mountain.

These cultural practices and understandings indicate the sacredness of the house to Andeans. It is a shrine to the earth and their ancestors. Any endeavor to stereotype such houses as "sick" is not entirely different to someone referring to one's religion as "sick." This explains why Andeans accept *vinchucas* as part of their households, not because they enjoy being bitten or getting sick, but because they are there, attached to the household. Insects in themselves have neither a positive nor negative value; they simply are part of the universe. The discovery that *vinchucas* are killer bugs is easy for outsiders; but, for Aymaras, they are "kissing bugs."

This adds an important consideration for anyone attempting to modify "sick" houses. Technicians in vector-control projects to improve housing have to respect these cultural values. Unfortunately, technicians of the pilot projects discussed in subsequent chapters paid little heed to the culture context of the house.

Conversely, cultural considerations can be assets in eliciting community members to participate to improve housing. These values can be used to help make houses *vinchuca*-proof. One culturally sensitive approach is to precede any construction with a ritual to the earth shrines of the home. In an even more practical vein, housing construction rituals, such as in laying the foundation, building walls, and thatching roofs can be used as occasions for instructing Andeans about preventing triatomine infestation.

Roof thatching is an important Andean institution, including a ceremony. Broadly, although there is much regional variation, this ritual as found among the Kallawayas, near Charazani, Bolivia, consists of a ritual to dispel the misfortunes of the surroundings, another to feed the earth shrines of the *ayllu* (communal land), the laying of the roof, and a festive banquet.

The first part is a symbolic sweeping of the house to dispel misfortunes (such as triatomine insects). A diviner arrives on a Friday night, throws coca leaves to discern what misfortunes are found within the house, and then goes throughout the house symbolically sweeping with ritual symbols and breaking string. As an adaptive strategy, the community health worker could participate in the coca seance to volunteer information about *vinchucas* and how this misfortune carries another tiny misfortune (*T. cruzi*) that injures the *chuyma* (heart and other central organs) and can cause *muerto subito* (sudden death) and *empacho* (constipation). The worker would instruct the inhabitants that this remedy requires continual vigilance, housing hygiene, and use of insecticides. After the shaman has ritually swept the household, the health worker could spray the house (see Bastien 1981, 1992). When the participants take the *kintos* (bundles of sacred items that attract the misfortunes) to the river, they could also take clothes to wash in efforts to dispel the evil. This ritual behavior could be used in this context to explain the importance of keeping the house clean.

The second part of the ritual consists of *misa sumaj suertepah wasi* ("Good Luck Table for the House"), where a *yachaj* (diviner) and the family prepare symbolic products corresponding to the head, trunk, and legs of the three major ecological levels of the *ayllu:* llama fat and fetus for the head, highlands, and herder; guinea-pig blood for the heart, central levels, and potato and oca fields; and coca leaves and chicha (corn beer) for the legs, lowlands, and cereal farmers (see Bastien 1978).

Implications for health workers include the fact that Andean peasants closely identify body and house concepts with community and environmental concepts. Health workers can assist at the *sumaj suerte* ritual to discuss erosion, deforestation, and animal depletion, and the relationship of these factors to migration, urbanization, impoverishment, and Chagas' disease. More readily than most Americans, Andeans thoroughly accept the relationship of bodily health to environmental well-being.

The House: An Economy of Exchange

Bolivians have a sacred economy centered around the house. They celebrate fiestas to the saints within their patios. They continually *ch'al-lar* (sprinkle) the courtyard, giving the initial drink to *Pachamama* (Mother Earth). Before they leave the house, they bless themselves and deposit an offering of coca leaves to the *cabildo* (shrine of the household). Good-luck tables featuring candies, coca, llama fat, qoa, tinfoil, and a llama fetus periodically are presented to the household shrines. The overriding concept is that, if they offer symbolic foods to the earth shrines, *Pachamama,* and earth, then the earth will bestow upon them an abundant harvest. Some would call this an imitation magic of reciprocity, but it can be seen as an economics of reciprocal exchange between beings who live on vertically distinct ecological levels, each with its unique products and resources. For rural Bolivians, a "sick" house is one that has turned in upon itself in selfish interest or that has been abandoned. It is sick like a body because it is not in centrifugal and centripetal motion with everything around it.

The economics of exchange fits into this in the following way: peasants throughout Bolivia pass through the countryside and observe that certain houses are *chullpa wasikuna* (tomb houses) and that certain communities are *chullpa llahta* (tomb communities). They refer to the fact that these places are without inhabitants, much like their ancient shrines (*chullpas*) to their ancestors, commonly found throughout Bolivia. They believe that anyone digging near a *chullpa* will die from *chullpa usu* (polio, or osteomyelitis). *Chullpa wasi* is the peasants' term for a "sick house." It is sick, not because of some intrinsic evil but because it is no longer an exchange unit between the people who inhabit it and the surrounding fields. It is a tomb of what was.

In contrast, *sayaña* is the Aymara word for house, and it refers to the bedrooms, kitchen, and storage rooms. It includes family members, alpacas, llamas, sheep, pigs, guinea pigs, and chickens. It contains the surrounding gardens and plots in the *qhapanas* (large fields). It includes the above sacred connotations and is considered a shrine. Pablo Regalsky graphically described this concept among the Quechua of Raqaypampa. After the harvest, the house is completely covered with corn so that it is symbolically no longer a building but a pile of corn. The Andean house is continually transformed by the cycle of activities surrounding it.

Sayaña is also founded on *ayni* and *turqasiña*, which are expressed in the ritual/work of thatching houses. These important Andean economic structures of the *sayaña* could be incorporated into housing-improvement projects to lower costs, increase community participation, and ensure continuity. Community members participate in a system of work exchange, *aynisiña*, and resource exchange, *turqasiña*.

Aynisiña is a basic Andean institution wherein peasants set up a system of mutual aid regarding work tasks. For example, someone helps another person thatch his roof; the recipient or his children now owe the helper an *ayni* for roof thatching or an equivalent task, due at some future time. A local health worker may donate a week at a training course or spray insecticides for a week. In exchange, members of the community owe the health worker an equivalency of work, such as herding the health worker's sheep or plowing a field.

Community health workers used *ayni* during the drought in Bolivia between 1982 and 1984 when they encouraged labor exchanges and cooperation in the communities of the Altiplano to prevent the hoarding of water as well as other conflicts (Bastien 1992). They coordinated the activities of digging wells, routing water, and building irrigation canals. One creative way they used *ayni* was to have the family of a treated sick person do some public-health service, such as building a latrine or digging a sewage ditch, in return for treatment provided by the local health worker.

Regarding housing improvement, similar festive and ritual ceremonies could be combined with *ayni*, extending the labor-exchange process to include construction of a new house or refurbishment of infested houses. In other words, housing projects need to be based on the peasants' economic and cultural institutions. Foreign aid and outside technicians can assist in this endeavor.

The other economic institution is *turqasiña*, which refers to bartering produce. Community health workers utilize this practice when patients cannot pay cash for medicine but can provide some produce instead. The health workers get the produce at a discount rate; they then consume, exchange, or sell it at markets, using the money to buy medicine.

Turqasiña can be employed in roof thatching. Participants arrive with supplies to thatch the roof: *jichu* (bunchgrass) gathered from the surrounding puna, rope woven from llama hide, and poles cut from eucalyptus trees. The implicit understanding is that the recipient can be expected to do the same for his helpful neighbor when that neighbor constructs his house.

Members of the agencies involved in vector-control projects could enter into the community under the terms of *aynisiña* and *turqasiña*. Whatever work and resources were provided to one community would be required to be performed by that community for another community, and so on.

Andeans have an interest in helping each other. Their survival is based on a long-standing formal system of replication and correspondence. Once a plan is presented to them that works, they will share it with others. They do this by celebrating a fiesta together, agreeing upon a common task, and cooperatively completing it. If models for triatomine-proofed houses are built that fit into their culture of the house, they will continue to build more of these houses. The culture of Andean housing is embedded within their cosmos and cosmogony. The ability of Andeans to survive at high altitudes has been partially explained by their relation of themselves and their social forms with the land, which is sacred and reproductive.

Global forces of privatization, capitalization, free trade, and individual capitalism have been centrifugal processes away from the communal community toward the world market, as discussed below. In Bolivia, as in the United States, private property and individual wealth are beginning to supplant shared land and cooperative movements. For the majority of Bolivians, this has led to loss of land, increased migration, and the growth of squatter settlements, as well as the loss of Andean traditions such as *sayaña, ayni,* and *turqasiña.*

Migration

The migration of infected people and increased domiciliary habits of *vinchucas* have expanded Chagas' disease to regions not environmentally considered optimal for this disease, which now is no longer limited to the natural environmental parameters for *vinchucas.* M. Goldbaum (1982) has shown the impact of migratory movements and Chagas' disease in Sao Paulo, Brazil, and Ciesielski et al. (1993) found 2 percent seropositivity for Chagas' disease among 138 Hispanic and Haitian migrant farmworkers in labor camps in eastern North Carolina.

Migrants spread Chagas' disease in a number of ways. Migrants can transport *vinchucas* in their baggage to nonendemic areas; infected peasants transfer *T. cruzi* in their blood to uninfected *vinchucas* in new regions. Peasants sell their blood to unwary buyers, passing the disease through blood transfusions. *Residentes* (urbanites) visit relatives in rural areas, where they become infected and return as hosts for Chagas' disease in the cities. Chagas' disease also has been imported into France and the United States (Brisseu et al. 1988; Kirchhoff, Gam, and Gilliam 1987).

Peasants migrate because their land has been sold, worn out, or expropriated. Some are ignorant of principles of sustainable agriculture; others lack money to improve productivity. Some Bolivians travel from the Altiplano to agricultural zones of Chile to pick fruit during the dry season and to pick coca leaves in the sub-Andean regions of the Yungas during the wet season. Many peasant families have daughters who work as maids for families in Cochabamba, Santa Cruz, and La Paz. Others migrate to cities to find employment in construction and domestic labor markets.

When peasants first settle an area they cut the brush and trees to farm the land. *Vinchucas* are forced out of their nests in bushes and trees where they have fed upon birds and rodents. They move into the corrals and huts of the invading peasants. The Department of Tarija, Bolivia, has suffered especially, with high percentages of *vinchuca* infestation reported in corrals (61.6 percent) and ovens (60.2 percent). This explains its high infestation rate (78.2 percent), infected *vinchucas* (50 percent), and people with Chagas' disease (60.6 percent).

Temporary Housing

Migratory peasants generally do not have the time and money to build a house that adequately protects them from the environment, so they construct temporary housing, which is often nothing more than a shack made from refuse. Cochabamba and Sucre had high numbers of refuse housing (41 and 44 percent, respectively), which are readily infested. Peasants invest little in shacks built on land that they do not own, may be evicted from, and are unable to sell. Outside of Cochabamba, peasants objected to participating in a housing-improvement program because they believed that once their houses were improved they would be confiscated and sold to someone else.

Peasants sometimes sleep in temporary shelters closer to their fields, which are becoming increasingly distant from their homes as traditional farming lands become barren. Peasants in these areas rapidly put together lean-tos of thatch and branches where they spend nights guarding their fields. This presents an additional problem: the peasant's main house may be *vinchuca*-proofed, but peasants remain at risk when they sleep in the fields.

The displacement of rural people is a growing social concern throughout Latin America. It has been brought about by overpopulation, depletion of natural resources, growth of corporations, and demand for mobile work forces. Migrating peasants essentially become foragers and gatherers. Frequent dislocation requires that they construct homes with available materials and that they invest little in nonmoveable property.[1]

Colonization

Since the 1953 Bolivian agrarian reform, national policies have encouraged colonization of unpopulated areas in Bolivia. The general movement has been away from the Altiplano and higher altitudes towards settlement in the lower regions of the Alto-Beni and Santa Cruz. Since the closing of mines in the 1980s, there has been an economic shift from Andean mining to tropical agriculture. These changes have brought about an increase in Chagas' disease.

Aymaras and Quechuas have lived in the higher mountains and valleys for millennia and are referred to as *Qollas*. Guarani tribes of many ethnic groups at lower altitudes are referred to as *Cambas*. *Qollas* and *Cambas* consider each other as inferior; for example, some *Cambas* extend their biases, teaching their parrots to cry out every time a *Qolla* passes, "Phew, what a stink." *Qolla* peasants, poor as they may be, consider themselves descendants of the Incas and heirs of that civilization.

There has been a mixing of *Qollas* and *Cambas* through colonization, more on the part of *Qollas*, who have settled in large numbers in the Departments of Santa Cruz and the Alto Beni. One consequence relating to the spread of Chagas' disease has been that the *Qollas* have brought their higher-altitude style of housing to these warmer and moist regions: thickly walled adobe construction, small openings for doors and windows, and thatched roofing—all of which hold the heat in and the cold out. The results are favorable for *vinchucas:* hot houses with little light and ventilation. The architectural style of *Cambas'* houses is characterized by a series of separated rooms around a central courtyard (*oca*). *Oca* housing allows more space between the buildings, which are separated from each other by outside work areas at the sides and within the center. This is different from *sayaña* housing with its fortress style of buildings tightly fitted together. The *sayaña* is metaphorically an extension of the earth, a mediator between that which is above and below, whereas the *oca* is a courtyard in the forest.

Oca houses also have become centers for *vinchucas*, partially because of colonization, which has brought crowding. People have moved their corrals, chicken coops, and storage areas closer together, in part to protect their animals from predators and thieves. However, this has also made it easier for *vinchucas* to get from the corrals to the dormitories.

National policy encourages peasants to live in clustered settlements to facilitate schooling, political consolidation, and the building of water and sewage systems. This in turn has created some unhygienic conditions, such as increased infestation, contaminated water supplies, and backed-up sewage systems. Health officials favor the development of water and sewage systems, because this is a marker most noted in world health standards, and Bolivian officials want to be recognized for improving their nation's health, especially now that they want to attract tourism.

Interestingly and fortunately, Chagas' disease has had little effect on nomadic Indian populations in lowland areas of the Amazon Basin in Bolivia and

Brazil, perhaps because they do not live for prolonged periods in the same dwellings (Coimbra 1992). Within the Department of the Beni, Bolivia, there are thirty-five ethnic groups. However, seminomadic and sedentary tribes are being infected with Chagas' disease at extraordinary rates, in part because their huts are made of thatched roofs and palm walls. For example, one community of Tupi Guarani Indians in Bolivia has a 100 percent rate of infection. Moreover, Tupi Guarani within the Department of Tarija will be seriously affected by the construction of a dam on the Pilcomayo River that will flood much of their land, further forcing them to become sedentary farmers.

Thatched roofs are used extensively throughout the Andean and tropical regions of Bolivia. Thatched roofs provide habitat for triatomines, especially for sylvatic species accustomed to living in trees, such as *Rhodnius prolixus,* whose preferred forest habitat is the branches of palm trees. When palm trees are cut down, this vector travels with the leaves used to weave roofs, and spaces within the woven palms provide homes for these insects (Gamboa and Pérez Ríos 1965).

Urbanization: Class and Ethnic Distinctions

According to the census of 1950, 74 percent of the Bolivian population lived in rural areas and 26 percent lived in urban areas. According to the census of 1992, 43 percent live in rural areas and 57 percent in urban areas. Bolivian cities were designed during the colonial period according to a grid system, with central plazas for *criollo* and *mestizo* classes. Indians lived on the periphery. The cities were designed for populations under 50,000 people. Within recent years, these colonial enclaves have expanded to include satellite cities with larger populations and resultant crowding. The result is a center of quaint colonial buildings on narrow streets that are packed with cars, people, and pollution, with a periphery of houses that are constructed piecemeal—beginning with shacks and progressing to adobe and walled enclosures, and finally to adequate housing, as finances and time permit. Although Bolivia does not have huge cities comparable to Argentina, Chile, and Brazil, the cities of La Paz, El Alto, Santa Cruz, and Cochabamba are large urban centers with similar problems. The rapid expansion of urban centers has been a major influence in the spread of Chagas' disease within the cities in Bolivia.

For migrants moving to cities, several strategies of shelter have been pointed out by Van Lindert and Van Westen (1991), who studied low-income housing in La Paz, Bolivia, and Bamako, Mali. The first strategy involves gaining access to shelter in the city for the first time and starts with a nonowned shelter that is shared with friends or relatives, for which something may be paid or given in exchange, often produce from the peasant's farm (Vaughan and Feindt 1973). The various households usually do not live under the same

Figure 20. Housing in the cities is frequently unavailable for the poor, who sleep in the streets, where they are particularly vulnerable to *vinchucas* and Chagas' disease. Urban transients are also the primary sources of blood transfusions, thus providing another source for spreading *T. cruzi*. (Photograph by Joseph W. Bastien)

roof, if possible, but houses are expanded horizontally, and new rooms are built away from the core unit. This is especially true in the settlements on the city's periphery. A gate in the fence which encloses the plot is the common entrance for the various domestic units, which are located in separate structures. Thus some protection is provided to all the families, as is more privacy and less crowding than is often the case in more centrally located districts. Settlement in the city's periphery has been common; the satellite city of El Alto, outside of La Paz, is the fastest-growing city in Bolivia, with a population of 350,000 in 1997, up from 25,000 in 1969. El Alto has ample land to expand on the extensive Altiplano, whereas La Paz with over 500,000 people is limited to a large crater. One observation in regard to Chagas' prevention is that housing improvement needs to focus on the core unit and all domestic units at the same time, rather than isolating certain domestic units.

After migrants have found housing in the city, they try to improve the household's position by moving the household and gaining home ownership (Van Lindert and Van Westen 1991). This greatly enhances their control over their living conditions. Because self-help construction is commonly engaged in Bolivia, this time is recommended to educate migrants about constructing houses that prevent triatomine infestation. Relocation decisions are greatly influenced by kinship networks. A fairly universal rule of intracity mobility of low-income households is that households will not move into a new urban space unless the conditions and (actual or potential) housing standards compare favorably with those of the vacated buildings.

Another strategy employed by the urban poor in their quest for adequate shelter is the *in situ* enlargement and improvement of the shelter they presently occupy. Security of tenure is the most important factor leading to this, which does not imply having a legal title as much as the assessment that their tenure is secure (see Turner 1963, 1968, 1969; Brett 1974). Low-income households may buy a house or plot to build on from the very start—provided they have some surplus income (Köster 1995). Having land is very important to Andeans, whether they live in the country or city. Land is also important to grow vegetables and raise animals, even if the plot is small.

The wealthy and middle-class *mestizo* people generally have uninfested houses; some have *campesina* or *chola* maids to keep them clean, but these maids could also carry *vinchucas* back and forth from rural and urban areas. The *mestizo*, or *mestiza*, class are the dominant upper-class Bolivians who speak Spanish and have adopted Western European ways. The *cholo*, or *chola*, class refers to peasants who have moved to the city, still speak Aymara or Quechua, and whose women wear traditional skirts, *pullera*, and hats. Processes of "cholification" are active in Bolivia, as *cholos* have taken over much of

Bolivian commerce and control the work force and certain political parties; one has even become president. *Chola* marketwomen have formed guilds with high solidarity that exert effective political pressure. Bolivia had its first native Aymara vice-president, Victor Hugo Cárdenas, from 1994 to 1997. *Campesino* (peasant) class refers to Aymara, Quechua, and Tupi-Guarani Indians who speak their native languages, wear distinctive clothing, and farm in rural areas.

The *cholo* class of Aymara and Quechua peoples is considerably better off in a material sense than the *campesino* class. *Cholos* have adapted sufficient Western ways to enable them to do business with the powerful *mestizo* class of Bolivians. *Cholos* are distinguished from *mestizos* in that the former still recognize their links with their Andean heritage, whereas the latter try to identify exclusively with the Western European tradition, although they may give some token acknowledgment to their Indian heritage. Certain *cholos* have accumulated great wealth as truckers, *cocainistas* (cocaine traffickers), *contrabandistas* (contraband traders), *chifleras* (herbalists), and *mercantilistas* (merchants).

Cholos have been able to link the peasant economy with the national economy. Peasants refer to them not as *cholos* but as *residentes* (residents), which implies residents of the city. Economists might initially infer that *residentes* exploit the *campesinos;* however, their gains as middle-men are leveled off by the need to pay for elaborate fiestas within the community where they trade. *Residentes* are also required to provide housing, hospitality, and legal assistance for peasants when they come to the city. The economic relationship between *cholos* and *campesinos* also depends upon kinship relationships—both real and ritual—Andean reciprocal exchange patterns, and capitalistic economics.

These relationships have affected housing patterns in interesting ways. Within the market area of Buenos Aires Street in La Paz live a group of related *cholo* truckers with kinship and origin ties to Aymara *campesinos* of Iquiqui who import electronic products from Japan. The goods arrive in containers and are transported by means of a new large truck across Bolivia, into Brazil, and over again into Bolivia on the border with Brazil, where they are put on a launch and transported upriver to a settlement within a swamp which is set upon stilts. Houses are constructed on three levels within the swampy area, so that if one area floods, the inhabitants move to the next floor, illustrating the ingenuity of the Aymaras. The goods are then sold to the tropical lowlanders, and the truck is also sold. One can estimate the dollar value of this exchange as close to $150,000.

Cholo housing also reflects their social class. *Cholos* have moved into neighborhoods of all classes in the cities of Bolivia. The size, shape, and exterior of their houses appears the same as other houses, but the interior often differs little from that of peasant housing, with unfinished walls, supplies stored in sacks throughout the rooms, walls covered with pictures, clothing hanging on pegs, newspapers used for wallpaper, and one or two rooms set aside for sleeping quarters. Even though many *cholos* have sufficient money to improve their houses inside, they perceive their living quarters from a different perspective. Poverty cannot be the only explanation for cluttered houses.

Cholo housing provides an insight into how Aymara and Quechua peoples use their housing: as depositories, for the processing of resources, to house cottage industries, for social gatherings, as symbols of ethnicity and class, and for dormitories, kitchens, and eating places. Their multifunctional housing appears cluttered to many Europeans and Americans. It also provides triatomines places to hide and people and animals to prey upon.

Upper socioeconomic classes of *mestizos* and *cholos* constitute only a small minority in Bolivia, and the vast majority of *campesinos* and *cholos* live in inadequate and unhygienic housing. Such is the case of impoverished urban migrants and dislocated peasants throughout Bolivia. Widespread poverty in Bolivia has created deterioration and crowding of domiciles to such a degree that urban settings have become optimal environments for triatomines and *T. cruzi.* The number of chagasic patients is increasing in the cities of La Paz, Cochabamba, Oruro, Sucre, Potosí, and Santa Cruz.

Chagas' disease is related to underdevelopment, overpopulation, poverty, inadequate housing, and the inequitable distribution of resources. The occurrence of Chagas' disease in Latin America corresponds to those rural areas most deprived of sanitation and primary health care and to the poorest rural regions. Moreover, victims of Chagas' disease are also being ostracized in certain areas, where being seropositive for the disease has a social stigma impeding employment.

Perhaps the most significant result of this is that it exacerbates the impoverishment and resulting lack of development in rural parts of Latin America. Modes of production on haciendas are semi-feudal; there is both difficulty in marketing products and a lack of technology in the subsistence economy. Communities are isolated, poor, and spread apart. The urban slum dwellers in cities, the landless workers, and those with tiny holdings in rural areas are at high risk for Chagas' disease, which in turn contributes to their plight.

Political Economy

Chagas' disease is related to economic, political, and social factors at broad political and economic levels. Lack of integration of peasants into politics and the economy, privatization of communal Indian land, the subsequent dislocation of peasants to areas with temporary housing and overcrowding, inadequate education in rural areas, and destruction of tropical areas are broader political developments which have contributed to the spread of Chagas' disease (see Briceño León 1990). Moreover, larger structural processes are more difficult to change than those at the individual or community level.

Microlevel analyses regard the causes within smaller units of society, such as the community, family, and individual. Housing hygiene is an effective way to prevent Chagas' disease at the microlevel, but this is also difficult to achieve because it involves changing peoples' values concerning animals (keeping dogs and cats outside), sleeping habits (not crowding together in bed), and basic hygiene (storing things in boxes and sweeping regularly). Changing behavior at the micro-sociocultural level is necessary for chagasic control, and this can be done by individuals and communities by means of specific projects.

Macrolevel factors are more difficult to change, in part because Latin American economics and politics are embedded in a colonial heritage of dependent relations to dominant countries, oligarchical hegemonies, bureaucracies, corrupt governments, elitism and class stratification, and ethnocide (destruction of tropical tribes to facilitate the extraction of forest resources—gold, timber, and game), to mention a few. Nevertheless, macrosocial factors need to be addressed by international organizations, and it is the responsibility of corporations and governments involved in the above to practice retributive justice by repairing damages incurred because of exploitative and environmentally destructive practices. The fact that Chagas' disease is becoming a worldwide problem illustrates that destruction abroad can cause problems at home.

Parasitic economic relationships between industrial countries and Bolivia developed in the nineteenth century (although indigenous peoples of Latin America supported others from Spain and Portugal centuries before), which was characterized by excessive exploitation of Bolivia's resources by foreign interests in collusion with Bolivian capitalists. Railroads were built early in that century for transporting rubber, quinine, tin, timber, oil, and cattle. Riverboats, railroads, and later trucks opened frontiers deep into Bolivia's forests. While Chagas' disease, malaria, and yellow fever somewhat held capitalist colonial intruders at bay, the same forests produced quinine bark to treat the illnesses (Bastien 1987a: 143–45). Effects upon the environment included large tracts of land destroyed by timbering, mining, and cattle grazing. A downward spiral began of decreasing biocultural diversity. At first this seemed insignificant amid the multitudinous natural riches of Bolivia; but it soon was out of control, devastating Bolivia's Indian populations, plants, and animals in tropical zones.

At the end of this millennium, Bolivia is on the crest of a free-market capitalistic wave of radical change (Raterman 1997). This has caused increased unemployment, poverty, environmental destruction, and grave social problems.

Since 1985, Bolivia has halted inflation, and government spending has been reduced to achieve an almost balanced budget. While national debt has grown from $3.3 billion in 1985 to $4.6 billion in 1995, it now takes a smaller percentage of the annual budget to pay for it.

After a series of military dictatorships,[2] in 1985 Gonzalo Sánchez de Lozada, minister of planning and finance, began a series of reforms with new laws to restructure Bolivian society. He later served as president from 1993 until 1997, when he further carried out the new laws. The laws advocate legal and social restructuring needed to support a free-market development model: new tax laws, new custom controls, new banking laws, and laws regarding investment and ownership. They are part of regional and worldwide moves toward economic integration that has culminated in the North American Free Trade Agreement (NAFTA) and the recent Summit of the Americas, with its call for complete economic integration by the year 2005.

Privatization and capitalization are the engines of this model, and there is an attempt to privatize state industries and at the same time keep the control and ownership in the hands of Bolivians. By 1997, state-owned enterprises such as the airlines, the petroleum industry, electric utilities, telephone companies, and mines had been sold to private investors. Downsizing often was necessary to make these corporations efficient, and thousands of workers were laid off. The plan was that revenue from the sale of these enterprises would be available to help start new industries and employ people.

Thus far, these changes have favored the wealthy and ruling classes, especially outside investors who have tapped into Bolivia's rich natural resources, especially for timbering, cattle raising, and large-scale agriculture. This has further opened the forests and reserves of Bolivia to capital development and helped incorporate Bolivia into the world market, where it is often cheaper to buy products from other countries than those produced by Bolivian peasants.

New laws and economic realignments only highlight Bolivia's huge social injustices, inefficiencies, and dependencies. The oligarchical leadership of centuries has left more than two-thirds of the people on the margins of economic life and further impoverished. Illiteracy, lack of health care, inadequate housing, increased migration, and high unemployment help reveal the racism and classism of the past. Indigenous people, even though they are the majority, count for very little, their women even less. An elitist class system of control and economic distribution which widens the gap between segments of the population is unsatisfactory. An elitist financial system eventually limits opportunities and hinders the formation of new enterprises.

An integrated market without an integrated society is a contradiction. Free markets need a level playing field, clear rules of the game, and maximum access to the market by all social players. Free markets and feudalism can't mix. Economic and political development are finally impossible in any given society without investment in and development of all national human resources. This development includes the education and training of workers in health measures.

Efforts at Incorporation

Questionably to his credit, Bolivian president Gonzalo Sánchez also led the passage of *Ley de Participación Popular* (Law of Popular Participation) as an endeavor to bring ethnic groups and peasants into the political economy of Bolivia. The law decentralized administrative authority and gave political authority to 380 municipalities throughout rural areas of Bolivia, giving peasants more possibility of political power. Sánchez also instituted health and education reform measures in rural areas.

The impact of these changes on Chagas' disease is mixed. Peasants now have improved access to national revenues through the municipalities for improving roads, schools, and houses. Proyecto Cardenal Maurer in Sucre is using municipal monies to improve houses to help control Chagas' disease. Peasants also participate in a national health plan that favors women and children and maternal health care, which indirectly helps restrict Chagas' disease. One of Bolivia's leading anthropologists, Xavier Albo, sees this as giving the peasantry more political involvement. Because global integration into world markets is a necessary economic trend in Bolivia, traditional Andeans are becoming involved in the political process of the nation.

On the negative side, however, another leading Bolivian anthropologist, Pablo Regalsky, represents Indian federations that violently oppose this new legislation as leading to the demise of autonomous Andean leadership centered in the community (Andean village) as opposed to the municipality (Bolivian village). Municipalities have replaced communities as political nuclei, and *vecinos* (*mestizos*) assume leadership roles over the peasants. Even if peasants get elected to power in the municipalities, critics believe it will only be after they are corrupted by the political parties.

These changes have had a less than positive effect on Chagas' disease. Peasants have lost large tracts of land to private corporations, for which they often work as migrant workers. In Misqui, Bolivia, for example, a large industrial dairy farm owned by investors has displaced fifty Quechua families who had previously held the land in common and through privatization laws were able to sell it to capital investors. Western property rights emphasize the rights of individuals, whereas Andean property rights emphasize ideas of commonality, exchange, and ecology. Whereas peasants traditionally held land in common and the community had a sense of social solidarity, emphasis now is placed on the individual, with few or no ties to the community. Individuals tend to think less of their commitment to the community than they did under Andean traditional patterns of work exchange, reciprocity, and shared land.

For example, if someone leaves the community to migrate elsewhere and leaves his house in disrepair, it will remain unattended and become a source of infestation for others in the community who have repaired their houses. It becomes more difficult to get community involvement in projects. Another concern is that peasants are rapidly becoming *jornaleros* (wage workers) for landowners after they sell or lose their land. This drastically changes the cultural constructs of how they perceive their homes and land, as discussed above. Finally, because of increased poverty, considerable numbers of peasants now work as migrant workers in Argentina, Chile, and Brazil. These and many other factors moved the Bolivian people to elect a new group of political leaders in 1997.

Suggestions

Endemic Chagas' disease in Bolivia is a symptom of its unpaid "social debt." Since 1985, Bolivians have paid more than $3 billion in debt repayment to institutions and international banks; but money must be reinvested in the environment and people of Bolivia. This must be done, if not for social justice, at least for economic survival, environmental protection, and disease prevention in Bolivia. Bolivia also must have equality of educational opportunity for all its people in order to compete in a global economy. A free market requires a radical educational reform which includes indigenous people and women in both rural and urban districts. Teachers to train other teachers are needed. The economic systems of Andeans need to be incorporated into free-market strategies. Andean communities can utilize their communal structure and economic exchange patterns to form strongly competitive cooperatives, which should be broad based to include credit and housing plans, consumer goods, and production goods.

There also is a need to change certain attitudes. The free market has brought new wealth to certain Bolivians, but this emerging middle class is driven by a consumerism that models itself after the few who are much richer and have no sense of nation building. They dissipate their wealth on such things as luxury homes and cars, investing the surplus in the United States. Bolivia's wealthy never have believed in themselves or in their own country. The poor of Bolivia have a "solidarity of suspicion" about world economic integration, both in theory and practice. Finally, a national policy is needed to combat Chagas' disease, because it debilitates members of the work force when they are most productive, leaves children without parental upbringing, and is costly to treat.

However, the political economy alone cannot be blamed for all unhealthy aspects of Bolivian housing. Chagasic control projects need to include the cultural economy of housing with the political economy, which will be the subject of subsequent chapters.

CHAPTER EIGHT
Pachamama Snatched Her: Getting Involved

Chagas' disease became a major concern for Ruth Sensano in 1989. She is director of *Proyecto Britanico Cardenal Maurer* (PBCM),[1] which sponsors Chagas' control projects in the Department of Chuquisaca. PBCM improved 452 houses between 1987 and 1991, another 400 in 1992, and by 1997 it had improved 2,600 houses.[2] PBCM improved the first 452 houses with a budget of U.S. $83,256, out of which the community contributed almost half, or $37,642. By the year 2005, Sensano predicts, she will have improved another 2,500 houses, counting on assistance from tax revenues given to the municipalities for regional improvement, as discussed in the previous chapter.

A native of Sucre and a *mestiza,* Ruth Sensano learned to be a project director. She controls the accounting process carefully so that there isn't any graft. Bolivians have a phrase in Aymara that translates roughly, "Sucking from above and sucking from below"; it refers to the mid-level Bolivian project personnel who steal from those above (foreign bosses) and from those below (peasants). Because of the great amount of graft in Bolivia, project directors need to scrutinize expenditures at every level.

Sensano is as shrewd as any native *chola* market woman and as accurate as an accountant: both skills enable her to deal with the bureaucratic economic systems of project supporters and the informal, dynamic economic systems of peasants. She was lured from a profitable accounting job in 1976 by Cardinal Maurer, a German immigrant and Bolivia's first Roman Catholic cardinal, to extend health care to peasants within the Department of Chuquisaca. Since then, Sensano has established a medical program that serves 54,500 people in 168 communities in three zones of Yotala, Yamparaez, and Tarabuco. She accomplished in fifteen years what the Bolivian Secretary of Health with triple the personnel and budget was unable to do in thirty years.

When I met Sensano one June morning in 1991 in Sucre, Bolivia, she told me why she became involved: "About twenty months ago, we started the Chagas' disease program. We found that *campesinos* came in with *bulbulos,* hardened and impacted intestines, and they couldn't go to the bathroom. They say that they eat cold food, their intestines fill, harden, and they can't defecate. This was caused by Chagas' disease." She also showed me a picture of a peasant with *bulbulos* who hadn't defecated for months (see Figure 9).

"We realized," Sensano continued, "that in many communities people were sick with Chagas' disease. The people are accustomed to *vinchucas* in their

Figure 21. Ruth Sensano is director of Chagas control in the Department of Chuquisaca, Bolivia. She has been a leader in the eradication of this disease, and her program is a model for other projects throughout Bolivia. (Photograph by Joseph W. Bastien)

beds, thirty to forty in their beds. They are used to the bites. They say, 'All night we are taking off their heads and destroying them. We have to sleep outside the huts to escape them. Sometimes we don't sleep all night because we have to kill *vinchucas.*' When *vinchucas* bite, they scratch it.

"*Campesinos* see a person working and then fall asleep and die with two or three drops of blood coming out of the nostril. They say she died '*asustado*' (frightened), or '*La Pachamama ha agarrado*' (Mother Earth snatched her!). In reality, *la vinchuca* got her, just as they got me!" (Sensano interview 6/17/91)

I noticed that her left eye had the carbuncular sore beneath the eyelid characteristic of acute Chagas' disease, Romaña's sign, so I asked her if she had Chagas' disease.

"I would be surprised if I wasn't infected," she replied, "seeing that I have slept in peasant huts many times. But that's my job! More than likely, all my workers have Chagas' disease. We are all in this together."

Before I parted, an old Quechua lady came in with a face twisted from Bell's Palsy. She was crying. Sensano hugged her, as a mother. Firmly, she advised the lady to take a taxi, providing her with the fare, to the Bolivian Supreme Court in Sucre.

"I'm also a social worker," she explained to me. "This lady was fired as a

Figure 22. Ruth Sensano assisting an Indian woman who had suffered Bell's Palsy and had been released as a maid because of her facial deformity. Sensano served as arbitrator in the Bolivian courts over this matter. (Photograph by Joseph W. Bastien)

maid after working thirty years for a wealthy family. They threw her out of the house because her disfigured face embarrassed them. They gave her no severance pay. Now, she is without a home and money." Sensano is contesting this in court, and she hired a lawyer to defend the woman. The case was prolonged for six months. Ruth Sensano sighed, "So much suffering and so little justice in Bolivia."

Charismatic Leadership versus Bureaucratic Technicians

I was encouraged to hear Ruth Sensano talk with such enthusiasm, which is not often the case with project directors and personnel. The bureaucracy of projects makes it difficult for technicians to become involved with peasants. Dr. Daniel Rivas, medical director, and Freddy Martínez, program development director, also shared Sensano's motivation. They believed in the Bolivian people and were dedicated to improving their country. Selfless dedication, persistence, and motivation are as important as funding in making health projects work; however, these leadership qualities are often overlooked in the assessment of health projects.[3]

Sensano's charismatic style is matriarchal. She follows the teachings of the Catholic church, especially concerning ideas of the Blessed Mother. As a matriarchal leader, Sensano has adapted Catholic teaching to Andean culture, with its prayers and rituals to *Pachamama*. At every step of a project, she has sprinkled Mother Earth, thrown coca leaves to divine success, and prayed a rosary to the Blessed Mother. The peasants revere this *Jacha Mama* (Big

Mother). When I asked her why she didn't become a nun like Mother Teresa, she replied that she had to be "top dog" and could never answer to a superior.

Religious motivation in health projects needs careful evaluation. Nongovernmental organizations (NGOs) currently administer health projects in Bolivia. Many projects receive funding from the United States government and other international sources. Some NGOs are religiously driven, so conversion strings are attached to the health care provided. This is one reason for the high rate of conversion to Protestantism among Aymaras of the Altiplano. Another problem with NGOs is their advocacy of other issues, such as family planning, pro-life positions, and biomedicine. These politically loaded agendas frequently divide the community; they can subvert the goals of Chagas' prevention and misdirect the project.

Sensano did not attempt to change the beliefs and practices of the peasants. She respected Andean beliefs and recognized the need for rituals. She invited shamans and *yachajs* to perform rituals at the beginning and end of the project. Her authoritarian style, however, made it difficult for PBCM to coordinate its efforts with other Chagas' projects in the Department of Chuquisaca. She admits this. However, she finished everything as she had promised, when the estimated rate of unfinished and unsustained development projects is 90 percent. Sensano's project was attuned to Chuquisaca peasants and was within their reach. This was partially because it fit into a working health program and also because she walked it through, step by step, developing and making it understood without any glitches.

Model for Chagas' Control in Bolivia

At a national planning meeting for Chagas' control in La Paz in November 1990, Sensano's project gained acceptance as an effective model for chagasic control to be used by other nongovernmental organizations (NGOs) in Bolivia.[4] Its attractiveness lay in its efficiency, effectiveness, low cost, and use of culturally accepted techniques.[5]

Primary health care is the primary objective of PBCM. Its goals, as ideally defined, are essential health care made universally accessible to individuals and families in the community, through their full participation and at a cost that the community and country can afford.[6]

Sensano had incorporated Chagas' control into PBCM's primary health care mission in 1989 for the Department of Chuquisaca. It wasn't until 1991 that Chagas' disease was even considered to be a part of primary health care in other parts of Bolivia. The Department of Chuquisaca is heavily infested with triatomine bugs and has a high percentage of infected chagasic patients: 78.4 percent of the houses are infested with *vinchucas*, 39.1 percent of the intradomiciliary *vinchucas* carried *T. cruzi*, as did 25.3 percent of the peridomiciliary insects (SOH/CCH 1994:19). Some 78 percent of the population tested in endemic rural areas were seropositive to Chagas' disease, and 26.6 percent were children from one to four years of age (SOH/CCH 1994:22). In Chuquisaca 9.4 percent of the inhabitants have latrines, 51 percent have potable water, and 2 percent have electricity.

Earlier referred to as the Department of Sucre, Chuquisaca has a population of 451,722 (rural, 305,201; urban, 146,521) people, according to the 1992 census. It covers 51,524 square kilometers, with a density of 9.6 persons per square kilometer. The annual population growth rate in Chuquisaca is low, 1.47 percent, compared to other departments: La Paz (1.6 percent), Santa Cruz (4.10 percent), Tarija (2.81 percent), and Cochabamba (2.66 percent). This department consists of high plateaus and valleys gradually descending down the eastern slopes of the Cordillera Central of the Andes. These valleys range in altitude from 2,425 feet to 9,200 feet above sea level. The fertile lands produce cereals, fruits, and vegetables and traditionally supplied the miners of Potosí with food.

Epidemiologists conducted studies in four communities where PBCM started Chagas' control projects to assess the rate of infestation and infection with Chagas' disease (see Appendix 14: Baseline Studies in Chuquisaca). Ninety percent of houses in the four communities were infested with *vinchucas;* 61 percent of these were transmitting the chagasic parasite (see Appendix 14, Table 5). Houses were classified as good, regular, and bad according to such factors as having straw and mud roofs; adobe walls partially plastered or without plaster; presence of cracks in walls, foundation, and roof; no ceiling; dirt floors; and poor hygiene (see Appendix 14, Table 6). The majority of the houses were found to be in poor condition and infested with *vinchucas;* a very high percentage of the population had Chagas' disease. Unhealthy houses correlate closely with infestation rates, both being about 90 percent. This being the case, in endemic areas housing conditions alone could serve as indicators of infestation rates.

Chagas' control projects are not easily incorporated into primary health care systems because of conflicting interests and inefficiency. A frequent conflict is that funding sources or advising institutions may be different: one organization may be responsible for primary health care, another funded for Chagas' disease control. Programs have to work together. Other possible infrastructures for Chagas' control include housing improvement projects (Plan International and Pro-Habitat) and credit cooperatives (Pro-Mujer and Pro-Habitat), discussed in the next chapter.[7]

PBCM's Chagas' control programs were based upon the following conclusions derived from baseline studies (see Appendix 14): Many peasants live in unhealthy houses that should be bug-proofed; peasants often do not know the danger triatomines present in their houses and therefore are in need of health education; peasants need technical assistance in home-improvement projects and in spraying insecticides. The goal was basically preventative—to break the transmission chain by means of education, house improvement and improved hygiene, and by spraying for insects. Of some consideration, PBCM lacked a therapeutic outreach program for those with Chagas' disease, even though its primary health care program assisted severe cases of heart disease and colonopathy.

Prevention breaks the transmission cycle of *T. cruzi* from triatomines to humans. In its most basic form, prevention against Chagas' disease involves the following objectives: periodically spraying with insecticides to destroy triatomines, improvement of housing and corrals to eliminate nesting areas of triatomines, and better housing hygiene. However, each of these objectives involves achieving many changes within the household which are difficult to accomplish. Because the house is the base for peasants' economy, where they eat, sleep, give birth, raise children, process food, store crops, and keep animals, Chagas' control projects have difficulty changing some of these cultural and economic practices. Project personnel often overly concentrate on health issues rather than on issues of productivity and economics.

Infrastructure for Chagas' Control

PBCM's infrastructure for a primary health care program served as an effective base for Chagas' control. Its infrastructure included three zones, each with a central hospital with three doctors (a director and two others to lead traveling teams), two health workers, and two social workers. These zones contained twenty-six *puestos sanitarios* (health posts) in the larger communities, each staffed with an auxiliary nurse and equipped with primary health care items (vaccines, antibiotics, bandages, and measuring instruments). Under Ruth Sensano's leadership, auxiliary nurses within the three zones were provided with training, technical support, and monetary incentives. Peasants at the village level were responsible for their health and were invited to support a community health worker (CHW), already discussed. CHWs assisted auxiliary nurses and health teams and later became principal links between the village housing-improvement committees and project technicians. CHWs usually serve for two or three years without pay; and they consider this part of their community service, *un cargo* (a load).

The *cargo* system is deeply embedded in Andean and Latin American culture; it predicates that leadership is a burden (*cargo*) to be carried voluntarily without material gain, but this service accrues towards one becoming a complete adult (*una persona muy completa*) in the community (see Bastien 1978, Metraux 1967, Wolf 1955). Adolescents grow into adulthood in part by serving the community. Adulthood is achieved by assuming tasks for the community.

The maturity of the individual relates to the community; the health of the community brings health to the individual. Throughout Bolivia, the *cargo* system has been used effectively to elicit community support, with some individuals accepting the load of overseeing the community's health as a community health worker (CHW).

Sensano had also trained traveling teams of technicians. Traveling teams from the hospitals educated and coordinated activities of the auxiliary nurses and CHWs and provided them with educational materials such as videos, slides, and posters. The traveling team consisted of a medical doctor, social worker, and health educator. Each hospital had two traveling health teams, so that one team was able to visit every village once a month while the other team worked at the hospital. Traveling teams initiated Chagas' control measures, completed base studies and evaluation studies, and provided technical assistance for housing improvement projects.

Peasants' Awareness of Chagas' Disease

When Chagas' disease control was begun in 1989, it presented additional challenges, which Sensano explains:

Adding Chagas' disease control to PBCM was a challenge, because it involved changing houses and habits of peasants. Deeply rooted cultural patterns needed to be changed and housing behaviors needed to be modified. Fumigation and housing improvement requires cost-sharing. Eradication of triatomines is only one step that needs to be followed up with vigilance, refumigating, and housing hygiene (Sensano interview 6/16/91).

With such complexity in mind, Sensano, Rivas, and Martínez decided to initially limit their Chagas' disease control efforts to four communities, which they selected according to the following criteria: high incidence of Chagas' disease, semi-nucleated communities, similar socioeconomic levels, little possibility of outside asistance, accessibility, and a favorable response to first efforts at *concientización,* or consciousness-raising (Rivas et al. 1990:4). They chose the communities of Puente Sucre (Yotala zone), Tambo Acachila (Yotala zone), La Mendoza (Yamparaez zone), and Choromomo (Tarabuco zone). The activities of the project consisted in *concientización,* forming house-improvement committees, and actually improving houses.

Concientización: Education

Sensano educated peasants by trying to change their perceptions so that they felt that they could do something about their impoverished conditions. In Bolivia and elsewhere, peasants often have a fatalistic attitude that discourages them from trying to improve their conditions, which in most instances is borne out by a history of exploitation. In *Chuquisaca,* for example, some peasants refused to improve their houses for fear that the landowners would then charge them rent. They also thought that the supplies would be another form of debt peonage, with interest rates at 12 percent per month. Diseases, such as Chagas' and tuberculosis, are facts of life for rural Bolivians; control over disease often is best initiated by means of rituals.

Concientización (consciousness-raising education, or CRE) was popular in Latin America during the 1980s. It implies that community members recognize the relationship of material conditions to behavioral, economic, social, and cultural factors by means of investigation and analysis of actual concerns.[8] *Concientización* attempts to help instill in poor people the hope of improving their situation. *Concientización* has premises in concepts of Christian social justice that relate the cause of the disease within the political and economic contradictions of Bolivian society. Therefore it is useful for looking at the connections between local causes of infestation and broader social concerns.

Even though Sensano proposed to look at the connection between broader concerns and causes of disease, she used an approach that scared peasants more than it made them reflect upon the political economy. As she describes it:

> ...*concientización* was, and still is, the key to our success. We used shock methods to make them realize that the bites of *vinchuca* cause *bulbosos* [welts] and heart problems. We traveled from house to house, showed them feces that the *vinchucas* left after they had sucked human blood, then became so full that they left traces of *mierda y sangre* [feces and blood] on the walls. We pointed out their eggs, hundreds of them, tiny white beads inside walls, mattresses, and clothing. The earth and straw of their houses were filled with *vinchucas*. Inside their straw roofs we showed them nests of sleeping *vinchucas*.
>
> We showed them the damage *vinchucas* do. We made them afraid. If you don't scare the *campesino*, he won't do any work. We also showed them the parasites with microscopes and pictures of people with intestines stretched out. We made them hear the irregular heart beats of chagasic patients, 1231234121234, with a stethoscope. We showed them radiographs of a normal heart and some of a chagasic heart. We had a video made and showed them that. We told them that they have a responsibility to take care of their children and that it is their responsibility if children suffer from Chagas' disease. Fathers and mothers cannot permit that their children die from *vinchucas*, it is just as necessary to get rid of *vinchucas* as it is to have their children learn to read and write. After educating and motivating them, they agreed to fix their houses (Sensano interview 6/17/91).

Concientización was used by Sensano to frighten people and instill in them a hate of *vinchucas*. Peasants now had another object to fear; a bug they once thought was a sign of fertility was now seen as a harbinger of death. Bolivians

Figure 23. Education of children about housing hygiene is important to prevent Chagas' disease. Traditionally children regard *vinchucas* as "toys" to play with.

realized the connection between *vinchucas* and some people with chronic heart disease, but life expectancy is not a major concern for peasants subsisting from day to day. Making peasants aware of disease-causing agents often is not enough to motivate them to do something. Disease and death are accepted facts of peasants' lives; they have become long accustomed to the unhealthy environments of mines and factories and being subjected to revolutions, reprisals, and military repressions.

Preventative health measures modify behavior to the degree that these measures produce some immediate and desirable effects. With Chagas' disease, once community members realized how nice their houses would be if they did not suffer from insect bites there and that they thus would have increased prestige, they were motivated to improve their houses. When I brought up the objection that peasants might revert to unhygienic conditions after the house was built, Sensano replied that this was not the case, because the women take pride in their new homes. They sweep them and put things away every day. Prestige is more motivational than is either injustice or economics.

Children and Women

The education of schoolchildren about disease is important because children and adolescents constitute half of Bolivia's increasing population, with a growth rate of 2.7 percent a year. Children share knowledge with their parents. Sometimes parents resist children advising them, but studies by Fryer (1991) show that even though many parents showed initial resistance, they eventually began asking children about their lessons and learned with them. When fathers migrate to work and mothers tend the fields, older children often are left to take care of the smaller children and the households.

An important factor for Chagas' disease lessons for children is making them applicable to household tasks (housing hygiene) and assisting children in educating their parents, such as assigning shared tasks for children and parents while calming parents' fears about their own inferiority in the face of their children's knowledge.

In Chuquisaca and elsewhere in Bolivia, inequality of women is increasing. Because of its social and cultural complexity, the division of labor among women, men, and children needs to be studied by anthropologists and sociologists so that education about housing improvement and maintenance and vector control can be carried out more effectively.

Andean women have always worked alongside men; but, because men have migrated to find work, women have had to assume men's traditional roles. Women often have become the sole agriculturalists, child raisers, and housekeepers of families. Some mothers work the fields carrying their babies; urban mothers take babies to their market stalls, where they are kept in cardboard boxes, being called "cardboard box babies." *Vinchucas* can take advantage of these babies. Toddlers remain at home, being cared for by slightly older siblings, usually girls. Thus, girls especially can spend less time at school. Peasant girls average four to six years of education, boys six to eight years.

Gender inequality also influences Chagas' disease, in that there is greater malnourishment among girls than among boys, because Aymara girls often receive less food than boys. This makes girls more susceptible to acute attacks of the disease than boys. Also disadvantaged with less schooling and less Spanish instruction, girls learn less about Chagas' disease.

One lesson observed from PBCM's educational approach is that more efforts need to be made to educate women about Chagas' disease and to address their increased responsibilities. This matter also needs to be discussed in group sessions with all community members.

House Improvement Committees

House Improvement Committees (HICs) were the functional units where plans and priorities for housing improvements were decided and where all participatory activities were coordinated. HICs consisted of a president and secretary who were responsible for organizing work groups of five to six villagers. HICs coordinated tasks with members of the community. These groups were assigned different tasks and were supervised by a master craftsman who taught members basic carpentry, about laying building foundations, tile making, and plastering. Local materials and personnel were used whenever possible. HICs and craftsmen supervised and coordinated the repair and/or construction of houses. They worked between the months of May and September, when agricultural work is least demanding and community members are most available. However, fiestas, popular during this time, delayed work for weeks at a time. Because of their success in Chuquisaca, HICs were adopted and modified as functional village units for other pilot projects in the departments of Cochabamba and Tarija (Ault et al. 1992:42, SOH/CCH 1994).[9]

Villagers worked to compensate for roughly half the cost of a house improvement ($75.00 per house) and provided supplies worth $18.75; and PBCM contributed supplies, fumigation, education, and supervision to the amount of $114.00. Each improved house cost $208.00, with villagers providing 45 percent and the project the remaining 55 percent.[10] Not counting free labor, the project improved a house for $114.00 and its total budget was $45,614 for 400 houses.[11]

As an evaluation, HIC failed to adapt to Andean labor and economic practices. Earlier, certain economic exchange principles of Andeans were discussed, such as *ayni* (labor debt), *mita* (community debt), and *turqasiña* (resource debt) that can be used to facilitate housing improvement. *Ayni* and *turqasiña* constitute a complicated system of exchange relationships that are socially embedded within familial and community relationships. *Aynis* are inherited and are considered more valuable than money, especially during harvest times and periods of hyperinflation. Thus, for example, if a roofer's family was deeply indebted to other commoners who had taken care of his or her harvest, then the roofer got a chance to return the work obligation by doing roofing for the project. Although *ayni* implies exchanging like-work, HIC has been able to negotiate with both parties alternative work assignments. The president and secretary of the committee literally keep the books concerning *ayni* and employ it to accomplish necessary work.

Pilot project models need to fit the projects into the political and economic systems of the community in order to become replicated models. It is perhaps a misnomer to refer to them as pilot projects; a more appropriate title might be isolated projects.

House Improvement

House improvement consisted of putting in a solid concrete foundation that would not crack, plastering the inside and outside adobe walls to cover existing cracks, whitewashing the walls with lime, installing glass win-

Figure 24a. House before improvement. A family standing in front of the remains of their previous house that had been infested with *vinchucas*.
(Photograph by Joseph W. Bastien)

Figure 24b. A community health worker distributing building supplies. (Photograph by Joseph W. Bastien)

Figure 25a. A neighbor helping mix plaster for walls. Exchange of labor is done through the concept of *aynisiña*. (Photograph by Joseph W. Bastien)

Figure 25b. A man hammering stones between the adobe blocks of his house to prevent entry of bugs. (Photograph by Joseph W. Bastien)

dows and metal screening, tiling the roof, and installing a ceiling to the interior. Bedrooms were first improved; later, dining and storage rooms. Depending on the condition of their houses, some families decided to demolish and reconstruct them, sometimes adding additional rooms, especially bedrooms. These improvements eliminated common nesting areas for triatomines. PBCM allotted supplies progressively in order to provide an incentive to complete each task and receive the next supply. Thus a temptation was removed to misallocate the materials. Households preferred to do the more favorable tasks first and neglected the less desirable, such as improving the surrounding area.

One criticism of PBCM is that for the first 400 homes it did not improve peridomicile areas, and, when they were evaluated, *vinchucas* were found in these areas. By 1992, however, bug-proofing of peridomicile regions became part of the program. The strategy was then adopted of starting with the peridomicile; if this was improved, then material was supplied for the house. This way both corrals and houses were bug-proofed.

Traditional methods and available resources were used together with more innovative techniques, tools, and materials whenever possible. Sand, earth, and cow dung were collected locally to make wall plaster. Workers prepared the lime by heating locally collected limestone rocks in an open kiln for twenty-four hours and then pulverizing the residue with a hammer. After plastering, they applied a white paste of lime and water to the walls to improve the appearance.[12] Wall plastering substantially reduces *vinchuca* infestation; but to be successful it has to be done thoroughly, so as to seal all the cracks and crevices in the house walls. The use of slow-release insecticide paints is another preventative measure.[13]

PBCM also taught villagers to make ceramic tile roofs to replace thatched roofs, greatly reducing a popular infestation area for triatomines. One community mastered tile making and began marketing their tiles to neighboring villages, thus developing a small local industry. Low-cost roofing material is needed in developing countries to provide a substitute for corrugated galvanized iron roofing, which is very noisy when it rains and heats up when it is hot, both common conditions in the tropics.[14] Sheet roofing also is extremely dangerous in windy climates when it becomes stripped from the house and is sent hurtling through the air with its sharp edges.

A stable concrete house foundation is necessary for each house to prevent water damage to the base of the walls and floor. Cement is expensive in terms of both price and transport costs, but a durable local substitute material was used in Chuquisaca. Soil stabilization was achieved by increasing the cohesion of the soil.[15] (This is one area where technical assistance is helpful.)

As an alternative, not utilized by PBCM, the mechanical compaction of

Figure 26. A woman and her children standing in front of their house after its improvement. (Photograph by Joseph W. Bastien)

adobe mix greatly increases its stability. An adobe press with a long handle used as a lever to compress the mud and clay in molds provides more leverage than the customary force of chest and arm muscles and results in a much harder adobe (Lunt 1980, Webb 1985, Webb and Lockwood 1987).[16]

Community Participation

Project success and sustainability are a function of community participation. As others have shown throughout Bolivia, community participation is more cost-effective than purely vertically structured programs (Bryan et al. 1994). Housing projects are more readily integrated into other programs if there is community participation. Community participation is active rather than passive involvement; it occurs when people make their own decisions and carry them out. Community participation refers to community members making decisions about, accepting, and complying with certain behavioral changes necessary in regard to combatting Chagas' disease. These include plastering cracks in the walls, keeping animals outside, and storing objects in containers to keep *vinchucas* from infesting the house.

Problems relating to community participation included the absence of skilled local labor for some tasks . There was some limited cooperation among households because of their distance from each other. Many peasants refused to cooperate because they didn't own title to land and homes. Certain adults refused to work with other adults. Poor sanitary conditions persisted in many areas. Peasants also had other tasks they considered more necessary things to do, such as plant and harvest crops. These problems in part indicated a lack of understanding of sociocultural issues and limited skills in cross-cultural communication from project workers.

Cross-Cultural Community Participation

Technicians in Chagas' control and other health projects sometimes confuse the idea of community participation when they imply that they have the solution to the problem. Technicians should endeavor to educate and activate peasants to participate in finding a solution. If technicians have already decided upon the solution, there is no room for alternative solutions. Cross-cultural community participation (CCCP) is a term that I have coined; it involves lengthy discussions with all members of the community (including women and children). CCCP does not have simple answers to prevent Chagas' disease; it allows people to arrive at solutions after they have been presented with the facts in terms that are meaningful to them. It involves serious discussion as to why peasants behave as they do. Why, for example, do they keep animals in the house? If this is not seriously considered, they will continue to do so no matter how nice their new house is. This has been the experience of the housing project in Tarija. CCCP demands that technicians negotiate change only after considerable discussion takes place and understanding is achieved about values and why people do what they do. CCCP is a pedagogy based upon an epistemology of exchange: knowledge is mutually arrived at between interested parties. This is essential for Chagas' disease, principally because of its social and cultural complexity that affords no unilineal or vertical approach.

Conclusion

The PBCM Chagas' control project was built upon an existing health program and consequently it attacked Chagas' prevention by focusing on the sickness.[17] *Concientización,* as practiced by PBCM, was exclusively about insect infestation and the sickness. The problem was not dealt with economically and socially: How are the people to take care of their cattle, pigs, and sheep? What can be done if someone abandons a house? What needs to be done to curtail migration? How can productivity be increased so as to lessen poverty?

When I last visited Ruth Sensano on June 13, 1997, I repeated the above criticism. She agreed with many of the points but added: "You have to begin somewhere and do something." More than anything, development projects have to be within the reach of the people.

She looked tired and weary. I took her picture and asked her if she had any parting words. She replied: "*Ama Kella* (don't be lazy), *Ama Sua* (don't be a thief), *Ama Lluya* (don't lie)." These are the words Mama Oqllo taught in ancient times to the women of the Incario.

CHAPTER NINE
Sharing Ideas

José Beltrán teaches children and adults about Chagas' disease. He is a model teacher for Chagas' prevention in the Department of Tarija and is the major educator for a number of communities that have improved over 1,350 houses by 1997. He succeeds because he communicates in culturally meaningful ways. José provided me with some examples:

I have good relations with the peasants because I am *Tarijeño* and speak their language, a dialect close to that of northern Argentina, *chapaco* style. *Tarijeños* share more and are much more open than *Qollas* (highland Andeans). Yesterday, for example, when I arrived late, they wanted to know why. It bothered them that they wasted time waiting for me. I always use simple language, *"Poque se han hui?"* "Why did you flee?" Or *"Le wa sumba hu un piedrada,"* "I am going to throw a stone." Other Bolivians can't understand *Tarijeños* because they speak a folk Spanish.[1]

I always use images. If I speak of parasites as something very small that you can't see, they are not going to understand this. The microscope is putting many lenses to the eyes of your *abuelita* [grandmother] so as to increase the size so that she can see. Teachers are too scientific. You have to have the mentality of the peasant, which is related to earth and all organisms in it. This is the foundation upon which we must build, otherwise we will get nowhere.

The chagas parasite is like us. It looks for different places. We want places that please us, and we remain in places that we like, that give us food and where the harvest is good. So too the parasite inhabits our organs to get food, develop, and multiply. It colonizes our body (Beltrán, interview 5/16/97).

José Beltrán has been a health educator for Tarija Chagas' projects for six years. Previously, he worked in health education for the Bolivian Ministry of Health for fifteen years. Tarija projects are noteworthy for their education about Chagas' disease and serve as examples for other programs.[2] The Department of Tarija has the same percentage—78 percent—of houses infested with *vinchucas* as does Chuquisaca. Percentages of *vinchucas* with *T. cruzi* are lower in Tarija with 20 percent, compared to 23 percent in Chuquisaca (SOH/CCH 1994). Tarija has 61 percent of its people infected with Chagas' disease, compared to 78 percent in Chuquisaca and 46 percent in Cochabamba. Tarija projects constructed 750 houses in five communities between 1992 and 1994, and

Figure 27. Chagas' control project worker checking a guinea pig house for *vinchucas*.
(Photograph by Joseph W. Bastien)

600 more in six other communities between 1994 and 1997. Chagas' control projects were placed in the Department of Tarija for both health and political reasons. Tarija has produced two presidents in recent years, Victor Paz Estenssoro (1985–1989) and Jaime Paz Zamora (1989–1993), both of whom made great efforts to address social concerns of their people.

Tarija's warm and temperate climate helps explain its high incidence of Chagas' disease. The Department of Tarija borders on Argentina to the south, Paraguay to the east, the Department of Chuquisaca to the north, and the Department of Potosí to the west. Its geography consists of lower valleys, plains, and a dry boreal forest (Gran Chaco), the scene of a disastrous war between Bolivians and Paraguayans from 1932 to 1935. The region is noted for its wheat, cattle, and grapes, which are pressed, fermented, and distilled to make wine, *singani,* and *pisco.* The climate is moderate, with altitudes of 1,000 to 3,000 feet, making it a vacation spot for tourists from within Bolivia and from neighboring countries.

Factors in the increase of Chagas' disease in the Department of Tarija have included the increase of population within urban areas. According to the 1976 census, the total population was 187,204 inhabitants, with 72,740 people (39 percent) living in urban areas and 114,464 people (61 percent) living in rural areas. The surface area of the department is 15,052 square miles, with a population density of 12.4 people per square mile (Muñoz 1977). According to the 1992 census, the total population was 290,851, with 159,841 inhabitants (55 percent) living in urban areas and 131,010 inhabitants (45 percent) living in rural areas (Censo Nacional 1992). This reflects a national trend in Bolivia—a marked decrease in the percentage of inhabitants living in rural areas. Between the years of 1976 and 1992, Tarija had a population growth rate of 2.81 percent, above the Bolivian national average of 2.03 percent. This movement of population from rural to urban areas and subsequent crowding in communities has spread *vinchuca* bugs to the cities, causing a marked increase in Chagas' disease.

Another factor in the spread of Chagas' disease has been the regular migration of Tarijeños to Argentina and Chile for farm work. Decreased agricultural production and loss of land has forced many Tarijeños to look for seasonal work elsewhere. They travel in large numbers to harvest sugar cane in the Department of Santa Cruz, Bolivia. Of ethnic concern, nomadic Guarani peoples have been displaced by dams and flooding of their land. Some of them now have infection rates of 100 percent, seriously endangering the survival of the last of these hunters and gatherers.

The Department of Tarija is culturally and ethnically rich. Colonial Spanish culture similar to that of Argentina predominates in Tarija. It is referred to as *chapaco* and has a wealth of proverbial sayings, songs, couplets, and a distinct Spanish dialect. Cowboys and Guarani Indians roam throughout the plains and forests. Local natives consider themselves descendants of Chiriguanos, a long-extinct ethnic group associated with lowland tribes of the Department of Santa Cruz. Aymaras and Quechuas consider themselves superior to lowland peoples. Aymaras and Quechuas further distinguish *Tarijeños* from *Cambas,* although both groups are lowlanders. People from La Paz and Cochabamba find *Tarijeños* amusing, slow-mannered, and not terribly *listo* (sharp). They often make them the butt of jokes, such as "Tarijeños are so lazy that their dogs bark lying down."

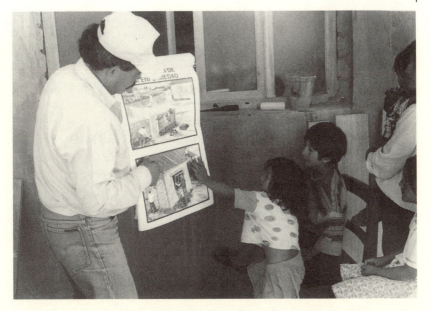

Figure 28. José Beltrán teaching children and adults about Chagas' disease. (Photograph by Joseph W. Bastien)

"Tarijeños have a sense of humor and a relationship with *vinchucas*," José Beltrán said, "best expressed in the following riddle":

Quien es? (Who is?)
Un capitán flautero (A capital flute player)
saco de clérigo, (cassock of priest)
ladrón por su gusto, (thief for pleasure)
médico por su deseo, (doctor for desire)
[answer:] *La Vinchuca.*

"A pointed analogy of musicians, clerics, thieves, and doctors for *vinchucas* with their needle-nosed proboscis, black-capped shell, thirst for blood, and blood-letting therapy" (Beltrán, interview 5/17/97).

I spent several days traveling with José Beltrán in his pickup truck and visiting homes, neighborhoods, and communities.[3] José was born to share ideas. Along the road, he stopped a stranger and, using a flip chart, gave him a short lesson about Chagas' disease. José later told me that he had missed this person on his previous visit. "You can't miss anybody, you have to go house to house to talk with people."

"Now, I have to spend more time educating and motivating peasants," José added, "because people have to invest more into improving their houses." By 1997, Pro-Habitat no longer had funds to improve houses and had adopted a credit plan to loan people money to fix their houses. Loans vary from U.S. $100 to $500 at 12.5 percent interest per year. José believed this to be a superior plan: "Providing credit is more sustainable than giving them supplies, we don't have the money to fix every house, and if we educate correctly and motivate them, then they will want to invest in their homes and keep them nice," he said.

Local experience gained from the Chuquisaca project as well as assistance from Vector Biology and Control Project (VBC), CDC, and SOH were used by SOH/CCH to implement similar pilot projects in the departments of Cochabamba and Tarija between 1992 and 1994. By 1994, approximately 3,100 houses in fifty-two communities had been improved in the three departments of Chuquisaca, Cochabamba, and Tarija (SOH/CCH 1994:54; Bryan et al. 1994). The average direct cost to the program in 1991 for each house improved was U.S. $251 in Cochabamba, $217 in Tarija, and $217 in Chuquisaca; but sums were reduced considerably for 1992 and 1993 (SOH/CCH 1994:17). A large percentage of project monies was spent for administrative offices, vehicles, consultants, and educational material—U.S. $4 million ($2.5 million from U.S. Public Law 480[4] and $1.5 million from CCH[5] (SOH/CCH 1994: 9)—which was about $1,300 per house.

One general criticism of the SOH/CCH pilot projects is that to satisfy project goals for fast results and monies to be spent during an allotted time, houses were hastily built and little education about Chagas' disease was provided. Some of these houses were not maintained; in others, the people moved their corrals alongside the houses and they became infested again. "Everybody wants a new house without much personal investment," José added, "and some have moved back to their run-down houses, and they use the new houses to show off during fiestas." He included Sensano's project in his criticism.[6]

I asked him, "How do you educate Tarijeños about house hygiene?" He replied:

My pedagogy is participatory education, basically. Peasants who listen to me are not receptive subjects of what I teach them. But they participate in reflecting on the visual charts, so that they understand what I want to communicate. This presents excellent results, as you saw last night (Beltrán, interview 5/17/97).

Well into midnight the night before, I had observed him teaching in *Rancho Norte*, a project community of about sixty families. The schoolroom was crowded, with the men standing back against the wall and women scattered around the room, seated on school benches. I sat with the women, exhausted from travel and interviews. José continually moved his body, raising his arms. He showed one elderly lady a picture, then pointed to a *vinchuca* illustration on the flip chart and asked her if she knew who "this fellow" was. She was confused. A few hands were raised, but José skated across the room to question someone about to doze off. "A *vinchuca*," the person quickly answered.

"And where do *vinchucas* live?" José continued.

"In the cracks and ceilings of our houses," someone answered.

"Have we invited them to eat with us?"

"No," the old lady answered, "they are very ugly and shit on the walls."

"They bite us and take blood from us," José added. "What happens if we see them full of blood and we squash them?" Everyone laughed at this, because they have squashed the bugs and seen blotches of blood.

A lady with thin arms, face wrinkled and leathery, wearing a derby hat, asked him about *vinchucas coloradas* (red *vinchucas*). She was the lady who at first had been slow to answer, because it turned out that she was not sure which type of *vinchuca* was illustrated. José picked up her skills, "I'll bet you $100, if the gringo loans it to me, that anyone can smash a *vinchuca colorada* and not find blood." The lady adds that these *vinchucas* are different from the bad *vinchucas*, whose bodies are black with orange marks on the sides.

José showed a slide picturing the harmful *vinchucas*, and then reminded them not to harm the good *vinchucas*, showing a keen sense of respect for beneficial insects. It was clear that peasants distinguished *vinchucas* as blood-eating, plant-eating, and insect-eating reduviids. Other educators have broadly declared war on all *vinchucas*, indiscriminately killing nectar and predator *vinchucas*. I wondered if insecticides also discriminated. José's pedagogical method emphasized the necessity of listening to the peasants, discussing matters with them, and letting them arrive at the solution.

To top off the evening in *Rancho Norte*, José showed the people a model of a house that they could build. They crowded around him, as he pulled off the roof to show them the floor plan. He began with simple questions:

"How many walls do you need for two rooms?"

"Four," they answered.

"No," he replied. He asked a *promotor* (CHW) to count the walls.

"Three," he answered.

"Counting the end wall," José continued, "the middle wall separating the two room, and the end room which begins another room. See, you save a room with this design."

"Notice the porch that extends in front of the rooms. There is a roof over this so you can work outside and not get wet if it rains or, if the sun is shining, you don't get hot," José added. "You can work preparing food and crops here. Look how open it is to let the air circulate. Your present rooms are dark with small windows. See how the air can circulate through the house. This is healthy and helps prevent tuberculosis."

"When you cook, where do you have to bring your food from?" José asked.

"We carry it across the patio to the eating room," someone answered.

"Yes," José replied, "and if it is raining, you get more soup!" They laughed at this.

Toward the end of the meeting, José asked me to say something, so we discussed Julio, who had recently died in *Rancho Norte* from Chagas' disease. I asked if they were taking care of his children and widow, and people replied that they had plowed a plot of land for them. Then I asked how many thought they had Chagas' disease. Six people out of thirty raised their hands. They had been diagnosed with Chagas' disease, but they were not taking chemotherapy. I suggested the possibility of using *Sangre de Drago*, and I asked Jaime Zalles to provide them with the names of plants to treat heart problems and stomach disorders. Zalles provided them with an ample list.

In parting, José asked me to take a picture of the group. I was out of film on the only occasion I was asked to take a photograph. All embraced one another and we departed. José entertained us with Tarijeño couplets on the journey back.

Development of Teaching Aids

José Beltrán collaborated with Irene Vance, director of Habitat, to produce educational material for Chagas' control.[7] Initial production costs were U.S. $80,000. They used a classic methodology for material development that included the steps of conducting baseline studies for assessing cultural and economic conditions, an assessment of community resources and needs, the development of preliminary materials based on this information, field testing of potential materials, modification and production of materials, and evaluation of the effectiveness of the materials used. They produced beautifully illustrated posters, comic books, and flip charts to teach people about Chagas' disease. They also produced slide shows and videos. By 1997, however, many of these teaching aids were no longer available in Tarija because the use and demand for them had been so great.

Although the success of these educational materials is unquestionable, critics have objected that this is an unsustainable resource which Bolivians cannot afford to continue. However, international funds are available for Chagas' prevention and certainly effective and attractive educational material is needed to educate peasants as well as CHWs, technicians, nurses, and doctors. Also, although Bolivia is a poor country, televisions are common, and there is a potential for image-based education that should be developed.

One concern with the visual aids was that they lacked cultural sensitivity, primarily because they were designed by professionals in La Paz for all Bolivians. A principal argument of this book is the necessity to design projects relating to the many different ethnic and cultural contexts in Bolivia.

Nonetheless, teachers like Beltrán are able to adapt teaching aids to the values of peasants, if they are creative and sensitive to the local culture. Because Bolivian educators normally follow strictly hierarchical models of teaching, they need to be encouraged to deviate from the formal texts and matter.

José Beltrán has his own style. He composes songs, sociodramas, and role plays to illustrate *T. cruzi, vinchucas,* and the infirm. His classes are part theater and games. He uses puppets for children and adults and contracts Bolivia's main puppeteer to do a show on *vinchucas* and parasites for the periodic health fair. Although it costs $100 to bring the puppeteer, the audience never forgets it. José spends several afternoons a week in the classroom, which he loves. "Children are curious about insects, creatures that are proportionate to their size," he continues. "They are easier to teach than adults who relate more to larger creatures."

José recognizes that cross-cultural communication is the major obstacle to health education. He stated:

> We had the best coverage for vaccinations in Tarija, almost 100 percent. Why? Because I went to the barrios with my loudspeaker. We brought puppets, charts, and posters. Even a portable video. I put the needle into my arm a dozen times to show them that it didn't hurt. They complained that when the Peace Corps was here, they used vaccinations to sterilize them. I don't know if this is true. But we had to discuss these matters with them. We had to overcome many difficulties. Peasants are smart and they listen. They want to be healthy too. Today, doctors, nurses, and technicians do not have the same enthusiasm. If three children are not vaccinated, they don't spend any time seeking them out. They look down upon peasants. They use a language that is sophisticated, abstract, and difficult for the peasants to understand. This is the most serious mistake. Why don't they talk to the peasants as their cousins and friends? They go to the community, but they don't communicate. I remember a nurse in Iskayachi who wanted to whip the children because they didn't line up for vaccinations. There is what we say in Tarija, *un desclacamiento,* and they don't want to identify with their people. They don't want to return, and they think that they are in another status or class, and the peasants are burros (Beltrán, interview 5/24/97).

Desclacamiento refers to the process of declassifying oneself from a lower class, but with the added notion of the nouveau riche, who look down upon the class from which they originated. Dr. Evaristo Mayda, director of Project Concern in Cochabamba, discussed this and added that the biggest obstacle in rural health improvement is the elitist attitudes of doctors, nurses, and technicians.

José Beltrán continued in even stronger terms:

> Peasants are considered burros because they haven't had the opportunity to

be educated as doctors have. Doctors do not want to see where they have come from. They think they are in another status and class. Doctors and technicians don't want the peasants to have health because that deprives them of sales and control. They are not interested in educating people, they want to increase the demand in health. They are also afraid that if they educate the CHWs and nurses they will know more than them. Education is power, not to be shared. Or they are going to lose their business. Because before calling the doctor or nurse to treat a patient for Chagas' disease, we instruct the CHW on how to do it, the doctor or nurse is going to lose the possibility of earning some money.

Once I brought a pregnant lady with a partial delivery (the placenta remained) twelve kilometers from a village to a hospital in Tarija. A woman doctor said to her, " *Que esta cochina, como va a dar luz!* ("What a sow, how is she going to birth? Why haven't you bathed her!"). They were insulting her. She began to cry. They refused to take her, fearing she might contaminate the hospital. I had to take her to my house, put her in a bed, and call a doctor who treated her. No one had educated her on how to prepare for birth. This was a bitter experience. I criticize and censure this behavior.

Stratified Classes

Beltrán highlights the problem of stratified classes to health projects. Chagas' projects bring together people from different social classes who have to communicate with one another to combat Chagas' disease. They often fail to achieve this goal because they perceive lower-class people as incompetent and inferior, thereby hindering community participation. The social dynamics of classes are important considerations for the success of any project.

Rural peasants generally are considered the lowest class. Since 1953 it has been against the law to refer to peasants as Indians—the accepted word is *campesino. Campesino*s have equal voting rights with all other classes. *Campesino*s traditionally speak Andean languages, follow an agricultural calendar, and, as of 1994, have their own political organization. *Vecinos,* or *residentes,* are the people who live in the city. They include the salaried workers, and most of them are not much better off than the peasants. Already mentioned, only 2,000 salaried workers make over U.S. $10,000 annually (*Presencia* 1997). The upper class, sometimes called *gente decente* (civilized people), is composed of distinguished families and wealthy people. These are broad distinctions; there are many finer class strata in each of these groups, such as the *cholo* and *mestizo* classes, already discussed. Race, as defined by skin color, is not as important a marker in Bolivia as is social stratum, which is determined by one's dress, behavior, family, and wealth. Consequently, such cultural markers as language, dress, and food habits are readily discarded to strip oneself from the lower peasant class. There is a tendency in peasants who have ascended to professional levels (doctors, nurses, and project personnel) to act out their perceived class superiority in dealing with peasants.

On the other hand, peasants have their own hierarchies, with certain members more distinguished than others; but this is based on completion of adult responsibilities within the community. Especially peasants from the Andean free communities (those that were not tied to haciendas) maintain a cooperative and communal spirit in their work. They help each other plow, seed, and harvest. If there is a fiesta, they all participate. If a project is to be completed, all members participate. When project personnel interact with such community members using class-stratified manners, they project upon the community political and social relationships that are offensive and counterproductive. Community participation in such groups is predicated on respect of differences and equality of participation; it is not based on paternalism, maternalism, classism, or racism.

José Beltrán's suggestions for better communication between doctors, nurses, technicians, and peasants include the fact that it is necessary that health professionals think in terms of cross-cultural communication and sharing of knowledge rather than having a superior form of knowledge. Doctors also have to internalize the reality of peasant culture and become motivated to work with these people as partners. This may necessitate spending several years in rural areas after medical school. It also involves learning native languages, colloquialisms, ethnomedicine, values, and economics.

At the conclusion of our last interview in 1997, José Beltrán sang a song that he had taught children concerning Chagas' disease. The tone is that of a *cueca* (popular dance of Chile), and the children dress like *vinchucas* and dance the *cueca* when they sing it.

Gracias a Dios que mi casa esta limpia y me curada.
Revocando las paredes combatimos las vinchucas.
Ordenada y revocada no hay mas bichos.
Thanks to God that my house is clean and I am healthy.
Plastering the walls we combat vinchucas.
Neat and plastered there are no bugs.

CHAPTER TEN

Culture Context Model for Chagas' Control
Oscar Velasco, M.D., coauthor

The following proposed culturally sensitive model attempts to lessen the gaps in cross-cultural communication between project personnel and community members. Pilot projects in Chuquisaca, Cochabamba, and Tarija failed to become models for other projects because they lacked a model themselves.[1] These projects were rapidly designed, generously funded, and built several thousand houses. However, they provided little in the way of evaluation of ways to improve them, thus failing as pilot projects. Another fault was that Chagas' prevention practices were barely integrated into the culture and economics of the community. Oscar Velasco and I have designed a program, called Culture Context Triangle (CCT), to be a model for Chagas' control and other health projects.[2]

The CCT model provides educators and health workers with a framework for cross-cultural communication and a guide for their activities. It recognizes that community members and ethnomedical practitioners are equal partners in Chagas' control. It integrates the subjects' ideas, values, and practices into the prevention and treatment of Chagas' disease, whenever possible and feasible. It includes treatment of patients with Chagas' disease; pilot projects in Tarija and Cochabamba detected cases of Chagas' disease but never did anything to treat these patients (patients were treated in Chuquisaca). These projects made people aware of their sickness without providing measures for treatment.

Successful cross-cultural communication strategies discussed in this book included the talks developed in Aymara and Quechua, the use of rituals to begin projects, educational material designed by Pro-Habitat, and José Beltrán's use of puppets and songs. Unproductive communication resulted from personnel who exhibited elitist and racist attitudes toward peasants, who didn't speak Andean languages or use colloquialisms and other culturally appropriate forms, and who used overly scientific language.

In the previously mentioned projects, there were various shortcomings. To cut costs, project personnel studied and used available resources for building materials whenever possible. They failed to consider ways that natives control *vinchucas* with plants and other practices, however. Project personnel sometimes overlooked peasants' work habits and calendar, ethnomedical beliefs and practices, economic exchange patterns, social and political systems, gender relationships, and role structures within the family. Omission of these cultural items jeopardizes project goals, because their inclusion makes it easier to implement projects and render them sustainable.

Community members failed to adopt Chagas' control measures into their lifestyle for a number of reasons. The material goal to have a new house overshadowed the necessity of serious behavioral changes in isolating animals, maintaining the structure, and improving house hygiene. Project demands to follow the fiscal budget forced personnel to improve houses at a rate faster than the subjects could internalize the reasons for doing so. Failure to follow community values created class distinctions, with better houses for certain members of the community. (In Tarija, the project matched what each household provided; so, for example, if someone put in $3,000, the project had to put in an equal amount. This resulted in project monies being used to fix up the houses of wealthy people, who demanded equal access to the program as peasants.) The greatest failure was not to incorporate economic development into the projects to deal with impoverishment and migration, which ultimately cause neglect and abandonment of houses. Thus, this housing improvement was a "Band-aid approach" to the problem, which also did not deal directly with the sickness.

After they had improved their houses, some people developed symptoms of Chagas' disease. Certain community members attributed this to the evil-eye; people envied those with new houses, so they gave them the eye. Other villagers refused to have their houses repaired because they didn't want the evil-eye. Technicians often shrug this off to the ignorance of peasants but then illustrate their own ignorance in neglecting these feelings. The incorporation of shamans into the project would have helped villagers to believe they could avoid the evil-eye. Along these lines, Ruth Sensano had diviners perform summation rituals.

Project personnel project a scientific world view on the traditional mythological and cosmological world views of Bolivians. Project personnel assume that scientific technology such as spraying and house construction is the sole answer to vector control. However, this excludes the wisdom and practices of ethnomedical practitioners—shamans, diviners, and midwives. Although *curanderos* do not follow scientific practices, their exclusion from health matters slights these respected community figures. It also makes them competitive, whereas their inclusion elicits their support. Because Bolivian communities have so many classes of *curanderos* (over thirty kinds of specialists), projects miss many opportunities to get support in what they are doing. For example, herbalists know certain plants that are insecticides and parasiticides. *Curanderos* often treat symptoms of Chagas' disease and refer patients to doctors.

Diviners serve as agents against the possibility of *mala suerte* (bad luck), so feared by Bolivians when someone tries to change things. Midwives may be able to detect babies born with Chagas' disease. Studies show that once ethnomedical practitioners are incorporated into biomedical projects they become an important asset (Bastien 1987a, 1992).

The pilot projects were exclusively concerned with spraying and housing improvement. They did not consider systemic relations between community health, agricultural production, economics, and the environment. Marco Antonio Prieto said that the pilot projects were *puntales* (isolated and unintegrated events), like an unsuitable but nice gift given to someone once or twice in a lifetime.[3] For a sustainable model of Chagas' prevention, isolated actions are not adequate; it is necessary to look at systemic relations, not at causality. Bolivians don't have enough money to solve all their problems; culturally sensitive community participation is necessary (Prieto, interview 5/25/97).

Another critic, Pablo Regalsky,[4] emphasizes the importance of understanding the native culture:

> For any Chagas' project, you need thirty years. You can't do it in five years. You have to begin by forming community teams who understand the sickness and can work with the community, who can be understood by the community according to terms that the peasants understand. If they don't understand how the disease functions, then it is impossible to be able to combat it. It is a long-term sickness and people will have to combat it for a long time. If a person becomes sick, what can he do? For example, Florencio, head of Sindicato, has been diagnosed with it. Florencio has to rest when he can, but he can't rest. "I am the leader of the peasant syndicate," he says, "and I have to travel, eating here and there, and not in my house." This is the problem that is not solved by plastering a wall.
>
> After forming a team, then you have to work for a long time in the community. We can't say that I am going to fix up a house in a year but that we are going to plaster in ten or fifteen years. Little by little, you go from house to house, explaining (Regalsky, interview 5/30/97).

These criticisms and suggestions are not meant to discredit the efforts of project personnel; rather, they are steps leading to the proposed model, the cultural context triangle.

This model triangulates upward from three corners; project personnel and technical assistance, community members' participation, and CHWs and ethnomedical practitioners form a pyramid whose apex is the prevention and treatment of Chagas' disease.[5] The elements converge toward common goals, maintaining distinct identities but operating within a shared cultural context distinct to the particular community. The base of the triangle is the culture of the community.

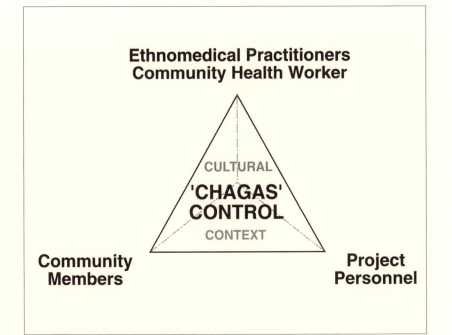

**Ethnomedical Practitioners
Community Health Worker**

CULTURAL
'CHAGAS'
CONTROL
CONTEXT

**Community
Members**

**Project
Personnel**

Figure 29. Cultural Context Triangle Model. This culturally sensitive model attempts to reduce the gaps in cross-cultural communication in health projects between project personnel and community members. This model triangulates upward from three corners. Project personnel and technical assistance, community members and participation, and CHWs and ethnomedical practitioners form a pyramid whose apex is prevention and treatment of Chagas' disease. The parts converge toward common goals, maintaining distinct identities, and operate within a shared cultural context distinct to the community.

This structurally interrelated approach posits culture as the cohesive element binding together the project, the community, and the local health team. It is distinct from one-sided and vertically directed approaches that implant outside project goals. Elements of what might be called biomedical imperialism are usually present in health projects that assume that science knows what is best for the natives. This usually translates into project managers dictating what aid various people should get and how it should be given. Nor should the proposed model be confused with a culturally sensitive model that employs anthropological knowledge as a tool to translate the project's goals into means acceptable to the community. In that type of project, goals take priority; in CCT, cultural context takes priority.

Developmental projects, programs to combat Chagas's disease, and other health projects often have not been sustained because they failed to integrate the project into the culture of the community. Such projects have produced clinics, hospitals, and houses in Bolivia, but in many cases the dust of unsustainability now covers these structures, making them monuments to misspent endeavors at international charity. Some programs actually have been countercultural, with ethnocentric religious, political, and economic views subtly embedded into project methods and goals.

Spokes of Culture Context

Like spokes of a wheel, the cultural context triangle has a number of spokes that hold it together. Broadly, culture context refers to the configuration of beliefs, practices, and material objects passed along through generations and considered by community members as their guides through life. Culture context is a dynamic structural relationship that provides continuity as well as incorporating change for community members. Certain spokes interrelate project personnel, community members, and ethnomedical practitioners within a culture context that accommodates innovations necessary for Chagas' control. These spokes connect the components and lead to the goal of culturally sustainable and workable solutions to Chagas' disease.

• The communication spoke connects personnel, community members, and ethnomedical practitioners in a dialogue as equal partners. It implies that project personnel be able to speak native languages and converse with men, women, and children in meaningful ways. It implies that community members can discuss matters with project personnel. Openness implies the ability to accept the community's point of view. It also implies integrity in stating one's objectives.

• The economic spoke links the cost of the project to the productivity of the household and community; for example, it integrates house repairs into a local economy. Peasant economies are not as needful of gifts as they are of credit, fair wages, and increased productivity. Increased productivity enables peasants to improve their homes. Communal land ideals, shared labor practices, and community service are means that can assist project personnel to improve houses at reasonable costs. Basic Andean institutions provide suitable systems upon which cooperatives can be formed. Examples are *aynisiña* (labor exchange) for house building, *turqasiña* (resource exchange) for materials, *mit'a* (community service) for environmental projects, and communal land, used for cooperatives to provide peasants with collective producing power. Examples here include CEDEC's assistance in agricultural and livestock productivity and Pro-Habitat and Plan International providing small loans for housing improvement (see Figure 30).

• The house spoke connects the physical and cultural environment of the house to the parasitic cycle of Chagas' disease. This involves removing material causes for infestation, but it also considers the values that household members

Figure 30. Martos Arredondo with family in front of his grease shop. Pro Habitat and Plan International provided him with small loans at reasonable credit to improve his house to make it *vinchuca* proof and to expand his oil-change business to include a truck wash. These loans average from $500 to $1,000 at 12 percent annual interest (compared to the usual 45 percent) and are guaranteed by neighbors who have similar enterprises. These micro-credit plans for house improvement provide a means to help eradicate Chagas' disease in Bolivia. (Photograph by Joseph W. Bastien)

place upon their homes. House uses include sleeping arrangements, gender re-lations, household activities, and celebrations. As an illustration, the house is considered as *sayaña* for Aymaras of the Altiplano; it has thickly built walls, a thatched roof, and is small. It protects them against the wind and cold, yet it is one with the earth. The Guarani of Santa Cruz consider the house *oca*, open, centered around a courtyard that brings together diversity. Amazonian tribes live in raised thatched huts adjacent to the forests for seven years and then move to another locale when the insects become unbearable. Some bring their lifestyles to environments that don't support them.

Chagas' control projects have concentrated too exclusively on the material improvement of houses, and they frequently follow architectural styles suit-able to *mestizos*. Personnel need to understand the house as a cultural institu-tion and as a connecting and controlling metaphor that integrates all elements of the triangle.

Physical aspects of the house touch upon cultural and social environments. Just as the parasitic cycle is dealt with in a total manner, so too housing changes need to be dealt with in a similar manner. This totality includes relationships of people to each other, to their animals and belongings, and to their shrines and household deities. For Andeans especially, the house is still revered as a place of the ancestors. Mummified ancestors were kept in houses well into the sixteenth century, until they were burned by missionaries. A few people still keep clothing of ancestors in their houses. Every house has a *cabildo* shrine for the male and another shrine for the female. The dead are said to return to the house at the celebratory Feast with the Dead.

• The spiritual spoke refers to the fact that many Bolivians include rituals and prayers in almost everything they do. If project personnel take a strictly secular and scientific approach to housing improvement, they will not be very motivational to peasants. However, project personnel should not use their re-ligion as the spiritual axis. The spiritual axis appropriate to the community is the sum of that community's religious beliefs and practices, including the cos-mology, myths, and rituals of the community. Examples discussed were the use of a roof-thatching ceremony to improve houses, the inclusion of divination rituals before building a house, and the use of a dispelling ritual to get rid of *vinchucas*.

• The temporal spoke coordinates people by scheduling events and ac-counting for the intervals between events. Aymaras follow the path of the sun for their daily clock, and they follow the rainy and dry seasons for their agri-cultural cycle. Frequently, diviners throw coca leaves to determine when and where to plant. In general, peasants follow natural processes rather than the Western calendar. Project personnel continually complain that villagers don't show up for agreed-upon tasks; however, the reason is that peasants have to take advantage of favorable natural conditions.

Peasants have very busy schedules with little free time to spend on outside projects. Women spin and weave, care for children, and listen to talks at the same time. Projects have to be woven into their schedule and according to their work load. Pilot projects had problems coordinating times with members of the community; often, either household members were absent when technicians were ready or materials weren't available when the people had time.

As an alternative, Roberto Melogno[6] finds that providing credit to contract skilled laborers is more cost- and time-effective than enlisting volunteer work of community members, who have to be trained and freed from their other activities, only to then do inferior construction.[7]

• The corporeal spoke includes the health of the individual. Health is defined not only as the absence of disease but also as the total spiritual, material, and psychological well-being of the person. Projects need to include doctors and nurses to administer to patients with Chagas' disease. They also need to include *curanderos* to deal with the cultural understanding of the symptoms of Chagas' disease, such as *empacho, cólico miserere,* and *mal de corazon.* How peasants perceive of their bodies is important, because it provides the basis of therapy. If, for example, it is important to them to balance the wet and dry or hot and cold, then symptoms of Chagas' disease need to be treated in a complementary manner.

• The ethnomedical spoke connects traditional practitioners to the project and creates a dialogue between biomedical and ethnomedical practitioners concerning the prevention and treatment of Chagas' disease. Examples discussed in the book include the work of Jaime Zalles, misfortune rituals used to treat Juana, and Kallawaya *mesas* to feed the earth shrines.

Ethnological research of native ethnomedical practices is necessary to help incorporate them into prevention and therapy measures for Chagas' disease. This includes surveys of medicinal plants and how they may be used to treat the symptoms of acute and chronic Chagas' disease. It also includes an understanding of how Chagas' symptoms are perceived as cultural illnesses and how they are treated by locals. Examples discussed were *cólico miserere, empacho, muerto subito,* and *chullpa usu.*

The CCT considers ethnomedical practitioners and project workers to be equal members of the elements composing the triangle, so they need to be incorporated into the planning, prevention, and treatment of Chagas' disease. If they are considered planners and players throughout the project, then they will more likely sustain it.

• The biomedical spoke is the scientific thread that relates biological facts to pathological, cultural, and social factors. The biological and medical sciences provide facts concerning the natural elements of Chagas' disease, and this indispensable knowledge needs to be incorporated into Chagas' control projects. Chagas' disease is extremely complex and requires some knowledge of biology, parasitology, immunology, pathology, and entomology. It is helpful to have an interdisciplinary team of experts design vector-control projects. The biomedical spoke can be blocked by any one specialist overemphasizing his or her position; for example, entomologists insisting upon insecticides as the only proper response. Some issues are uncertain or are being revised, such as the concept of Chagas' disease being an autoimmune disease.

Project personnel need scientific knowledge about Chagas' disease. Many doctors are confused about its treatment, partial immunity, indeterminate phases, and therapy. Recently, the biomedical community in Bolivia has come to better recognize the prevalence of Chagas' disease; nonetheless, however, many authorities believe that Chagas' disease is not a major problem and that Chagas' control projects have been overemphasized.

The biomedical spoke connects project personnel with people suffering from Chagas' disease—doctors and nurses treat patients. Pilot projects developed a protocol for treating the acute phase of Chagas' disease in children younger than fourteen years; however, resources were not provided to treat them. A major concern is to treat the symptoms of heart disease and colonopathy.

• The technical spoke concerns the connecting links of methods, tools, and materials that bring people together to help prevent and treat Chagas' disease. Sometimes imported technologies separate personnel from community members; the standard guide is to use available technology, native resources, and personnel as much as possible in order to make community members less dependent upon outside sources. Bolivia has skilled laborers in the fields of construction, fumigation, and repair of houses. When household members themselves do such tasks they need to be instructed in proper techniques to make their houses *vinchuca* proof. Examples cited include the use of cow dung in plaster, improvement of the consistency of adobe, employment of insecticides in paint, and the formation of tile factories. Research is needed to discover drugs and insecticides from medicinal plants that can prevent or treat Chagas' disease (see Bastien et al. 1996).

• The environmental spoke connects humans with biotic factors related to the parasitic cycle. Animals and plants are important in controlling the Chagas' parasitic cycle. Its spread throughout the Americas is related to depletion of land, deforestation, and destruction of various species of plants and animals. Noted for their environmental practices, Aymara and Quechua cultures have adapted to mountainous environments in harmonious ways that other cultures can emulate. Lowland peasants of the departments of Santa Cruz and Tarija also understand their environment, and, once they are presented with information about the parasitic cycle of Chagas' disease, they can assist in discovering ways to break this cycle. Andean concepts such as that of Kallawayas who feed earth shrines of their mountain so that the mountain will feed them are useful images to teach people about the relationship of humans to the land.

Reaching the center is done along all spokes, which intersect within the context of culture. A culture context is the central hub of the spokes. When housing improvement and hygiene are considered part of the culture context, people build these houses with their own resources and continue to maintain them while incorporating their aesthetic, social, and spiritual values. One reaches the center along another spoke when housing hygiene becomes second-nature to the majority of the community and ethnomedical practitioners have adapted features of biomedicine into their native practices and rituals. The CCT model will truly be a success when communities throughout Bolivia incorporate Chagas' control measures into their communities.

The culture context model is a culturally sensitive and effective plan for the prevention of Chagas' disease. It respects the culture of people, utilizes their cultural resources, and uses culture as a focal point and dynamic for innovative responses to the problem. Culture context can be seen as the "owner's manual" of a community.

This model recognizes that a community may be a mix of ethnic classes and groups, such as Aymara and Quechua, with a mix of urban and rural features. Essentially, project personnel learn by participation and by observation about the culture context of the community where they intend to work. Moreover, they then should discuss matters with the people and let them help decide upon a course of action.

Future Hope

Several nongovernmental organizations have recently adopted a culture context model for projects other than Chagas' disease, and directors of these projects helped me design the culture context model for Chagas' disease. As already discussed, Oscar Velasco directs a health project in Potosí that includes biomedical and ethnomedical practitioners on an equal basis. They have incorporated biomedicine into the culture context of Andean ethnomedicine (see Bastien 1992). Antonio Prieto, also discussed, has developed an economic development project for peasants of Chuquisaca that focuses on the relationship of productivity to national and international economics within the culture context of the community; and Pablo Regalsky has renovated the culture context of the people of Raqaypampa, Department of Cochabamba, by reintroducing age-old practices of agroproduction that had been lost.

Evaristo Mayda has formed a strong organization of ethnomedical practitioners that serves the needs of the Quechua of Cochabamba. More than 130 community health workers of the Department of Oruro have separated from any
institutional affiliation to form their own organization, with their own projects, within Aymara and Quechua culture contexts.

These Bolivians mentioned have recognized the failures and problems of
vertically designed and biomedically oriented projects.[8] They are keenly aware
of the pressures of global economics, privatization, and capitalization upon the
production of peasants. They are actively involved in issues of peasant productivity, microcredit, and the formation of cooperatives. Many of these Bolivian
leaders speak Andean languages, have studied anthropology, and have lived for
years in peasant communities, appreciating the culture context of the community. Their projects fit the culture context of Bolivian communities; the
programs' success lies in the fact that they are generated by Bolivians with
knowledge and sensitivity to the culture context.

For future projects, it is necessary that specialists from all relevant disciplines work together with members of the community and ethnomedical
practitioners to reach solutions within the culture context of the community.
Solutions should not be ready-made formulas.

International funding sources should seriously consider the following criteria before allocating funds for the prevention of Chagas' disease. The institution should be knowledgeable about (and able to work within) the cultural,
social, and economic systems of the community for which the project is
planned. Project personnel should be able to speak the native language and
communicate effectively with all members of the community while employing
a balanced interdisciplinary approach.

The following pages will examine "cultural correctness" in development
projects. One issue to be examined is the integrity of an institution's objectives
in carrying out a project within a culture context. Frequently, nongovernmental organizations (NGOs) use projects to advance their moral, political, or religious objectives. For example, the Roman Catholic relief organization *Caritas*
distributes food donated by the U.S. government and has organized *Clubes de
Madres* (mother's clubs) in Bolivia while at the same time teaching these mothers the church's position on family planning. Some medical institutions oppose ethnomedicine and ethnomedical practitioners in their endeavors to
bring primary health care to the people. Fortunately, many NGOs in Bolivia
now recognize the value of ethnomedicine and include it within their health-
care programs. Perhaps the biggest obstacle is the Western mentality that scientific biomedicine is the only answer to eliminating sickness and bringing
about health. However, if one accepts the World Health Organization's definition of health as not merely the absence of sickness but also the total well-be-

ing and happiness of the person, then culture needs to be considered in health programs.

The culture context triangle does not imply that everything within the culture is productive towards the absence of disease. Regarding Chagas' disease, many types of behavior and values may have a negative impact. The CCT model, however, acknowledges that the culture context is dynamic and that it both can and should accept beneficial changes. Importantly, these changes need to fit into the systems of the culture (economic, social, political, and religious) in order to become permanent. The change must be a culturally acceptable negotiated agreement between project personnel, members of the community, and local ethnomedical practitioners.

CHAPTER ELEVEN
Solutions

The challenge of Chagas' disease is not insurmountable. There are solutions, and this chapter contains some possibilities. Previous chapters addressed housing improvement and hygiene as ways to prevent the disease. I now consider solutions to socioeconomic and environmental issues that have helped precipitate this epidemic. The good news is that many Bolivians recognize these solutions and are applying them.

Interdisciplinary Approach

An interdisciplinary approach is necessary to deal with socioeconomic and environmental factors in the spread of Chagas' disease. A major problem of the pilot projects was that Chagas' disease was narrowly considered from a biomedical perspective, with little if any consideration of the cultural, economic, environmental, and social factors involved in this epidemic.[1] These pilot projects thus pointed to the importance of including the social and economic sciences in the effort to prevent Chagas' disease. Narrowly focused approaches of particular disciplines are insufficient to deal with its complexity. If this book has shown anything, it is that Chagas' disease is complicated by issues of biology, chemistry, parasitology, pathology, entomology, economics, ecology, sociology, and ethnology. Each of these studies is necessary to deal with Chagas' control and disease. Detailed and varied perspectives need to be brought together within the culture context. The CCT model converges toward an apex of prevention and treatment of Chagas' disease.

Anthropologists look at Chagas' disease from a cultural perspective. Culture is seen as the major influence upon people's behavior. Anthropologists examine the relationship of people's values and behaviors with environmental factors related to *vinchucas* and *T. cruzi*. They study the etiology of Chagas' disease and how people deal with its symptoms. They are able to explain the cultural dynamics of shamans, midwives, and *curanderos*. Anthropologists can be seen as the translators and negotiators between the technical-scientific world views of project personnel and the cultural practices of peasants.

The following anthropologists have contributed to the prevention of Chagas' disease. Oscar Velasco integrates ethnomedicine and biomedicine in the treatment of Chagas' disease. Alan Kolata and Charles Ortloff (1989) have shown that the raised-field technique in about A.D. 500 at Tiahuanaco, an archaeological site on the Altiplano, was a more productive farming technique than that used now by the Aymara, which was introduced by the Spaniards. Raised-field techniques also provided better nutrition. Applying this archaeological knowledge, Kolata is reintroducing raised-field techniques to Altiplano Aymaras.

Social anthropologist Xavier Albo has studied Aymara and Quechua political and economic systems to assist his public policy advocacy of their interests, and his studies greatly assist project personnel in these matters. Cultural anthropologist Pablo Regalsky leads an institute that promotes the ethnoscientific knowledge and traditional agricultural systems of peasants in the valleys of Cochabamba and Misqui. He has helped Quechua peasants of Ragaypampa restore traditional methods of crop rotation to enhance production and to maintain adaptive varieties of potatoes within the Misqui region. This has offset the trend for single-crop production of russet potatoes, caused by the demand for larger potatoes to make french fries in Cochabamba.

Sociologists deal with social stratification and ways to deal with divisions between peasants, city dwellers, *cholos,* and *mestizos.* Bolivian sociologists have been very helpful in the understanding of gender and age roles. There is a body of statistical information available that provides quantitative information about demographics, migration, income, and social stratification. Project sociologists are needed to assist in group dynamics, enlisting community participation, and providing leadership. Social psychologists are helpful in assessing motivational factors and social behavior.

Juan José Alva, for example, works in rural sectors of the city of Cochabamba on housing concerns and Chagas' control. He is also a professor of sociology at the University of San Simon in Cochabamba. He teaches rural teachers and has been influential in getting them to use educational material that is adaptable to the people in these areas.

Roberto Briceño-León and Silverio González analyze economic and social conditions leading to infestation of triatomines in villages of Venezuela. They introduced locus of control theory into the SOH/CCH pilot projects in Bolivia. Locus of control implies that an individual's general expectations about his or her ability to control the future greatly influence that individual's response to house improvement programs (González Tellez, interview 10/15/91). People's notion of whether the future is controlled by themselves, the state, fate, or luck greatly influences their desire to act to prevent anything or improve houses. González helped project personnel deal with the fatalistic attitude of peasants. He also found that, after they improved their houses, many people gained a sense of empowerment.

Economists devise ways that projects can be financed by community members. They also help to increase productivity in rural areas. Many factors in vector infestation are related to economic problems. Migration and inadequate housing are caused in part by low productivity, unemployment, debt peonage, and impoverishment. Chagas' disease has increased because poverty in Bolivia and other countries of Latin America has increased, especially in cities.

Innovative economists are forming microcredit institutions and cooperatives to assist community members to develop free trade. As an example, Marco Antonio Prieto analyzes problems within the rural communities of Chuquisaca and devises economic measures such as microcredit and cooperatives to deal with these problems. Ronald Gutiérrez, an economist for Plan International, studies how the political economy affects migration and housing development in the Department of Tarija. Plan International and Pro-Habitat provide credit for housing improvement in the barrios of Tarija. Ruth Sensano has introduced the production of tile roofing to certain communities. It serves not only to prevent *vinchucas* but also as an additional source of income to the community. The parish in San Lorenzo, Territory of Lomerío, has a housing cooperative that provides credit to Chiquitano Indians to build houses and a tile-and-brick cooperative to provide them with building materials.

Agriculturalists study land to increase productivity, decrease depletion, and improve farming and herding. They have introduced rotational planting. Livestock suffer similar symptoms of Chagas' disease, and its toll on sheep, cattle, goats, horses, alpacas, llamas, and guinea pigs is very great. Percentages of livestock infection are proportional to percentages of human infection wherever animals are kept near dormitories, which is almost always the case among peasants. Chagas' disease's toll on animal productivity is a concern that Bolivians generally haven't even begun to consider. At the present, the major concern is that domiciliary animals attract *vinchucas* and are carriers of *T. cruzi*, adding yet another infected blood source for uninfected *vinchucas*. Agriculturalists deal with ways that livestock can be kept so that they do not serve as reservoir hosts for parasites. Bolivian agriculturalists also practice veterinary medicine and are necessary to treat infected and ill livestock.

Linda Gregg, an expert in animal husbandry, studies goat and cattle herding among the Quechuas of Misqui, Bolivia, an area where Chagas' disease is 70 percent endemic. She provides medical care for sick animals and has found that imported cattle brought hoof-and-mouth disease to cattle in the region. She is introducing ways to increase herds, produce healthier animals, and improve herding techniques to minimize erosion caused by goats. She also is assessing the loss of productivity in livestock as caused by *T. cruzi*.

Community health workers have been trained in agriculture and animal husbandry in the Department of Oruro. They have introduced *carpas solares* (solar gardens) to hundreds of communities of the Altiplano, where previously because of the cold nights and altitude of 12,500 feet the growing of tomatoes, cabbages, onions, and carrots was not feasible. Now these communities have vegetables to help balance their diet of potatoes. Workers also have introduced new types of seeds and rabbits.

Naturalist Jaime Zalles studies the economical uses of wild plants throughout Bolivia. He and ethnologist Manuel de Luca have published popular books on the medicinal and nutritional uses of plants. Written in the Aymara, Quechua, and Guarani languages, these books are well-illustrated and helpful guides to members of the community, CHWs, and ethnomedical practitioners. Zalles gives presentations to peasants about Chagas' disease and informs them about native plants that can be used to treat its symptoms or as insecticides. He cultivates medicinal plants for export and is involved with scientists trying to find herbal cures for Chagas' disease, AIDS, and cancer.

These specialists, many of whom are Bolivians, may provide innovative and unique solutions to Chagas' disease, and many could be employed for less than the cost of one consultant from the United States. They constitute an interdisciplinary team for dealing with Chagas' disease. Bolivians should be able to provide a more integrated interdisciplinary and culturally sensitive approach to the prevention of Chagas' disease than could international agencies or nongovernmental organizations. However, they too must avoid Bolivia's inherent class and race stratification. They too need to be trained in the culture context triangle. Their endeavors do bear out the premise of the culture context model: that people within a community know best how to solve their own problems once they are educated about them. The role of project workers is to meaningfully educate them.

Decreased Productivity

Economic and social costs of Chagas' disease are huge for Bolivians and other peoples of Latin America. Chagas' disease helps creates a downward spiral of productivity; it is a debilitating disease at all stages. At its early stages parasites sap vital nutrients and dispel toxic waste products; at its later stages diseased organs totally disable workers. Most notably, peasants suffer fatigue, especially those working at higher altitudes, where they often must stop farming their plots or leave the work to relatives and children. The inability to work results in decreased crops, which causes malnourishment that leads to increased susceptibility to Chagas' disease.

Even more costly, many adult victims die during their most productive years. Children are left without mentors and families without breadwinners. Remaining members of the community then must assume responsibility for the survivors. For this reason, Chagas' disease is a major obstacle to development in Latin America. The World Bank considers it the fourth most serious health problem in Latin America (after respiratory and diarrheal illnesses and HIV infection), as measured by years of life lost adjusted for disability (see Fig-

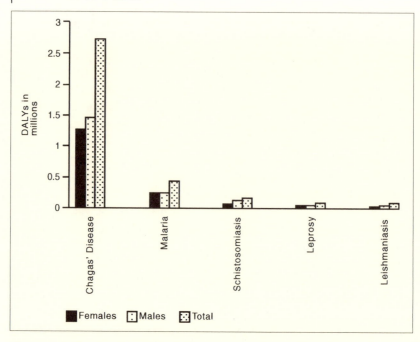

Figure 31. Disease burden in Latin America in disability-adjusted life years (DALYs), from five tropical diseases. (From *World Development Report 1993: Investing in Health*. World Bank.)

ure 31). From a cost-benefit analysis, it is cheaper to build a house for every Bolivian family than to cover the cost of Chagas' disease to the economy from loss of production (not including the loss of animals).

Agrarian productivity also has declined in the Altiplano because of environmental and economic factors. Vast deforestation of the Altiplano caused widespread loss of other vegetation and water shortages. Insect populations shifted from wooded areas to houses. Highland peasants moved to lower, more disease-infested regions of the Alto-Beni and Santa Cruz. Bolivian peasants are having problems competing against large-scale commercial farmers. Rural Bolivia lacks electricity, secondary-education facilities, and adequate health care. These factors also have discouraged children from taking over the family farm. As a result, rural-to-urban ratios have plummeted from 74–26 percent in 1950 to 42–58 percent in 1992.

Life in urban areas is not much better for Aymara, Quechua, and Guarani Indians who go from being independent agriculturalists to becoming dependent and low-paid *jornaleros* (hired workers). Many are not even that lucky— unemployment in Bolivia is at 20 percent and rising. Bolivia is a poor and unhealthy country.

Transported pathogens have a distinct advantage with the migration of people in generally being able to colonize and reproduce in new territories. Seasonal migration can lead to a biotic exchange of pathogens between regions, exposing populations to diseases from many regions. In other words, Chagas' disease, AIDS, tuberculosis, and malaria accompany these movements and spread back and forth from home territories to colonized or work areas. Globalization brings colonization not only of humans but of insects, parasites, and viruses. Chagas' disease in Bolivia provides a microcosmic illustration of what is happening on a global scale.

Increased Productivity

Chagas' disease will likely decrease to the degree that productivity is increased among peasants in Bolivia. This is an axiom seldom considered by health workers, however. Nearly half the population of Bolivia is involved in small-scale agricultural production of various species of vegetables, fruits, and grains; together, they produce large quantities of produce. Small-scale production is a feasible economic alternative along the valleys and mountainsides of the Andes. Large-scale farming has not been economically feasible in many of these regions.

Productivity can be increased by utilizing the capacity of peasants to produce on a small scale. Small farm and cottage industries are the basic productive units in Bolivia. Bolivia's cities are being fed to a large extent by market women who sell foods and produce from sidewalk stalls and markets. There is an economic system involving planter, harvester, trucker, and vendor, these roles frequently being filled by relatives and members of the household. Productive units are the family, relatives, and community; they function on small scales—sales are small and profits are little. Combined, however, these smaller units have considerable economic leverage and resources. Their economy is held together by religious fiestas, reciprocal exchange, and community bonds. A similar situation is found in the production of goods. Cottage industries produce clothes, foods, various goods, and jewelry. Bolivia has been called the land of free enterprise.

This productivity of rural and urban peoples is the basis for economic development in Bolivia. Small-scale productivity can drive a country's economy if it is used to produce specialty goods that cannot be found elsewhere. Bolivia's farms and cottage industries produce items in demand by many countries, such as cañiwa and quinua (France imported 150,000 tons of quinua in 1996). Peasants farm plots on mountainsides too steep for plows in order to produce these high-protein native cereals. *Chifleras* (women herbal vendors) in Oruro sell $1 million worth of medicinal plants throughout the world. A naturalist and a chemist in La Paz export herbal medicines to other parts of the world. They work with peasants in many communities who grow the herbs in gardens, providing them with seeds, medicine to sell, and profits. The two also teach the peasants about the prevention of Chagas' disease.

Politicians frequently overlook the importance of smaller productive units in the economic development of Bolivia. Small-scale producers need less credit, generally amounts from $500 to $1,000, with annual interest rates below 13 percent. Presently many peasants cannot get loans; for those who can, interest rates often are so high (up to 50 percent) that many cannot repay them and are kept in debt peonage. Farmers need credit to maintain operations during an unproductive year as well as to buy tools, improve seed crops, and purchase livestock. Their children need school supplies and clothing. Some sell their produce in the cities; but they are unable to do this at municipal markets without licenses (RUCs), which are expensive, so they end up selling their goods on the streets. One credit union in Sucre provides farmers with credit so they can purchase licenses and sell at markets, where they have increased sales in a shorter amount of time. Community members individually took out loans to jointly buy a truck in which they could transport their produce to market without having to sell it to a middle-man trucker who formerly made most of the profit.

Six neighboring families in the Tomatita barrio of Tarija co-signed for one other as guarantors to repay the loan if another fails. Individual families have then invested in production: one woman purchased a refrigerator and a television set for her household store and lounge to better serve neighborhood clientele. She makes more money than her carpenter husband, who is frequently unemployed.

An example on a larger scale: three families took out separate loans to purchase a taxi for U.S. $3,000, which they operate between them. The taxi's monthly income is U.S. $400. Half is budgeted for expenses, so that within two years the car will be paid for, and the owners plan to buy other taxis until every participating family has one.

Cooperatives have been mentioned a number of times as very adaptable to Andean economics. Cooperatives fit into concepts of *aynisiña* (labor exchange), *turqasiña,* and the fiesta system. Cooperatives add an institutional and economic framework that fits into the formal economy of Bolivia. Housing cooperatives have been very successful in Puno and Lima, Peru, with more than 5,000 houses being built. The housing cooperative in San Lorenzo has enabled more than sixty families to build homes. These and other cooperatives have also served to provide loans for capital investment in the production of goods.

Cooperatives, credit unions, neighborhood associations, and the new "Laws of Popular Participation" provide Bolivians with ways to increase production. These measures are better solutions for rural peasants than is large-scale industrial farming, which takes the land away from the peasants and re-duces them to migrant workers.

Land Holdings

Productivity is linked to land holdings, which present long-standing problems for peasants. Like Chagas' disease, the issue is environmen-tally and historically complex, with no easy solution. Presently, small-scale production has become even smaller because land holdings are being divided into smaller plots, going from the *minifundio* to the *surcofundio* (furrow farm). After the agrarian reform of 1954, many land holdings went from the *latifundio* (hacienda) to plots of several acres, allotted to each peasant family who worked as peons on the hacienda. These three-acre plots then gradually decreased as the land was subdivided to provide for offspring of the landholders. In the eastern lowlands of Bolivia there still exist pre-agrarian reform conditions of *pongeaje* (peonage), where native peoples have to work for free for owners of large land estates. Until 1960, Chiquitano Indians were held as slaves in some lowland areas.

In contrast, members of free communities continued to hold land in com-mon, and every year leaders allotted parcels to households according to their needs. This long-existing pattern of communal land distribution has never been very popular with Western reformists, many of whom equated it with communism and socialism. Eventually the passage of *Las Leyes de Participación Popular* in 1994 required that members of free communities register their land as private property, with the provision that, if they don't, this land will revert to the municipalities to be sold. This created a traumatic situation for many peas-ants who were unsure of how to divide the land and under which families to register it. Certain communities refused to declare their land as private prop-erty and are vigorously fighting confiscation. Pablo Regalsky, director of CENDA, has supported their endeavors with notable success. Peasant unions have united in this endeavor, which has solidified Aymara and Quechua Indi-ans throughout Bolivia in a common cause. As a result, peasants have entered the political arena with notable success, electing an Aymara speaker as vice-president in 1994. Since his victory, however, he has done little to assist them.

According to the agrarian reform laws of 1954, members of free communi-ties and individual peasant property owners are not required to pay taxes if they work the land. Individuals with large land holdings are required to pay taxes if the land is productive. To avoid paying taxes, some large land owners leave land fallow, although, also according to the same laws, unworked land should be distributed to the neighboring peasants. Rarely, if ever, has this hap-pened with large tracts of fertile land lying fallow, however. Now, in fact, some of these landlords are selling the land to private corporations. After these corporations begin to farm, they gradually take over more land, inducing neighboring peasants to sell their land and then work as farm workers on the larger farms.

A strong indigenous peasant movement has arisen in Bolivia affecting land tenure and productivity. Beginning in 1982 indigenous peoples participated in the making of a law that was finally passed in 1996—INRA (*Instituto Nacional de Reforma Agraria*)—which guarantees the sovereignty of indigenous people and their land holdings. Foreigners are not permitted to enter their land without permission. Many tribes in eastern Bolivia occupy regions east of the Andes that include vast plains and tropical forests. Parts of this land have been altered from tropical hardwood forests to grassy savannahs for cattle raising. Thousands of acres of forests were cleared to farm soy beans which were never grown, leaving dusty flatlands.

Theoretically, the new laws protect native peoples, who are proven caretakers of the forest preserves; however, one problem is that many Bolivian people have not been socially trained to understand these laws. They also have few means to enforce them, as is also the case with Bolivia's environmental laws. Organizations would do well to teach Bolivians about their laws and help them use modern technology to enforce the laws. Lowland tribes have been given laptop computers to help them communicate with networks of environmentally concerned groups that can help them survive against miners and loggers.

Another favorable aspect of *Las Leyes de Participación Popular* of 1994 is that it provides government recognition of territorial units as municipalities. Previously, the government strongly favored urban areas, now it has decentralized in favor of regionalization. There currently are 380 municipalities, and these municipalities provide increased flexibility in regard to addressing cultural and social factors, climatic and agricultural conditions, soil conditions, and community problems. Most importantly, federal funds are now being distributed to the municipalities for agricultural and community development.

Environment

Bolivia has perhaps the greatest biodiversity and beauty of any country in the Americas. It is a gem of the world, noted for its beauty and wealth. From the top of the Andes to the Amazon basin, Bolivia has climatic and ecological zones that are equivalent to those from Alaska to Panama. From La Paz, one can travel up to a 17,000-foot pass with its near arctic conditions and then down to tropical forests housing parrots, monkeys, and snakes. Bolivia has more species of birds than any other country in the world, and it is still possible to visit areas where the animals are unaccustomed to humans, such as the Noel Kempf Preserve, a 2-million-square-mile preserve accessible only by helicopter.

Bolivia's natural resources have been among the most exploited in the world. Its gold, silver, tin, and antimony mines have made others rich. Its eastern Andean slopes have been stripped of large, elegantly flowered chinchona trees in the eighteenth and nineteenth centuries to provide quinine bark to treat malaria throughout the world. In the twentieth century, the United States has virtually destroyed Bolivia's coca crop and other vegetation in its effort to win the cocaine war at home. Amazonian forests have lost trees slashed for rubber, Tajibo trees stripped for bark to fight cancer, and palms bled for their resin to treat AIDS. Centuries-old mahoganies are cut down in a day and transported across roads that erode forest floors to urban centers of the world to build desks. *Vinchucas* and *T. cruzi* are also part of the equation.

In *The Coming Plague*, Laurie Garret (1994:619) sounded a warning call: "Human beings stomp about with swagger, elbowing their way without concern into one ecosphere after another. The human race seems equally complacent about blazing a path into a rain forest with bulldozers and arson or using an antibiotic "scorched earth" policy to chase unwanted microbes across the duodenum.... Time is short."

Ecosystem disruption and subsequent loss of species have profound implications for human health (see Grifo and Rosenthal 1997). Damage to the ecosystem has caused changes in the equilibria between hosts, vectors, and parasites in their natural environments; for example, *T. cruzi* has switched from animals to humans as its primary host. In addition to global warming, acid rain, and pollution, Chagas' disease warns us of a potential huge epidemic.

Chagas' disease has increased as biocultural diversity has decreased in Bolivia. It may be part of the environment's barometer indicating rising pressure upon the forests. Bolivian natives recognize this, and they attribute many sicknesses to ecological abuses of animals and plants. Andeans have an environmental wisdom that sees humans, plants, animals, and land as ideally in balance. Andean Indians have rituals to feed the earth, the mother. Traditionally, they refer to alpacas and llamas on the same plane of existence as humans, the only difference being that humans now speak and herd them, whereas formerly it was the other way around. A major deity of Andeans is Pariya Qaqa (Igneous Rock), a god who became a rock, the mountain upon which they live. To native Bolivians, then, the earth is sacred; it is to be fed with ritual foods and worked in such a way that it continues to produce. They have developed elaborate systems of rotating fields and crops for three years and then letting them lie fallow as herd grounds so they will be fertilized. This has been practiced for over 1,000 years. Highland Andeans and lowland Indian tribes remain guardians of the mountains, valleys, and forests of Bolivia.

Huarochiri legends were recorded in 1608 by Father Francisco de Ávila, and they reveal prehispanic religious traditions. These legends unfold a landscape alive with diverse sacred beings, mountain deities, and prophetic animals. They express the sacredness of animals, plants, and land. The following myth relates how overpopulation caused hunger in ancient times. The brocket deer reproduced until food became scarce. The conditions of their life became a problem.

Now, in ancient times, brocket deer used to eat human beings.

Later on, when brocket deer were very numerous, they danced, ritually chanting, "How shall we eat people?"

Then one of their fawns made a mistake and said, "How shall people eat us?"

When the brocket deer heard this they scattered. From then on brocket deer became food for humans (Huarochiri ms., Chapter 5, 71, ed. and trans. Salomon and Urioste 1991).

This myth illustrates the closeness of Andeans to animals. At first deer ate humans; but, after a fawn made a linguistic mistake, humans ate deer.

The following myth discusses a time when this world wanted to come to an end, but Andeans and animals were saved by the prescience of llamas:

In ancient times, this world wanted to come to an end.

A llama buck, aware that the ocean was about to overflow, was behaving like somebody who's deep in sadness. Even though its owner let it rest in a patch of excellent pasture, it cried out and said, "In, in," and wouldn't eat.

The llama's owner got really angry, and he threw the cob from some maize he had just eaten at the llama.

"Eat, dog! This is some fine grass I'm letting you rest in!" he said.

Then that llama began speaking like a human being.

"You simpleton, whatever could you be thinking about? Soon, in five days, the ocean will overflow. It's a certainty. And the whole world will come to an end," it said.

The man got good and scared. "What's going to happen to us? Where can we go to save ourselves?" he said.

The llama replied, "Let's go to Villca Coto mountain. There we'll be saved. Take along five day's food for yourself."

So the man went out from there in a great hurry, and himself carried both the llama buck and its load.

When they arrived at Villca Coto mountain, all sorts of animals had already filled it up: pumas, foxes, guanacos, condors, all kinds of animals in great numbers.

They stayed there huddling tightly together.

The waters covered all those mountains and it was only Villca Coto mountain, or rather its very peak, that was not covered by the water.

Water soaked the fox's tail.

That's how it turned black.

Five days later, the waters descended and began to dry up.

The drying waters caused the ocean to retreat all the way down again and exterminate all the people.

Afterward, that man began to multiply once more.

That's the reason there are people until today.

Regarding this story, we Christians believe it refers to the time of the Flood.

But they believe it was Villca Coto mountain that saved them (Huarochiri ms., Chapter 3, 29–34, ed. and trans. Salomon and Urioste 1991).

Villca Coto Mountain was the most beautiful *huaca* (earth shrine) at the Inca court in Cuzco. A *huaca* is any material thing that manifests the superhuman: a mountain peak, a spring, a union of streams, a rock outcrop, an ancient ruin, a twinned cob of maize, a tree split by lightning (Salomon and Urioste 1991:17). The world imagined by Andeans is not made of two kinds of stuff—matter and spirit—like that of Christians. *Huacas* are energized matter. This myth gives the earth dynamic shape by mapping onto it *huacas* that symbolize idealized environments and relations between animals and humans. Humanity, the superhuman, society, and earth forms relate to each other in a structure of correspondence.

Andean legends offer us a map to reorder things. Brocket deer serve to warn about overpopulation and overconsumption; a llama predicts impending destruction of the earth and is carried on the herder's back to Villca Cota, where they are saved.

A modern sequel to brocket deer and llama is *vinchuca*. *Vinchuca* brings humans *Trypanosoma cruzi* to remind them that they are in a state of eternal competition. Humans have beaten out virtually every other species to the point that humans now talk about protecting their former predators (Joshua Lederberg 1994). *Vinchucas* warn humans that they are not alone on top of the mountain. *Trypanosoma cruzi* and scores of other microbe predators are adapting, changing, evolving, and warning humans that any more rapid change might come at the cost of human devastation. Humans have been neglectful of the microbes, among other things, and that is coming back to haunt us. The world really is just one village. *Vinchucas* warn us to return to *huaca* Villca Cota.

Trypanosoma cruzi

The full taxonomic name of the Chagas' disease parasite is *Trypanosoma (Schizotrypanum) cruzi* (Chagas 1909). In its biological classification, *Trypanosoma cruzi (T. cruzi)* belongs to subkingdom Protozoa, phylum Sarcomastigophora, subphylum Mastigophora, class Zoomoastigophorea, order Kinetoplastida, family Trypanosomatidae, genus *Trypanosoma*, and species *cruzi*. Each of these categories reveals something interesting about this parasite.

Trypanosomes fit into the order Kinetoplastida because they are flagellar organisms with a kinetoplast, an organelle unique to this order which contains the mitochondrial DNA and gives rise to the mitochondrion. Sausage- or disc-shaped, a kinetoplast has a single mitochondrion that contains enzymes for respiration and energy production. The DNA fibers run in an anterior-posterior direction and are organized into a network of linked circles, with up to 20,000 mini-circles and 20 to 50 maxi-circles in the kinetoplast network (Battaglia et al. 1983). Like a minuscule computer, these circles program the replication rate and survival activity of the mitochondrion during the cell cycle. Trypanosomes have one nucleus. Although there is indirect evidence of sexuality, it has not been observed directly (Tait 1983), and the organisms reproduce asexually by binary fission.

Trypanosoma cruzi belong to the family Trypanosomatidae, or trypanosomes, which are classified together because during one stage of their lives they live in the blood and/or tissues of vertebrate hosts, and during other stages they live in the intestines of bloodsucking invertebrate vectors (Schmidt and Roberts 1989). They also belong to the subgenus *Schizotrypanum,* which is a category adopted for trypanosomes that multiply in vertebrates via intracellular stages. Technically speaking, all species are hemoflagellate and heteroxenous and (except *T. equiperdum)* are transmitted to animal hosts.

Trypanosoma cruzi belong to the stercorian section (A. *stercoria)*, a subspecies, because its infective stages develop in the vector's digestive tract and contaminate the mammalian hosts through the vector's feces. Important factors in the transmission of *T. cruzi* to humans are lack of personal hygiene, invasion of human habitations by vectors, and a close temporal relationship between the taking of the blood meal and defecation by the vector. Chagas' disease also has been transmitted by insect feces falling from the ceiling and contaminating foods. *Triatoma infestans* is a particularly efficient vector because it defecates close to the bite wound, providing *T. cruzi* easy access to enter the wound.

In comparison, *T. rangeli*, which is not associated with human pathogenicity, belongs to the salivary section (B. *salivaria*) because it infects hosts through saliva as well as feces. Because the two parasites can be confused in diagnosis, one way to distinguish *T. rangeli* from *T. cruzi* is to examine by xenodiagnosis if the parasite is found in the insect's saliva. If so, it is *T. rangeli*, which does not cause Chagas' disease. The highly pathogenic (to humans) salivary trypanosomes belong to the *T. brucei* group, which are transmitted through the saliva of tsetse flies and cause human sleeping sickness.

Trypanosoma cruzi pass through different forms at various stages in their life cycle, of which three are important in the human context: trypomastigotes, amastigotes, and epimastigotes (see Figure 5). *T. cruzi* become metacyclic trypomastigotes in the hindgut of the *vinchuca* bug, and they are the infectious forms for animals and humans. Metacyclic trypomastigotes are 20 microns long, 3 microns wide, and can change positions very rapidly. (A micron equals .001 millimeters.) They are flat on the sides, with a free flagellum (tail) attached to an undulating membrane on the body (Manson-Bahr and Bell 1987). They have a central nucleus and a posterior kinetoplast. Trypomastigotes occur in peripheral blood of hosts and multiply by splitting lengthwise, with the kinetoplast and nucleus dividing before the cytoplasm and a new flagellum developing from the new kinoplast. Amastigotes are intracellular round and oval forms, 1.5 to 5 microns long, without an external flagellum. They occur within hosts.

All trypanosome species are either elongate with a single flagellum or rounded with a very short, nonprotruding flagellum. The flagellum arises from a kinetosome (core or basal body), is attached to the parasite's membrane, and pulls the organism by undulating along its side and, at certain life stages, extending forward from its prow. This makes the organisms agile swimmers and intruders into cells. The flagellum may also be used to attach the organism to the insect's gut wall or salivary glands.

Epimastigotes are easily distinguishable from trypomastigotes, because, in epimastigotes, the flagellum begins near the center of the parasite between the nucleus and kinetoplast, extends along the anterior undulating membrane, and protrudes from the prow (Schmidt and Roberts 1989:57). In trypomastigotes, the kinetoplast and kinetosome are found in the posterior tip, from where the flagellum begins, flows along the membrane of the parasite, and extends from the prow. The epimastigotes in the midgut of the insect are small, 10 to 20 microns, multiply profusely by binary fission, provide a reservoir of parasites, and thus maintain the infection in the bug (Molyneux and Ashford 1983:168).

Longer epimastigotes (35 to 40 microns) travel from the midgut to the rectum of *vinchucas*, where they adhere to the epithelium of the rectal glands with their flagella. Epimastigotes develop into metacyclic trypomastigotes, which swim freely in the rectal lumen. Metacyclics are 17 to 22 microns long. They no longer divide and are very active. This life cycle takes anywhere from six to fifteen days, depending on the stage of the bug which ingests the parasite and the temperature at which the bug lives (Molyneux and Ashford 1983:168). This reproductive and infective cycle of *T. cruzi* continues throughout the life of the bug and apparently does no harm to it.

In observation, *T. cruzi* have no stages outside the gut of insects and the blood and cells of vertebrates. Drugs aside, once host and vector are infected, they generally remain so throughout their lives. This is because *T. cruzi* can reproduce asexually by binary fission in both the vector and the definitive host.

After metacyclic trypomastigotes enter a mammal's cells, they reproduce by binary fissions into amastigotes. Amastigotes cluster into cysts—tiny, entangled snakelike bundles of evolving forms that burst cells, exploding amastigotes into the bloodstream, once again to repeat the process in another cell with such speed that industrial mass production looks slow in comparison. Meanwhile, they also produce stumpy trypomastigotes that circulate in the blood in order that they can be absorbed by blood-ingesting *vinchucas*. This reproductive cycle is constant, so that infected humans have trypomastigotes permanently circulating within their blood and amastigotes reproducing in their cells.

Amastigotes frequently develop into short and stumpy trypomastigotes, which are found in chronic phases of the disease. Stumpy trypomastigotes are thought to be the most infective stage to triatomine bugs (Molyneux and Ashford 1983:167). As with African trypanosomes, the morphological form of the trypomastigotes that the insect ingests with blood influences the level of infection: "stout" forms seem to be more infective than are "slender" forms (WHO 1991:22). During the acute phase, triatomines are less likely to ingest trypomastigotes in the blood of the host because the host's immune system is attacking these forms and driving them into the sanctuary offered by host cells. In the chronic phase, the slower, short, stumpy trypomastigotes can leisurely wait for ingestion by "kissing bugs," because immunosuppression has reduced the risks of attack in the circulation system of the host. Although the numbers of trypomastigotes seldom reach the levels seen in the blood during the acute phase of Chagas' disease or during African trypanosomiasis, the trypomastigotes of *T. cruzi* are able to increase their numbers in the peripheral circulation system of the chronic patient.

The advantage of circulating in the blood is that *T. cruzi* can then readily transmit its progeny to insects, who provide another environment for development and transportation to other hosts. This strategy assures that even though *T. cruzi* ultimately destroy the host in which they presently reside, their offspring will carry on in another host. Their migration between cells within the same host ensures a ready supply of new nurseries for their offspring, while transmission via insects promotes their movement from one host to another, whether sylvatic or domestic animals or humans. The disadvantages of circulating in the blood are that *T. cruzi* are under attack by the humoral immune system, and one strategy the organism has developed is to spend as little time in the blood as possible.

Trypanosome cruzi employ an important adaptive strategy seen with many parasites in that they try to maintain their own population levels within the carrying capacity of the host organism. It is not to their advantage to destroy their hosts too quickly, or, as George Stewart says, "They don't want to burn down their home before they have acquired a replacement."[1] With sound practicality, then, Chagas' disease has a relatively low incidence of parasitemia in its acute phase.

After the *vinchuca* bug has ingested trypomastigotes, another reproductive process takes place within the insect's gut. Insects do not get sick or suffer from *T. cruzi* except for the loss of nutrients (WHO 1991:22). In contrast, however, a closely related parasite, *Trypanosoma rangeli,* which is harmless to humans, has a pathogenic effect on insects. After trypomastigotes have traveled to the anterior intestine, they take on epimastigote forms, then travel to the midgut and change into amastigotes and proliferate. Amastigotes next give birth to metacyclic trypomastigotes in the rear of the intestines and from there are transported through the feces the next time the insect takes a blood meal. Delay time between ingestion of a blood meal and defecation is a large factor in infection rates of triatomine vectors; *Triatoma infestans, vinchucas,* have a rapid time period.

Within the insect, *T. cruzi* go through their reproductive cycle in eight to ten days and produce as many as 100 protozoa. The number produced is affected by the blood-meal size, the number of parasites ingested, the stage and age of the insect vector, the ability of the parasite to establish rectal gland infections in the vector, and the kinetics of parasite transformation in the insect's digestive tract (WHO 1991:22).

The susceptibility of triatomine vectors to infection with *T. cruzi* varies greatly among different vector species and with their interaction with strains of *T. cruzi* (WHO 1991:22). The presence of three main isoenzymic strains (zymodemes) within *T. cruzi* was discovered in Brazil (Miles et al. 1977; Ready and Miles 1980) and more have been found in Bolivia (Tibayrenc et al. 1984) and Chile (Gonzalez et al. 1995). The geographic frequency of occurrence of the principal isoenzymic strains has been described in these countries and is important to pathogenicity (Brénière et al. 1989, Miles, Provoa, Prata, et al. 1981) and genetic variability of *T. cruzi* (see Appendix 2).

APPENDIX 2
Strains of *T. cruzi*

T. cruzi strains are classified into schizodemes and zymodemes: schizodeme classification is based on electrophoretic mobility of kinetoplast DNA (see Gonzalez et al. 1995 for description of methodology). Electrophoresis indicates characteristic mobility in an electric field by the DNA of various strains. Zymodeme classification is based upon enzymatic profiles of parasite strains (see Miles et al. 1977, Ready and Miles 1980). Metacyclic trypomastigotes are examined *in vitro* for genetic variation indicated by isoenzyme analysis (Breniere et al. 1991).

Zymodeme (schizodeme) classification is useful for identifying strains of differing pathogenic potential and for distinguishing between organisms which cause human diseases and those that cause animal diseases (Breniere 1989). Genetic interpretation of zymograms of *T. cruzi* from various hosts over a broad geographical range (from Argentina to the United States) has revealed great genetic variability (WHO 1991:13). Supposedly, these characteristics are fairly stable in a strain, but this is not always the case.

Schizodemes or zymodemes are important classifications to determine in infected patients because different strains show affinity for different tissues and cause varied pathologies. The fact that patients in Sucre, Bolivia, have a high incidence of colonopathy may be explained by zymodemes distinct from those found in La Paz, which favor cardiopathy (Brénière et al. 1989). In highly endemic areas of Santa Cruz, patients are often infected with more than one strain. These strains may cause differing pathologies in the same individual. This implies that humans may be challenged by different strains even after developing so-called partial immunity to one strain.

In the Amazonian basin of Brazil, zymodemes Z1 and Z3 have been isolated from sylvatic sources, principally with armadillos (*Dasypus*) and opossums (*Didelphis*) as hosts and reduviids (*Panstronglyus megistus*) as vectors that are associated with these mammals (Miles, Provoa, Prata, et al. 1981 and Miles, Provoa, de Sovza, et al. 1981). Z1 is also found in some domestic environments of Venezuela, where megasyndromes infrequently occur. These sylvatic zymodemes are more frequently associated with acute Chagas' disease than are Z2 zymodemes. Zymodeme Z2 has not been identified with a sylvatic source and is the primary source of the domestic transmission cycle; it has been found in domestic situations in acute and chronic cases with cardiac and digestive symptoms being associated with megasyndromes.

Significant research on zymodemes has been done in Bolivia by investigators from a branch of Pasteur Institute in La Paz, Instituto Boliviano de Biología de Altura (IBBA) (see Brénière et al. 1989, Tibayrenc et al. 1984). In earlier studies, Tibayrenc and colleagues collected 132 *Trypanosoma cruzi* stocks in southern Bolivia—in Tupiza and Tarija—that were characterized using enzymes. Five different isoenzymatic strains (IS) were found that are distinguishable from those found in Brazil. The incidence of IS 2 is higher (60 percent) in Tarija (altitude 6,400 feet) than it is in Tupiza (31 percent; altitude 8,528 feet), which suggests that IS 1 seems to be more frequent at high altitude and that IS 2 seems to be more frequent at lower altitudes (Tibayrenc and Desjeux 1983). Genotype frequencies demonstrated the lack of Mendelian sexuality among stocks of *T. cruzi* from southern Bolivia, which supports a clonal theory of propagation for trypanosomatids (Tibayrenc, Hoffman, et al. 1986, Tibayrenc, Ward, et al. 1986).

All strains were transmitted by *Triatoma infestans*, in contrast to Brazil, where strains were transmitted by different vectors, perhaps suggesting that different *T. cruzi* strains were adapting to particular vector species (Miles, Provoa, de Sovza, et al. 1981). Different strains were found in the same suburb and house in Tupiza. Forty-four houses were examined: nine had two different isoenzymic strains, two had three different strains, and one had four different strains. The migration of triatomine bugs from house to house is important; flights of several kilometers are possible (Lehane and Schofield 1981).

In a later Bolivian study (Brénière et al. 1989), researchers at IBBA performed serological and pathological studies on 495 patients with Chagas' disease from different areas of Bolivia. Eighty-nine *Trypanosoma cruzi* strains were isolated by xenodiagnosis and characterized by twelve isoenzyme loci; they were related to the presence of cardiac changes and enteric disease with megacolon. There was high heterogeneity of human zymodemes, presenting evidence of two predominant zymodemes genetically dissimilar from each other and ubiquitous in Bolivia. Researchers observed mixtures of different zymodemes within the same patients, and there was no apparent difference of pathogenicity between the two more frequent zymodemes isolated from humans.

In the Andean northern region of Chile, a recent study was completed concerning the biochemical, immunological and biological characterization of *T. cruzi* (González et al. 1995). Within this region (at Quebrada de Tarapaca, discussed in Chapter 2), autopsies performed on mummies dated around A.D. 500 revealed the presence of clinical manifestations of Chagas' disease (Rothhammer et al. 1985), which indicates a very early adaptation of *T. cruzi* to human habitats.

Clinical surveys indicated that in the lower Andean region of northern Chile the infection rate was low and great evidence of cardiac involvement was detected by alteration of electrocardiograms (Arribada et al. 1990). In the higher Andean region a very high infection rate was detected, but cardiac involvement was lower than that of the lower region (Apt et al. 1987). This indicates the importance of altitude factors in the *T. cruzi* infection causing cardiac involvement (Villarroel et al. 1991). The more benign character of Chagas' disease detected in Chile compared to other endemic areas (Neghme 1982) is significant, either because of the *T. cruzi* strain circulating in each area and/or because of the ancient adaptation of the parasite to the human host in this country and particularly on the Andean highlands of Quebrada de Tarapaca (González et al. 1995:126).

Researchers found more than one type of *T. cruzi* parasite strain in the Chilean highlands; they also found that the different strains had higher or lower parasitemia levels. Each *T. cruzi* strain displayed a unique characteristic. González and colleagues (1995:131) hypothesize that tissue tropism of individual *T. cruzi* strains and geographic distribution of different strains and their source (sylvatic or domestic) may play a role in the wide variety of clinical signs encountered in Chagas' disease (Rassi 1977). Conclusions from the Andean northern of Chile study are as follows:

> Finally, the parasite sample studied here from humans resembles the main ones circulating in humans of other endemic areas of Chile as described before (Solari et al. 1992; Hendriksson et al. 1993; Muñoz et al. 1994), in spite of the fact that other *T. cruzi* populations are also transmitted by the insect vectors and their poor infective capacity in the murine experimental models. This observation probably is explained by a special adaptation of the Zymodeme 30 parasite type in human hosts from the presumably mixed infective *T. cruzi* populations circulating in nature. This observation and the early adaptation of *T. cruzi* to humans in the [Andean] highlands and other endemic areas of Chile as well, compared to other countries, could explain the more benign character of Chagas' disease in this geographic area. The biochemical characterization shows that several *T. cruzi* subpopulations exist in the endemic area of Chile, but it remains to be demonstrated whether the clinical evolution of this parasitism on humans varies depending upon the infective strain involved (Gonzalez et al. 1995:132–33)

Immunization against *T. cruzi*

Immunization against trypanosomes needs to be targeted at the surface membrane of the parasite, which presents a number of considerations. American trypanosomes, such as *T. cruzi*, differ from African trypanosomes and do not employ the dramatic surface modulation seen with African trypanosomes, such as *T. brucei gambiense* and *T. b. rhodesiense*, that cause sleeping sickness. *T. cruzi's* evasive strategies are to share antigens with host cells and to alter host antigens so that when host antibodies attack the parasites they simultaneously attack host cells (Ávila 1994, Brener 1994). This is an evasive function of the surface membrane.

A most vital part of any parasite is its surface, which is the site of nutrient acquisition, the site of dealing with host immunity, and the site where it protects itself from biotic and abiotic components of the environment. The surface membrane of *T. cruzi* as well as similar protozoa exhibits a wide variety of housekeeping functions. For example, it is responsible for ion balance, nutrient transport, and resisting the physical and chemical perils offered by the *vinchuca's* gut. The parasite's surface is also a key participator in the adherence to and penetration of host cells. Moreover, it is this organelle that deals effectively with the host's immune response.

The more that is known about *T. cruzi's* surface, the more we can learn about how it penetrates cells, what it eats, and how it eats. Consequently, extensive research is being done concerning the biochemistry of *T. cruzi's* surface, especially on how it interacts with the host's immune system.

T. cruzi has a very complex life cycle, which is composed of various stages that pass through a multitude of microenvironments within its mammalian and insect hosts. These microenvironments present many hostile elements which must be overcome since they are essential to the parasite as home or transportation and provide the protozoan with the space and nutrients to survive and reproduce. The capabilities of the organism cannot be assumed to be the same in each environment, since the environments differ so dramatically. If *T. cruzi* alters its surface to deal with environments, it also consequently alters the basis for attack by the host immune system. *T. cruzi's* basic survival strategy is alteration of its surface as it passes through various stages within the vector insect—from trypomastigotes in the foregut, to epimastigotes in the midgut, and to metacyclic trypomastigotes in the hindgut, which are passed in the feces and deposited on the skin of the animal/human host, and, within the host, from metacyclics in the blood, to amastigote forms in tissues, to trypo-mastigotes circulating in the blood (see Figure 7).

In comparison, African trypanosomes pass through only two stages, trypo-mastigote and epimastigote. Within a vertebrate host, African trypanosomes multiply as trypomastigotes in the blood and lymph, whereas *T. cruzi* multi-plies intracellularly as amastigotes. African trypanosomes survive by contin-ually varying their coats and presenting new antigens, thereby exhausting the immune system and setting the stage for secondary infections.

African trypanosomes change their surface coat to defeat the immune sys-tem, but American trypanosomes have taken up an intracellular existence and interacted with several broad modulations of vertebrate immune function to evade immunity in more subtle but equally effective ways in terms of its sur-vival. *T. cruzi* doesn't undergo a dramatic alteration of the glycoprotein coat as do African trypanosomes, but it does have many different strains (See Appen-dix 2: Strains of *T. cruzi*). In Bolivia well over a hundred strains of *T. cruzi* have been identified which have different surface architecture. *T. cruzi* uses its sur-face architecture as an immunoprophylactic. For example, once *T. cruzi* trypo-mastigotes have penetrated host cells, surface components protect it from lysosomal enzymes and products of oxidative burst.

The adaptive successes of African and American trypanosomes lie with their surface coat, which is quite able to outsmart immune systems of the host. Generally speaking, the outer surface of any parasite is one of the most impor-tant organs in its symbiotic relationship because it provides an interface be-tween the parasite and its vertebrate and invertebrate hosts. A large measure of the success of trypanosomes lies in their ability to modulate their outer surface in response to attack from host antibodies and immune cells and to hostile components from the environment they encounter in the insect gut and in the cells, fluids, and tissues of a vertebrate host. If prophylactic vaccinations are developed against *T. cruzi* and the African trypanosomes, they will probably have to somehow alter or incapacitate the outer surface of the parasite.

African trypanosomes have coats of glycoprotein, which are capable of pro-ducing thousands of antigenic variations. After African metacyclic trypo-mastigotes have infected a person, the humoral immune system responds by producing antibodies primarily of two classes, IgM and IgG. The IgM class is the first of these defense proteins produced in response to infection. They de-stroy by agglutination and lysis all antigenically identical organisms within a given population of parasites. Some trypomastigotes escape because they have different surface antigens, however, and they quickly reproduce until there is another attack by a new variety of IgM antibodies. Another group survives with antigenic variations on their surface coats, and another IgM antibody contin-gent rushes out to kill them. Eventually, the parasites win this battle because their possibility of variation and survival is greater than the strength of the host's immune system, continually weakened by the stress of the attacks. Moreover, continual lysing of antigens releases toxic substances into the victim's body. Every wave of antibodies quickly becomes useless because the trypanosomes have selected new coats with new antigens which evade the previous antibodies (Katz, Despommier, and Gwadz 1988). In short, African trypanosomes display a "moving target," a continual variation of antigenic coatings, so that just as the host mounts an antibody response to one, another type proliferates (Schmidt and Roberts 1989).

Glycoproteins on *T. cruzi's* Surface

In the parasite *Trypanosoma cruzi*, mucin-like glycoproteins play an important role in the organism's interaction with the surface of the mammalian cell during the invasion process (Di Noia, Sánchez, and Frasch 1995). Mucins are highly glycosylated proteins expressed by most secretory epithelial tissues in vertebrates; but recent research has shown that these gene-encoding molecules have been detected in *Leishmania major* (Murray and Spithill 1991) and in *Trypanosoma cruzi* (Reyes, Pollevick, and Frasch 1994). These mucin-like genes have a defined basic structure and sequence, which allows their inclusion in a gene family.

Trypanosoma cruzi has a family of putative mucin genes whose organization resembles the ones present in mammalian cells (Di Noia, Sánchez, and Frasch 1995). Different parasite isolates have different sets of genes, as defined by their central domain. Much work has been done on the biochemical and functional characterization of mucin-like surface glycoconjugates (Schenkman et al. 1994). These heavily O-glycosylated molecules are Thr-, Ser-, and Pro-rich and are attached to a membrane by a glycophosphatidylinositol anchor (Schenkman et al. 1993). Mucins in *T. cruzi* are the major acceptors of sialic acid in a reaction catalyzed by trans-sialidase. These molecules are involved in the cell-invasion process, probably mediating adhesion of the parasite to the mammalian cell surface (Ruiz et al. 1993, Yoshida et al. 1989). A putative mucin gene in *T. cruzi* has been identified (Reyes et al. 1994), having a small size and encoding five repeat units with the consensus sequence T_8KP_2. In a later study, Di Noia, Sánchez, and Frasch (1995) establish that *T. cruzi* does in fact have a putative mucin gene family resembling the one present in vertebrate cells. Their members have a Thr/Ser/Pro-rich central domain, which might or might not be organized in repetitive units, and highly conserved non-repetitive flanking domains.

In earlier studies (e.g., Snary 1985:144–48), the following glycoprotein or antigens have been found on *T. cruzi's* surface. Lipopeptido phosphoglycan (LPPG) is a complex surface component found on the membrane of epimastigotes. This large complex molecule includes three glycoproteins with a molecular weight (MW) of 37,000, 31,000, and 24,000 (referred to as GP-37, GP-31, and GP-24, respectively). Indirect evidence indicates that LPPG may also be found on amastigotes, because antibodies against LPPG have been found in the serum of patients with Chagas' disease. Generally, epimastigotes are thought to occur only in insects and not in the vertebrate host, although this conclusion is not definitive. The presence of LPPG antibodies in hosts apparently indicates that this glycoprotein is also found on trypanosomes in the host. It is not clear why the current reasoning is that it is found on amastigotes alone and not also on trypomastigotes.

The function of LPPG in *T. cruzi* is not known, but it is postulated that it provides some protection for free-living protozoa from the macroenvironment. Epimastigotes face an environment in the insect's gut with many hostile components. LPPG, then, may be part of the baggage still carried by *T. cruzi* from among the characteristics displayed by free-living ancestors of the parasite. Once the ancestors of American trypanosomes gave up their free-living life-style, perhaps they kept LPPG because it came in handy inside the insect's gut. In other words, it was a pre-adaptive feature allowing them to settle in what would otherwise be a hostile environment.

Glycoprotein (GP-90) is another cell-surface antigen found on all three life-cycle forms—trypomastigote, epimastigote, and amastigote. One parasite-promoting function of GP-90 is that it interferes with complement-mediated lysis of the parasite. Antibodies to GP-90 are found in all patients, and these antibodies do not cross-react with leishmaniasis antigens. Consequently, GP-90 shows great promise as a diagnostic tool to differentiate between Chagas' disease and leishmaniasis in Bolivia, where patients are subject to infection from *T. cruzi* and from *Leishmania* sp. and where diagnostic testing frequently does not discriminate between them.

Another useful glycoprotein, GP-72 (MW 72,000) is specific for epimastigote and metacyclic trypomastigote (infective parasites) insect stages, but it is not found on blood trypomastigotes or intracellular amastigotes. GP-72 is very useful for isolating different strains (zymodemes) of *T. cruzi,* because each strain shows a different concentration of GP-72—the higher the concentration of GP-72, the more pathogenic the strain. Moreover, different strains of the parasite cause different clinical syndromes: some strains tend to megavisceralize and cause megasyndromes; others might concentrate in the heart and nerves.

Antigenic Targets for Immunizations

Glycoprotein (GP) antigens found on *T. cruzi's* coat are considered as antigenic targets for immunizations. Because GP-90 is found in all stages of *T. cruzi's* life cycle, it may be a candidate target of a vaccine against the parasite. Experimentally, acutely infected chagasic mice were vaccinated with such an antibody and did not die; however, they remained infected. Although this vaccine may be suitable to curtail the ravages of acute infection in infants, it is less than adequate for adults who are suffering with chronic infections.

Because GP-72 is found on the surface of infective trypomastigotes, it would be a good antigen to target in the development of a vaccine. The function of GP-72 is demonstrated by the fact that if GP-72 is stripped from the surface of epimastigotes, they are unable to transform into metacyclic trypomastigotes. GP-72 is essential for this transformation process.

Entomologically, GP-72 is valuable for the making of maps plotted according to geographical areas where various strains (zymodemes) of *T. cruzi* are found. The pathology of Chagas' disease is related to zymodemes. From the different regions of Bolivia, triatomines are collected, epimastigotes extracted from infected bugs, and GP-72 measured. This provides a guide to the prevalent strains and pathologies in the departments of Bolivia. Glycoprotein GP-25 is useful in immunodiagnosis and appears on epimastigotes and trypomastigotes.

Another possibility for vaccine involves GP-85, which is thought to be a glycoprotein that allows the parasite to attach itself to the host's cell membranes. If a vaccine can destroy GP-85, the parasite cannot penetrate and attach itself to cells.

With any of these possibilities, a major problem is that antibodies specific to *T. cruzi* antigens also cross-react with human host cells. Therefore, even if it worked in mice, there is the possibility that a vaccine may aggravate the situation by inducing antibodies that cross-react with host cell antigens. Autoimmunity is considered to play a central role in the pathology of Chagas' disease.

Conclusions from research on various biochemical coatings on surfaces of *T. cruzi* indicate that immunoprophylaxis does not appear to be possible for the following reasons (Snary 1985:144–48): scientists have not found a vaccine that induces sterile immunity, and, furthermore, in regard to experimental vaccines, scientists have not established that those tested would not also induce autoantibody production in the host.

The conclusion is that *Trypanosoma cruzi* has evolved to fit an intricately complex niche in the organic world. The biology of this organism is complex, involving intimate interactions with two different hosts which include a variety of different life-cycle stages that exhibit major differences in structural and functional biochemistry. The organism's survival involves highly successful evasive strategies against the human immune system as well as the extraordinary ability to survive in a variety of hostile environments inside insects and humans and to make use of the complex relationship between insects and mammals in the reproduction and transmission of the species.

Prospects for Immunizations

The facts that most of the pathology from Chagas' disease relates to the immune response and that living organisms are necessary for acquired partial immunity present slim possibilities for developing a vaccine against Chagas' disease. To produce a vaccine for Chagas' disease, the following requirements are necessary:

1) Any vaccine should not induce active infection; therefore, immunization with living *T. cruzi* is out of the question. Reasons include the facts that even weaker strains could elicit autoimmune pathology and that weaker strains are not found, only less virulent strains. Moreover, the risk would be much too great to be undertaken by international health organizations.

2) Any vaccine must confer total and sterile protection. Vaccines that have been tried in mice employing either live and attenuated (weakened) parasites, killed intact organisms, or cell homogenates were able only to delay mortality. These vaccines produce partial protection from acute infections and do not provide protection from chronic infections, which in some cases are a more horrible way to die. Nonetheless, partial protection may be important to prevent the high incidence of deaths of children from acute infections.

3) Any vaccine cannot induce an autoimmune response, so the vaccine has to be very specific and exclusionary in targeting *only* parasite antigens and not those that the parasite shares with the host. Any misdirection could lead to creating EVI antibodies that are in themselves sources of pathology in the host. Moreover, the targeted parasite antigen must be essential to the parasite and on its surface throughout its trypomastigote and amastigote forms. This implies highly complicated research and very involved testing of vaccines, with the result most likely being high-cost vaccine production that will be unaffordable to people in endemic areas.

If and when a suitable antigen is found and vaccines are developed with it, there are most likely some strains of *T. cruzi* to which the chosen antigen may be ineffective in inducing protective immunity. Even if all strains are affected, there will be mutant individuals which the vaccine will not affect, leading to the evolution of resistant strains of the parasite. These "super" *T. cruzi* will continue on.

4) Any vaccine should not be immunosuppressive. Because *T. cruzi* antigens induce polyclonal activation, they are followed by a period of immunosuppression. Implications are that if children are vaccinated and immunosuppression follows, they are subject to other infections. A related problem is that polyclonal activation can also cause severe inflammation, lesions, and fever.

Conclusions include that a vaccine for *T. cruzi* cannot be a crude extract, and that to fulfill the above criteria the vaccine is going to have to feature a highly sophisticated, very carefully selected, and very specific and essential antigen of *T. cruzi* found on all its forms. Moreover, the antibodies produced from this vaccine antigen must be able to destroy 100 percent of trypomastigotes within minutes after the bite of a triatomine bug. If one trypomastigote gets into a cell, it can reproduce there and establish an infection.

Regarding Bolivia and many tropical areas, administration of such a vaccine will be difficult because of its inevitable high cost. Vaccine administration in underdeveloped countries is a problem; improper storage and/or administration can result in contamination or destruction of the vaccine or its selection for resistant individuals in parasite populations.

Triatoma infestans

Most people, except perhaps entomologists, would describe *Triatoma infestans* as ugly. It is about one inch long (equal to the combined length of 12,500 T. cruzi trypomastigotes). It has two pairs of long, bent legs covered with fine hairs protruding from an oval-shaped abdomen. A third pair of legs extends like arms from a trapezoidal, horny thorax adjacent to protruding bulbous eyes (see Figure 3). The legs are angularly bent, with thick femurs, long tibias, and short tarsus and nails, enabling it to rapidly move across floors and walls, cling to ceilings, and carry many times its weight in blood. Transparent parchmentlike wings cover the center of its back like a cloak. Extended, they are inadequate for flying, but are used for gliding from heights and for mounting during sex. A pincher-shaped head protrudes from the thorax, with a proboscis folded back underneath which swings down, half-open like a jack-knife, to pierce the skin and suck blood.

A principal biological characteristic of *Triatoma infestans,* as well as other triatomines, is obligate bloodsucking by nymphs and adults of both sexes. Their great success in obtaining blood meals is due primarily to their being nocturnal predators as well as to the biochemical and physiological adaptation of species members to profoundly different ecological niches. They insert their prosces into sleeping mammals, employing a generalized anesthetic so as not to alarm their victims while they leisurely fill up on blood. Different hormones such as ecdysone and juvenile hormones regulate the biochemical and physiological changes in the tegument as they molt and transform through five stages to adulthood.

Blood provides triatomines with a protein- and lipid-rich diet (Brenner 1987). Their metabolism has adapted to this diet, and their energy requirements and ATP (adenosine triphosphate) production are provided largely by fatty acid metabolism and the tricarboxylic acid cycle. Consequently, lipid metabolism is more important than carbohydrate metabolism in triatomines. Their use of fatty acids as a source of ATP production in substitution of carbohydrates has many advantages including large fuel stores and high ATP yield per molecule.

Triatomines vary in color and size, according to species. Colors vary from light yellow to black; some animals have different patterns of grey, green, orange, white, or yellow spots, principally on the connexivum. Size varies within the subfamily from 5 to 45 millimeters (about the size of an average cockroach) and is a key characteristic in distinguishing species as well as sex, with adult males being larger than females.

Triatomines make a squeaky shrill sound by rubbing their suction tube against ridges in its protective sheath under their bellies. Their front wings are leathery and their back wings are membranous, at best serving to glide several hundred meters. Although there is great variation between species in the use of wings for flight, some are capable of flying considerable distances, which is important in the colonization of new habitats and in the spreading of Chagas' disease.

Nymphs are wingless and remain in the area where the eggs are deposited. Nymphs, as well as adults, are superb crawlers, with three pairs of highly developed legs. Because the nymphs are small, they can more easily hide, enter through bedding, and take a blood meal than the larger adults. Mosquito netting is ineffective against nymphs, which can crawl underneath the netting or arise from under the mattress.

Triatomines search out warm-blooded animals in rooms and corrals by means of temperature gradients detected by their antennae. Carbon dioxide produces increased activity of the bugs. Another factor attracting them are feces left by a previous bug. *Triatoma infestans* and *Rhodnius prolixus* habitually defecate after a blood meal, and pheromones have been found in their feces. (Pheromones are hormones whose presence communicates certain biological activity response between members of the same species; a good example is a bitch in heat attracting male dogs.) Pheromonal attraction can be greatly lessened by house and personal hygiene, thus eliminating fecal matter for the insects' sensors.

Pheromones not only attract unfed bugs to a blood source, their aggregation toward fecal matter may also be important in the maintenance of the correct gut fauna by coprophagy (Molyneux and Ashford 1983:79). As is the case with many hematophagous insects, *Triatoma infestans* and *Rhodnius prolixus* need bacterial and fungal symbionts for digesting blood.

Instar and Life Stages of Triatomines

Using *Rhodnius prolixus* as an example, the sex life of female triatomines begins one to three days after the bug's emergence into the adult stage (Molyneux and Ashford 1983:81). Males develop a bit more slowly and inseminate females five to nine days after their emergence as adults. As mentioned, wings are sprouted and used only at the adult stage, primarily for copulation and reproduction purposes. Flying necessitates large amounts of energy. The male flies on top of the female to embrace her with his legs, and then slides alongside, inserting his reproductive organ into her. Females are inseminated shortly after molting and can produce viable eggs for one year after separation from males (Perlowagora-Szumlewiecz 1969). Multiple copulation does not affect egg production. Although blood meals are necessary for viable egg production, unfed mothers may lay fertile eggs if they maintained a high nutritional status as nymphs.

Within ten to twenty days, the female deposits her eggs. In laboratory conditions, the eggs of *T. infestans* are clearly visible—ivory colored and about half the size of a grain of rice. Laboratory-fed females lay anywhere from 80 to 150 eggs; in natural environments the crucial variable for egg production is the availability of blood meals. Egg production also varies among species, with certain species producing up to 2,000 eggs (Molyneux and Ashford 1983:80). *Triatoma infestans* adults live from eight to sixteen months and lay an average of 240 eggs (Zeledón and Rabinovich 1981). The life span of *T. infestans* in Bolivia has been estimated at three years (Jemio Alarico and Ariel Sempertegui, interview 6/18/1991).

Females lay their eggs in their microhabitat, in such places as cracks or crevices in the homes, burrows, or nests of the mammalian or avian hosts of the bugs. Some eggs are laid loose and others are glued in clumps to a surface. The eggs hatch in from one to two weeks, depending on the temperature. The emergent triatomine will pass through five nymphal instars on its way to growing wings and becoming an adult. An instar is the period between the nymph stages in the life of an insect. During the nymph stages, triatomines crawl. The nymph stages can take anywhere from four to forty-eight months, depending on the temperature, humidity, and frequency and volume of blood meals. Nymphs can imbibe between six to twelve times their own weight in blood.

Triatomines need an adequate blood meal for growth and development during each of the five immature stages and for oviposition by the adult females (Marsden 1983:266). The content of blood meals increases with each nymph stage, adult bugs drinking about 100–300 mg of blood, if possible. Among certain species, fifth-instar nymphs can consume more blood than adults, and female adults more than male adults (Molyneux and Ashford 1983:81). Instars from the third to fifth stage are frequently used in xenodiagnosis. At all stages they take many times their weight in blood, and the molt from a fifth-stage larva to an adult is particularly dependent on a large blood meal.

Although triatomines can go for months without blood meals, many take their meals after seven days, which provides sufficient time for *T. cruzi* to have multiplied in the bug with its six-to-fifteen-day reproduction cycle. When their hindgut becomes extended with feces, triatomines seek out blood meals, which is a distinct advantage for the parasitic *T. cruzi*.

Triatomines can live a long time without blood; *T. infestans* is able to tolerate longer periods of starvation throughout the later instars. During the fourth and fifth instars the organism can survive up to seven months without food. Younger nymphs need blood meals more frequently in order to pass through the stages to adulthood. Long periods of starvation don't affect the persistence or viability of trypanosomes in the insect's gut (Molyneux and Ashford 1983:80). *T. cruzi* have no known pathological effects on *vinchucas,* and to what degree this parasitic relationship negatively affects a triatomine's metabolism is not known. Conversely, *T. cruzi* have adapted to the gut of *vinchucas,* an environment equally as hostile as that of their human hosts.

Of epidemiological significance, *vinchucas* are capable of being vectors for *T. cruzi* throughout all their nymph stages. However, they have to become initially infected from ingestion of the parasite in a blood meal from a host; they are not infected from birth. It follows that there will be lower degrees of infection among early nymph stages, because some have not taken as many blood meals. Significantly, the proportion of infected bugs rises with age, and the adult infection rate can be used as a convenient measure of transmission risk in the field (Minter 1978b; Marsden et al. 1982).

In Tarija, Bolivia, for example, *vinchucas* within the nymph stages had an infection rate of 25 percent, whereas within the adult stage it was 37 percent (Valencia 1990a). The infection rate of vectors, however, greatly depends on the degree of infection found in hosts. In certain regions of Bolivia, as high as 90 percent of adult *vinchucas* are infected, as are 50 to 60 percent of the nymphs. Thus, variables affecting the rate of bugs infected with *T. cruzi* are its developmental stage, access to blood meals, and the incidence of infected hosts. In a household colonized with *vinchucas* which has one person with Chagas' disease, it is only a matter of time until all members will become infected.

Although the feeding activities of domestic vectors are not well known, Rabinovitch et al. (1979) have calculated that within a house with a typical insect population of *Rhodnius prolixus,* an adult would be bitten an average of nine times each night and in exceptional circumstances up to fifty-eight times. Bolivians can take some encouragement from the fact that *Rhodnius prolixus* is much more voracious than *Triatoma infestans,* whose populations average only two bites per adult per night. The least bothersome is *Panstrongylus megistus;* Marsden (1983:258) sat for two nights in a house with many *P. megistus* present on the walls and was approached by only a single bug. Some bugs remained on the same spot of the wall for as long as forty-eight hours.

Triatomines are biologically equipped to find blood meals. Heat-sensitive antennae and pheromonal communication direct them to sleeping mammals and birds at night. Frequently, they glide back and forth across a room, detect warmth from a human and gently land upon his or her body or face. Probing the warm surface to sample underlying fluids, sensilla in the insect's proboscis search for adenosine triphosphate (ATP) or other appropriate engorgement factors. If successful, the *vinchuca* injects its needle-sharp proboscis coated with a general anesthetic and decoagulant so that it can easily and leisurely (up to thirty minutes) drink blood, as much as seven times the bug's weight, until its gut is filled to a certain capacity determined by abdominal stretch, which triggers the molting cycle in nymphs (Molyneux and Ashford 1983:79). Abdominal stretch of the midgut with blood also triggers peristalsis and the triatomine defecates on its victim's face, adding insult to injury (as well as exchange of parasites for blood).

Genetic factors of different triatomine species regulate their susceptibility to parasites, parasite density in the feces, and defecation time (WHO 1991). Defecation time of triatomines is crucial for the transmission of parasites to hosts. Scratching the wound, the victim spreads the fecal matter over the bite site, allowing parasites to enter through the wound or the irritated surrounding skin.

After filling up with blood, *T. infestans* defecates within minutes near the bite site. Other triatomines defecate some time after the blood meal and away from the bite site, which lessens chances of spreading infection (Wood 1951). Studies of three species have also shown important differences not only between species but also between the different instars and sexes within the species (Dias 1956, Zeledón et al. 1975, Pippin 1970). After a blood meal, *R. prolixus* was the first to defecate; it also defecates more frequently, within one-, five-, or ten-minute intervals, than other species. The mean times for the first defecation and the percentage of individuals which defecated within this species was surpassed only by the adult stages of *T. infestans*. *T. dimidiata* was slower to defecate and did so less frequently after meals than the other two species. However, *T. dimidiata* defecated more during the meal, taking longer to feed and interrupting the blood meal more frequently to defecate. Females of all three species defecated sooner, more frequently, and in greater number than did males. *T. dimidiata* females and fifth-instar nymphs had the highest defecation average. *T. infestans* defecated throughout all instar stages but mostly so during the fourth instar stage and less so as an adult. *R. prolixus* also defecated throughout all instar stages, with the males defecating decisively less.

A defecation index has been established by Zeledón (1983:329) for each of the instars, which permits an easy visualization of the differences between instars of the same species or of different species. The index is the mean number of defecations in ten minutes, multiplied by the percentage of insects which defecate in ten minutes divided by 100. The high defecation index of *T. infestans* and *R. prolixus* is a major reason why these triatomines are so successful in transmitting *T. cruzi*.

Nonetheless, defecation at later times also presents health hazards in that

House Infestation in Bolivia

A national epidemiological study of housing and Chagas' disease in Bolivia was completed by Angel Valencia, Abraham Gemio Alarico, and John Banda Navia in 1990. They studied various localities from 1,000 to 11,500 feet above sea level and populations stratified into urban populations, dense population centers, and dispersed populations. Moreover, they also considered the ecological factors of microenvironments. In all, they studied 109 localities and 3,236 houses. The populations within these houses were 18,172 people (an average of 5.6 per household) and 17,588 animals (25 percent dogs, 13 percent cats, 27 percent pigs, and 35 percent guinea pigs). From the human population, they obtained 9,547 serological samples on filtered paper and also conducted 7,996 electrocardiographic studies (Valencia 1990a:7).

Regarding housing infestation, Valencia (1990a:29–30) and co-workers first noted the exact time that their searches began, then they started in the dormitory, going from left to right in the room, and then proceeded in a clockwise pattern to inspect the other rooms. Employing flashlights, they examined every surface, including walls, ceiling or roof, bedding, furniture, stored clothing, wall hangings, and domestic items. Wearing plastic gloves and using anatomical pinchers, they captured the *vinchucas* by the thorax and placed them in separate boxes designating where they had been captured. They annotated house number, date, name of the head of the household, locality, province, department, and how the specimen was caught.[1] Likewise, inspectors proceeded outside the house (peridomicile). Wearing thick leather gloves, they removed rocks, uncovered logs, removed firewood, and turned over adobes to capture *vinchucas*. Averages were computed from how many *vinchucas* were captured per hour per inspector, not counting time spent explaining procedures to household members or in filling out forms. At no time were irritants used to drive out bugs.

Indices were established in the following manner: the index of infestation for a particular locale was determined by the percentage of the places examined in relation to the places infested; the index of infestation of houses was determined by the percentage of the houses examined in relation to houses infested; the index of density was determined by the percentage of houses examined for triatomines in relation to the number of triatomines captured; and the index of accumulation was the percentage of houses infested with triatomines in relation to the total number of triatomines captured (Valencia 1990a:27).

These indices are at best estimates, given the variables of the investigators' ability to catch bugs and various environmental factors, including the accessibility of hiding places and the temperature. A more accurate but methodologically unrealistic accumulation index would be one in which the house is enclosed in plastic, sprayed, and dismantled, as was done in Panama for one house, which contained a reported 100,000 triatomines (Sousa and Johnson 1971). Another method would be for entomologists to study the carrying capacity of different environments in Bolivia for *vinchucas*, which then could be used as a guide. An area's carrying capacity implies that *vinchucas* maintain fairly stable populations determined by the availability of hiding places and blood meals. If they overpopulate, they are unable to nourish themselves and do not progress along the instar stages to adulthood, when they are able to lay eggs.

A national epidemiological study by Valencia (1990a) found that rates of infestation varied greatly according to the type of housing and density of population throughout Bolivia. This suggests that the presently high rates of Chagas' disease are as much a function of improper housing, crowding, and poverty as they are of climatic zones. It has long been commonly believed in Bolivia that Chagas' disease was limited to lower regions in Bolivia. To evaluate housing and population variables, the following classifications were made (see Table 1): category "x" were superior houses, with improved floors, stuccoed walls, and ceilings with metal roofs; category "y" were houses with improved floors, walls plastered with earth, a ceiling of wood or cloth, and a metal roof; category "z" were houses with dirt floors and straw or palm roofs without ceilings. Densities of population were classified into strata. Stratum "A" (urban population) consisted of communities with 5,000 or more inhabitants. Stratum "B" (populated centers) were communities of varying sizes, with clusters of houses (some urbanization, a plaza, church, school, etc.). Stratum "B" was divided into "B^1," with populations of from 1,000 to 4,999 inhabitants, and "B^2," with populations from 200 to 999 inhabitants. Stratum "C" consisted of dispersed populations of less than 199 inhabitants.

In general, Table 1 indicates that 28 percent of the total houses investigated in Bolivia were infested by triatomine bugs, with an accumulation index of ten (9.97) triatomines per infested household. The accumulation index varies little between the different strata, indicating that triatomines populate to a carrying capacity (the optimal population size that a particular environment can support). Urban centers, Stratum A, have the lowest infestation rate (10.81 percent), accumulation index (7.6), and density index (0.8). These lower figures are also attributable to the fact that investigators disproportionately studied category x housing (1,045 houses), compared to category y (129 houses) and category z (219 houses) found within urban centers. A counter objection, how-

TABLE 1
INDEX OF COMMUNITY AND HOUSE INFESTATION IN BOLIVIA
(adapted from Valencia 1990a:36)

	TOTAL	STRATA			
		A	B^1	B^2	C
TYPE OF HOUSING	3,286	1,393	358	309	1,226
Category x	1,454	1,045	139	58	212
Category y	638	129	84	82	343
Category z	1,194	219	135	169	671
Infested Houses	930	150	99	138	542
Entomology Indices:					
Infestation (percent)	28.3	10.81	27.71	45.51	45.41
Density (number)	3.4	0.8	2.5	5.2	5.4
Accumulation (")	9.97	7.6	9.0	11.4	11.9

ever, is that urban centers have fewer houses in category y and z; however, this is unlikely in Bolivia with its massive urban migration and its accompanying poverty. Peri-urban areas of Cochabamba, Santa Cruz, and La Paz (El Alto) indicate rising rates of *vinchuca* infestation and Chagas' disease.

Within Stratum B^1, communities from 1,000 to 4,999 inhabitants, the infestation rate was 27.71 percent, which was close to the national average. These communities are market, provincial, and regional centers scattered throughout the plains, valleys, and mountains of Bolivia. Some communities have pre-Columbian origins, while others were founded during the colonial period as *reducciones* and *pueblos* to administer the colonies. Spanish *conquistadores* attempted to control Andeans by clustering them into religious indoctrination centers *(reducciones)* and municipal centers *(pueblos)*. These houses are constructed of adobe, with thatched roofs and dirt or brick floors, and many stand as architectural monuments to another generation. They have become centers for triatomines. Rarely does one find that the *vecinos* (villagers from *pueblos,* as distinct from *campesinos,* or farmers) replace these antiquated buildings with new ones; rather, they build alongside the old ones, thus providing areas for triatomines. This helps explain why 139 families are living in category x housing and an almost equal number, 135 families, are living in category z housing. It also explains why the density index (which is derived from the number of bugs captured divided by the houses investigated) is high (2.5). The fact that housing in B^1 is fairly divided between categories x, y, and z places all residents at risk, because triatomines will travel over 1,000 meters in search of blood meals.

Similar explanations more readily apply to stratum B^2, which has 45.51

percent of the houses infested, a density rate (5.2) double that of B^1, and an accumulation index of 11.4. Within B^2, 55 percent of the homes fall within category z and 27 percent within category y, which increases the probability for infestation.

The peasants in stratum C suffer the same risk as those in stratum B^2, with similar indices for infestation (45.51 percent), density (5.2), and accumulation (11.9); also, 55 percent of households fall within category z. The major difference is that the sample (1,226) in stratum C is much larger than the sample (309) in B^2. An obvious conclusion is that Bolivians living in small communities (200 to 1,000 inhabitants), smaller hamlets, and farms suffer from high rates of triatomine infestation due to their living conditions and large number of domestic animals. More than half the houses within these strata have dirt floors, thatched roofs, cloth ceilings, and adobe walls, usually unplastered. Also, 17,588 animals were counted (25 percent dogs, 13 percent cats, 27 percent pigs, and 35 percent guinea pigs). The census did not include poultry such as chickens, ducks, and geese that attract and provide blood meals for triatomines but are not subject to, or hosts of, Chagas' disease. Bird nests also provide favored hiding places for triatomines.

Even though lower-class strata have a higher incidence of infestation than other strata, within urban centers and peri-urban peripheral areas triatomines are spreading because of massive migration, both permanent and seasonal, from rural areas in Bolivia to industrialized areas. Housing can be even worse in these crowded areas, with scores of people living in rapidly constructed dwellings.

The percentage of vectors positive for *T. cruzi* in parts of Bolivia was indicated by a study done in 1991 by the SOH/CCH Chagas Control Pilot Program (1994). It conducted a baseline study within the departments of Chuquisaca, Cochabamba, and Tarija of 1,037 houses (93.6 percent coverage of the areas' 1,108 houses); examined 4,128 blood samples from persons living in the houses (64 percent were seropositive for Chagas' disease); and collected 13,000 peri- and intradomiciliary vectors. My analysis of these results indicates that Cochabamba had the lowest percentage of houses with basic services (only 3 percent had latrines, and none had potable water and electricity) and the lowest percentage (38.6) of houses infested by vectors positive for *T. cruzi*, with 46 percent of the insects carrying the parasite. The availability of latrines, potable water, and electricity does not appear to correlate with infection rates. Tarija has the highest percentage of electricity, 55.6 percent, and the highest percentage—50 percent—of intradomiciliary vectors positive for *T. cruzi*. This calls into question the notion that lighting would keep photosensitive triatomines outside of the house.

Environmental and climatic factors play a key role in the epidemiology of

Chagas' disease. The Department of Tarija is a sub-Andean region, around 6,400 feet in elevation, with a warm, dry winter season. Temperature fluctuates from 64 to 77°F, and the area receives 28 inches of rain a year, beginning in October and subsiding in March (Muñoz 1977). This climate is preferred by triatomines, as there are no severe cold spells to immobilize the insects. The principal cultivation is of semitropical fruits, coca, coffee, grapes, and cocoa, and many of these plants provide nesting sites for triatomines. Some of this region has been cleared for cattle range, destroying wildlife and plants and forcing triatomines to invade houses. Less hospitable to *vinchucas,* the Department of Cochabamba is a mesothermic valley (at 8,310 feet) of the Cordillera Cochabamba. Temperatures fluctuate from 54 to 72°F, and rainfall is 26 inches, falling mainly between November and March. Principal cultivation is of corn, potatoes, wheat, barley, fruits, and vegetables. The Department of Chuquisaca is a sub-Andean temperate zone with a median temperature of 59°F and an average altitude of 8,200 feet above sea level. This department also includes lower regions, which might explain its high triatomine infestation and infection rates discussed in Chapter 8.

House Infestation in Latin America

Similar statistics to those in Bolivia (see Appendix 5: House Infestation in Bolivia) are found in endemic areas for Chagas' disease in other countries of Central and South America (Briceño-León 1990). For Central America, equally high infestation rates of from 30 to 70 percent are reported for three-fourths of El Salvador (OPS 1982:3); 25 percent of *vinchuca* bugs examined there were infected with *T. cruzi*. In endemic areas of Honduras 15 percent of houses are infested (Ponce 1984), and one vector, *T. dimidiata*, has spread to urban settings of the capital, where a family of middle-class professionals reported an acute case of Chagas' disease in 1989 (Briceño-León 1990:24). In Costa Rica, 35 percent of the houses are infested, with an average of 22 triatomines per house (Zeledón et al. 1975). Some 31 percent of the triatomines and 12 percent of the people of Costa Rica are infected with *T. cruzi*. Six percent of the population in Guatemala are infected with *T. cruzi;* and, in Panama, 3 to 22 percent are infected (WHO 1985). (See Appendix 7.)

In South America, 100 percent of the houses in endemic areas of Argentina are infested with *T. cruzi*, and 8 percent of children under eight years are infected with Chagas' disease (Pavlone et al. 1988:103–5). Around 30 percent of the houses in the northern half of Chile are infested with *vinchucas*, and 17 percent of the insects carried *T. cruzi* (Schofield, Apt, and Miles 1982; Flores et al. 1983; Schenone et al. 1985). In Uruguay, Chagas' infection rates range from 1 to 7 percent for people over twelve years old (Salvatella 1986); and, in Paraguay, all rural areas are endemic for the disease, with infection rate percentages between 22 and 72 percent being reported (Arias et al. 1988; WHO 1985).

Even though Brazil has made a concerted effort to prevent Chagas' disease, it ranks as one of the most endemic areas in Latin America. About 4.5 percent of the rural population have antibodies against the parasite; 5 million Brazilians have Chagas' disease and another 25 million are at risk. In the Federal District of Brazil, 4.3 percent of all deaths are attributed to Chagas' disease (Dias 1987, Pereira 1984).

In Peru, endemic regions are Arequipa, Moquegua, and Tacna, with 12 percent infection rates. Colombia has an even higher infection rate of 16 percent of the houses infested with triatomines, and 30 percent in the Departamento del Norte de Santander.

Venezuela has more than 1 million people with Chagas' disease. Roberto Briceño-León (1990) presents a carefully researched analysis of the relationship of housing to Chagas' disease in Venezuela. Within the last fifty years, Venezuela has had zones where 54 percent of the people were seropositive for Chagas' disease. One epidemiological study conducted between 1959 and 1965 indicated that within the 35-to-44-year-old age group 79 percent of those tested had antibodies against *T. cruzi*, and within the 5-to-14-year-old age group 15 percent were infected. Fortunately, these figures have dropped significantly since the 1970s because of the use of insecticides: within the group from birth to 9 years of age infection rates have lowered from 20.5 percent in 1959–1965 to 1.3 percent in 1980–1982; the rates have dropped from 28.4 percent to 2.7 percent in the group aged from 10 to 19 years. Levels of house infestation have also lowered considerably—from 73.2 percent of the huts and 31.1 percent of the houses at the beginning of the program in 1970 to 22.1 percent of the huts and 5.6 percent of the houses being infected in 1976 (Sequeda et al. 1986).

In Venezuela, initial success in the late 1970s led to diminishing insecticide use in the 1980s; it dropped from 74 percent coverage in 1980 to 11 percent in 1984 (Briceño-León 1990:29). Houses again became increasingly infested, in part because depletion of forests and sylvatic animals in Venezuela pressured triatomines to search for domestic sites for blood meals. This has been demonstrated in the Municipal Bergantín, Estado Anzoátegui, where insecticides were used from 1970 until 1973, followed by three years without spraying insecticides. The rate of house infestation by triatomines increased from 2.8 percent to 11.4 percent, and hut infestation went from 10 percent to 50 percent.

Vector Species of *T. cruzi* in the Americas

Vinchucas belong to the Triatominae subfamily of the Reduviidae family of the order Hemiptera, which contains over 4,000 species of large bloodsucking insects. *Vinchucas* are like squash bugs, another species of reduviid, but not a vector of *T. cruzi,* found on garden plants in the United States. Being hemipteran, *vinchucas* possess two pairs of wings and characteristic mouth parts adapted to piercing and sucking; they also undergo incomplete metamorphosis. There are 105 species of Triatominae in the Americas; they are clustered into tribes with thirteen genera, and over half of these species have been reported to be infected with *T. cruzi* (see WHO 1991:81–86 for list and location).

The Triatominae species most responsible for Chagas' disease in South America are, in order of importance, *Triatoma infestans, Rhodnius prolixus, Panstrongylus megistus, Triatoma brasiliensis, Triatoma sordida,* and *Triatoma dimidiata*—with *Rhodnius pallescens* as the principal vector in Central America and Panama. The principal reason for their abundance is that these triatomines have adopted domiciliary habits.

The interaction between the different vectors, different strains of *T. cruzi,* and hosts is an important parameter affecting the susceptibility of a vector to infection (WHO 1991). The vectors' ability to adapt to a domiciliary habitat and its susceptibility to harboring *T. cruzi* are principal determinants of its vectorial capacity. Factors influencing the vector's susceptibility include genetic factors which regulate variances for each species concerning the susceptibility and intensity of infection, parasite density in the feces, and time of defecation. Local parasite strains more readily infect local vector species than do strains from other endemic areas, and vectors are capable of "selecting" subpopulations of *T. cruzi* from a natural heterogeneous population, which affects the parasite's pathogenicity in human hosts. The morphological form of the trypomastigote ingested also influences the infection in that the "stout" forms seem to be more infective to the vector than are the "slender" forms, which seem to be more infective to the host. Feeding habits of vectors also influence vector infection.

Other important susceptibility factors include the stage and age of the insect vector, the climate, the blood-meal size, the number of parasites ingested, the ability of the parasite to establish rectal gland infections in the vector, and parasite transformation in the insect's digestive tract. After triatomines are infected, they remain carriers of *T. cruzi* for the rest of their lives, and they show no significant biological differences from uninfected triatomines. The insect apparently is not affected pathogenically (WHO 1991).

Within the triatomine subfamily there are fourteen genera and 111 species of blood-sucking bugs. The vast majority are found in Central and South America, where thirteen genera and 103 species of triatomines have been reported and over half have been reported naturally infected with *Trypanosoma cruzi:* sixty-eight species have been recorded as infected with *Trypanosoma cruzi,* twenty-three with *T. rangeli,* two with *T. vespertilionis,* one with *T. conorrhini,* and four with *Blastocrithidia* (Carcavallo 1987:15–17; Molyneux and Ashford 1983:78–84). Asian triatomines have not been reported as carrying *T. cruzi,* and the only known Asian vector of a trypanosome is *Triatoma rubrofasciata,* which is associated with the transmission of the rat trypanosome *T. (Megatrypanum) conorrhini* in Japan.

The three genera with the greatest epidemiological significance are *Rhodnius,* which is distinguished from other genera of Triatominae by its long head, with antennae inserted at the front (Lent and Wygodzinsky 1979); *Triatoma,* which have intermediate-length heads, with antennae inserted midway between the eyes and the clypeus; and *Panstrongylus,* which have short, robust heads with antennae extending immediately in front of the eyes.

Triatoma infestans is the most widespread domestic species and the most important vector of Chagas' disease in Argentina, Chile, Bolivia, Brazil, and Uruguay (also discussed in Appendix 4: *Triatoma infestans*). Generally adaptable, *T. infestans* has the unique advantage of being euribiotic (adaptable to many ecologic zones), eurithermic (adaptable to different temperatures), euriphagic (adaptable to a wide variety of hosts and feeding habits) as well as being relatively eurihydric (adaptable to varying humidity). It occupies the greatest climatic range of triatomines, from arid highlands in Andean countries and temperate plains in Argentina to the dry tropics in northeastern Brazil. It is the oldest-domiciliated triatomine species, being now restricted to artificial human ecotopes in most of its distribution area but still thriving in sylvatic ecotopes.

Triatoma infestans' long-standing adaptation to human habitations and its ability to tolerate many ecotopes have enabled it to disperse with migrating human populations. Most common in poor adobe houses, it nests in the thatched or straw roofs, in cracks in the mud walls, and in areas between the roof and walls. It also colonizes cement-block or brick houses, getting into crevices or breeding in household belongings. In Bolivia, blood meals commonly are taken from resident hosts (humans, chickens, dogs, cats, and guinea pigs) 84–99 percent of the time. In Chile, 69 percent of *T. infestans'* blood meals are from humans, who act as the main reservoir host of the parasite. In

Argentina, 25–49 percent of triatomine feeds are from dogs, which have become the main parasite reservoir for domestic transmission of Chagas' disease there (WHO 1991).

Rhodnius prolixus is the next most important vector of Chagas' disease in much of tropical America. Like *T. infestans*, it has evolved and adapted to domiciliary habitats. *R. prolixus* is a native of northern South America, where it occupies many sylvatic arboreal habitats associated with mammals and birds that nest in palm trees or bromeliads (WHO 1991). However, it is present exclusively inside houses in a number of Central American countries and in parts of Mexico. In its domiciliary habitat, it feeds mainly on the blood of humans and chickens, and to a lesser extent on cats and dogs. In its sylvatic habitat, it feeds mainly on opossums and rodents. Because of its preference for nesting in palm trees, it also likes to nest in palm-thatched roofs as well as in cracks in walls and in household goods.

Panstrongylus megistus is a distant third to *Triatoma infestans* and *Rhodnius prolixus* as a carrier of *T. cruzi*, being limited to Central America, northern South America, and the forests of coastal Brazil. It is a stenohydric species, endemic in sylvatic ecotopes and sometimes in peridomestic structures. In northeastern Brazil, humans have deforested its natural ecotopes, thus helping make it an important domiciliary species. One indication of this is that in southern and central Brazil blood meals from humans account for only 14–30 percent of the total feeds of bugs collected in domestic and peridomestic sites (birds and rodents were more important blood sources); while toward the northeast intense deforestation has destroyed the natural habitats of *P. megistus* and it has become an important domiciliary species, taking an increasing number of blood meals from humans (WHO 1991).

Also in northeastern Brazil, *Triatoma brasiliensis* is the most important vector of *T. cruzi*, being highly susceptible to infection. It is found in sylvatic and peridomestic habitats, especially rocky areas and cattle shelters, and it has infected rodents and goats. Birds are its principal blood source, followed by humans.

T. sordida is another species found throughout southern Bolivia, Paraguay, northern Argentina, and central and southern Brazil that has extended its range northwards and southwards because of intense deforestation of its original home. Originally a sylvatic and peridomestic species that fed mainly on birds, it is becoming increasingly domiciliated in southeastern and central Brazil, taking 16–32 percent of its blood meals from humans (WHO 1991).

Triatoma dimidiata is an important vector in Central America and parts of Mexico. It is a domiciliary species found in wooden houses, woodpiles, and earthen floors. It prefers to feed upon human blood, but it also feeds upon rodents, dogs, chickens, and opossums.

Rhodnius pallescens has become increasingly domiciliated, invading houses from its breeding places in palm trees. In Panama, 59 percent of its blood feeds were from humans, followed by preferred feeding on opossums and poultry. Chagas' disease has been more on the increase in central Panama than in western areas of that country because of the association of *R. pallescens* with the opossum (*Didelphis marsupialis*). In western Panama, the principal vector of Chagas' disease is *Triatoma dimidiata.*

In the United States, triatomines thus far have not adapted to household ecotopes (Ryckman 1986). *Rhodnius prolixus* and *Triatoma dimidiata* are the most important vector species from Mexico to northern South America. In Ecuador, *Triatoma dimidiata* is the primary domiciliary vector species. *Rhodnius prolixus* is the main vector in Colombia, French Guiana, Guyana, Suriname, and Venezuela. *Triatoma venosa* and *T. maculata* are found in homes in Colombia but have only secondary importance. In Peru, major vectors are *Panstrongylus lignarius* in the north and *T. infestans* in the south. *P. megistus* is found in limited areas in Bolivia and Paraguay. *T. sordida* covers the eastern part of Bolivia, a broad band in southern Brazil, and areas in Argentina, Paraguay, and Uruguay (WHO 1991).

Several species of triatomines are naturally infected with *T. cruzi* in Brazil. As in Bolivia, *T. infestans* is the most important, and it has dispersed northwards, reaching the northeastern states of Pernambuco and Parába. Second in importance, *P. megistus* has a wide geographical distribution and high rates of natural infection. It is domiciliary in parts of northeastern and eastern Brazil. In northeastern Brazil, *T. brasiliensis* is the main vector, with *T. sordida* and *T. pseudomaculata* generally replacing the main domiciliary species after fumigation. *T. sordida* and *T. pseudomaculata* have low rates of natural infection with *T. cruzi.*

Percentages of infected triatomines are smaller in countries of Central America than in South America, especially Bolivia and Brazil, where averages are around 50 percent. Table 2 shows the infection rate of triatomine bugs with *T. cruzi* parasites in Central America.

T. dimidiata and *R. prolixus* frequently harbor the Chagas' parasite in Central America. *T. dimidiata* has a much higher rate of infection than *R. prolixus* in El Salvador and Nicaragua; but, in Honduras, the rates of infection of both species are similar, 34.7 percent and 32.2 percent, respectively, for *R. prolixus* and *T. dimidiata*. In Costa Rica, *T. dimidiata* is the principal vector, with an infection rate of 30.9 percent; and, in Panama, *R. pallescens* is the principal vector, with an infection rate of 32.7 percent. Within the Panama Canal zone and the provinces of Panama, Colon, Chiriquí, and Bocas del Toro, percentages of infected *R. pallescens* ranged from 68.7 to 84.1 percent (Sousa and Johnson 1971). In one house alone, approximately 100,000 triatomines were found.

Table 2
Rates of T. cruzi Vectors in Central America
(Cedillos 1987:47)

Countries	Triatomine Sp.	Number	% pos.	Source
Costa Rica	*T. dimidiata*	3276	30.9	Zeledón et al. 1975.
El Salvador	*R. prolixus*	2068	13.6	Peñalver et al. 1965.
	T. dimidiata	1767	30.8	Peñalver et al. 1965.
Guatemala	*T. dimidiata*	5747	23.4	Peñalver, Fajardo Aguilar 1953.
Honduras	*R. prolixus*	3238	34.7	Ponce and Zeledón 1973.
	T. dimidiata	791	32.2	Ponce and Zeledón 1973.
Nicaragua	*R. prolixus*	282	9.6	Urroz 1972.
	T. dimidiata	18	39.0	Urroz 1972.
Panama	*R. pallescens*	3283	32.7	Pipkin 1968.

The parasite *T. rangeli* is also found along with *T. cruzi* (but in lesser percentages) in triatomine species *R. prolixus* and *R. pallescens* in El Salvador, Honduras, and Panama (Sousa and Johnson 1971, 1973). *T. rangeli* is nonpathogenic in humans, and its precise identification is important to determine the true occurrence of *T. cruzi*. In El Salvador, one study indicates a higher percentage of triatomines (*R. prolixus*) infected with *T. rangeli* (21.4 percent) than with *T. cruzi* (0.5 percent), which suggests the possible displacement of *T. cruzi* by *T. rangeli* when both trypanosomes occur in the same insect (Cedillos 1975, 1987). Another possibility, especially in earlier studies, is that the identification of *T. cruzi* from *T. rangeli* was incorrect because it was primarily made by direct microscopic examination of an insect's intestinal content, and Giemsa stain was seldom used (Cedillos 1987:49).

The severity of *T. cruzi* infections is only moderate in Central America, where the parasite does not cause the significant myocardial damage, megaesophagus, and megacolon that it does in Bolivia and central parts of Brazil (Cedillos 1987:54). Although this geographical variation could be related to genetic and nutritional conditions, it is most probably a function of the prevalence of different infective *T. cruzi* strains in the two regions. One virulent strain, *T. cruzi* Zymodeme 2 (Z2), is common in central Brazil and is associated with severe cases of megasymptoms. The Z2 strain has not been found in El Salvador and Panama, where Zymodeme 1 (Z1) and Zymodeme 1 and 3 (Z1, Z3), respectively, are identified (Miles, Provoa, Prata, et al. 1981:1338, Kreutzer and Souza 1981:30).

In Bolivia, thirteen species of triatomines have been found (Valencia 1990b: 9). Within the subfamily Triatominae, three of its five tribes are reported: Tribe

Rhodniini Pinto, 1926, with genera *Rhodnius* Stal, 1859, and *Psammolestes* Bergroth, 1911; Tribe Triatomini Jeannel, 1919, with genera *Triatoma* Laporte, 1832, *Panstrongylus* Berg, 1879, and *Eratyrus* Stal, 1859; and Tribe Bolborderini Usinger, 1944, with genera *Microtriatoma* Prosen and Martinez, 1952. Not recorded in Bolivia are Tribe Alberproseniini Martínez and Carcavallo, 1977, and Tribe Cavernicolini Usinger, 1944.

Triatomine vectors of *Trypanosoma cruzi* in Bolivia are principally those reduviids that have adapted to living in peridomicile and domestic environments and to sucking blood from humans and domestic animals (see Figure 13). These species are *Triatoma infestans, Rhodnius prolixus,* and *Panstrongylus megistus,* which show a long relationship with humans as hosts. Approximately eight other species of triatomines are infected with *T. cruzi;* they are in the process of changing biotopes from sylvatic to domestic environments as their preferred hosts, smaller wild animals, are depleted and forests are cut down. As human groups migrate, they spread triatomines to other biotopes—for example, bringing *T. infestans* to higher altitudes in Bolivia. Also, as nomadic groups become sedentary, they provide sylvatic triatomines time to colonize their communities. The vector, host, and parasite relationship is changing daily in Bolivia and no rigid classification can be maintained. Important variable factors include the degree of adaptability of a species, the passive transport of bugs by humans, destruction of a species habitat and hosts, and personal and household hygiene. (See Appendix 5.)

Triatoma infestans has become such a major transmitter of *T. cruzi* in Bolivia because it cohabits with humans and can live at altitudes between 1,000 and 11,000 feet (Valencia 1990b:9); it has been found at sea level and as high as 12,500 feet in Lallagua, Bolivia (Carcavallo 1987:17). Entomologists captured 10,070 triatomines in Bolivia from domiciliary and peridomiciliary areas within environments ranging from 1,000 to 11,000 feet; 98.5 percent were *T. infestans,* 1.35 percent were *T. sordida,* and 0.2 percent were *Eratyrus mucronatus* (Valencia 1990a:39). As already mentioned, the adaptive features of *T. infestans* enable it to live within the various ecologic zones of Bolivia, a country noted for its many different life zones, from the Amazon basin to the crested Andes, including every ecotope. Although *T. infestans* thrives best within temperatures ranging from 60° to 80°F and altitudes from 1,200 to 6,000 feet, it has followed migrating human populations to most parts of Bolivia. At higher temperatures and altitude, however, these bugs reproduce at a slower rate. (See Appendix 4.)

Although only a few species of Triatominae are principally responsible for the transmission of *T. cruzi,* a variety of other insects, including ticks, bedbugs, and mosquitoes, can incubate *T. cruzi* in the laboratory (Brumpt 1912); however, their role in the transmission of the parasite to humans appears negligible.

Nevertheless, further research needs to be done concerning the possibility that after insecticide application bedbugs may proliferate and transmission might be possible if infected insects were crushed on the skin (Marsden 1983:257). *Trypanosoma cruzi* remains infective for months in dead triatomines kept refrigerated (Soares and Marsden 1980).

The ability of these bugs to adapt to artificial ecotopes illustrates a dynamic process (Zeledón 1983:327). Certain species with higher adaptability invade new territories, while other, less-adaptable, species are passively transported by humans to other regions where they begin their process of adaptation. Some species have adapted very well to peridomestic and domestic niches. This phenomenon is occurring in South and North America and, more recently, in some areas of Asia. The adaptive skills of trypanosome-carrying assassin bugs make it certain that Chagas' disease will spread to areas where it was not known before.

In summary: *Triatoma infestans* is by far the most common vector of Chagas' disease in Bolivia and Brazil, with *R. prolixus* and *P. megistus* running a distant second; however, *T. infestans* does not appear to be a principal vector in Central America. Also, *T. infestans* carries more virulent strains of *T. cruzi* associated with megasyndromes than the strains found in Central America. Although this leads to the impression that the severity of *T. cruzi* infections is only moderate in Central America, no studies have been done in Central America to ascertain what proportion of those infected develop the chronic phase of the disease (Cedillos 1987:54). Other factors relating to geographical variation in pathology include genetic and nutritional conditions, incidence of infection, socioeconomic conditions, climatic factors, and reservoir hosts.

Ecological factors, such as climatic factors and reservoir hosts, also affect vectorial transmission of *Trypanosoma cruzi* (WHO 1991). Climatic factors, mainly temperature, affect the rate of increase of triatomine populations. Where maximum and minimum annual temperatures show little variation in central Brazil (Goís), *T. infestans* populations produce two generations a year (WHO 1991). The rate of female fecundity, development rates of nymphs, and adult emergence rates are highest during the summer (December and January), followed by a minor peak in the winter (June and July). Adults and fourth- and fifth-instar nymphs mainly compose the winter population. Molting and reproduction are resumed at the beginning of spring.

The proportion of infected vectors has been found to be higher at the beginning of the hot season (WHO 1991). Seasonal changes in age structure and density of populations produce changes in the proportion of infected vectors. In temperate regions, transmission of *Trypanosoma cruzi* is concentrated in the warm season; in warm climates, transmission occurs throughout the year, with the highest level in the summer. The frequency of acute cases of Chagas' disease markedly increases during the summer months. These features of infection rates and of population dynamics should be considered when agencies program control operations and primary health care measures.

Fortunately for humans, many species of triatomines are sylvatic and feed on animals and birds; consequently, relatively few triatomine species feed on humans. Most of the species of triatomine bugs are prevalent in tropical and subtropical areas at altitudes between 200 and 1,500 meters (600–4,500 feet) above sea level, although eighteen species are found in near arctic biomes (*T. patagonica* is found in the Patagonian region of Argentina), twenty-three species in xerophytic forests, sixteen in desertic and semidesertic plains and plateaus (most notably the Altiplano, where *T. infestans* is found), and eleven in temperate foothills and valleys (Carcavallo 1987).

APPENDIX 8

Hosts for *T. cruzi*

Although triatomines are opportunistic blood feeders, the seven most important vector species (see Appendix 7: Vector species of *T. cruzi* in the Americas) show a preference for blood meals, with humans being the most desirable, then chickens and pigeons, and dogs and cats to a lesser degree. The nocturnal activity of cats saves them to a degree from these nocturnal predators. Guinea pigs are a delicacy to *vinchucas* in Bolivia and Peru, where Andeans traditionally raise them inside the kitchen. Guinea pigs have also been a factor for the spread of Chagas' disease throughout Andean countries. Rats and mice play a lesser role in providing blood meals and a major role as predators of triatomine bugs, as are chickens and cats, thus somewhat suppressing triatomine populations.

An important ecological factor influencing transmission of Chagas' disease is the association of triatomines with synanthropic animals (WHO 1991). Synanthropic animals are those animals that live around humans. They range from pets, livestock, and rodents to opossums, raccoons, foxes, deer, and other animals that, in part because of deforestation and encroachment upon forests, live close to humans. Because these animals serve as blood sources, they contribute considerably to maintaining or increasing population densities of domiciliary and peridomiciliary vectors. Animals also serve as vehicles to disperse triatomines to other parts of the world. The migratory wood stork (*Mycteria americana*), as one known example, carried *Rhodnius prolixus* from the north of South America to Central America and Mexico.

Epidemiologically, sylvatic and synanthropic animals serve as reservoir hosts for *Trypanosoma cruzi*. (Humans have become the principal hosts.) After Carlos Chagas (1909) found *Trypanosoma cruzi* in house-dwelling triatomines, *Panstrongylus megistus,* he discovered that the two important mammalian hosts in the domestic environment in the transmission cycles were humans and cats. Three years later, Chagas discovered infections in armadillos and recognized *Panstrongylus geniculatus* as the vector in this purely sylvatic cycle in armadillos. Subsequently, throughout the countries of Latin America, a wide variety of mammals and triatomine vectors have been identified as involved in the transmission cycle of *T. cruzi* and related flagellates. More than 150 species of wild and domestic mammals have been found to be reservoirs of *T. cruzi* (see WHO 1991: Annex 4 for list).

Certain animals are better reservoir hosts than others. Dogs, cats, and rodents are the prime reservoir hosts within the peridomestic arena, and opossums (*Didelphis* species) and armadillos within the sylvatic arena. *T. cruzi* infections in dogs have been reported from fifteen countries and infections in cats from seven, with great variability in infection rates (from 4.5 percent to 100 percent in dogs and from 0.5 percent to 60.9 percent in cats). Dogs are important reservoir hosts due to their close contact with humans during the night, the age-independent persistence of parasitemia in dogs, and the possibility of congenital or lactogenic infection of dogs, as has been indicated by a study in Argentina. Guinea pigs are bred indoors in Bolivia and Peru, where high rates of infection have been reported (Bolivia, 10.5–61.1 percent; Peru, 19.2 percent [Gürtler et al. 1990; WHO 1991]).

Other domestic animals—cattle, goats, pigs, donkeys, and horses—have rarely been found infected. They are not considered to play an important role as reservoirs because of their low population density, their less-close contact with humans, and their low rates of parasitemia (WHO 1991:25). Some species, such as goats and certain rats, appear to be able to eliminate the infection. Although they serve as blood meals, chickens, turkeys, ducks, and pigeons are not susceptible to *T. cruzi* infection (see Appendix 10: Immune Response). This is also true for all other birds as well as reptiles. Chickens are used in laboratories to blood feed sterile *vinchucas* that are used for xenodiagnosis. Veterinary researchers and animal environmentalists need to assess the considerable impact Chagas' disease has upon domestic and sylvatic animals.

APPENDIX 9

Acute Chagas' Disease

In 1909 Carlos Chagas diagnosed a child named Rita as having an acute attack of parasitemia caused by *T. cruzi,* and accurately described its symptoms:

> Among the chief clinical symptoms of this child, whose fever had come on some eight or ten days before examination, were the following: axillary temperature 40°C (105°F) spleen enlarged and to be felt under the edge of the ribs; liver also enlarged; groups of peripheral lymph nodes swollen etc. Most noticeable was a generalized infiltration, more pronounced in the face, and which did not show the characteristics of renal oedema but rather of myxoedema. This last symptom, which I later found to be one of the most characteristic of the acute form of the disease, already then revealed some functional alternation of the thyroid gland, perhaps affected by the pathogenic action of the parasite (Chagas 1922).

Rita died three days later. The pathology of acute Chagas' disease varies from a mild to a virulent infection. Some symptoms of acute Chagas' are related to inflammation, which is one of the body's defenses against *T. cruzi* and tissue damage, facilitating repair of the damage. Inflammation often includes fever, general malaise, and swelling and soreness of the lymph nodes and spleen, which contain large numbers of macrophages and T and B lymphocytes activated to combat antigens peculiar to *T. cruzi.* Inflammation's redness and warmth result from the increased amount of blood in the area. Swelling results from more proteins and fluids escaping into the tissue (Schmidt and Roberts 1989:27).

Definite symptoms of acute Chagas' are the ophthalmo-ganglial complex (Romaña's sign) and chagoma of cutaneous inoculation, which occurs near the bite site in 90 percent of the people recently infected (WHO 1991; see Figure 4). However, Borda (1981) claims lesser percentages of from 1 to 3 percent. Romaña's sign is not frequently found in Bolivia; if found, it is usually confused with an eye irritation. Appearing suddenly, Romaña's sign is the swelling of the upper and lower eyelids in one eye. An infection occurs through the skin of the eyelid, developing into inflammation around the eye with edema and inflammation of the local lymph nodes. The swollen eyelids are firm to the touch, purple, and not painful. There can be an inflammation of the conjunctiva or the mucous membrane that lines the eyelids (Katz, Despommier, and Gwadz

1989:174). Moderate swelling extends to the same side of the face, which, if touched, is found to be hard. This swelling gradually disappears after a month. The duration and durability of Romaña's sign set it apart from the swelling of other minor eye irritations.

Chagomas also appear at the infected bite sites of other parts of the body, especially on uncovered areas—hands, forearms, feet, calves, and legs. Nodulelike protrusions, chagomas are cutaneous tumors beneath the skin, resulting from the hardening of skin and subcutaneous cells. Chagomas are painful, firm, feverish, and abnormally red, which is due to capillary congestion in inflammations. When chagomas slowly disappear after a month, they leave a depigmentation, like a burn wound.

Acute infections also alter the cardiovascular system, with tachycardia (without correspondence to the intensity of fever), cardiac enlargement, hypotension, and heart failure (Andrade 1994, Köberle 1968:80). Heart alterations vary from slight to severe, as registered by electrocardiogram, but disappear after the acute phase (Borda 1981). Seventy percent of acute cases show no electrocardiographic or radiological abnormalities due to acute myocarditis of different stages (Laranja et al. 1956, WHO 1991:3). The remaining 30 percent indicate such electrocardiographic irregularities as sinus tachycardia, low QRS voltage, prolonged P-R interval, and primary T-wave changes. Chest x-rays can reveal cardiomegaly of varying degrees of severity.

About 2–3 percent of the acute cases with myocarditis die. Infants under two years constitute the greater number in this group. Also common to children of this age group is meningoencephalitis, another severe complication of the acute stage. Patients suffer convulsions, with or without fever, and lose consciousness to varying degrees (WHO 1991:3). The death rate for acute Chagas' with meningoencephalitis can be as high as 50 percent (WHO 1991).

For the remaining cases, the symptoms subside spontaneously within one to two months, without clinical symptoms in the short or medium term. Sometimes the frequency of tachycardia is extremely high and continues to increase after the remission of the temperature during the recovery process (Köberle 1968:80).

For those who survive the acute phase or who do not experience it, death from subsequent acute phases is frequently prevented by the presence of the parasite and the complement immune system. This is referred to as partial immunity, and it is important to consider in attempts to destroy the parasite during initial attacks within the acute stage—which may not be a good idea if the patient is to be subjected to new infections and subsequent violent acute phases. However, even with partial immunity over time, there is molecular mimicry between *T. cruzi* and the host's nervous tissue (Ávila 1994), rendering

Chagas' an autoimmune disease in that its antibodies destroy nerve cells. As one bonus, research concerning Chagas' disease adds to the scientific understanding of autoimmune diseases.

Pathology of the Acute Phase

The pathology of the acute phase begins with an increase of trypomastigotes circulating in the blood (George Stewart, interview 2/21/92). During this phase, trypomastigotes can be detected in blood samples, whereas in later phases very few circulate and either serodiagnosis for antibodies or xenodiagnosis for circulating parasites is needed to test for infection.

Trypomastigotes spread through lymphatics, with resulting lymphadenopathy. Initially, trypomastigotes actively penetrate host cells, but they may also enter through phagocytosis by host macrophages, reproducing as amastigote forms (Schmidt and Roberts 1989:65). The trypomastigotes lose their undulating membrane and flagellum inside the host cell and begin reproducing by means of binary fission—eventually producing so many amastigotes that the host cell is ruptured and killed. Amastigotes form into cystlike pockets, called pseudocysts, within the muscle cells. Some amastigotes evolve into trypomastigotes and find their way into the bloodstream, where they are picked up by *vinchucas* to be passed on to another host. All cells are susceptible, but parasites show great affinity for fixed macrophages of the spleen and liver and muscle cells (especially the myocardium). Myocardial fibrosis (myocarditis) is the most serious clinical consequence.

The pathology of the acute phase is the least understood because the phase is very short and not everyone infected passes through it. As parasitologist George Stewart (interview 4/15/92) explains it: cellular response on the part of macrophages encapsulating trypomastigotes at the site of the bite results in inflammatory responses that set off the acute phase. The invasion by macrophages results in a cascade of events. One such event alters the immune system. During the acute phase there are dramatic alterations in macrophage and lymphocyte cell populations, along with T-cell and B-cell responses. Macrophages are antigen-presenting cells (APCs) that consume the antigen, partially digest it, and display its epitope and class-II protein on their surfaces. T-cells recognize the antigen's epitope found on antigen-presenting macrophages and activate B-cells to produce plasma cells that secrete antibodies specific to the antigen. Throughout the acute infection period, parasites can be detected in most tissues, including trypomastigote forms in fairly large numbers. The sites of the growth are characterized by inflammatory cellular infiltrates. Wherever the parasite is growing—in lymph nodes and locally in the skin—macrophages, T-cells, and B-cells massively invade these cells. This invasion does not continue into the chronic phase.

This pan-lymphocyte proliferation is accompanied by severe immunodepression—the immune system becomes exhausted and specific antibodies against the parasite are inadequately produced. Very few antibodies are produced against the parasite, because there is massive polyclonal non-specific B-cell stimulation. Suppression is achieved by polyclonal B-cell activation early in the infection; many subtypes of B-cells are stimulated to divide and to produce nonspecific IgG and autoantibodies (Schmidt and Roberts 1989, Kobayakawa et al. 1979).

The result is a random, nonspecific impact on the parasites. It acts more like a bombing in a blitzkrieg than targeting bombs with radar and aiming at a specific site. Suppression of the immune system is indicated to some degree by the fact that all this activity is ineffectual. Experimentally, chagasic antigens have been injected into the host during the acute phase of the disease, resulting in the nonresponse of antibodies to these antigens and further indicating the parasite's ability to alter the immune system.

Experiments with mice indicate that if scientists destroy T-helper cells by injecting mice with T-helper cell antibodies, polyclonal B-cell activation will be stopped. This implies that such activation is T-helper-cell mediated and that trypomastigotes alter the T-cells; so it is not simply mitogenic stimulation of B-cells. As mentioned, acutely infected patients respond with a massive proliferation of B- and T-cells, but the T-cells don't live up to their reputation and are deficient in their cytotoxic influence. Causing this are suppressor T-cells that are highly active during the acute phase and figure in the immunosuppression, but the major players are the macrophage subpopulations. When the trypomastigotes initially enter the body, antigens are consumed by macrophages that partially digest the antigen. The macrophages initiate cytokene communication that leads to enormous proliferation of T-helper cells and B-cells and that probably stimulates suppressor T-cell activity. T-suppressor cells interact with T-helper cells by dampening the immune response and by lessening the effect of cytotoxic cells, which have an effect opposite those of T-helper cells (Schmidt and Roberts 1989).

Researchers at IBBA in La Paz, Bolivia, also have been studying the pathogenesis of acute Chagas' disease among high-altitude patients (Carrasco and Antezana 1991). They provide an alternative explanation: after the parasite penetrates the blood in the acute phase, it produces septicemia with hematogenous metastasis, which refers to the presence of *T. cruzi* in the blood and its entrance into other parts of the body, especially the muscles, through the blood. Trypomastigotes are guided to cells. As to what guides them, Carrasco and Antezana provide one explanation. Trypomastigotes need carbohydrates to survive, and it is possible that they have a product in their metabolism that searches the blood, acting like a "trigger" and informing trypomastigotes of cells rich in glycogen, such as muscles. After trypomastigotes leave the blood by perforating the walls of the capillaries, they penetrate the plasmatic membrane of cells. Inside cells, metacyclic trypomastigotes lose their tails and evolve into small, round, and tailless shapes called amastigotes. Amastigotes develop into trypomastigotes in these cystic cavities.

Maturation of trypomastigotes is uniform, but not all leave the cyst to become active at the same time. Maturity of the nascent trypanosomes requires adequate biochemical conditions. Mature trypanosomes return to the blood, where they circulate throughout the body searching out other cells to continue their cycle or to be picked up by *vinchucas* (Carrasco and Antezana 1991).

Other trypomastigotes remain in the cysts and self-destruct, leaving behind an array of toxic materials, dead parasitic material, pseudocysts, and destroyed cells that produce inflammations and tumors underneath the skin, such as chagoma and Romaña's sign. According to Carrasco and Antezana (1991), the inflammatory process is self-limiting and does not attack other organs. Other researchers, however, referred to in Carrasco and Antezana, indicate effects upon the central nervous system. Viana in 1911 described an alteration of ganglion cells and their disintegration corresponding to the velocity of broken pseudocysts within the central nervous system of acute patients (Brénière et al. 1983). Monckeberg mentioned in 1924 severe lesions of nerves and ganglions in the hearts of dogs experimentally infected with *T. cruzi*. Degenerative and inflammatory lesions coexisted during the rupture of the pseudocysts, with degenerative lesions apparently appearing first. Köberle in 1957 and 1959 suggested the presence of a neurotoxin, that would be released after the destruction of trypomastigotes and that would act locally or at short distances (Pereira Barreto 1985, Köberle 1970). The fact that approximately 80 percent of the ganglion cells could be destroyed in the acute phase constitutes the fundamental revelation of Köberle's neurogenesis theory (Köberle 1970). However, first Andrade in 1958 and later Dominguez and Suarez in 1963 did not find a similar correlation in their experiments (Carrasco and Antezana 1991).

According to neurotoxic theory, it is the trypomastigotes that remain in the pseudocysts and self-destruct that produce the toxic materials within the tumors and cause the inflammations. *T. cruzi* alters cell permeability and thus dramatically increases calcium levels that are toxic to human cells. The parasite needs high levels of calcium for its own cytoplasm, but extra calcium alters cell metabolism and could explain some of the cellular necrosis (George Stewart, interview 2/4/94).

A more scientifically acceptable theory holds that damages during acute phases are due to an overreaction, as well as ineffective reaction, of the auto-immune system (see Brener 1994). Pathogenesis during the acute phase is the result of a cascade of events involving the immune system in which pan-lymphocyte proliferation is accompanied by a severe immunodepression: the immune system becomes exhausted and specific antibodies against the parasite are inadequately produced. The fact that the human immune system is impli-cated within the pathogenesis indicates, as in AIDS, the deficiencies of the hu-man body's defenses against viruses and parasites and the need for more research into the complexities of the immune system and how it sometimes becomes our own worst enemy. Simplistic theories of antigens and antibodies have been replaced by complex synergetic interactions of events and cascades of events between complex parasitic and human immune systems.

When symptoms of Chagas' disease appear among patients in endemic ar-eas, health workers should test for acute Chagas'. At this stage, parasitological examinations are more easily performed because *T. cruzi* are circulating in the blood and can be observed in drops of blood examined under the microscope. Antibodies are also in high number, assisting in the detection through use of ELISA immunosorbent assay. Xenodiagnosis is often necessary during indeter-minate and chronic stages of the disease because parasites circulating in the blood are fewer in number. As discussed, in contrast to other means of testing such as through extraction of blood in a syringe, xenodiagnosis uses sterile *vinchucas* to feed in the armpit of the patient for thirty or more minutes, pro-viding the bugs with time to ingest *T. cruzi* and blood. It is often difficult to catch *T. cruzi* in the bloodstream because its natural habitat is intracellular. Xenodiagnosis can also determine the zymodeme and population size of *T. cruzi*, which is important for treating latent and chronic stages. (See Appen-dix 12.)

Detecting Acute Stages

In endemic areas of Chagas' disease it is important to detect acute and even asymptomatic infections in children so that specific therapy can be started immediately. Serologic profiles of eighty-six chagasic children and fifty-six healthy children from a highly endemic area in Cochabamba, Bo-livia, indicate that alpha-2-macroglobulin (A2M) and C-reactive protein (CRP) were significantly increased in acute chagasic children (Medrano-Mercado et al. 1996). Because parasites are commonly present in blood and tis-sues during the acute phase, it is possible that the high levels of A2M may act as inhibitors of a high level of proteinases, derived from the parasites, from host cell damage, or from both. These results open a route to discern different stages in the acute infection by examination of sera and using humoral criteria:

1) an early acute stage, with an increase only in specific anti-*T. cruzi* im-munoglobulin M (IgM) levels (group 1);

2) an intermediate acute stage having high specific IgM levels and/or high

immunoglobulin G (IgG) levels and/or high anti-galactose (anti-Gal) levels and increased A2M and/or CRP levels;

3) a late acute stage, with low IgM levels but high A2M, CRP, anti-Gal, and specific IgG levels.

The detection of high immunoglobulin G alone is indicative of the chronic/indeterminate stage of Chagas' disease (Medrano-Mercado et al. 1996).

In Bolivia, however, serological methods involve many problems, including difficulties in sample collection and storage until the time of screening; difficulties in the standardization of the diagnostic methods commonly used, such as the indirect hemagglutination test, the indirect immunofluorescence test, ELISA, or complement fixation; and the absence of a clear correlation of the results of tests performed in different laboratories (Pless et al. 1992). The procedures and techniques to quantify five relevant proteins are easy to perform and to automate for large-scale screening, in contrast to other immunologic techniques that are used for serodiagnosis of Chagas' disease. They would consititute a tool in detecting acute Chagas' disease, especially in endemic rural areas.

APPENDIX 10

Chronic Heart Disease

Symptoms of chronic Chagas' disease are insidious and progressive (see Figure 8). After recovering from acute phases, many people, perhaps the majority, remain asymptomatic for the rest of their lives, while others remain in good health for many years before developing symptoms and signs of the chronic stage of disease. The chronic phase is characterized by widespread damage to the organ(s) and the multiform chagasic syndrome, with its digestive (aperistalsis, megaesophagus, megacolon), respiratory (megatrachea, bronchiectasis), urinary (megaloureter), cardiac (denervation), and neurological (myelopathy, encephalopathy) components (Köberle 1968, Iosa 1994).

Cardiac abnormalities range from types of rhythm disturbances to various forms of heart block, including right- and left-bundle branch block, hemiblocks and atrioventricular blocks (see Andrade 1994, Iosa 1994). Some tested patients show a normal electrocardiogram (ECG) reading, particularly in the early stages, but stress testing may reveal ECG abnormalities such as heart block or arrhythmias which might not be seen in resting ECGs. Sometimes available in urban centers, echocardiography may also be useful in evaluating cardiac chamber size and left-ventricular function and in following the progression of the disease.

Although electrocardiographic abnormalities related to Chagas' disease have been estimated as high as 87 percent (Hurst 1986:1170), 33 percent seems a more reasonable figure from studies in Brazil. Almost one-third of 2,000 subjects examined by ECG in endemic areas of Brazil indicated abnormalities, and 9 percent of chest x-rays showed enlargement of the cardiac shadow (Braunwald 1988:1447; Hurst 1986:1170).

Pedro Jáuregui and Alberto Casanovas (1987:30–33) analyzed electrocardiographs from people living in endemic chagasic areas throughout Bolivia to see how many indicated electrocardiographic abnormalities characteristic of chagasic-related heart disease. They studied 4,108 electrocardiographs from patients of rural communities in the Departments of La Paz (280), Tarija (258), Potosí (311), Cochabamba (1,818), Santa Cruz (1,185), and Chuquisaca (256). They found that 436 (9.4 percent) strongly indicated Chagas' disease from the total number of 853 (20.8 percent) of ECG abnormalities. Of the 853 total abnormalities found, 469 (55 percent) were in men and 384 (45 percent) were in women, with 761 (89 percent) being adults and 92 (11 percent) being youths.

Criteria used to indicate chronic chagasic myocarditis among the ECG abnormalities were left anterior hemiblock (29 percent), block of the right bundle branch (27 percent), and sinal bradycardia (16 percent). There were 152 patients who had combined abnormalities of block of the right bundle branch and left anterior hemiblock. Including other abnormalities, 61 percent suffered from heart block, 22 percent from arrhythmias, 10 percent from repolarization disorders, 2 percent from overcharges, and 2 percent from other alterations. Youths indicated light disorder of conduction of the right bundle branch or sinal bradycardia with repolarization suggestive of vagotonia. Vagotonia is a disorder that results from overstimulation of the vagus nerve, causing a slowing of the heart rate, fainting, and dizziness.

Diagnostic tests were not given to verify what percentage of these people were infected with *T. cruzi,* so conclusions are indefinite; however, some hypotheses can be suggested, such as the relationship of altitude to chagasic heart disease. Altitude appears to affect the manifestations of chronic chagasic heart disease. Lesser oxygen intake at high altitude (hypoxia) puts additional stress on chronic chagasic patients emigrating from lower to higher regions of Bolivia. Twenty-three percent of ECG alterations were found in patients from mesothermic zones as compared to 14 percent from those in subtropical zones. Mesothermic zones in Bolivia are mountains, plateaus, and valleys at altitudes from 8,000 to 14,000 feet. Although triatomine vectors are infrequently found above 13,000 feet, Bolivians move from the lower areas where they were infected to higher altitudes where hypoxia combines with chagasic stress to produce ECG abnormalities.

Although research is needed to correlate the incidence of ECG abnormalities with seropositive chagasic patients in higher altitudes, one clinical conclusion is that patients with myocarditis in La Paz are at greater risk than those at lower altitudes. The aerobic effect of living at high altitude that has traditionally endowed Andeans with strong hearts is counterproductive to Andeans suffering with hearts infected with *T. cruzi.* Traditionally, Andeans have referred to leishmaniasis as *"el mal de los Andes";* it now appears that Chagas' disease may be the curse of Andeans.

Therapeutically, patients with chronic Chagas' disease stand a better chance of living longer at lower altitudes if they can avoid becoming superinfected. However, at lower altitudes there is a greater risk of superinfection, as there are more *vinchucas* and infected people. This leads to an auxiliary research question: to what degree does superinfection precipitate chronic Chagas' disease myocarditis among lowland Bolivians? Apparently, it has a limited negative effect, considering that only 14 percent of patients from mesothermic zones had ECG abnormalities.

Immune Response

George Stewart, coauthor

The human immune response to *T. cruzi* infection is inadequate and complex, providing at best partial protective immunity during the chronic phase and at worst causing severe immunopathology which may play a significant role in the morbidity and mortality rates of the disease. Pathology associated with *T. cruzi* includes immunopathology, an inflammatory response that causes chronic myocarditis and degeneration of the heart and gastrointestinal system. Even more insidiously, *T. cruzi* immunizes humans to their own antigens so that defensive antibodies become offensive and destroy myocardial and neural cells. As one favor, *T. cruzi* provides chronically infected patients with immunity from acute infections, but only as long as *T. cruzi* is present; it is as if to say: "Without me, you're subject to acute infection from another bite!"

Natural Resistance

Amphibians and birds are completely resistant to *T. cruzi* under natural conditions, and the reasons for this could give a clue as to how to manipulate human immunology to block this parasite. Amphibians and birds have an innate immunity. When infective bloodstream forms of *T. cruzi* are injected into chickens during experiments to attempt infection, the trypomastigotes are rapidly destroyed within one minute, scarcely enough time to become intracellular and reproduce as amastigotes and then change into infective trypomastigotes. When infective trypomastigotes are placed in fresh human blood or serum from other mammals *in vitro* they are not destroyed, and the parasite may remain alive for several weeks *in vitro* until antibodies are formed that activate complement. (Complement is a series of enzymatic proteins in normal serum that, in the presence of a specific activator—the parasite—destroys the invader.) This delay provides enough time for *T. cruzi* to become firmly established in the mammalian host.

Experiments have shown that the natural resistance of birds to *T. cruzi* infection is antibody independent and related to complement. It is antibody independent because birds kill bloodstream forms immediately, before antibodies can form. Components on the surface of trypomastigotes activate complement in chickens but not in mammals. Proof that complement kills *T. cruzi* in chickens is provided by experiments in which cobra venom is used to destroy complement in chickens. In chickens treated in this fashion, the parasites stay alive for long periods of time, although they do not infect the chicken. Other factors may be involved that alter the parasites' ability to survive, such as high body temperature of birds.

Complement in mammals is not directly activated by the parasites: such activation in these hosts is antibody dependent. That is, the only way that human complement will destroy *T. cruzi* is after specific antibodies have been formed against *T. cruzi* antigens and have attached to the surface of the parasite. Human complement is activated by a specific antibody bound to *T. cruzi* antigens; then its enzymes punch a hole in the parasite and kill it. Already discussed, the formation of effective antibodies is delayed for several weeks following introduction of the parasite, providing a window of time for *T. cruzi* to infect the person.

Humans appear to have no natural resistance to *T. cruzi*. Epidemiological factors, such as house hygiene, sleeping arrangements, and use of insecticides, explain the occurrence of uninfected individuals in highly endemic areas, but these preventative measures do not constitute natural resistance. The misconception of natural human resistance may arise from the fact that the host may respond differently to different strains of the parasite and that Chagas' disease manifests itself in a wide variety of pathologies, creating the impression that certain people are more resistant than others. During the acute phase, some patients manifest mild symptoms or none at all; but, again, this may be due to differing strains of *T. cruzi* as well as to individual immune responses. In patients displaying relatively minor acute symptoms, seroconversion (in which a previously negative-testing individual suddenly tests positive) documents that infection has taken place and that *T. cruzi* is moving slowly and surely. Therefore, significant factors that influence pathology are parasite strain and individual immune competence.

One other factor influencing pathology appears to be the length of time humans have been exposed to Chagas' disease. As discussed in Chapter 2, Andeans in the highlands of Chile had a very high infection rate, but their cardiac involvement was lower than that detected in other endemic regions (González et al. 1995). Within this same region, scholars had earlier uncovered mummies of early Andeans from about A.D. 500 with clinical symptoms of Chagas' disease. The more benign character of Chagas' disease is explainable in the context of either the *T. cruzi* population circulating in the area and/or the ancient adaptation of the parasite to the human host in this area, particularly in the Andean highland.

Acquired Resistance to the Acute Phase

Although human hosts have no natural resistance to the acute phase of Chagas' disease, infected humans usually acquire resistance to the severe pathology of the acute phase from subsequent infections, either of the same or different strains. Acquired resistance (partial immunity) is an immunity that slowly develops after the establishment of the acute phase and is antibody dependent. Acquired resistance primarily protects hosts from the mortality associated with initial contact with the parasite (acute phase) and from consequences of future acute phases by a quick and vigorous immune response. But acquired resistance remains only as long as *T. cruzi* is present.

An important consideration for doctors is whether or not to completely kill all the parasites in the body of someone living in an endemic area, where that person is at high risk of being reinfected and possibly subject to the acute pathology. An alternative is to help the immune system manage the number of parasites throughout the chronic phase. Paradoxically, the one bonus *T. cruzi* provides to infected individuals is protection from the frequently deadly attacks of parasitemia in the acute phase. However, even this resistance wanes and waxes, as evidenced by exacerbations of the infection with repeat acute attacks in some individuals throughout life.

Parasites have many strategies for evading host immunity. Some evasive strategies are less refined, such as destruction of T4 cells by HIV, while others are more fine-tuned, such as getting inside cells and hiding, acquiring or synthesizing hostlike surface components, modulating the immune system so that it doesn't destroy them, or developing antigenic variation. *Trypanosoma cruzi* can incorporate certain host plasma proteins onto its surface to escape immune recognition. It can also cleave antibody molecules attached to its surface, rendering them ineffective as markers for immune cells and complement. As already discussed, *T. cruzi* are unable to antigenically vary their surfaces as effectively as their African counterparts. Rather than face the immune system, *T. cruzi* runs for cover, employing an evasive strategy of quickly entering into host cells, where it hides and reproduces as amastigotes (an intracellular, non-flagellated form; see Figure 5). Thus, *T. cruzi* uses intracellular localization to evade immunity, a strategy that appears important during the chronic phase of infection when the majority of parasites are intracellular. Post-mortem examinations indicate that chronic patients have amastigotes within their heart cells years after the initial infection.

The human immune system is as sophisticated, perplexing, and capable as are the parasites against which it acts. The human immune system is how the host defends itself against nonself entities (viruses, bacteria, protozoa, etc.). It also serves as an internal janitor, assigned the job of cleaning up self components that have been altered. The immune system also preserves body integrity, monitors internal changes, attacks foreign organisms, degrades and passes on information about nonself intruders, and remembers the information for future attacks. The human immune system is broadly classified into cellular and humoral components, which can act independently as well as interact in varying degrees of complexity. Cellular response depends on the action of cells, whereas humoral immunity depends on antibody molecules, which are present in the blood and body fluids. Both cellular and humoral responses are mounted during *T. cruzi* infection.

The basic components of the humoral immune system are immunoglobulins, which are closely related but not identical proteins that interact with the specific antigens promoting their production. Out of five major types, immunoglobulin M (IgM) and immunoglobulin G (IgG) are featured in the host response to *T. cruzi*. IgM is the body's first reaction to the parasite and is relatively ineffective in Chagas' disease. Appearing later and being more effective against blood-form trypomastigotes, IgG is the principal antibody in the blood. *T. cruzi*–specific IgG and IgM are crucial to driving the parasite into an intracellular existence, terminating the acute phase of the disease. This antibody attack is T-cell-dependent. That is, T cells recognizing *T. cruzi* antigen stimulate B cell proliferation and differentiation into plasma cells, actively producing parasite-specific antibodies. Among activated lymphocytes are long-lived memory cells which respond rapidly to secondary infection with *T. cruzi*, producing quick and effective humoral and cellular responses against the parasite.

Antibodies bound to the surface of *T. cruzi* trigger contact killing of bloodstream forms of *T. cruzi* by host cells, a process referred to as antibody-dependent, cell-mediated cytotoxicity (ADCC). ADCC elicits response by eosinophils, macrophages, and neutrophils, when antibodies are present, against bloodstream forms of *T. cruzi* (Kierszenbaum 1979; Kierszenbaum, Ackerman, and Gleich 1981). Macrophages phagocytize the parasite, and granules in the eosinophils and neutrophils fuse with the phagosome and kill *T. cruzi* (Okabe et al. 1980:344–53). When macrophages are not activated by IgG antibodies specific to *T. cruzi*, then macrophagic engulfment works to the parasites' benefit in that trypomastigotes are not killed but rather multiply within the macrophages and spread throughout other parts of the body. In fact, certain strains of *T. cruzi* prefer macrophages as first cellular sites for reproduction for the very reason that macrophages are mobile and ineffective until IgG antibodies are produced against them several weeks after the first infection.

When *T. cruzi* infects humans, it frequently invades monocytes, which are circulating macrophages important in phagocytosis. Phagocytosis is a process of engulfment of the invading particle within a vacuole created from the white blood cell's membrane. The cell then empties digestive enzymes from organelles called lysosomes into the vacuole to destroy the particle (Schmidt and Roberts 1989:21). When blood monocytes move into the tissue, they differentiate into macrophages. As already discussed, macrophages are effective in destroying *T. cruzi* only in the presence of specific antibodies. Until the T cells are able to orchestrate the antibodies and macrophages, *T. cruzi* multiplies and spreads to other cells.

The dual role of macrophages makes them metaphorically similar to the fox guarding the hen house. Monocytes and macrophages first serve as host cells which support the parasites' intracellular multiplication as amastigotes and differentiation into infective trypomastigotes. Macrophages are very mobile cells, so *T. cruzi* spreads throughout the body until macrophages are told to stay where they are; but this takes the assistance of T helper cells, which elaborate chemical messages (cytokines) that instruct macrophages to destroy the parasite. By this time, *T. cruzi* has entered many other types of cells and become ensconced within these other cells.

The belief that macrophages need ADCC to kill *T. cruzi* has been supported with naive (immunosuppressed) mice that were deprived of immunoglobulin production and infected with *T. cruzi*. These mice could not produce antibodies against the trypanosomes, and their macrophages engulfed but were unable to destroy the parasites. The parasites multiplied within the macrophages. With similarly immunosuppressed mice, trypanosomes were first exposed to immunoglobulin outside of the mice and then injected into the naive mice. Trypanosomes with antibodies were engulfed and destroyed by macrophages, so opsonization is an important process in phagocytosis of *T. cruzi*. Opsonization implies that antibodies mediate destruction of parasites by first binding the open end (FAB) of their Y-shaped molecule to the parasite's antigen. Phagocytic macrophages then recognize the projecting stem (Fc) of the antibody, engulf, and lyse the parasite.

However, it has not been established that antibodies on the parasite's surface are the only factor involved in the opsonization process. In another experiment with immunocompetent mice, researchers stimulated the production of macrophages by injections of Bacillus Calmette-Guerin (BCG), which is a protein similar to TB in its macrophage-stimulating actions. This caused an activation of macrophages that were non-specific for *T. cruzi* antigens. These macrophages engulfed *T. cruzi*, limited their multiplication, but did not kill them. This experiment indicated that BCG activates macrophages to at least the level of controlling reproduction but not to the top level as specific *T. cruzi* antibodies do. It takes cytokines, which are substances released by sensitized lymphocytes when they contact specific *T. cruzi* antigens, to reach that top level of macrophage activation. Cytokines help to produce cellular immunity by stimulating macrophages and monocytes. Cytokines cause macrophages to go one step farther and be trypanocidal.

A combination of T cells and macrophages is needed to destroy *T. cruzi*. Without this balance, problems arise: if a person has a lot of macrophages and fewer T cells, then this person will suffer a much more severe infection than one with a balance of the two or a surplus of T cells. One obvious conclusion is that immunosuppressed people, such as AIDS patients with depleted T cells, can suffer severe infections of Chagas' disease.

Macrophage activation also demonstrates an important feature of the immune system: that there are different levels of macrophage activity, ranging from merely engulfing *T. cruzi,* which enables it to multiply and spread, to engulfing it and inhibiting its multiplication and spread, and, at the highest level, to involving T cells, with which the parasite is destroyed. It is not all or nothing in macrophage activation; rather, there are degrees of effectiveness and interacting processes.

Protective and Nonprotective Antibodies

During Chagas' disease, both protective and nonprotective antibodies are produced. Lytic antibodies (LA) recognize epitopes (specific markers) on the surface of *living* trypanosomes, attach to these epitopes, and initiate the complement cascade, which includes enzymes that lyse the parasite. Among chronically ill patients, there are varying levels of lytic antibodies. Those patients that show the least clinical manifestations have the greatest number of lytic antibodies that react with epitopes exposed on the surface of living trypanosomes. This explains why acquired immunity from severe symptoms of the acute phase requires the continual presence of living trypanosomes.

The nonprotective antibodies are called CSA (conventional serological antibodies) and do not recognize epitopes of *T. cruzi*. Patients with the most dramatic clinical manifestations have the greatest number of CSA, which are not inert antibodies but contribute to pathogenesis. Experiments have been performed giving people ground-up antigens of *T. cruzi*. These antigens from nonliving *T. cruzi* organisms induced nonspecific T- and B-cell polyclonal activation and thereby vast amounts of ineffective antibodies that cause more damage to hosts than parasites, similar to what happens to the body in African sleeping sickness and malaria infections.

In this experiment, as well as among chronic patients with severe clinical manifestations, the immune system is being inundated with many different *T. cruzi* antigens, a few of which are vulnerable targets but the vast majority of which are no more than smoke screens. A person's humoral immune system produces high levels of anti-trypanosomal antibodies, but these antibodies are not targeted against epitopes on the surface of living parasites. Rather, these CSA are targeted against antigens that are not important to the parasite, or are unable to be reached, so the CSA are unable to lyse the organism. In popular terms, *T. cruzi* antigens stimulate polyclonal activation, which is like throwing in a large group of antigens and confusing the system, which then overreacts with too many ineffective punches that do more damage to living cells than to parasites by causing inflammation, fever, and lesions.

The fact that Chagas' disease patients vary greatly in their proportions of LA and CSA antibodies partially explains the wide range of clinical manifestations exhibited. As already discussed, acute patients with severe symptoms have high levels of CSA and low levels of LA; conversely, those with high levels of LA frequently do not suffer symptoms of the acute phase. This may explain why only about one-third of infected patients suffer the acute phase. The key variable is how each individual immune system deals with specific surface epitopes of antigens that are important in acting against the parasite. Another factor contributing to the LA/CSA response may be the strain of the parasite; different strains sometimes elicit sharply different antibody responses.

Because low levels of LA correlate with clinical manifestations and because individuals vary in the amount of LA produced, it is important to determine the presence of lytic antibodies in infected patients. ELISA, complement fixation, indirect agglutination tests, and radio immunoassays are not specific enough to distinguish which particular antibody is able to kill *T.* cruzi. One serological test is complement-mediated lysis, in which the patient's serum is bound to trypomastigotes *in vitro* and exposed to complement. If the complement lyses the parasites, then LA is present in the blood. Indirect immunofluorescence with living trypanosomes is another assay that can determine the protective effect of serum: technicians study antibodies fixed to the surface of living trypanosomes with immunofluorescence to see if they are interacting with epitopes on the surface of the parasite. A third method is serum neutralization, in which living trypanosomes are exposed to a patient's serum. If the parasite is neutralized, then the serum contains lytic antibodies.

These tests are important to determine a patient's progress against *T. cruzi* infection and whether chemotherapy should be used. Patients with low LA levels will not be helped as much by chemotherapy as those whose antibodies are assisting in lysing the parasite. Moreover, as patients are being treated and being cured, LA levels decline rapidly, giving an indication of effective treatment.

This also explains why an active infection is required to stimulate protective immunity: cured patients no longer have LA in their systems. LA are manipulated by parasites so that they are produced at certain times and released under certain circumstances. Parasites regulate their number and degrees of infection in order that overpopulation does not become a problem for their survival and that their hosts remain alive until they can complete their own life cycles.

Also influencing the severity of symptoms, strains and stages of *T. cruzi* vary in their susceptibility to complement-mediated lysis. Some strains are lysed more effectively by human complement than are other strains, and the virulence of strains conversely may be related to the parasites' susceptibility to complement. Regarding *T. cruzi* stages, blood-form trypomastigotes are more susceptible than are metacyclic trypomastigotes and intracellular amastigotes. Metacyclic trypomastigotes are initially exposed to complement, and in chickens these parasites are lysed. Metacyclic trypomastigotes quickly go intracellular, especially into macrophages, where they transform and multiply into amastigote forms. Because of their intracellular location, amastigotes resist complement-mediated lysis. After several generations, amastigotes transform into trypomastigotes that circulate in the human blood. Not many trypomastigotes are released into the blood; many of them go into cells. These trypomastigotes show a wide variation in their resistance to complement-mediated lysis, but they are much more susceptible to complement-mediated lysis in the presence of specific *T. cruzi* antibodies than are other forms.

Evasive Strategies

Intracellular hiding is a very important evasive strategy of *T. cruzi*, because the blood is the primary battleground of the humoral immune response. If *T. cruzi* trypomastigotes remained in the blood for a month, this would give the T and B lymphocytes sufficient time to activate very specific IgG immunoglobulins against them. During the acute phase, polyclonal stimulation occurs and parasites are chased into cells. After polyclonal activation subsides, immunosuppression follows, which provides more time for trypomastigotes to enter cells.

Some lesser strategies are evident. Trypomastigotes show rapid surface turnover, capping, shedding, and some interstrain antigenic variation of their coats, but not to the degree exhibited by the *T. brucei*– complex of organisms. If antibodies attach to trypomastigotes, trypomastigotes can shed them if they act quickly enough.

Trypomastigotes are also able to evade host antibodies by binding to the Fc (crystallizable fragment) portion and by fabulation. *T. cruzi* have a surface component that enables their antigens to bind to the Fc end and not to the FAB (antigen-binding fragment) end of the immunoglobulin molecule. If antigens bind to the Fc end, then this end is blocked from activating complement, which is necessary to lyse the parasite. This is especially true for antibodies directed specifically at nonsurface epitopes, which they cannot reach, since antigens on the trypomastigote's surface bind to the Fc portion of IgG. Antibody-dependent cell-mediated cytotoxicity (ADCC) and antibody-dependent complement lysis are both dependent on the Fc portion being exposed. Trypomastigotes become coated with host antibodies clinging to antigens on their surfaces, but with their FAB extended and nonfunctional.

Fabulation is when trypomastigote antigens bind to the FAB end of the molecule and cleave off the Fc portion, which literally disables the antibody. Trypomastigotes have surface proteases (protein-eating enzymes) that cleave off the Fc end of the antibody. Without its Fc end, the antibody is left with an ineffective little piece of protein dangling from its surface that is unattractive to complement or to cells.

Although it is not surprising that *T. cruzi* has all these mechanisms for evading the host immune system, African trypanosomes rely most heavily on antigenic variation. African trypanosomes don't have the need to use anything but antigen variation, which is enough to enable them to avoid the destruction of all their number by host immunity measures. A parasite may have four or five mechanisms for evasion, and then another one appears that is better than the others, but the parasite doesn't then get rid of the less-effective ways, at least not for many, many generations. These mechanisms will be selected in those organisms that don't have the better one. *T. cruzi*, then, has not attained such a refined mechanism of evasion as antigenic variation, and so it utilizes more than one evasive mechanism. All of which work toward the same end: the survival of the species.

Autoimmune Components of Pathogenesis

The severe symptoms of Chagas' disease come in large part from autoimmunity responses (see Andrade 1994, Brener 1994, Iosa 1994). Thus, most of the pathology associated with *T. cruzi* infection is referred to as immunopathology. Throughout the chronic phase, a tremendous inflammatory process accompanies cells invaded by *T. cruzi* amastigotes, especially the amastigotes that live for a long period of time. This inflammatory process most frequently focuses in the heart, causing chronic myocarditis, but it also occurs within the esophagus and colon. This inflammatory response is directed against amastigotes that, over a period of time, slowly release themselves from the cells that they have invaded. This begins an inflammatory process against the escaped amastigotes and destroyed cells left behind. Monocyte or mononuclear infiltrates focus within specific locations where the parasites emerge and eventually invade other tissues, including the heart and neuron tissue. These infiltrates also enter myocardial plexes and plexes that serve the digestive tract. Plexes are nerve nets that serve various organs. Neuronal degeneration can occur during the acute phase in those who are experiencing severe attacks, especially children under the age of five, but this degeneration most frequently occurs during the chronic phase of the infection.

During the acute phases, polyclonal activation incites T and B cells, which produce antibodies not directed against the parasite in ways that will protect the host but rather against epitopes the parasite possesses and may share with host cells. These CSAs or nonproductive antibodies damage heart and nerve cells, frequently leading to death.

During the chronic phase, *T. cruzi* protects itself by mimicking host antigens which are shared with heart and nerve cells. Molecular mimicry between *T. cruzi* and host nervous tissue is the most current and acceptable theory of how the immune system is responsible for tissue lesions on infected organs (see Ávila 1994 and PAHO 1994 for a discussion of this theory). *T. cruzi* have on their surfaces various host plasma proteins and immunoglobulins (antibodies), as well as shared heart- and nerve-cell antigens. During the chronic phase, damage of the cardiac system leads to conduction abnormalities, which can be detected through the measurement of cardiac function. Gastrointestinal damage begins with the reduction of muscle tone and ends with muscular atrophy of the smooth muscles of the gut, esophagus, and colon so that these organs dilate and cannot contract to pass food through, resulting in blockage. Patients suffer chronic dysphagia (difficulty in swallowing) and constipation, which can include an enormously enlarged colon (megacolon) and esophagus (megaesophagus).

These severe clinical manifestations, however, cannot adequately be explained by inflammatory responses of the immune system to a few parasites being attacked with a focal inflammation. During the chronic phase, *T. cruzi* reproduces in numbers, and the immune system attempts to keep them in check; but, at some point, the inflammation process rapidly spreads out from focal areas where parasites are emerging, to attack human cells. This diffusion heralds the critical point for chronically infected patients.

This is not just a matter of parasite antigens attaching to self cells and rendering them nonself cells so that human antibodies mistake human cells for parasite cells, but rather it is a situation where human antibodies attack self cells simply for what they possess. *T. cruzi* immunizes people to their own antigens: it causes the human immune system to create antibodies that target antigens belonging to cardiac and neuronal cells and which then lyse them with complement. The immune response attacks self cells in two ways: parasites frequently alter the normal structure of host cells or attach parasite antigens to these cells; or, using an even more effective method, these parasites can get the immune system to think that it is attacking the parasite while it is in fact attacking itself. *T. cruzi* can do this because it has surface molecules that mimic those on the surface of host cells.

This has been demonstrated in experiments with rabbits. When lymphocytes from chronic chagasic rabbits were injected into healthy rabbits, these lymphocytes bound to and destroyed heart cells. This provided evidence that a cell-mediated autoimmune response is involved in the generation of cardiomyopathy and other pathogenic events that occur with the disease. If spleen cells from *T. cruzi*-infected rabbits are placed *in vitro* with normal rabbit heart cells, the heart cells are killed. Spleen cells from the infected rabbit contain both lymphocytes and monocytes sensitized to the parasite antigen.

Further proof is found in the fact that serum from chagasic patients invariably contains autoantibodies that attack heart and neuronal cells *in vitro*. These autoantibodies attach and bind to cardiac epithelium and interstitial tissue, blood vessels, and muscle tissue, and are technically referred to as EVI antibodies (endothelial, vessel, and interstitial). EVI antibodies are detected at high levels in the serum of chronically ill chagasic patients and at extremely high levels in the serum of those with cardiac abnormalities.

The question is, how does *T. cruzi* make human antigens look like *T. cruzi* antigens? When the host immune system attacks *T. cruzi*, it recognizes many epitopes on the parasite's surface that are nonself and belong to the parasite. The surface of *T. cruzi* has many molecules on its surface which have epitopes that allow macrophages to attach to the surface and phagocytize the parasite. Macrophages pick up epitopes unique to *T. cruzi* as well as others the parasite shares with the host; so, when T cells develop and receive this information, they confuse parasite and human epitopes. Human cells can also be rendered nonself by attaching to them something that is nonself, such as a parasite antigen. The human immune system then attacks its own cells. When the immune system begins to attack its own cells, it also processes information about this system of antigens and includes all those that are related to it macromolecularly. It is clueing-in on some antigens that are *not* nonself and develops a response against its own cells. Therefore, when the immune system goes after *T. cruzi*, which has on its surface some antigens that are similar to those of the host, the immune system picks up epitopes of self cells that have been disarranged because they are in close association with these nonself antigens and produces antibodies against the human cells. The immune system response is not specific enough to determine which molecules belong to the parasite and which to itself.

The antigenic epitope involved in this autoimmune reaction against cardiac cells contains laminin (a basement membrane glycoprotein). Tested sera from infected humans and monkeys contained high levels of EVI antibodies that reacted with laminin. EVI antibodies are anti-laminin antibodies. This was detected by pouring serum down a sepharose (gel) column with laminin bound to it so that only anti-laminin antibodies would stick to it. This affinity chromatography test is called a laminin sepharose affinity column. Laminin is a very important glycoprotein on the surface of many cells, especially those of the heart. If rabbits are immunized with laminin, they produce antibodies that cross-react with *T. cruzi* and EVI cells. Conclusions are that laminin may be the major antigenic component inducing EVI antibodies and that laminin is found on the surface of *T. cruzi* and cardiac cells.

However well laminin explains myocardiopathy, it is not found in large amounts on the surfaces of neuronal tissue, so there must be another cross-reacting antibody to explain the degeneration of neuronal tissue and muscles of the gut.

In conclusion, *T. cruzi* is a complex organism that has elaborate mechanisms for survival in its host. Within its millions of years of existence, *T. cruzi* has evolved a number of strategies for evading and manipulating mechanisms of the human immune response. In an elaborate chess game of moves and countermoves, *T. cruzi* has literally checked the king, although the game is not over, as scientists rapidly are uncovering complexities of the relationship between *T. cruzi* and the vertebrate immune system. The second theme implicates the human immune system for sometimes doing more damage than good: the fact that a protozoan such as *T. cruzi* can turn this system around so that it attacks itself is a strategy any warrior could learn from, but the most important lesson from *T. cruzi* is that it provides us with information and the stimulus to do more research on this process. Parasitology and immunology are extremely complex disciplines needing more study, and Chagas' disease has proven to be an important and interesting model in both areas of study.

Diagnostic Tests

In 1909, when Carlos Chagas took a sample of the child Rita's blood and examined it under the microscope, he saw trypanosomes. He was able to find them because they were abundantly present at this time, although, generally speaking, it is more difficult to find them in a blood sample. Trypanosomes of *T. cruzi* can be found in patients during the acute phase of Chagas' disease by direct examination of the blood and later by centrifugation of clotted blood, xenodiagnosis, and animal inoculation. One problem is the possible misidentification of parasites in examination of the blood—for example, the spirochete of syphilis has been confused with *T. cruzi*. If *T. cruzi* is reported in blood samples, retesting is recommended. Tables 3 and 4 concisely provide a list of the different tests and their validity.

Much less popular, but still common, xenodiagnosis appears to be a technique from the Middle Ages akin with the use of leeches; but it is an effective available resource. Uninfected *vinchucas* are placed within a jar, tucked under the patient's armpit, and allowed to consume blood for thirty minutes. Their feces are examined thirty and sixty days later for *T. cruzi*. Obviously, xenodiagnosis has its problems, primarily, obtaining uninfected bugs. This technique is rarely used on children for obvious reasons. Many adults also have phobias and would rather go untested. However, sometimes medical examinations are as painful as the illness. Xenodiagnosis can be an excellent examination for the determining of parasite populations and strains.

Indirect tests that look for *T. cruzi* antibodies have recently been devised, but they usually are not used during the acute phase because the immune system is in the process of producing chagasic antibodies. Similar to that used for AIDS, an ELISA test has been designed to detect the presence of *T. cruzi* antibodies; however, the chagasic ELISA sometimes fails to differentiate antibodies of *T. cruzi* from those of either *T. rangelii* (a harmless cousin) or *Leishmania braziliensis* (the causative agent of the mucocutaneous form of leishmaniasis, common in Andean regions where Chagas' disease is also found). Chronic patients should be tested both ways, even when ELISA comes out negative, to determine the rate of infection. People without noticeable symptoms living in chagasic areas are encouraged to have an ELISA test. If it comes out positive, xenodiagnosis is encouraged to determine the nature of the infection and form of treatment. The Ministry of Public Health and IBBA in La Paz, Bolivia, provide these tests for Bolivians at a reasonable cost (five dollars in 1997).

TABLE 3

PARASITOLOGICAL METHODS FOR THE DIAGNOSIS OF CHAGAS' DISEASE

(adapted from WHO 1991:38)

Methods	Type of laboratory[a]	Percentage of Sensitivity[b]	
		Acute stage	Chronic Stage
DIRECT			
Thin Smear	A/B	>60	<10
Thick blood smear	A/B	>70	<10
Fresh blood examination	A/B	80–90	<10
Strout	A/B	90–100	<10
Buffy coat on slide	A/B	90–100	<10
INDIRECT			
Xenodiagnosis	B	100	20–50
Blood cultures	B	100	40–50

[a]A: Health center laboratories located in areas at risk of vectorial and nonvectorial transmission (the infrastructure is that from the first level of medical care upwards). B: Specialized laboratories for parasitological diagnosis. A and B laboratories are found at MSSP and IBBA in La Paz, MSSP in Cochabamba, and MSSP in Santa Cruz. Since 1991 USAID has helped improve these laboratories for chagas diagnosis. Sucre lacks an adequately equipped B laboratory.

[b] As compared to xenodiagnosis for the acute stage of the infection and to serological diagnosis for the chronic stage.

Relatively few Latin Americans are tested for *T. cruzi* due to a combination of factors including cost, pain, and a fatalistic attitude that, if they test positive, medications are prohibitively priced and only partially effective, with the probability that they will be again be parasitized. There is also the social cost of being ostracized, although this is less true in Bolivia than in some other places. Epidemic diseases frequently lead to old and new prejudices surfacing that lead to ostracism of the victims (see Foege 1988, and Lederberg 1988, in regard to AIDS in the United States). It would not be a very popular decision for immigrants to the United States to let others know they are seropositive for *T. cruzi*.

TABLE 4

Serological Methods for Diagnosis of Chagas and Antigens Used
(WHO 1991:40)

Complement-fixation test (CFT). Aqueous or methanol extracts of whole *T. cruzi* have been widely used but have been replaced by purified fractions of the parasite in an attempt to standardize the sensitivity and specificity measures.

Indirect immunofluorescent antibody test (IFAT). Formol-fixed epimastigotes are stable antigens. The IFAT has the advantage that it can be used for differentiating IgM from IgG antibodies.

Indirect haemagglutination test (IHA). The antigens are polysaccharide or glycoprotein fractions from epimastigotes. Red cells sensitized with those antigens can be stored lyophilized or in suspension.

Direct agglutination test (DA and 2-MEDA). The antigen consists of whole epimastigotes treated with trypsin, and fixed with formaldehyde and filtered to prevent autoagglutination. The test can be used for detection of IgG or IgM antibodies.

ELISA. The antigen consists of peroxidase, or phosphatase-labeled conjugates or fractions of *T. cruzi* adsorbed to polyvinyl plates or other materials, and is stable. The test can be used for detection of IgG or IgM antibodies.

Latex agglutination. Polystyrene particles absorbed with *T. cruzi* extracts are used.

APPENDIX 13
Chemotherapy

The first chemical solutions against Chagas' disease with sufficient activity to justify clinical trials, the bisquinaldines, were not discovered
until 1937 (Jensch 1937), and it was not until 1972 that the first drug to combat
the disease, nifurtimox, was announced and launched by Bayer for use in some
countries of Latin America in 1976 (Bock et al. 1972). (Bayer has discontinued
producing the drug as of 1997). Nifurtimox is a 5-nitrofuran derivative (synonyms: Bayer 2502, Lampit) with antiprotozoal activity, and it is also used
to treat leishmaniasis and African trypanosomiasis (Reynolds 1986:673; see
Figure 32).

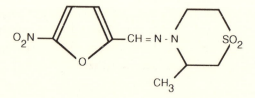

Figure 32. Nifurtimox.
(From W.E. Gutteridge, *Existing Chemotherapy and Its Limitations*, 1985.)

Nifurtimox is administered as a yellow powder that a patient is to dissolve
in water and drink three times a day after meals for sixty to ninety days at a
daily dose of 8–10 mg per kg for adults, 15–20 mg per kg for children aged one
to ten years, and 12.5–15 mg per kg for children aged eleven to sixteen years.
Dosages may be as large as 25 mg/kg for severe complications such as acute
meningoencephalitis (WHO 1991). Children tolerate the drug better than do
adults. Nifurtimox is readily absorbed and rapidly metabolized, with a peak
plasma concentration at one to three hours, which declines to zero by twenty-
four hours. Some doctors prefer to stagger the treatment in two-month intervals (Jáuregui, interview 6/22/91). Although the usual treatment extends for
120 days, it can be effective when given for sixty days (Macedo 1982).

The earlier the diagnosis is made and treatment initiated, the greater is the
chance that the patient will be parasitologically cured (Cancado and Brener
1979). Drug therapy is highly recommended to minimize parasitic invasion of

vital tissues (McGreevy and Marsden 1986:117). Good results are achieved early in treatment, as indicated by the disappearance of circulating trypanosomes, remission of disease signs and symptoms, and occasional reversion to a serologically negative condition. Serological tests tend to become negative from six to eight months after treatment, and the cure is considered successful when both parasitemia and serological tests become negative and remain so for at least a year after the end of treatment.

Nifurtimox does have side effects, including nausea, skin rashes, peripheral neuritis, bone-marrow depression, loss of weight, loss of memory, and sleeping disorders, which may lead to depression and general malaise to such a degree that few patients actually complete the treatment period (Gutteridge 1985). When nifurtimox was given to animals in high doses, it produced cancer; but no such effects have been described in human patients (McGreevy and Marsden 1986:117). In one study using nifurtimox in Brazil, all treated patients had weight loss, 70 percent had anorexia, and 33 percent had peripheral neuritis during treatment at 7–8 mg/kg per day for sixty days (McGreevy and Marsden 1986:117). Peripheral neuritis and psychosis depend on dosages of nifurtimox and usually occur at the end of high-dose treatment (15–20 mg/kg per day). Nifurtimox will cause hemolytic anemia in glucose 6-phosphate dehydrogenase (G6PD)-deficient individuals.

The efficacy of nifurtimox varies in different geographical areas. Cure rates appear to decrease going from south to north in Latin America, and this is probably due in part to variation in the sensitivity of different strains of *T. cruzi* (see Appendix 2: Strains of *T. cruzi*). Studies of both acute and chronic Chagas' disease show that patients from central Brazil are relatively unresponsive to nifurtimox as compared with patients from Argentina, Bolivia, and Chile (Cancado and Brener 1979, Brener 1979). The cure rate is about 92 percent in Argentina, Chile, Bolivia, and southern Brazil, and about 53 percent in central Brazil. Low concentrations of circulating parasites are difficult to detect, and monthly xenodiagnosis or blood culture is required.

Regarding acute patients in central Brazil, xenodiagnosis is usually negative during nifurtimox treatment, but it converts to positive in 60–70 percent of the patients over a four-year period. Post-treatment serodiagnosis usually remains positive in chronic patients, suggesting that parasites persist even when xenodiagnosis is negative.

Nifurtimox's action has been explained by two hypotheses. The first implicates biosynthetic reactions, especially nucleic and protein synthesis (see Sims and Gutteridge 1978, 1979), as a consequence of interaction with nucleic acids, especially DNA, in which single- and double-strand breaks occur (Gugliotta et al. 1980). This mechanism is similar to that suggested for the antibacterial action of similarly acting drugs and also explains the known mutagenicity and

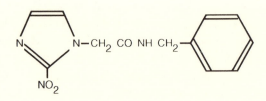

Figure 33. Benznidazole.
(From W.E. Gutteridge, *Existing Chemotherapy and Its Limitations*, 1985.)

carcinogenicity of many 5-nitrofurans (Gutteridge 1985). The second hypothesis explains the lysing of the parasites as a result of drug metabolism, of superoxide anions and hence hydrogen peroxide, which accumulates to cytotoxic levels in *T. cruzi* because of the absence of catalase (Docampo and Stoppani 1979, Docampo and Moreno 1984). This hypothesis explains the ultrastructural lesions that these drugs produce (Sims and Gutteridge 1979), and *T. cruzi* does indeed generate free radical metabolites from nifurtimox at physiological drug concentrations (Docampo and Moreno 1984). Neither hypothesis is mutually exclusive—drug metabolism produces both types of activity. Research on the effects of nifurtimox on intact *T. cruzi* is required to resolve this debate.

Benznidazole was announced in 1974 and released by the Roche pharmaceutical company in Latin America in late 1978 (Barclay et al. 1978; see Figure 33). Benznidazole's synonyms are R07-1051, Radanil, and Rochagan. It is a 2-nitroimidazole derivative with antiprotozoal activity (Reynolds 1986:660). Also a yellow powder, it is taken in water and is rapidly absorbed and distributed through the body tissues (Macedo 1982). Recommended dosage is 5 mg/kg/day (10mg/kg/day for children) for sixty days (Gutteridge 1985). It is claimed to be effective in curing more than 80 percent of both acute and chronic Chagas' disease patients. There is no clear evidence that it has any advantage over nifurtimox, and the efficacy of the two drugs is similar, though it has been claimed that benznidazole has less geographic variation in cure rates (Ribeiro-dos-Santos, Rassi, and Köberle 1980).

Initial clinical studies with benznidazole used higher doses, and serious side effects such as polyneuropathy and progressive purpuric dermatitis occurred. Adverse effects of benznidazole include nausea, vomiting, abdominal pain, peripheral neuropathy, and severe skin reactions (Reynolds 1986:660). It causes erythematous light-sensitive skin rashes, which can be severe, in half of the patients (Boainain 1979). A study involving twenty patients with chronic Chagas' disease who were given benznidazole in a dosage of 5 mg per kg of body weight daily had to be stopped because of the high incidence of

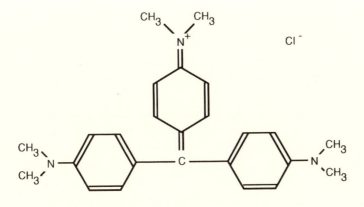

Figure 34. Gentian violet.
(From W.E. Gutteridge, *Existing Chemotherapy and Its Limitations*, 1985.)

skin rashes and neurological symptoms (Apt 1986:1010). Benznidazole also causes a marked thrombocytopenia in humans and depresses thymus-dependent immune functions in rabbits (Teixeira et al. 1983).

As possible new drug leads, another nitroimidazole (2-amino-5-[methyl-5-nitro-2-imidazolyl]-1,3,4 thiadiazole) has shown remarkable efficacy in mice, curing 89 percent of cases with a single dose (Filardi and Brener 1982). It is also active against parasite strains that are resistant to nifurtimox and 2-nitroimki-daxole derivatives. Trypomastigotes are cleared from the bloodstream in six hours, and destruction of amastigotes occurs in eighteen to thirty-six hours (Almeida et al. 1984). This drug is presently being tested on humans (Mc-Greevy and Marsden 1986:118).

Another promising drug, allopurinol, is presently being researched, with initial studies indicating trypanosomicidal action at daily doses of 600 mg given for thirty to sixty days. Research is still being conducted concerning its efficacy and toxicity.

Another drug, gentian violet, is used to prevent transmission of the disease through blood transfusions. Although gentian violet is effective in destroying trypomastigotes in blood supplies, people dislike receiving a transfusion of violet-colored blood, and it is still being evaluated for safety. Gentian violet (crystal violet) is a cationic dye (see Figure 34) that demonstrates photodynamic action in visible light to produce hydrogen peroxide (Docampo et al. 1988). It is readily soluble in water. First used in 1953, it rapidly lyses trypomastigote forms of *T. cruzi* in whole blood and thus prevents the transmission of Chagas' disease through blood transfusion (Nussenzweig et al. 1953). The dosage is 25 cc of solution gentian at 0.5 percent in glucoside isotonic solution for each 500 cc of blood for twenty-four hours, but blood is rarely, if ever, held long enough in Bolivia to be treated with gentian violet (Nussenzweig et al. 1953, Schumuñis 1991). At the University of Brasilia in Brazil, this technique has been used to treat seropositive blood for many years without mishap (Marsden 1983:255). However, it does not work against all strains of *T. cruzi* (Brener 1979).

Gentian violet exhibits photodynamic action against parasites (Docampo et al. 1988). Visible light causes photoreduction of gentian violet to a carbon-centered radical, and under aerobic conditions this free radical autooxidizes generating anion whose dismutation yields hydrogen peroxide.

Side effects for patients who receive blood with gentian violet are being studied (see Ramírez et al. 1995 for alternative methods under research). Gentian violet causes microagglutination and rouleaux formation of erythrocytes *in vitro*, and it has never been subjected to current safety testing standards. The concern shown by patients towards the coloration (Gutteridge 1982, 1986) is a factor to be considered and discussed with patients receiving a transfusion, as they are likely to encounter this at a time when psychological disturbances should be kept to a minimum.

In highly endemic areas of Chagas' disease where serology is occasionally unreliable and little screening is done, addition of gentian violet to all blood before transfusion has been recommended (Carrasco et al. 1990, Rassi and Rezende 1976).

Presently, nifurtimox and benznidazole are effective in controlling the acute stage of Chagas' disease to prevent damage to vital organs. A cure rate of near 90 percent is claimed if these drugs are administered at an early stage and in prescribed dosages. Nifurtimox and benznidazole have effectively treated congenital Chagas' disease in newborns and infants in Argentina, Bolivia, Brazil, Chile, and Uruguay. Severe side effects, questionable safety, and availability provide serious limitations that need to be resolved by research to provide more adequate drugs and more funds to provide these drugs to the impoverished in Latin America. In endemic areas with high risks of reinfection, it may be advisable to use these drugs in lesser dosages to limit the damage of *T. cruzi* rather than attempt to completely eradicate it.

None of these drugs, including gentian violet, is ideal (Gutteridge 1985, Ramírez et al. 1995), and our ability to control and treat, let alone eradicate, Chagas' disease is severely curtailed. The obstacles are formidable on the scientific side and relate not only to finding trypanocides that lyse the parasites in their different stages and differing strains but also to getting the drug to the vicinity of the *in vivo* sites of trypanosomes without destroying human cells.

The cost of discovering a drug and developing it to product registration is on average about ten years and millions of dollars, with about one successful drug resulting from 10,000 tested compounds. The problem is further aggravated with Chagas' disease because the human commercial market is small in comparison to the number of people infected, so pharmaceutical companies are unlikely to invest in drug development when the potential return on their investment is risky. However, as Chagas' disease continues to become worldwide in scope through immigration, vertical transmission, and blood transfusions, the marketability of treatment drugs will increase. The discovery of the nematocidal and ectoparasiticidal activities of the avermectins, and the commercial success of Ivermec, ensure that increasing attention will be paid to trying to find similarly successful drugs for Chagas' disease. Pharmaceutical companies, international agencies such as World Health Organization and the United Stages Agency for International Development, and governments of Andean countries are beginning to work together with scientists in the development and distribution of drugs to treat Chagas' disease.

Very encouraging news has come from a group of scientists at the Instituto Venezolano de Investigaciones Científicas, the London School of Hygiene and Tropical Medicine, Janssen Research Foundation, and the Swiss Tropical Institute (Urbina et al. 1996). They have screened hundreds of compounds and found a compound code-named D0870 to be effective against both short- and long-term Chagas' disease. It is an inhibitor of sterol biosynthesis and as such was identified first as an anti-fungal agent. Inhibitors of sterol biosynthesis also affect *T. cruzi*, which has similar steroid metabolism to fungi. Earlier *in vitro* studies showed that D0870 causes the parasite's natural sterols to be replaced by 14 α-methyl sterols. The new compound is able to cure a large percentage of both acute and chronic *T. cruzi* infections in mice—blocking parasite growth and reproduction and penetrating cells infected by parasites in chronic infections. D0870 has been found to be effective against six different strains of *T. cruzi* in mice as well as *T. brucei* (responsible for African trypanosomiasis) *in vitro*. These results provide a sound basis for further pre-clinical development of D0870 as an anti-*T. cruzi* compound (toxicology and pharmacokinetics studies). After that, clinical studies using this compound for treating Chagas' disease may be initiated. But the compound is in its early phases and it will be years before Zeneca Pharmaceutical makes it available for human treatment (*TDRnews* 1996:4-4).

APPENDIX 14

Baseline Studies in Chuquisaca

Baseline studies were completed in four communities of the Chuquisaca region where *Proyecto Británico Cardenal Maurer* was working. Project members surveyed seropositivity to Chagas' disease, infestation rates and percentage of infected vinchucas, and types of housing. Meeting some resistance, doctors and nurses extracted blood samples from thirty-seven people in the community of Choromomo. Andeans frequently fear that blood lost will not be restored, based on beliefs that they have only a limited supply of blood. Blood and bugs were shipped by air to a laboratory in Cochabamba, where they were analyzed for *T. cruzi*. Results indicated that 61 percent (403) of the bugs (660) and 32 percent (12) of the blood samples (37) were positive for Chagas' disease. Significantly, 27 percent (9) were from people between the ages of eight and twenty-six years (CRS-PROCOSI 1990:16).

Additional baseline studies in 1990 gave project workers some idea of infestation rates and conditions of housing for four characteristic communities (see Table 5).

TABLE 5
BASE STUDY OF TRIATOMINE INFESTATION IN CHUQUISACA
(CRS-PROCOSI 1990:8)

Community	Houses Examined	Triatoma Infected Houses		Triatomas Captured	Triatomas with *T. cruzi*	
	No.	No.	%	No.	No	%
Puente Sucre	21	18	86	73	32	44
Choromomo	32	32	100	120	104	87
La Mendoza	66	59	89	215	134	62
T. Ackachila	60	52	87	252	133	53
TOTAL	179	161	90	660	403	61

Ninety percent of houses in the four communities were infested with *vinchucas*, of which 61 percent were transmitting the chagasic parasite. Comparing the four communities, when infestation rates increase 10 percent, going from an average of 90 to 100 percent, the percentage of infected triatomines increases at a greater percentage, going from an average of 61 percent to 87 percent, as illustrated in Choromomo. Communities with 60 to 80 percent bug infestation rates also indicated similar infection rates. This suggests the hypothesis that at a nearly complete infestation rate, the parasite approximates this percentage.

Another study was completed to assess type of housing within the Department of Chuquisaca (see Table 6).

TABLE 6

CLASSIFICATION OF HOUSES IN FOUR COMMUNITIES OF SUCRE

(CRS-PROCOSI 1990:9)

COMMUNITY	Type I Good	Type II Regular	Type III Bad	TOTAL	Closed Houses
Puente Sucre	0	2	20	22	1
Choromomo	0	4	28	32	2
La Mendoza	0	3	63	66	2
T. Ackachila	0	9	53	62	3
TOTAL	0	18	164	182	8

Dwellings were categorized into three types: Type 1—good, Type 2—regular, and Type 3—bad. Houses were classified into types according to such factors as having straw and mud roofs; adobe walls partially plastered or without plaster; presence of cracks in walls, foundation, and roof; no ceiling; dirt floors; and poor hygiene. This grouping was relatively easy to apply, because most houses fit into the bad category and none fit into the good category, with 18 regular and 164 (or 90 percent) bad (see Table 6). Unhealthy houses correlated closely with infestation rates, both being 90 percent. This being the case, in endemic areas, housing conditions alone could serve as indicators of infestation rates.

Baseline studies provided personnel with figures to evaluate progress and to what extent fumigation, house improvements, and housing hygiene lowered the infestation rates. After spraying and house improvements were completed, a new study of house infestation was done. Periodic surveys indicated that continued vigilance was essential to Chagas' disease control. Since *vinchucas* kept colonizing homes if houses became run down, PBCM concluded that spraying was necessary every six months; however, this is costly.

Notes

Introduction

1. This research is summarized in the following articles and books: concerning Aymara rituals (Bastien 1989), Kallawaya herbal curing (Bastien 1982, 1983a, 1983b), ethnophysiology (Bastien 1985), Kallawaya herbalists (Bastien 1987), cultural perceptions of neonatal tetanus and programming implications (Bastien 1988), integration of ethnomedicine and biomedicine (Bastien 1992), and training of community health workers (Bastien 1990).

2. Some of these positions were coordinator with Project Concern for community health workers and biomedical personnel of the Department of Oruro, Bolivia, (Bastien 1987b, 1990a); educator with Project Concern for diarrhea control and oral rehydration therapy (Bastien 1987a: 81–84); researcher with Resources for Child Health concerning prevention of neonatal tetanus (Bastien 1988); anthropologist working with Bolivian radio schools (1990); and ethnologist advisor to USAID projects: Community and Child Health (1987a, 1991), Bolivian Forestation Project (1995), and Chagas Control Project, Bolivia (1991).

3. The acronym in Spanish is SNS/CCH, Programa Piloto de Control de Chagas; in English it is SOH/CCH, Chagas Control Pilot Project.

Chapter 1

1. For the medical history of Chagas' disease see Chagas 1909, 1911, 1921, 1922, 1988; Chagas Filho 1959, 1968, 1988, 1993; Kean 1977; and Lewinsohn 1979, 1981.

2. "La vinchuca incommode beaucoup ceux qui voyagent de Mendoza à Buenos-Ayres....C'est un escarbot ou scarabée, dont le corps est ovale e très-aplati, et qui devient gros comme un grain de raisin, du sang qu'il suce....Cet insect ne sort que de nuit; les individus ailés peuvent avoir cinq lignes de long, et volent; ce qui n'arrive pas aux petit."

3. Concerning the debate whether Darwin had Chagas' disease see Browne 1995:280; Keynes 1988:315; Goldstein 1989:586–601; and Woodruff 1965.

Chapter 3

1. Castor oil is a fixed oil expressed from the seed of the croton plant, *Croton tiglium*. Although commonly used fifty years ago in biomedicine, Taber's *Cyclopedic Medical Dictionary* (1985:400) says, "Action: Drastic cathartic, externally as a rubefacient. This chemical has no place in medicine and should not be used."

2. Biomedical ethics in Bolivia at the time treated lightly the fact that doctors used Indians as trial subjects. The most noted transgression was a La Paz oculist's experiments on Aymara Indians, who were noted for their excellent vision, in the early de-

velopment stages of radial kerometry. In other Latin American countries, prisoners have been experimentally infected with *T. cruzi* and treated with potential remedies (G. Stewart, interview, 1993).

3. This name is purposely withheld for legal reasons. One of Bolivia's most reputed naturalists, Jaime Zalles, claims that the patented formula from Regenerator has had millions of dollars in drug sales. I have been unable to verify this.

4. As one example: "Fifth Case.- Margarita Vidaurre. First analysis from Laboratorio de Salud Pública on October 24, 1966. Complement Fixation: positive. Second analysis from Laboratorio de Salud Pública on July 12, 1970, negative."

5. Scientists discussed below discount *floripondio* as an insecticide.

6. Leading this research are Dr. Gonzalo Tapia, director, and biologist Jose Luis Alcázar, both of Proyecto Chagas of the Universidad Mayor San Simon, Cochabamba; Dr. Gene Bourdy of *Instituto Boliviano de Biología de Altura* (IBBA); and botanist Suzanna Arrazola of the Herbario, Cochabamba.

7. There is hope that a novel compound code-named D0870, which has been shown to cure both long-term and short-term Chagas' disease in mice (Urbina et al. 1996), will do the same in humans; however, it is in the early phases of clinical development for other infections. (See Appendix 13.)

Chapter 4

1. Meningoencephalitis due to *T. cruzi* has been reported in pharmacologically immunodepressed patients and in patients with AIDS (Jost et al. 1977; Corona et al. 1988; Del Castillo et al. 1990). (See Appendix 11.)

2. In addition to these practical considerations, *T. cruzi* have unique properties that make them evasive targets for potential chemotherapeutic agents and therefore present formidable challenges to pharmacologists and medical chemists. *T. cruzi* are intracellular parasites, found in a variety of tissues. The effectiveness of a chemical compound depends on its capacity to cross the vascular endothelium and cell membranes into the cytoplasmic compartment of the parasite. *T. cruzi* is not a homogenous species—there are geographic strains which vary in tissue tropism and response to chemotherapy and biochemical parameters such as electrophoretic profiles of isoenzymes and peptides. The value of a particular drug depends on its effectiveness against both the amastigote and trypomastigote stages of all geographic strains (McGreevy and Marsden 1986:115–27). (See Appendix 13.)

3. In another study, Bryan and Tonn (1990:14) report higher rates of *T. cruzi* infection in captured (domestic) triatomines, with averages from 40 to 50 percent and infection rates of 70 to 90 percent in rural areas of the Cochabamba and Chuquisaca departments of Bolivia. (See Appendix 5.)

4. A recent study analyzed hemotherapy and the problem of transfusional Chagas' disease in 850 Brazilian municipalities from 1988 to 1989. It found that some type of hemotherapy was practiced in 68.8 percent of these municipalities (Moraes-Souza et al. 1995). Prior screening of donors was carried out by 75.2 percent of the services for syphilis, 65.4 percent for hepatitis, 53.8 percent for AIDS, and 66.8 percent for Chagas' disease. In the case of Chagas' disease, only 10.3 percent of services used the chemoprophylaxis of gentian violet. Most services used only one serologic technique to screen

donors, and the proportion of potential donors with positive serology for anti– *T. cruzi* was around 1 percent. (See Appendix 13.)

5. Although the potential problem of the blood supply in the United States has been recognized for some time (Schmuñis 1985), the recent diagnosis of Chagas' disease acquired through blood transfusion in the United States (Grant et al. 1989) and Canada (Nickerson et al. 1989) has significantly highlighted the seriousness of this problem (Skolnick 1989, Kirchhoff 1989).

6. In Brazil in 1911 Carlos Chagas considered the possibility of congenital transmission of *T. cruzi* when he found trypomastigotes in the blood-smear of a two-month-old child whose mother was also infected (quoted in Howard and Rubio 1968). In Venezuela in 1949 Dao reported other cases of congenital Chagas' disease in Latin America (quoted in Bittencourt 1976). In Chile, Howard (1962) observed that 0.5 percent of premature babies weighing less than 2,000 grams (4.4 pounds) suffered from congenital Chagas' disease. In Salvador, Bahia, and Brazil, Bittencourt and colleagues (Bittencourt and Barbosa 1972, Bittencourt, Barbosa, et al. 1972) found that 2 percent of stillborn babies were infected with *T. cruzi;* and, in Argentina, Salem and colleagues found slightly higher rates, 2.35 percent among stillborn infants (quoted in Bittencourt 1975). By 1979 the number of described cases had reached 100, giving the impression that congenital transmission of Chagas' disease is infrequent. However, this impression is misleading, because the registered cases are only of fetuses and premature stillborns and do not include congenital Chagas' disease in newborns delivered at term (Bittencourt et al. 1974). The varying degrees of fetal and neonatal pathology in such countries as Argentina, Brazil, and Chile may be related to inherent characteristics of the parasite (Moya 1994). The fact that the incidence of infection remains the same in each of these countries and geographic regions suggests that population-related factors are not involved. Various factors having to do with the mother, the fetus, and the parasite are more likely implicated in transplacental transmission.

7. The newborns were delivered at the Percy Boland Maternity Hospital in the city of Santa Cruz and observed from August 1979 until July 1980. Blood samples from newborns and mothers were used to investigate the presence of *T. cruzi* by means of the modified Strout concentration, which has the highest sensitivity (95.2 percent; but only for acute cases) when compared to other direct parasitological testing methods (Flores et al. 1966; Cerisola 1972:97–100). (See Appendix 12.)

8. Fetal infection can occur when the mother is in acute, indeterminate, and chronic phases of infection. Most infected pregnant women experience the chronic, or inapparent, form of the disease during their pregnancy, although cases of acute infection have been reported (Moya 1994). The fetus of an infected pregnant woman is usually unaffected, with no observed alterations in the growth or viability of the fetus, nor is the newborn predisposed to exhibit specific disorders. Chagas' disease in the mother poses little risk to the baby during the perinatal period, which is after the twenty-eighth week of pregnancy through twenty-eight days following birth (Moya 1977, 1994; Moya and Barousse 1984; Castilho and Da Silva 1976).

If the fetus is infected, the outcome of pregnancy may be spontaneous abortion, fetal death, premature birth, low birth weight for gestational age, and even full-term delivery (Moya 1994). Congenitally infected infants present a broad spectrum of clinical manifestations—from grave illness with multisystem compromise (usually in premature neonates) to a total absence of symptoms at birth. Some infants remain asymptomatic; others present manifestations of the disease several weeks or months later. Clinical manifestations are encephalitis, meningoencephalitis, lesions in the retina or choroid, and elevated protein levels and cell counts in cerebrospinal fluid (Muñoz and Acevedo 1994).

9. Another route for *T. cruzi* is through the blood, by hematogenous spread, and through crossing of the placenta, with multiplication of the parasite in the Hofbauer cells (Bittencourt 1975). The amniotic fluid may provide another vehicle for *T. cruzi* to travel to fetuses as well as to obstetricians and gynecologists (Apt, Tejada, and Atrozz 1968; Bittencourt et al. 1981; Nattan-Larrier 1921). Contact of the skin with infected amniotic fluid could allow penetration of the skin, and *T. cruzi* has been found in the skin (Bittencourt 1976). Research is needed to evaluate the exact mechanisms of congenital transmission.

10. In laboratory experiments, animals have been infected by eating infected triatomines or mammals, but this has not been documented in experiments with humans (WHO 1991:34).

Chapter 5

1. Volvulus is found among Andeans at high altitudes (13,500 feet) and its predisposing cause is a prolapsed mesentery intestine, which may be caused by *T. cruzi* within this organ.

2. This doctor's behavior represents an elitist attitude that some Bolivian doctors exhibit in their treatment of peasants. There has been a considerable change within the 1990s with other Bolivian doctors who are able to communicate cross-culturally with the peasants (see Bastien 1992: 173–91).

3. See Marcondes de Rezende and Ostermayer 1994; Teixeira et al. 1980; Ribeiro dos Santos and L. Hudson 1980; Petry and Eisen 1989.

4. Dr. Mario Barragan Vargas conducted a five-year study of megacolon in Viacha, elevation 13,123 feet, located twenty miles from La Paz on the Altiplano. He found many cases of megacolon, which he attributed to altitudinal and genetic dispositions, not to Chagas' disease.

5. See MacSweeney, Shankar, and Theodorous 1995; Cutait and Cutait 1991; and Da Silveira 1976 for a discussion of current procedures.

6. See Rezende and Rassi 1958; Godoy and Haddad 1961; Vieira and Godoy 1963; Morales Rojas et al. 1961; and Iñiguez-Montenegro 1961.

7. In Brazil, chagasic esophageal problems are well known to the people, who refer to it in Portuguese as *Mal de Engasgo* ("Sickness of Choking"), *Entalo* ("Stuck"), and *Embuchamento* ("Engorgement"). The most frequent symptoms expressed are difficulty in swallowing, 99 percent; regurgitation, 57 percent; painful swallowing, 52 percent; belching, 41 percent; hiccups, 38 percent; sensation of plenitude, 32 percent; and coughing, 26 percent (Köberle 1968:90–91). Loss of weight, heartburn, and sour eructations are also very frequent, occurring in 70 percent of the cases. Advanced cases show elongation of esophagus muscles that can reach twenty-six times their normal weight. Advanced cases also have a predisposition to carcinoma, which may occur in 10 percent of the cases (Camara-Lopes 1962).

8. Nerve cells are decreased along the whole extension of the esophagus, resulting in loss of the coordinated peristalsis and sensitivity of the denervated musculature. This phenomenon, which occurs in the denervated hollow muscular organ, is called "aperistalsis" and describes the absence of esophageal motility (Brasil 1956). The denervated structure becomes supersensitive to any stimulus, inducing diffuse and severe spasms of the esophagus, which occasionally needs an urgent application of atropine.

9. The consistency of what is ingested is very important, because the transport of solids requires a more coordinated peristalsis than does the movement of liquids; also, excessive solid transport can cause a high overload to the damaged organ. In addition, increased consistency (reduced liquidity) of the contents of the esophagus favors the development of megaesophagus. Patients often drink large quantities of liquids to aid the passage of solids through the organ. Generally either very hot or very cold food intensifies difficulties in swallowing, and perhaps the associated abundant salivation constitutes a type of auxiliary mechanism for the deficient deglutition.

Chapter 6

1. This center began in 1984 with assistance from Banco InterAmericano Desarrollo (BID) and a contract with the Universidad El Salvador de Buenos Aires, Ministerio de Previsión Social y Salud Pública, and La Universidad de Sucre.

2. Figures have been adjusted to the 1992 census.

3. Such pathologies include cardiac enlargement, mitral and tricuspid valve insufficiency, and pulmonary embolization. An abnormal left ventricular impulse may reflect the frequent apical aneurysm formation. Right-bundle-branch block is frequent. Complete heart block, high-grade ventricular ectopy, and atrial fibrillation have a grave prognostic significance, both aggravating the congestive heart failure and enhancing predisposition for sudden cardiac death (see Iosa 1994). (See Appendix 10.)

4. Ventricular arrhythmias are a prominent feature of chronic Chagas' disease. Ventricular premature depolarization, often with multiple morphologies, is seen frequently. Bouts of ventricular tachycardia and arterial hypertension may occur as well as bradycardia and arterial hypotension (Braunwald 1988:1447; Iosa 1994).

5. See Brener (1994) and Appendix 11 for an overview of current theories on pathogenesis.

6. Investigators have found autoantibody and self-reactive T-cell formation in human and experimental *T. cruzi* infections (Teixeira, Teixeira, and Santos-Buch 1975; Cossio et al. 1974). Cross-reactive autoantibodies were mainly directed toward ubiquitous and evolutionary conservative molecules (Levin et al. 1989, Kerner et al. 1991, Van Voorhis et al. 1991) which lack clinical and biological significance for the different clinical forms of chronic Chagas' disease.

7. The presence of an antibody against cardiac myosin is correlated with the development of chronic inflammatory cardiopathy in *T. cruzi*-infected mice (Tibbetts et al. 1994). Immunization with cardiac myosin HC induces aggressive myocarditis (Neu et al. 1987b). Cunha-Neto and colleagues (1995) have recognized a heart-specific *T. cruzi* cross-reactive epitope, with chronic heart lesions further indicating the involvement of cross-reactions of myosin and B13 in the pathogenesis of chronic Chagas' disease.

8. See Voltarelli, Donadi, and Falcao 1987; Cunningham, Grogl, and Kuhn 1980; Mosca, Briceño, and Hernández 1991.

9. These antigens include many stress proteins with sequence homology to those of living organisms (Young, Lathigra, and Hendrix 1988).

Chapter 7

1. An appropriate technology for chagasic control is to teach peasants how to prevent *vinchuca* infestation by means of readily available materials, such as the use of cow dung in plastering and the use of bottle caps with nails through them to secure roofing and sheeting. For an excellent study on housing in La Paz, see Köster 1995.

2. Bolivia has traditionally had authoritarian governments, a carryover from colonial times. Presidents enjoyed power akin to the concept of the "divine right of kings." By 1985, Bolivians had suffered a series of military dictators, the most brutal being Luis García Meza, presently serving thirty years in prison for his crimes. In 1997, Bolivians voted for another "old time" military leader, General Hugo Banzer.

Chapter 8

1. Another acronym for the organization is PSBB, which refers to *Proyecto Social Boliviano-Británico "Cardenal Maurer."* By 1994, the British government no longer partially financed this project, so it was shortened to the Cardenal Maurer Project (CM).

2. The *Proyecto Británico Cardenal Maurer* project in Chuquisaca was included in 1991 as one of three pilot projects sponsored by the Bolivian Secretariat of Health (SOH) and Community and Child Health (CCH), with assistance from the United States Agency for International Development (USAID) and the Centers for Disease Control (CDC). The SOH/CCH Chagas Control Program ended on December 31, 1994.

3. Other successful health projects in Bolivia support this conclusion. Enthusiastic leaders include Gregory Rake with the CHW program in Oruro, Oscar Velasco with Project Concern in Potosí, Evaristo Mayda with ethnomedicinal practitioners in Cochabamba, Irene Vance with Pro-Habitat in La Paz, and José Beltrán with Plan International in Tarija.

4. These nongovernmental organizations (NGOs) include Pro-Habitat (Tarija), Plan-International (Tarija), and Proyecto Chagas (Cochabamba).

5. As authorities on the control of Chagas' disease in Bolivia, Bryan and Tonn (1990) wrote: "PBCM in Sucre is the best project of Chagas' disease control. It is a small project but well organized, with emphasis on community participation, health education, fumigation, and improvement of housing. It serves as a model for other chagasic control projects."

6. See WHO and UNICEF 1978:2–3; Coreil and Mull 1990; Phillips 1990:150–77.

7. USAID in Bolivia subcontracts many of its projects to nongovernmental organizations such as Project Concern, Save the Children, Operation Hope, Caritas. These organizations have their own goals underlying proposed humanitarian objectives of the project. As one measure, PROCOSI was formed in Bolivia in the 1980s and serves

as a coordinating board of NGOs in Bolivia through which USAID-Bolivia channels developmental monies.

8. Paulo Freire initiated *concientización* in Brazil, and spread it throughout Latin America by his writings, most notably, *Pedagogy of the Oppressed* (1970) and *Education for Critical Consciousness* (1973). See Luft (1983) and Hope and Timmel (1987) for detailed descriptions of *concientización* pedagogy. Although *concientización* has been identified with Karl Marx's analyses of the contradictions inherent in matter and the exploitation of the peasant by the capitalist classes, it also reflects the teachings of Jesus. Freire's 1970 book became a "Marxist's bible," as some saw it, for liberation-theology priests forming base communities. Severe military repression, both by Latin American and U.S. military forces, has extinguished these priests and their base communities. For a different interpretation see Berryman (1987:34–38, 71, 73, 130).

9. These pilot projects modified the role of community health workers (CHWs). A plan was adopted where each CHW was responsible for forty to ninety (average sixty) houses, and their fundamental role was to visit each family weekly to provide motivation and technical education (SOH/CCH 1994:16). This required too much time from CHWs, however, who were required to spend from thirty to sixty hours a week visiting families, considering that they have other responsibilities and are unpaid. In contrast, PBCM's practice of having traveling teams and CHWs meet together with the community members was more effective. Community leaders were motivated to assume responsibility for seeing that every family carried out its assigned task. The community accepted responsibility to carry out the project and CHWs served as liaison between the house improvement committees and PBCM personnel.

10. The total cost for 400 houses was $83,256, out of which villagers provided $37,642 in work and materials, and collaborators in the project provided $45,614, of which PBCM gave $10,814, Catholic Relief Services $5,000, the British embassy $5,000, and PROCOSI $24,800. PROCOSI (Programa de Coordinación en Supervivencia Infantil) is funded by USAID and the Bolivia Child Survival program. It is a supervisory and administrative organization for many nongovernmental health agencies and projects in Bolivia.

11. Volunteer labor is figured in to the cost of each house to indicate to providers of funds that what they contribute is matched. However, this gives the impression that house improvement is much more costly to the taxpayer or contributor.

12. The addition of vermifuge plants to wall plaster is another possibility, and insecticide paints are now being used effectively in Brazil (Pinchin et al. 1978a, 1978b).

13. Slow-release insecticide paints used during house building have shown lasting properties of killing 100 percent of 5th instar *T. infestans* after a ten-minute period of contact more than five years after being applied and subsequently exposed to environmental conditions in Brazil (Oliveira Filho, Deus, and Brasil 1987). Structures of a house were painted with black bitumen paint containing 9.7 percent clorpyrifos-ethyl (Dursban) before covering them with mud. This technique could be used in areas where houses are being built or restored. Using Dursban insecticide for painting walls presents problems of toxicity for humans, however.

14. An alternative low-cost roofing for tropical areas of Latin America involves the conversion of fibrous agricultural residues, such as bagasse from sugar cane, into a corrugated fiber roofing panel, which requires a relatively low capital investment and is labor intensive (Bryant 1978). Cost per square foot is about fifteen cents in U.S. money (1978).

15. Because of its clay content, walls built of unstabilized soil will swell on taking up water and shrink on drying (Briceño-León 1987:384). This results in cracking, which provides nesting areas for *vinchucas*. Soil stabilization is achieved by increasing the strength and cohesion of the soil, reducing the movement of moisture in the soil, and by making the soil more waterproof. Strength of a soil can be increased by the addition of cementious materials, such as Portland cement or other materials that include hydrated lime and lime-pozzolana mixes. A pozzolanic reaction is the reaction between lime and certain clay minerals to form various cementlike compounds. Lime also reduces the extent to which clay absorbs water, thus making the soil less sensitive to changes in moisture.

16. In Venezuela and Brazil, workers use metal presses to compact the mud within the cane to assure greater durability for cloth coverings or cement later placed on the walls (Schofield et al. 1990 and Briceño-León 1990:137). All these devices produce low-cost building blocks of about 12 x 6 x 4 inches, similar in size to traditional handmade adobe blocks (Briceño-Leon 1987:384).

17. Marco Antonio Prieto, director of Centro por Estudios por Desarollo Chuquisaca (CEDEC), provided this critique.

Chapter 9

1. See Victor Varas Reyes' study *El Castellano Popular en Tarija* and Ananias Barreto's work *Costumbres y Creencias del Campo Taijeño* for more examples.

2. A number of institutions, including Caritas (Catholic Relief), Pro-Habitat (UNICEF), SOH/CCH (Secretaria Nacional de Salud and USAID), and Plan International, have been involved in several projects in the Department of Tarija to improve houses. Each institution has contributed to solving the problem: Caritas (formation of CHWs), Pro-Habitat (educational material), SOH/CCH (evaluation studies and financial support), and Plan International (a micro-credit system). The projects have had different sponsoring organizations through their tenure.

3. I first met José Beltrán in 1991 and admired his teaching skills. During our last visit in 1997, he was even more proficient using the colorful charts and posters that he had helped design for other projects sponsored by SOH/CCH.

4. U.S. Public Law 480, according to which funds in host-country national currency derived from the sale of U.S. agricultural products are retained in the host country for use in development-assistance projects.

5. The five-year, $20 million Community and Child Health Project from 1989 until 1994 was funded by USAID, whose objectives were maternal and child health, primary health care, improvement of water and sanitation facilities, agricultural sustainability, and family planning. In 1991, Chagas' disease control was added, mostly through the efforts of Dr. Joel Kuritsky and President Jaime Paz, who during his inaugural visit to Washington, D.C., asked President George Bush for additional monies to combat Chagas' disease.

6. Project personnel are prone to criticize people doing other projects, although Beltrán's remarks reflected the opinion of other observers. He is considered the foremost expert on Chagas' control in Tarija.

7. For an outline of procedures, see Table 2: Production of Educational Materials, and Table 3: Phases of Educational Process (SOH/CCH 1994:36–37).

Chapter 10

1. Pilot projects were supported by the Bolivian Secretariat of Health (SOH) and the USAID Community and Child Health Project (CCH). The SOH/CCH Chagas' Disease Control Program lasted from 1991 to 1994, cost U.S. $4 million, and sponsored housing-improvement projects in Tarija, Cochabamba, and Chuquisaca, improving 3,135 houses (see SOH/CCH 1994).

2. Dr. Oscar Velasco is mentioned in Chapter 5. He is a Bolivian medical anthropologist and is presently director of Project Concern in Potosí. Velasco and I also designed the CHWS program and the articulation of biomedicine and ethnomedicine in the Department of Oruro (see Bastien 1992).

3. Marco Antonio Prieto is director of Centro por Estudios por Desarollo Chuquisaca (CEDEC). His criticism was primarily directed at the project in Chuquisaca, which, of the three pilot projects, attempted most to become integrated with the culture.

4. Dr. Pablo Regalsky is director of Centro de Comunicación y Desarollo Andino (CENDA) in Cochabamba.

5. Dr. Evaristo Mayda suggested the triangle diagram. Dr. Mayda is director of Project Concern Cochabamba and has been a leader in integrating ethnomedicine and biomedicine in the Department of Cochabamba.

6. Melogno is director of *Fundación de Programas de Asentamientos Humanos,* a housing project in the Alto Beni. He was interviewed on May 13, 1997.

7. SOH/CCH allocated a dollar amount to this volunteer activity as a form of cost-sharing; thus, when a household matched the money donated, their share was calculated according to what they would have earned if they had been paid. Cost-sharing was helpful in negotiating for matching funds from institutions.

8. All are native Bolivians, except for Regalsky, who was born in Buenos Aires but who speaks the Quechua language fluently and has done fieldwork among the Quechua of Ragaypampa. Quechua leaders work with him on matters concerning the new laws and popular participation. He has been an advocate for Quechuans for ten years.

Chapter 11

1. The SOH/CCH projects were directed by biologists from Vector Biology Control and a medical doctor and epidemiologist from the Centers for Disease Control, with only token considerations from anthropologists, economists, and sociologists. As a result, these projects narrowly focused on house improvement and spraying as the immediate solution to control *vinchucas*. Afterwards, with the exception of some communities in the Chuquisaca project, infestation began anew because peasants improved their houses for reasons other than *vinchuca* control.

Appendix 1

1. Dr. George Stewart, professor of Biology at the University of Texas at Arlington, has done extensive and noted research on parasites and disease. Many of the ideas and

facts in the appendices are from his lectures. Nonetheless, I am totally responsible for the content of the appendices.

Appendix 5

1. For a comparison of sampling techniques for domestic populations of triatomines see Schofield and Marsden (1982:356), who used another method for studying house infestation. Inspectors examined a house for bugs at approximately monthly intervals for two and a half years. Two men, each equipped with a flashlight and long forceps, searched the house for forty-five minutes and collected all the live bugs they could find. These bugs were sorted, counted, and then destroyed. Bug population estimates were then made by the Zippin (1956:163–89) withdrawal method. Within the house being studied 92 adults and 169 fifth instars were collected. The number of the other stages present could not be estimated, but life-table studies indicate that these figures are consistent with a total bug population (including eggs) of approximately 2,200 individuals.

Bermúdez et al. (1978) examined a henhouse in Gutiérrez, in a rural area of the Department of Santa Cruz, Bolivia, and found 1,524 triatomines; less than 1 percent were infected with *T. cruzi*. One explanation is that these *T. infestans* predominantly fed on chickens, which cannot become hosts for *T. cruzi*.

Glossary

acute infection—Refers to initial infection with *Trypanosoma cruzi,* which may not be clinically apparent. If apparent, it is characterized by inflammation caused by the infiltration of mononuclear cells and may include fever, general malaise, swelling and soreness of the lymph nodes and spleen, and Romaña's sign. Acute phase begins four to twelve days following the introduction of the organism and ends after approximately two months (sometimes up to four months). This phase can be deadly for infants, who do not have fully developed immune systems.

adenosine triphosphate (ATP)—An enzyme found in all cells. When this substance is split by enzyme action, energy is produced. Triatomines effectively acquire this through blood meals.

African trypanosomiasis—Another name for African sleeping sickness caused by trypanosome parasites that are *salivaria* (travel from the mouth of the insect).

Altiplano—A high plain or plateau (12,500 feet) between the eastern and western ranges of Bolivia and Peru. It is where Aymara- and Quechua-speaking Andeans live.

amastigote—A stage of trypanosoma found in the host that lack long flagella. Amastigotes are round and smaller than trypomastigotes. They are intracellular, forming cysts in muscle and neuron tissue. Within this stage, trypanosomes reproduce into more amastigotes and trypomastigotes.

American trypanosomiasis—Another name for Chagas' disease, caused by trypanosome parasites that are stercoria (travel from the intestines and fecal matter).

antibody—A protein produced in the immune system that responds to a foreign substance or antigen. See Immunoglobin.

auxiliary nurses—Medical personnel who manage health posts in rural areas of Bolivia. They receive six months training in primary health care and emergency medicine.

ayllu—Distinguishable groups in the Andes whose solidarity is formed by religious and territorial ties (*llahta ayllu*), by permanent claim to land and lineage (*jatun ayllu*), by affinal ties (*masi ayllu*), and by work (*mitmaj ayllu*). Kallawayas understand *ayllu* as the vertical triangular land masses divided into high, center, and low ecological zones where communities live. They also perform healing rituals to the earth shrines of the *ayllu.*

Aymaras—A civilization and ethnic group of Andean peoples who speak the Aymara language and live in the highlands of Chile, Bolivia, and Peru.

aynisiña (ayni)—A basic Andean institution wherein peasants set up a system of compensation regarding work tasks. An *ayni* would be an amount of work, such as thatching a roof, that someone owes another because he or she has done the same or an equivalent task for that person.

barbeiro—A popular Brazilian name for *vinchucas,* or triatomine vectors of Chagas' disease.

baseline study (survey)—A collection of initial epidemiological, entomological, and social data concerning incidence of disease, infestation of insects, and condition of housing that is used as a basis to determine the effectiveness of Chagas' control projects.

Benznidazole (synonyms are R07-1051, Radanil, and Rochagan)—A drug used to treat Chagas' disease. It is a 2-nitroimidazole derivative with antiprotozoal activity.

Bolivian agrarian reform—It marks the end of feudalism in Bolivia and began after the April 1952 revolution. It divided the haciendas, distributed land to the peasants, and abolished the tribute system. It restored to indigenous communities the lands which had been usurped from them, and it cooperated in the modernization of agriculture. After the Agrarian Reform law was signed, 90 percent of the landlords abandoned their estates and the countryside essentially belonged to the Indians.

campesinos (peasants)—A word used to refer to traditional Andeans and the vast majority of Aymara and Quechua farmers and herders throughout the Andes. They speak native languages and generally dress in traditional clothes.

capitalization—Influx of investment funds for capital development.

cargo system—A deeply embedded Andean political institution in which leadership is seen as a burden (*cargo*) to be carried voluntarily without material gain but which accrues toward becoming a complete adult (*una persona muy completa*) in the community. It entails a number of leadership responsibilities for each person: leading the village, taking care of fiestas, being a secretary, and, lately, being involved in community health work.

carrier (also carrier host)—One who harbors disease organisms in his body without manifesting symptoms—thus acting as a carrier or distributor of infection. Many Bolivians do not suffer from Chagas' disease but are infected with Chagas' disease and thus are carriers from which uninfected bugs can contract the parasite.

chagoma—A carbuncle sore or painful node covered by tight reddened skin that often, but not always, appears at the site where *T. cruzi* enters the skin. The most characteristic of these is Romaña's sign, which appears arround the eye.

chapaco—A popular name given to people of the Department of Tarija, Bolivia.

cholos—Aymara and Quechua people who have adopted some Western ways but who continue to hold on to many Andean traditions. Many speak Spanish, and the men wear Western clothing, whereas many women continue to wear stove-pipe and derby hats and *pullera* (traditional skirts). In a hierarchical, class-stratified society, *cholos* are higher than *campesinos* (peasants) and lower than *mestizos*. The *cholo* class has become a dominant merchant class in Bolivia, excelling as truckers, traders, market vendors, merchants, and politicians. See *campesinos* and *mestizos*.

chronic phase (also called Tertiary Chagas' disease, classic chronic)—A result of gradual tissue destruction, usually of the colon, esophagus, and heart. Some patients remain relatively asymptomatic until this phase when organ damage appears. Other patients who have suffered severe acute infections pass immediately into the chronic phase because of initial organ damage. The chronic phase is considered incurable, with only its symptoms being treated.

chuyma usu ("sick heart")—A phrase used by Andeans to express heart disease, which often indicates *T. cruzi* infection.

cólico miserere ("miserable colic")—Refers to enlarged colon, often caused by obstruction or entangled intestines (volvulus) or denervation of intestinal tissue from *T. cruzi* infection.

colostomy—The opening of some portion of the colon onto the surface of the abdomen to release feces. This is performed when it is impossible for the feces to pass through the colon and out the anus due to damage caused by *T. cruzi* or other pathological conditions.

Community Health Workers (CHWs, *promotores*)—Members of an outreach program in which community members become involved in their own health delivery and elect some resident to be trained in providing primary health care. Many rural communities in Bolivia have CHWs, who play an integral part in the prevention of Chagas' disease.

community participation—Involvement of community members in decision making involving acceptance of and compliance with certain social and behavioral changes in regard to Chagas' disease.

concientización (consciousness-raising education, CRE)—A pedagogy of development that helps community members recognize the relationship of material conditions to behavioral, economic, social, and cultural factors by means of phenomenological investigation and analysis of concerns.

congenital transmission—Vertical transmission of *T. cruzi* from an infected mother to her infant, through the birth canal, blood, or maternal milk.

contamination—The deposit of *T. cruzi* in the fecal matter of triatomine bugs on the skin where the parasite enters through an abrasion or by scratching. This mode of infection is distinct from that of malaria parasites directly injected into the skin by mosquitos. Hygiene thus is an important factor when contamination is the primary route for infection.

cross-cultural communication—The ability of people from different cultures to be able to effectively express their concepts with terms that each side will understand and be able to fit into their culture.

cross-cultural community participation (CCCP)—Active involvement of technicians and community members from different cultures (such as Western biomedicine and Andean ethnomedicine) to discuss differences and be able to arrive at acceptable solutions to both.

cultural epidemiology—The study of cultural factors affecting the transmission, distribution, prevalence, and incidence of disease, which attempts to explain values, behaviors, and ethnomedical practices as they relate to the spread and curtailment of a disease. (Cultural epidemiology is a study initiated by the author, and it is the methodology employed in this book.)

culture—The sum total of artifacts, behaviors, beliefs, practices, technology, material objects, and values that societies hold and pass from one generation to the next. Cultures can be compared to "owner's manuals" that one receives at birth from other members of the society, although cultures are dynamic and continually changing.

culture context— Configurations, patterns, or structural relationships characteristic of any culture that provide members with themes, values, and functional arrangements perceived as very important to them.

culture context model—A development model that considers culture context as the primary basis for adopting change, such as Chagas' prevention.

culture context triangle—A model of development based on equal participation of 1) ethnomedical practitioners and community health workers, 2) community members, and 3) technical personnel within the cultural context of a community.

curandero—A generalized term used throughout Latin America to refer to traditional healers.

Darwin's disease—Sometimes used to refer to Chagas' disease on the assumption that Charles Darwin suffered and died from Chagas' disease; discussed in Chapter 1.

defecation time—The length of time after the triatomine bug feeds until it defecates. An important index, because certain triatomine species, such as *Triatoma infestans,* are much more infective than others like *Panstrongylus megistus,* because the former defecates sooner, thereby depositing infected fecal matter near the bite site.

disease burden—Refers to productive years that a worker loses because of a certain disease or disability; also known as disability-adjusted life years (DALYs). Chagas' disease is very high in this regard, because many workers die young from it; moreover, children are left without parents.

electrocardiogram—A record of the electrical activity of the heart that provides important information concerning the spread of excitation to different parts of the heart. It is valuable for Chagas' disease treatment in that it detects abnormal cardiac rhythm and myocardial damage.

empacho (constipation)—A culturally defined condition that includes the inability to defecate, which may be a sign of megacolonitis caused by Chagas' disease.

endemic—The continuous presence of a disease in a region for long periods of time. Chagas' disease is endemic in most of Bolivia.

entomologist—One who studies insects; medical entomologists study insects and their relationship to human diseases.

epidemic—An infectious disease that attacks many people at the same time in the same geographical area.

epidemiology—The study of the various factors relating to the transmission, distribution, prevalence, and incidence of disease. This study attempts to explain or anticipate an outbreak of disease. See cultural epidemiology.

epimastigotes—A transformative stage of *T. cruzi* found within an insect that follows the ingested trypomastigote stage and leads eventually to the metacyclic trypomastigote stage. Epimastigotes are distinguishable from trypomastigotes because in epimastigotes the flagellum begins near the center of the parasite between the nucleus and kinetoplast, extends along the anterior undulating membrane, and protrudes from the prow.

flagellate protozoa—Protozoa having a flagellum, such as *T. cruzi*.

flagellum—A whiplike extension attached to the parasite's membrane that propels the organism by undulating along its side and at certain life stages extending forward from its prow, making parasites agile swimmers and intruders into cells. The flagellum may also be used to attach to the insect's gut wall or salivary glands.

gentian violet—A dye used to destroy trypomastigotes in blood supplies.

hematophagous insects—Insects that live off blood.

host—The organism from which a parasite obtains its nourishment. Hosts in Chagas' disease include mammals, some other animals, and humans. Hosts refer to organisms where the parasite is infective and primarily reproduces. See vector.

house improvement committees (HICs)—The functional units at the community level in the PBCM project where plans and priorities for house improvements were decided and where all participatory activities were coordinated.

house infestation—Refers to the number of triatomine insects found in a house.

hypoxia—High-altitude stress from decreased oxygen.

ileostomy—Excision of the ileum.

immune system—The defensive protective reaction of the body to substances that are foreign or are interpreted as being foreign.

immunization—The process of rendering a patient immune to, or protecting individuals from developing, certain diseases.

immunocompetence—Being capable of developing an antigenic response to stimulation by an antigen.

immunodeficiency—The decreased or compromised ability to respond to antigenic stimuli, which may be caused by malnutrition and diseases such as AIDS.

Immunoglobin G (IgG)—Antibody involved in the secondary immune response.

Immunoglobin M (IgM)—Antibody involved in the primary immune response.

immunopathic medicine—The practice of ways to build up the immune system and to help it deal with organisms within and outside it.

Inca empire—An early Andean civilization that flourished between 1275 and 1532 and spread across the Andes from Chile to Ecuador, with its capital in Cuzco, Peru. Quechua was the lingua franca. Chagas' disease likely was present during these times, as indicated by an Inca mummy in which *T. cruzi* was found.

infection—The condition resulting when a pathogen (e.g., *T. cruzi*) becomes established within a host after invasion.

infestation—The presence of insect vectors in a given location.

instar—The period between the five nymph stages in the life of triatomines, or *vinchucas*.

interdisciplinary approach—A developmental approach that includes the biomedical perspective as well as cultural, economic, environmental, and social factors involved in Chagas' disease.

intradomiciliary—Within the house; in Bolivia this includes bedrooms, kitchen, and storage areas.

jampiri—An herbal curer in the Andes.

Kallawayas—An Andean ethnic group of approximately 15,000 people who live in northwestern Bolivia within the Province Bautista Saavedra. They speak both Aymara and Quechua and are noted for their pharmacopeia of medicinal plants and herbs.

latent Chagas'—An asymptomatic stage of Chagas' disease. Latent Chagas' presents several possibilities: 1) the infection is arrested at this stage; 2) it develops later to late latent Chagas' with minor clinical findings; and 3) it develops into classic indeterminate Chagas' disease.

Leishmania braziliensis—The causative agent of the mucocutaneous form of leishmaniasis, common in Andean regions where Chagas' disease is also found. It resembles lepromatous leprosy, producing disfigurements of the nose and lips. Andeans refer to it as *"lo mal de los Andes."* It is common in lower regions of the Andes, and, diagnostically, it may be confused with *T. cruzi* infection.

macrolevel processes—Larger units of social analysis, such as the nation, international community, and environment, affecting diseases.

macrophages—Cells capable of destroying particular substances within early stages of the immune reaction.

mal de corazon (heart problems)—A term commonly used by Bolivians to refer to symptoms of Chagas' disease, which causes heart diseases.

matrilateral cross-cousin marriage—A marriage-exchange system in which children marry their mother's brother's children.

matrilineal—A lineage-descent group in which children belong to their mother's group.

megasyndromes—Enlarged organs, usually heart (megacardia), esophagus (mega-esophagus), and colon (megacolon), caused by *T. cruzi* infection.

meningoencephalitis—Inflammation of the brain and its meninges. *T. cruzi* frequently causes this during the acute phase of Chagas' disease, especially in children, either killing them or leaving lasting effects.

mesa—A traditional Andean ritual in which foods symbolic of people, places, and intentions are offered to earth shrines.

mestizo—Refers to middle- and upper-class Bolivians who have completely adopted Western dress, traditions, and the Spanish language. *Mestizo* is a broad category that includes many Bolivians who are not *campesinos* and *cholos*. Bolivia is a highly class-stratified country with many classes determined by race, ethnicity, language, dress, economics, politics, and appearance; however, *campesino* and *cholo* classes predominate and are very well defined.

metacyclic trypomastigotes—A stage of *T. cruzi* which develops from the epimastigote stage within the triatomine's intestine and is infective to animals and humans. Immediately after introduction into the bite site or mucuous membranes, metacyclic trypomastigotes penetrate a variety of cells and become transformed within these cells into amastigotes. After several divisions, the parasite transforms into trypomastigotes that are released into the bloodstream. These trypomastigotes are different from metacyclic trypomastigotes and are taken up by triatomines, where they then transform into epimastigotes and eventually metacyclic trypomastigotes.

microlevel processes—Smaller units of social analysis, such as the community, family, and individual, that relate to diseases.

mountain-body metaphor—Kallawaya Andeans understand parts of their body as relating to places on their *ayllu* mountain; therefore, if they ritually feed earth shrines corresponding to these parts, their bodies will be healthy.

muerto subito (sudden death)—A term frequently used by Bolivians to describe death caused by heart failure brought about by Chagas' disease. A person suddenly drops dead and a drop of blood emits from the nose.

myxoedema—A decreased function of the thyroid gland, accompanied by swelling, anemia, lethargy, slow speech, mental apathy, et cetera. Carlos Chagas considered this to be one of the most characteristic manifestations of the acute form of Chagas' disease.

neuron cell—A nerve cell; the structural and functional unit of the nervous system. Neuron cells function in the initiation and conduction of impulses for organic processes. *T. cruzi* prefers to inhabit neuron cells, consequently impairing the conduction of impulses to the organs related to the neuron cells.

nifurtimox (synonyms: Bayer 2502, Lampit)—A drug commonly used to treat Chagas' disease. Nifurtimox is a 5-nitrofuran derivative with antiprotozoal activity; it is also used to treat leishmaniasis and African trypanosomiasis.

nymphs—Refers to triatomines going through one of five nymph stages before becoming adults, at which time they grow wings. During the nymph stages, triatomines crawl. The nymphal stages can take anywhere from four to forty-eight months depending on the temperature, humidity, and frequency and volume of blood meals. Nymphs can imbibe between six and twelve times their own weight in blood. Nymphs become infected with *T. cruzi* and spread Chagas' disease.

Panstrongylus megistus—Triatomines that belong to the genus *Panstrongylus;* they are vectors of *T. cruzi.*

parasite—A plant or animal that lives upon or within another living organism in order to absorb nutrients from the host. Parasites include multi-celled and single-celled animals, fungi, bacteria, and, possibly, viruses. Parasites can be pathogenic (disease causing) or nonpathogenic.

Parasitemia—The condition of being actively infected by a parasite. This occurs early in Chagas' disease but is very difficult to detect, even with microscopic analysis. Also refers to the acute phase of the disease, with intense inflammatory reactions manifested in high fever, chagomas, Romaña's sign, lymphadenopathy, hepatomegaly, splenomegaly, myocarditis, and meningoencephalitis.

parasitic cycle—Refers to the parasite, vector, and host relationship.

parasitic protozoas—Unicellular animals that infect and live off many species of vertebrates and invertebrates and that have adapted to life in nearly all available sites within the body of the host. There are about 10,000 different protozoan parasites. Some of the disease-causing parasitic protozoa include those in the genera *Plasmodium* (malaria), *Trypanosoma* (Chagas' disease, African sleeping sickness), and *Entamoeba* (amebic dysentery). Parasitic protozoa greatly influence humans, society, and culture.

partial immunity—A condition in which people infected with *T. cruzi* will usually not suffer another acute attack if they remain infected. One implication is that it may not be wise to rid someone of *T. cruzi* parasites if that person is likely to be infected again and possibly suffer the deadly effects of another acute phase. The presence of the parasite inhibits strong infections from newly colonizing parasites.

pathogen—A microorganism or substance capable of producing a disease.

patrilineal descent—A social grouping held together by descent through the father.

peridomicile—Areas outside the house including corrals, animal shelters, sheds, and walls.

pilot project—A project developed primarily to serve as a model for future projects. For example, houses may be improved in one village by development workers to show peasants how they can replicate these endeavors. The success of a pilot project is indicated by the degree to which it is replicated.

political economy—The relationship of political-economic factors in bringing into physical proximity parasites, vectors, and hosts. Houses can become "sick" because of overarching economic and political problems that cause impoverishment, migration, and low productivity.

prevalence—The number of cases or people infected with a disease at a specific time within a well-defined area.

privatization—Refers to pressure from capitalistic Western nations on Andean nations and communities to divest state-owned enterprises and community-held property and allow for private enterprises and individuals to buy and maintain them.

promotores—Spanish for community health workers.

protozoa—A phylum comprising the simplest animal forms—single-celled organisms ranging in size from 1.5um to 50mm. Of the 66,000 known species, 10,000 are parasitic and 56,000 are free-living. They are found in every ecological niche.

pyrethroid insecticides—Chemical insecticides synthesized to resemble extracts of pyrethrum, a plant-derived compound used for centuries for insect control in the Andes and Asia.

qollas—An indigenous word used to refer to highland Aymara and Quechua speakers of Bolivia, as distinguished from *cambas,* another indigenous word used to refer to Guaranis and others who live in lower regions of Bolivia, especially those in the Department of Santa Cruz.

Quechuas—A civilization and ethnic group who speak the Quechua language, which was spread at the Inca conquest, and live in the valleys and highlands of the Andean mountains of Chile, Bolivia, Ecuador, and Peru.

Reduviid—From Reduviidae, a large family of predaceous insects, sometimes referred to as assassin bugs; most members are insectivores. One subfamily, the Triatominae, is found mainly in the Americas; its members are hematophagous and vectors of Chagas' disease.

reinfestation—The reappearance of insect vectors from an outside source in a location from which they had previously been eliminated by control measures.

residentes—A term used by rural peasants to refer to friends and relatives living in urban areas.

residual effect—The period of time that an insecticide is effective.

Rhodnius pallescens—The principal vector of *T. cruzi* in Central America and Panama.

Rhodnius prolixus—Triatomines that belong to the genus *Rhodnius* and are vectors of *T. cruzi.*

Romaña's Sign (*Signo de Romaña*)—A symptom of acute infection by *Trypanosoma cruzi,* consisting of edema (marked swelling) around the orbit of the eye and in the lymph node on the face in front of the earlobe. It is present only in a minority of infections.

Sajjra mesa "misfortune table"—A ritual performed by *warmi yachaj* to remove illness in the Kallawaya region of the Bolivian Andes.

salivaria—Refers to trypanosomes, such as *T. rangeli,* that develop in an insect's saliva or mouth and are injected by biting. The highly pathogenic human salivary trypanosomes belong to the *T. brucei* group, which are transmitted through the saliva of tsetse flies and cause human sleeping sickness. See *stercoria.*

sayaña—Aymara concept for house, which includes the house, its surrounding territory, and attendant livestock.

schizodeme—A classification of *T. cruzi* strains based on electrophoretic mobility of kinetoplast DNA. See zymodeme.

Schizotrypanum cruzi—An early classification of *Trypanosoma cruzi* by Carlos Chagas that was later changed because the parasite fit better into the trypanosome genus.

Secretaría Nacional de Salud—Bolivia's ministry of health, which sponsors clinics, hospitals, and medical personnel throughout rural and urban areas of Bolivia. It was previously called *Ministerio de Previsión Social y Salud Pública* (MPSSP) until 1993 when the name was changed.

seropositive—Positive results in a serological test; i.e., shows the presence of specific antibodies to *T. cruzi.* These tests are indirect in that they do not detect the parasite, nor are they capable of determining the prevalence of the parasite. People who test seropositive for Chagas' disease usually have a direct examination of xenodiagnosis to determine the population and strain of the parasite.

shamans—A generalized term used to refer to traditional healers who use rituals and magical paraphernalia to heal.

sindicatos—Regional political organizations with vested power from the government.

Signo de Romaña—See Romaña's Sign.

Spanish Conquest—In 1532 Spaniards conquered Andean regions and began europeanizing Andean ethnic groups by imposing the Spanish language and Western economic systems (e.g., encomiendas, haciendas, work tribute, taxes) and by missionization. Effects of this colonization continue today. Many in the Andean ethnic groups have strongly resisted these efforts at Westernization and continue to follow deeply rooted Aymara and Quechua traditions.

stercoria—Refers to trypanosomes, such as *T. cruzi,* that develop in an insect's intestines and are deposited in its fecal matter. See *salivaria.*

superinfection—A second infection of a host that already is infected by the same species of parasite.

surveillance—The periodic collection of data in an area to detect changes in infection rates, prevalence, and vector infestation.

sylvatic cycle—The existence of vectors, parasites, and wild-animal hosts in a cycle not dependent on humans, human habitation, and domestic animals.

synanthropic animals—Animals that live close to humans, such as cats, dogs, mice, rats, oppossums, et cetera.

transfusional transmission—Infection with *T. cruzi* from transfused blood or other blood products.

Triatoma—A genus of insect, along with the genera *Panstrongylus* and *Rhodnius*, that are vectors of Chagas' disease; common names include triatomid and reduviid.

Triatoma brasiliensis—A triatomine vector of Chagas' disease in Latin America.

Triatoma dimidiata—A triatomine vector of Chagas' disease in Latin America.

Triatoma infestans (T. infestans)—The most important vector of Chagas' disease in Bolivia, where it is called *vinchuca*.

Triatoma sordida—A triatomine vector of Chagas' disease in Latin America.

triatomines—Refers to members of the Triatominae, a subfamily of the family Reduviidae. Triatomines are characterized by their bloodsucking (hematophagous) ability, and certain species carry the parasite *T. cruzi*. Sixty-eight species are recorded as infected with *Trypanosoma cruzi*.

Trypanosoma brucei gambiense—A flagellate protozoan that lives in the blood of cattle and humans, causing African sleeping sickness; tsetse flies are the vectors.

Trypanosoma cruzi (T. cruzi)—The causative agent of Chagas' disease in many animals and humans. It is transmitted by bloodsucking insects (triatomines) belonging to the family Reduviidae. It is a flagellate protozoan that transforms within the triatomine's gut into metacyclic trypomastigotes that are infective to mammals, where it transforms into intracellular amastigotes and trypomastigotes.

trypanosomes—Protozoa parasites which are classified together because during one stage of their lives they live in the blood and/or tissues of vertebrate hosts, and during other stages they live in the intestines of bloodsucking invertebrate vectors (Schmidt and Roberts 1989). Includes *T. cruzi, T. gambiense,* and *T. rhodesiense,* which cause diseases of man, and *T. brucei, T. congolense,* and *T. evansi,* which cause diseases of domestic animals.

trypanosomiasis—Infection caused by trypanosomes, protozoa parasites from the genus *Trypanosoma (T.). T. gambiense* and *T. rhodesiense* cause African trypanosomiasis, commonly referred to as African sleeping sickness; *T. cruzi* causes American, or South American, trypanosomiasis, commonly referred to as Chagas' disease.

trypomastigote—The form of *Trypanosoma cruzi* which can exist in the blood of humans; it is typically C-shaped with a large kinetoplast and free flagellum. Also called Tryps.

tsetse—A bloodsucking fly of the genus *Glossina,* known as the carrier, or vector, of *Trypanosoma gambiense* and *Trypanosoma rhodesiense,* the protozoan parasites that cause African sleeping sickness.

Tupi-Guarani—A term used to refer to many ethnic groups that live in the departments of Tarija, Santa Cruz, Beni, and Pando in Bolivia. It is a broad term that it is not very culture specific.

turqasiña—An Andean institution which refers to bartering produce for produce of equivalent value.

uxorlocal—A situation in which, after marriage, a husband goes to live with his wife.

vaccine—A suspension of infectious agents or some part of them, given for the purpose of establishing resistance to an infectious disease.

vector—An agent of transmission; a biological vector is a carrier, especially the animal which transfers an infective agent from one host to another. The vectors in Chagas' disease are triatomine insects, especially *Triatoma infestans,* or *vinchucas.*

vinchucas—A popular name in Andean countries for triatomine insects carrying the *T. cruzi* parasite.

vólvulo (volvulus)—A twisting of the bowel upon itself, causing obstruction. Although a prolapsed mesentery is frequently the cause in high altitudes, this term has also been applied to megacolon symptoms associated with *T. cruzi.*

Wankaris—A name given to semisedentary farmers, herders, and gatherers who lived at the Quebrada de Tarapacá (northern Chile, southern Andes) around A.D. 500 and whose mummies have been found with megasyndromes suggesting, although not proving, the existence of Chagas' disease during those times. Chagas' disease is still found in these regions; but it has less severe effects, suggesting a long-term adaptation to *T. cruzi.*

warmi yachaj—A woman diviner and ritualist in the Kallawaya region of Bolivia who performs rituals to the river to remove sicknesses.

xenodiagnosis—A method of diagnosis in which an uninfected (sterile) vector is fed on a suspected host and later examined for the presence of the parasite. In the case of Chagas' disease, this is done by placing about twenty-five sterile triatomine insects in a jar under the arm of a person and allowing the insects to blood feed for thirty minutes. Thirty and sixty days later, the feces of the bugs are inspected microscopically to see if they contain *T. cruzi.* This examination is usually done after someone has tested positive with ELISA tests; and it is effective in determining the parasites' population size and strains (zymodeme). (See Appendix 12.)

yachaj—Quechua for diviner or soothsayer in the Andes; (*yatiri* is Aymara for the same). Literally, "one who knows." *Yachajkuna* (pl.) and *yatirinaca* (pl.) perform divination rituals with coca leaves and the intestines of guinea pigs to determine causes of illness. They also perform rituals to remove the causes of the illness.

Yungas—Region of eastern Andean slopes from around 2,000 to 6,000 feet; it receives ample rainfall and is noted for its lush vegetation and production of fruits, vegetables, and coca leaves.

zymodemes—Classifications of *T. cruzi* based upon enzymatic profiles of parasite strains, over 100 of which have been classified. It is suggested that certain zymodemes prefer particular organs and manifest varying degress of sickness. Also referred to as isoenzymatic strains (IS) of *T. cruzi*. (See Appendix 12.)

Abbreviations

ATP—adenosine triphosphate

CCH—Community and Child Health Project (1989–1994), sponsored by US-AID-Bolivia and the Bolivian Secretariat of Health (SOH). This project included primary health care, nutritional care, vaccinations, water projects, maternal and child health care, and Chagas' control in 1990.

CCCP—Cross-cultural community participation

CCT—Culture Context Triangle

CDC—Centers for Disease Control (Atlanta, Georgia)

CEDEC—Centro por Estudios por Desarollo Chuquisaca

CENDA—Centro de Comunicación y Desarollo Andino, Cochabamba

CHW—Community Health Worker

DALYs—disability-adjusted life years

ECG—electrocardiography

Habitat—United Nations Center for Human Settlements

HICs—House Improvement Committees

IBBA—French/Bolivian Institute for High Altitude Biology and Parasitology, affiliated with Pasteur Institute in France.

IS—isoenzymatic strains of *T. cruzi*

MPSSP—Ministerio de Previsión Social y Salud Pública, Bolivia's ministry of health until 1993, when its name was changed to Secretaria Nacional de Salud (SNS).

NGOs—Nongovernmental organizations, privately operated but often with funding from international agencies that are involved in development projects. Bolivia currently has over fifty NGOs working in public health matters.

PAHO—Pan American Health Organization

PBCM—Proyecto Británico-Cardenal Mauer; name later changed to Cardenal Mauer (CM) after Britain discontinued funding this project in the Department of Chuquisaca.

P.L. 480—U.S. Public Law 480 allows for funds in host-country currency derived from the sale of U.S. agricultural products to be used in the host country in development projects. Some $2.5 million was provided to pilot projects of SOH/CCH Chagas program in Bolivia.

Pro-Habitat—United Nations Center for Human Settlements in Bolivia

PROCOSI—Programa de Coordinación en Supervivencia Infantil Organizaciones Privadas Voluntarias, which assumes the role of coordinating NGOs in

Bolivia by allocating funds contributed by USAID and other agencies and by evaluative studies.

SNS—Secretaría Nacional de Salud (Spanish name for Secretariat of Health—SOH)

SOH—Secretariat of Health. New name replacing MPSSP in 1993, after the Bolivian government enacted legislation to decentralize the administration of health from La Paz to regional locations.

SOH/CCH—Secretariat of Health (SOH) and Community and Child Health (CCH) Chagas Control Program in Bolivia (1991–1994), sponsored by US-AID-Bolivia and the Bolivian Secretariat of Health.

USAID—United States Agency for International Development

VBC—Vector Biology and Control Project (USAID, Washington, D.C.)

WHO—World Health Organization

References

Acquatella H., J. Gomez-Mancebo, F. Catalioti, V. Davalos, L. Villalobos, J. Alvarado
  1987 Long-term control of Chagas' disease in Venezuela: Serologic findings, electrocardiographic abnormalities and clinical outcome. *Circulation* 76:556–62.
Adler, S.
  1959 Darwin's illness. *Nature* 184:1102–3.
Alarico, Jemio, and Ariel Sempertegui
  1991 Interview by J. Bastien, Sucre, Bolivia, June 18, tape recording.
Albo, Xavier
  1985 Desafios de la solidaridad aymara. La Paz: CIPCA.
Allen, J.R.F., and B.R. Holmsted
  1980 The simple beta-carboline alkaloids. *Phytochemistry* 19:1573–82.
Almeida, Maria T., L.S. Filardi, and Z. Brener
  1984 Alterações ultra-estruturais dos estagios intracelulares e efeito sobre as formas sanguineas induzidas in vivo pelo 2-amino-5-(1-methyl-5-nitro-2-imidazoly-10-1,2,3-thiadiazole. *Revista Sociedade Brasileira de Medicina Tropical* 17:89–93.
Alvarenga, N.J., and P.D. Marsden
  1975 Estudos sobre persistencia de infectividade do *Trypanosoma cruzi*. I. Efeito da termperature sobre a infectividade de flagelados de amostra Peru de *T. cruzi* obtridos de fezes de triatomíneos. *Revista Sociedade Brasileira de Medicina Tropical* 9:283–87.
Amando Phillippi, Rodolfo
  1860 *Viaje al Desierto de Atacama hecho de orden del Gobierno de Chile en el verano 1853-54, publicado bajo los auspicious del Gobierno de Chile*. Sajonia: Libería de Eduardo Anton.
Andrade, Z.
  1958 Anatomic patologia da doença da Chagas. *Revista Goiana Medicine* 4:103–19.
  1994 Pathology of the autonomic nervous system in Chagas' cardiopathy. In *Chagas' Disease and the Nervous System*, 212–22. Washington, D.C.: Pan American Health Organization.
Apt, Werner
  1978 Ciclo evolutivo del *Trypanosoma cruzi*. In *Enfermedad de Chagas*, Alfredo Romero Davalos, ed., 69–77. La Paz: Editorial Los Amigos del Libro.
  1986 Letter. *Transactions of the Royal Society of Tropical Medicine and Hygiene* 80:1010.
Apt, W., A. Arribada, H. Sagua, J. González, and J. Araya
  1987 Cardiopatía chagásica en el altiplano chileno. Estudio clinico, epidemiológico y electrocardiográfico. *Revista Médica de Chile* 115:616–23.
Apt, Werner, C. Naquira, A. Tejada, and L. Atrozz
  1968 Transmisión congénita del *Trypanosoma cruzi*. II. En ratas con infección aguda y crónica. *Boletín Chileno de Parasitología* 23:9–15.

Arata, Andrew A.

1992 Work Plan and Technical Assistance to Bolivian Chagas' Disease Control Program of the CCH Project (511 -0594). In Vector Biology and Control Project Report No. 82236A. Arlington, VA: Vector Biology and Control Project.

Arias, A.R., J.M. Rosner, M.E. Ferreira, P. Galeano, M. Maldonado, and R. Henning

1988 Chagas' Disease in Paraguay. XII International Congress for Tropical Medicine and Malaria.

Arnold, D.Y.

1992 La casa de adobes y piedras del Inka. In *Hacia un orden andino de las cosas,* ed. Denise Arnold, D. Jünénez and Juan de Dios Yapita, 31–108. La Paz: Hisbol.

Arriaza, B.

1995 Chile's Chinchorro mummies. *National Geographic* (March): 71–88.

Arribada, A., W. Apt, X. Aguilera, A. Solari, and J. Sandoval

1990 Cardiopatía chagásica en la Primera Región de Chiloe. Estudio clinico, epidemiologico y parasitologico. *Revista Médica de Chile* 118:846–54.

Ashburn, Percy M.

1947 *The Ranks of Death: A Medical History of the Conquest of America.* New York: Coward McCann.

Astruc, J.A.

1754 *A Treatise of Venereal Disease.* London: Innis, Richardson, Davis & Cox.

Atias, A.

1980 Enfermedad de Chagas digestiva en Chile, experiencia de 20 años. *Boletín Hospital Civil de San Juan de Dios* (Quito) 27:251–57.

Ault, Steven, Jesse Hobbs, Robert Klein, and Rodrigo Zeledón

1992 Technical Evaluation of USAID CCH-Chagas' Disease Control Project Bolivia—August 1992. In Vector Biology and Control Project Report No. 82061. Arlington, VA: Vector Biology and Control Project.

Ávila, José Luis

1994 Molecular mimicry between *Trypanosoma cruzi* and host nervous tissue. In *Chagas' Disease and the Nervous System.* Scientific Publication No. 547, 250–72. Washington, D.C.: Pan American Health Organization.

Azara, Félix de

1809 *Voyages dans l'Amérique méridionale, par don Félix de Azara, commissaire et commandant des limites espagnoles dans le Paraguay depuis 1781 jusqu'en 1801.* 4 vols. & atlas. Paris: Dentu.

Azogue, E.

1982 Transmisión congenita de la enfermedad de Chagas en Santa Cruz, Bolivia II—hallazgos patológicos. *Boletín Informativo del CENETROP* 7 (1): 19–23.

Azogue, E., and G. Urioste.

1985 Transmisión congenita de la enfermedad de Chagas. III aspectos clínicos y anatomo-patológicos del recíen nacido. *Boletín Informativo del CENETROP* 11 (1): 21–30.

Azogue, E., C. La Fuente, and Ch. Darras

1981 Transmisión congénita de la enfermedad de Chagas en Santa Cruz Bolivia. I: Epidemiología. *Boletín Informativo del CENETROP* 7(1): 23–29.

1985 Congenital Chagas' disease in Bolivia: Epidemiological aspects and pathological findings. *Transactions of the Royal Society of Tropical Medicine and Hygiene* 79:178–80.

Bachelard, Gaston

1969 *The Poetics of Space.* Trans. by Maria Jolas. Boston: Beacon Press.

Balderrama, H., A. Romero, J.A. García, H. Bermúdez, R. Serrano, C. La Fuente, and F. Romero

1981 Estudio epidemiológico de Chagas crónico en la población de El Trigal, Santa Cruz, Bolivia. *Boletín Informativo del CENETROP* 7:16–22.

Barclay, C., J. Cerisola, H. Lugones, O. Ledesma, J. Silva, and C. Morego

1978 Aspectos farmacológicos e resultados terapéuticos do Benznidazol novo agente quimioterápico para tratamiento de infección de Chagas. *Prensa Médica Argentina* 65:239–44.

Barrera Moncada, G.

1987 Desarrollo mental en niños con infección chagásica crónica. *Archivos Venezolanos de Puericultra y Pediatría* 50:106–11.

Barreto, Ananias

1993 *Costumbres y Creencias del Campo Tarijeño.* Tarija: Editorial de la Universidad Juan Misael Saracho.

Bastien, Joseph W.

1973 *Qollahuaya Rituals: An Ethnographic Account of the Symbolic Relations of Man and Land in an Andean Village.* Ithaca: Cornell Latin American Studies Program.

1978 *Mountain of the Condor: Metaphor and Ritual in an Andean Ayllu.* American Ethnological Society, Monograph 64. St. Paul: West Publishing Company. (Reissued in paperback by Waveland Press in 1987.)

1981 Metaphorical relations between sickness, society, and land in a Qollahuaya ritual. In *Health in the Andes,* ed. Joseph W. Bastien and John Donahue, 19–37. Monograph 12. Washington, D.C.: American Anthropological Association.

1982 Herbal curing by Qollahuaya Andeans. *Journal of Ethnopharmacology* 6:13–28.

1983a *Las plantas medicinales de los kallawayas.* Oruro, Bolivia: Proyecto Concern.

1983b Pharmacopeia of Qollahuaya Andeans. *Journal of Ethnopharmacology* 8:97–111.

1985 Qollahuaya-Andean body concepts: A topographical-hydraulic model of physiology. *American Anthropologist* 87:595–611.

1987a *Healers of the Andes: Kallawaya Herbalists and Their Medicinal Plants.* Salt Lake City: University of Utah Press.

1987b Cross-cultural communication between doctors and peasants in Bolivia. *Social Science and Medicine* 24:1109–18.

1988 Cultural perceptions of neonatal tetanus and programming implications, Bolivia. Resources for Child Health Project. Arlington: REACH, John Snow, Inc.

1989 A shamanistic curing ritual of the Bolivian Aymara. *Journal of Latin American Lore* 15 (1): 73–94.

1990 Community health workers in Bolivia: Adapting to traditional roles in the Andean community. *Social Science and Medicine* 30:281–88.

1992 *Drum and Stethoscope: Integrating Ethnomedicine and Biomedicine in Bolivia.* Salt Lake City: University of Utah Press.

Bastien, J.W., W. Mahler, M. Reinecke, W. Robinson, J. Zalles-Asín, and Yong-Hua Shu

1990 Testing of anti-HIV compounds from Bolivian-Kallawaya medicinal plants. Paper presented at the 2nd International Congress of Ethnobiology, Kunming, China, October 22–28.

Bastien, J.W., W. Mahler, M. Reinecke, W. Robinson, F. Valeriote, J. Zalles, and Qi Jia

1994 Phytochemical studies of Kallawayan medicinal plants as potential anti-tumor drugs. *Abstracts, Southwest Regional Meeting of the American Chemical Society* 50:165.

Bastien, J.W., S. Abdel-Malek, Jia Qi, M. Reinecke, T.H. Corbett, F. Valeriote, W.F. Mahler, W. Edward Robinson, and J. Zalles-Asín

1996 New drug leads from Kallawaya herbalists of Bolivia: Background, rationale, protocol and anti-HIV leads. *Journal of Ethnopharmacology* 50:157-66.

Battaglia, P.A., M. del Bue, M. Otaviano, and M. Ponzi

1983 A puzzle genome: kinetoplast DNA. In *Molecular Biology of Parasites,* ed. J. Guardiola, L. Luzatto, and W. Trager, 107–24. New York: Raven Press.

Beauchamp, Tom L., and James F. Childress

1983 *Principles of Biomedical Ethics* (2nd ed.). New York: Oxford University Press.

Behrhorst, Carroll

1983 Introduction. In *Health in the Guatemalan Highlands,* ed. Ulli Stelzer, xi–xxxv. Seattle: University of Washington Press.

Beltrán, José

1991 Interview by J. Bastien, Tarija, Bolivia, June 12, tape recording.

1997 Interviews by J. Bastien, Tarija, Bolivia, May 15–25, tape recordings.

Bermúdez, H., A. Garrón, and A. De Muynck

1978 Infestatión del peridomicilio por *T. infestans* en Gutiérrez (Prov. Cordillera, Depto. Santa Cruz). *Boletín Informativo del CENETROP* 4 (1-2): 48–51.

Bernstein, Richard J.

1992 *The New Constellation: The Ethical-Political Horizons of Modernity/Postmodernity.* Cambridge: MIT Press.

Berryman, Philip

1987 *Liberation Theology: The Essential Facts About the Revolutionary Movement in Latin America and Beyond.* New York: Pantheon.

Bertha (pseudonym)

1991 Interview by J. Bastien, July 22, tape recording.

Bittencourt, A.L.

1975 Aspectos anatomo-patológicos da pele na enfermedade de Chagas congénita. Estudo de 29 casos. *Revista do Instituto de Medicina Tropical de São Paulo* 17: 135–39.

1976 Congenital Chagas disease. *American Journal of Diseases of Children* 130: 97–103.

Bittencourt, A.L., and H.S. Barbosa

  1972 Incidencia da transmissão congenita da doenca de Chagas em abortos. *Revista do Instituto de Medicina Tropical de São Paulo* 14:257–59.

Bittencourt, A.L., H.S. Barbosa, T. Rocha, I. Sodre, and A. Sodre

  1972 Transmissão congenita da doença de Chagas em partos prematuros na maternidad Tsylla Balbino (Salvador-Bahia). *Revista do Instituto de Medicina Tropical de São Paulo* 14:131–34.

Bittencourt, A.L., H.S. Barbosa, I. Santos, M.A. Ramos

  1974 Incidencia da transmissao congenita da doença de Chagas em partos a termo. *Revista do Instituto de Medicina Tropical de São Paulo* 16:197–99.

Bittencourt, A.L., L.A. Rodríguez de Freitas, M.O. De Araujo Galvao, and K. Jacomo

  1981 Pneumonitis in congenital Chagas disease. A study of ten cases. *American Journal of Tropical Medicine and Hygiene* 30:38–42.

Bittencourt, A.L., M. Sadigursky, A.A. Da Silva, C.A. Menezes, M.M. Marianetti, S.C. Guerra, and I. Sherlock

  1988 Evaluation of Chagas' disease transmission through breast-feeding. *Memórias do Instituto Oswaldo Cruz* 83:37–39.

Boainain, E.

  1979 Tratamento etiologico da doença de Chagas na fase crônica. *Revista Goiana de Medicina* 25:1–60.

Bock, M., A. Haberkorn, H. Herlinger, K.H. Mayer, and S. Petersen

  1972 The structure-activity relationship of 4-(5'-nitro-furfurylidene-amino)-tetrahydro-4H-1,4-thiazine-1, 1-dioxides active against *Trypanosoma cruzi*. *Arzeimittel-Forschung* (Aulendorf) 22:1564–69.

Borda Pisterna, Mario

  1978 Breves referencias a la sistemática, bioecología, y morfología externa de los triatomíneos. En especial *Triatoma infestans* y *Triatoma sordida*. In *Enfermedad de Chagas*, ed. A.R. Davalos, 83–97. La Paz: Los Amigos Del Libro.

  1981 *Conozca El Mal De Chagas*. Cochabamba: Centro de Investigaciones Ecológicas del mal de Chagas, Universidad Mayor De San Simón.

Borges, Jorge Luis

  1977 *Obras Completas*. Buenas Aires: Emecé Editores.

Bos, R.

  1988 The importance of peridomestic environmental management for the control of the vectors of Chagas' disease. *Revista Argentina de Microbiología* (Buenos Aires) 50:56–62.

Bottasso, O.A., N. Ingledew, M. Keni, J. Morini, J.F. Pividori, G.A.W. Rook, and J.L. Stanford

  1994 Cellular immune response to common mycobacterial antigens in subjects seropositive for *Trypanosoma cruzi*. *The Lancet* 344 (December 3): 1540–41.

Boyle, T.C.

  1990 *If the River Was Whiskey*. New York: Penguin.

Brasil, A.

  1956 Etiopatogenía da aperistalsis do esófago. *Revista Brasileira de Medicina* (Rio de Janeiro) 13:577–90.

Braunwald, Eugene

1988 *Heart Disease: A Textbook of Cardiovascular Medicine* 1:1445–48. Philadelphia: W.B. Saunders Company.

Brener, Zigman

1975 Chemotherapy of *Trypanosoma cruzi* infections. *Advances in Pharmacology and Chemotherapy* 13:1–44.

1979 Present status of chemotherapy and chemoprophylaxis of human trypansomiasis in the western hemisphere. *Pharmacology and Therapeutics* 7:71–90.

1994 The pathogenesis of Chagas' disease: An overview of current theories. In *Chagas' Disease and the Nervous System,* Scientific Publication No. 547, 30-46. Washington, D.C.: Pan American Health Organization.

Brénière, S.F., M. Bailly, R. Carrasco, and Y. Carlieranti

1983 Transmission transplacentaire des anti-corps *anti-Trypanosoma cruzi.* Serie *Entomologie Médecine et Parasitologie* 21:139–40. Montpellier, France: Cahier UMR CNRS/ORSTOM. Also in Spanish in *Annuario IBBA* (La Paz) *1986–1987,* 207–8.

Brénière, S.F., M.F. Bosseno, C. Barnabe, S. Urdaneta-Morales, M. Tibayrenc

1993 Population genetics of *Trypanosoma cruzi* and *Trypanosoma rangeli:* Taxonomical and epidemiological purpose. *Biological Research* (BSA) 26 (1–2): 27–33.

Brénière, S.F., P. Braquemond, A. Solari, J.F. Agnese, and M. Tibayrenc

1991 An isoenzyme study of naturally occurring clones of *Trypanosoma cruzi* isolated from both sides of the West Andes highland. *Transactions of the Royal Society of Tropical Medicine and Hygiene* 85:62–66.

Brénière, S.F., R. Carrasco, S. Revollo, G. Aparicio, P. Desjeux, M. Tibayrenc

1989 Chagas's disease in Bolivia: Clinical and epidemiological features and zymodeme variability of *Trypanosoma cruzi* strains isolated from patients. *American Journal of Tropical Medicine and Hygiene* 41:521–29.

Brénière, S.F., R. Carrasco, G. Antezana, P. Desjeux, M. Tibayrenc

1989 Association between *Trypanosoma cruzi* zymodemes and specific humoral depression in chronic chagasic patients. *Transactions of Royal Society of Tropical Medicine and Hygiene* 83 (4): 517.

Brenner, Rodolfo R.

1987 General aspects of reduviidae biochemistry. In *Chagas' Disease Vectors* vol. 3, *Biochemical Aspects and Control,* ed. Rodolfo Brenner and Angel de la Merced Stoka, 2–8. Boca Raton, FL: CRC Press.

Brett, S.

1974 Low-income urban settlements in Latin America: The Turner model. In *Sociology and Development,* ed. E. De Kadt and G. Williams, 171–96. London: Tavistock Publications.

Briceño-León, Roberto

1987 Housing for control of Chagas' disease in Venezuela. *Parasitology Today* 3:384–87.

1989 Vector control: House improvement and sanitary measures. Geneva: World Health Organization, unpublished data.

1990 *La Casa Enferma: Sociología de la Enfermedad de Chagas.* Caracas: Fondo Editorial Acta Científica Venezolana Consorcio de Ediciones Capriles C.A.

Brisseu, J.M., J.P. Lebron, T. Petit, M. Marjolet, P. Cuilliere, J. Godin, J.Y. Grolleau

1988 Chagas disease imported into France. *The Lancet* (7 May): 1046.

Browne, Janet

1995 *Charles Darwin: Voyaging.* New York: Alfred A. Knopf.

Brumpt, E.

1912 Le *Trypanosoma cruzi* evolue chez *Conorhinus megistus, Cimex lenticularis, Cimex boutei,* e *Ornithodorus moubata:* Cycle évolutif de ce parasite. *Bulletin de la Société de Pathologie Exotique et de ses Filiales* (Paris) 5:360–67.

Bryan, Ralph, Fanor Balderrama, Robert J. Tonn, and João Carlos Pinto Dias

1994 Community participation in vector control: Lessons from Chagas' disease. *American Journal of Tropical Medicine and Hygiene* 50 (6): 61–71.

Bryan, Ralph, and Robert J. Tonn

1990 *Bolivia: Current Status and Potential Development of Control Strategies for Chagas' Disease.* Area Report 123-4. Arlington, VA: Vector Biology and Control Project.

Bryant, Ben S.

1978 Corrugated roofing panels from agricultural residues. *Appropriate Technology* 4 (4): 26–28.

Burgdorfer, W., R.S. Lane, and A.G. Barbour

1985 The western black-legged tick, *Ixodes pacificus:* A vector of *Borrelia burgdorferi. American Journal of Tropical Medicine and Hygiene* 34:925–30.

Calkins, Abigail, and Jason Coughlin

1993 Credit schemes for home improvements and sustainability mechanisms for the Chagas' disease control project—Bolivia. In Vector Biology and Control Project Report No. 82235. Arlington, VA: Vector Biology and Control Project.

Calvo, Daniel, Oswaldo Elío Valdivia, and Alfredo Romero Dávalos

1978 Transmisión del *Trypanosoma cruzi.* In *Enfermedad de Chagas,* ed. Alfredo Romero Davalos, 79–82. La Paz: Editorial Los Amigos del Libro.

Camara-Lopes, L.H.

1962 The endemic South-american megaesophagus. *Second World Congress of Gastroenterology* (Munich) 1:79–85.

Cancado, J.R., and Z. Brener

1979 Terapêutica. In *Trypanosoma cruzi. Doença do Chagas,* ed. Z. Brener and Z. Andrade, 362–424. Rio de Janeiro: Guanabara Koogan.

Carcavallo, R.U.

1987 The subfamily triatominae (Hemiptera, Reduviidae): Systematics and some ecological factors. In *Chagas' Disease Vectors,* vol. 1, *Taxonomic, Ecological, and Epidemiological Aspects,* ed. R. Brenner and A. de la Merced Stoka, 1–18. Boca Raton, FL: CRC Press.

Carcavallo, R.U., and R.J. Tonn

1985 *Rhodnius Prolixus* STAL. In *Factores Biológicos y Ecológicos en la Enfermedad de Chagas,* vol. 1, 209–17. Buenos Aires: Centro Panamericano de Ecología y Salud/Servicio Nacional de Chagas.

Carrasco, Roxanna, and Gerardo Antesana

1991 Enfermedad de Chagas. Mimeograph. La Paz: Instituto Boliviana de Biología de Altura.

Carrasco, Roxanna, H. Míguez, C. Camacho, L. Echalar, S. Revollo, T. Ampuero, and J.P. Dedet

1990 Prevalence of *Trypanosoma cruzi* infection in blood banks of seven departments of Bolivia. *Memórias do Instituto Oswaldo Cruz* 85:69–73.

Carrasco Capriles, Nicolás

1984 *Regenerator y Sistema Inmunológico*. La Paz: Editorial Los Amigos del Libro.

Carter, William

1964 *Aymara Communities and the Bolivian Agrarian Reform*. Gainesville: University of Florida Press.

Carvalho, M.M.

1950 Mal disfágico cárdio-esofágico. Coimbra, Brazil: Imprensa de Coimbra, Limitada.

Castilho, E.A. de, and G.R. Da Silva

1976 Maternal Chagas infection and prematurity. *Revista do Instituto de Medicina Tropica de São Paulo* 18:258–60.

Cavin, J.C., S.M. Krassner, and E. Rodríguez

1987 Plant-derived alkaloids active against *Trypanosoma cruzi*. *Journal of Ethnopharmacology* 19:89–94.

Cavin, J.C., and E. Rodríguez

1982 Ethnopharmacology of Amazonian psychoactive plants. In *Aspects of American Hispanic and Indian Involvement in Biomedical Research*, ed. J.V. Martinez and D.I. Martinez, 169–77. Bethseda: Society for the Advancement of Chacanos and Native Americans in Science.

Cedillos, R.A.

1975 Chagas' disease in El Salvador. *Bulletin, Pan American Health Organization* 9 (2): 135–41.

1987 Current knowledge of the epidemiology of Chagas' disease in Central America and Panama. In *Chagas' disease vectors,* vol. 1, ed. Rodolfo Brenner and Angel de la Merced Stoka, 41–55. Boca Raton, FL: CRC Press.

Censo Nacional

1992 *Censo nacional de poblacion y vivienda: Recuentos preliminares. Republica de Bolivia*. La Paz: Ministerio Planeamiento y Coordinación, Instituto Nacional de Estádistica.

Centers for Disease Control (CDC)

1991 Morbidity and mortality weekly report. U.S. Department of Health and Human Services. Epidemiology Program Office at CDC, Atlanta, GA.

Cerisola, J.A., M.C. Russo, C.E. Del Prado, L.B. de Jozami, and R.W. Rhowedder

1972 Estudio comparativo de diversos métodos parasitológicos en la enfermedad de Chagas aguda. Simposio Internacional sobre enfermedad de Chagas, Buenos Aires.

Chagas, Carlos

1903 Estudos hematológicos no impaludismo. These Inaugural de Carlos Chagas. Rio de Janeiro: Faculdade de Medicina do Rio de Janeiro.

1909 Nova tripanozomiase humana: Estudos sobre a morfologia e o ciclo evolutivo do *Schizotrypanum cruzi* n. gen. n. sp. Agente etiológico de nova entidade mórbida do homen. *Memórias do Instituto Oswaldo Cruz* 1:159–218.

1911 Nova entidade mórbida do homen: Resumo geral de estudos etiologicos e clinicos. *Memórias do Instituto Oswaldo Cruz* 3:219–75.

1912 Sobre um tripanozoma do tatu Tatusia novencincta transmitido peolo Triatoma geniculata (Latr 1811). *Brazi-Médico* 26:305–6.

1921 American trypanosomiasis. *Proceedings, Institute of Medicine of Chicago* 3: 220–42.

1922 The discovery of *Trypanosoma cruzi* and of American trypanosomiasis. *Memórias do Instituto Oswaldo Cruz* 15:1–11.

1935 *Discursos e conferências.* Rio de Janeiro: Officina de Obras Gráphicas da S.A.

1988 A short chronicle of the discovery of Chagas' disease. *Pacing and Clinical Electrophysiologoy* 11 (July): 1108–13. Reprint of Chagas's diary.

Chagas Filho, Carlos

1959 *Carlos Chagas (1879–1934).* Rio de Janeiro: Officina Gráfica da Universidade do Brasil.

1968 Histórico sobre a doença de Chagas. In *Doença de Chagas,* ed. J. Romeu Cançado, 5–21. Belo Horizonte, Brazil: Imprensa Oficial do Estado de Minas Gerais.

1988 A short chronicle of the discovery of Chagas' disease. *Pacing and Clinical Electrophysiology* 11 (July): 1108–13. Reprint of Carlos Chagas's diary.

1993 *Meu Pai.* Rio de Janeiro: Casa de Oswaldo Cruz

Chapuis, Y.

1973 Acute Chagas disease in children at Cochabamba, Bolivia. *Annales des Sociétés Belges de Médecine Tropicale, de parasitologie et mycologie humaine et animale* 53 (6): 581–93.

Chocair, P., R. Sabbaga, V. Amato Neto, M. Shiroma, and G.M. de Goes

1981 Transplante de rim: nova modalidade de transmissâo de Docença de Chagas ao homen. *Revista do Instituto Medícina Tropical de São Paulo* 23:280–82.

Ciesielski, S., J.R. Seed, J. Estrada, and E. Wrenn

1993 The seroprevalence of cysticercosis, malaria and *Trypanosoma cruzi* among North Carolina farmworkers. *Public Health Reports* 108 (6): 736–41.

Cieza de León, Pedro de

1959 *The Incas of Pedro de Cieza de León,* ed. V.W. von Hagen, trans. Harriet de Onis. Norman: University of Oklahoma Press.

Clark, Julia B., Sherry F. Queener, and Virginia Burke Karb

1986 *Pharmacological Basis of Nursing Practice.* St. Louis: C.V. Mosby Company.

Coimbra, Jr., Carlos, R.V. Santos, M.M. Borges, N.M. Flowers, and R.F. Plazza

1992 Seroepidemiological survey for Chagas' disease among Xavante Indians of central Brazil. *Annals of Tropical Medicine and Parasitology* 86 (5): 567–68.

Colk, Ralph

1977 *To Be An Invalid.* Chicago: University of Chicago Press.

Coreil, Jeannine, and J. Dennis Mull

1990 *Anthropology and Primary Health Care.* Boulder, CO: Westview Press.

Corona, S., C. Amanales, M.A. Avario, et al.

1988 Granuloma chagásica del cerebro en un paciente con leucemia linfoblástica. *Revista Médica Chilena* 116:676–80.

Cossio, P.M., C. Diez, A. Szarfman, E. Kreutzer, B. Candiolo, R.M. Arana
  1974 Chagasic cardiopathy: Demonstration of a serum gamma globulin factor which reacts with endocardium and vascular structures. *Circulation* 49 (January): 13–21.
Cossio, P.M., R.P. Laguens, and C. Diéz
  1974 Chagasic cardiopathy: Antibodies reacting with plasma membrane of striated muscle and endothelial cells. *Circulation* 50 (6): 1252–59.
Coura, J.R., L.L. Abreu, J.B. Pereira, and H.P. Willcox
  1985 Morbidade da doença de Chagas; IV, Estudo longitudinal de dez anos em Pains e Iguatama, Minas Gerais, Brazil. *Memórias de Instituto Oswaldo Cruz* 80:73–80.
Crosby, Alfred W.
  1972 *The Columbian Exchange: Biological and Cultural Consequences of 1492.* Westport, CT: Greenwood.
  1976 Notes and documents: Virgin soil epidemics as a factor in the aboriginal depopulation in America. *William and Mary Quarterly* 33 (2): 289–99.
CRS-PROCOSI
  1990 *Evaluación de medio termino proyecto control de chagas en Chuquisaca.* Sucre: PBCM, CRS, PROCOSI.
Cruz, F.S, J.J. Marr, and R.L. Berens
  1980 Prevention of transfusion induced Chagas' disease by amphotericin B. *American Journal of Tropical Medicine and Hygiene* 29:761–65.
Cuellar, C.J., and A. De Muynck
  1980 Factores condicionantes de la transmisión de la enfermedad de chagas en Gutierrez e Ipita, Chaco Boliviano. *Boletín Informativo CENTROP* 6:10–14.
Cunha-Neto, Edécio, Márcia Duranti, Arthur Gruber, Bianca Zingales, Iara de Messias, Noedir Stolf, Giovanni Bellotti, Manoel E. Patarroyo, Fulvio Pilleggi, and Jorge Kalil
  1995 Autoimmunity in Chagas disease cardiopathy: Biological relevance of a cardiac myosin-specific epitope crossreactive to an immunodominant *Trypanosoma cruzi* antigen. *Proceedings of the National Academy of Science USA* 92 (April): 3541–45.
Cunningham, D.S., M. Grogl, and R.E. Kuhn
  1980 Suppression of antibody responses in humans infected with *Trypanosoma cruzi. Infection and Immunity* 30:496–99.
Curtis, C.G., ed.
  1990 *Appropriate Technology in Vector Control.* Boca Raton, FL: CRC Press.
Custred, Glynn
  1979 Inca concepts of soul and spirit. In *Essays in Humanistic Anthropology,* ed. Bruce Grindal and Dennis Warren, 277–302. Washington, D.C.: University Press of America.
Cutait, D.E., and R. Cutait
  1991 Surgery of chagasic megacolon. *World Journal of Surgery* 15:188–97.
Darwin, Charles
  1837-1839 Zoology notes, Edinburgh notebook. In *Charles Darwin's Notebooks, 1836–1844,* ed. Paul Barrett, Peter Gautrey, Sandra Herbert, David Kohn, and Sydney Smith. Ithaca, NY: Cornell University Press, 1987.

Da Silveira, G.M.
   1976 Chagas' disease of the colon. *British Journal of Surgery* 63:831–35.
Dauelsberg, P.
   1983 Tojo Tojones: Un paradero de cazadores arcaicos. Caractéristicas y secuencias. *Chungara* 11:11–30.
Deane, M.P., A.M. Goncalves, N.M. Pererira, H. Nomen, and C.M. Morel
   1981 Coexistence of distinct strains of *Trypanosoma cruzi* in experimentally infected mice as investigated by schizodeme and zymodeme analysis. *Pesquisas Básicas Doença de Chagas.* Reuniao Anual 8, Abstract 89 (Minas Gerais).
Del Castillo, M., G. Mendoza, J. Oviedo, R.P. Bianco, A.E. Anselmo, and M. Silva
   1990 AIDS and Chagas' disease with central nervous system tumor-like lesion. *American Journal of Medicine* 88:693–94.
De Muynck, Aimé, Angel Garron, Hernán Bermudez, Hugo Zuna, Alfredo Romero, Freddy Romero, Antonio Garcia, Jorge Prado, Luis Queirolo, and Benjamín Ribera
   1978 Estudio Epidemiologico de la enfermedad de Chagas en porongo, departmento de Santa Cruz, Bolivia. *Boletín Informativo del CENETROP* 4(3): 88–7.
Dias, E.
   1956 Observações sobre eliminacao dejecoes e tempo de sucção em algums triatomíneos sul-americanos. *Memórias do Instituto Oswaldo Cruz* 54:115–24.
Dias, J.C.P.
   1985 Aspectos socioculturales y económicos relativos al vector de la enfermedad de chagas. In *Factores Biológicos y Ecológicos en la Enfermedad de Chagas,* ed. R. Carcavallo. Buenos Aires: Servicio Nacional de Chagas.
   1987 Control of Chagas disease in Brazil. *Parasitology Today* 3 (11): 336–41.
   1988 Rural resource development and its potential to introduce domestic vectors into new epidemiological situations. *Revista Argentina de Microbiología* 50: 81–85.
   1991 Chagas' disease control in Brazil: What strategy after the acute phase? *Annales des Sociétés Belges de Medecine Tropicale, de parasitologie et mycologie humaine et animale* 71 (suppl. 1): 75–86.
Dias, J.C.P., and R.P. Dias
   1982 Housing and the control of vectors of human Chagas' disease in the state of Minas Gerais, Brazil. *PAHO Bulletin* 26:117–28.
Dias, J.C.P., and Z. Brener
   1984 Chagas' disease and blood transfusion. *Memórias do Instituto Oswaldo Cruz* 79 (suppl.): 139–47.
Dias, J.C.P., C.C.P. Loyola, and Z. Brener
   1985 Doença de Chagas em Minas Gerais: Situaçâo atual e perspectivas. *Revista Brasileira de Malariologia e Doenças Tropicals* (Rio de Janeiro) 37:7–28.
Dillehay, Tom
   1995 *Tombs for the Ancestors.* Washington, D.C.: Dumbarton-Oaks.
Di Noia, Javier M., Daniel O. Sánchez, and Alberto Frasch
   1995 The protozoan *Trypanosoma cruzi* has a family of genes resembling the mucin genes of mammalian cells. *Journal of Biological Chemistry* 270 (41): 24146–49.
Di Primio, E.
   1971 Erros e deficiências no diagnóstico da Doença de Chagas no Rio Grande do

Sul. O problema da provável contaminação por via oral de *Trypanosoma cruzi* em Tuetonia, RS. *Hospital* (Rio de Janeiro) 80:150–65.

Dobyns, Henry F.

1963 An outline of Andean epidemic history to 1720. *Bulletin of the History of Medicine* 37: 493–515.

1966 Estimating aboriginal American population: An appraisal of techniques with a new hemispheric estimate. *Current Anthropology* 7:395–449.

Docampo, R., and S.N. Moreno

Free radical metabolites in the mode of action of chemotherapeutic agents and phagocytic cells on Trypanosoma cruzi. *Review of Infectious Diseases* 6:223–38.

Docampo, R., and A.O.M. Stoppani

1979 Generation of superoxide anion and hydrogen peroxide induced by nifurtimox in *Trypanosoma cruzi. Archives Biochemistry and Biophysics* (New York) 197:317–21.

1984 Free radical metabolites in the mode of action of chemotherapeutic agents and phagocytic cells on *Trypanosoma cruzi* microbodies. *Experientia* 32: 972–75.

Docampo, R., S.N. Moreno, F.R. Gadelha, W. de Souza, F.S. Cruz

1988 Prevention of Chagas' disease resulting from blood transfusion by treatment of blood: Toxicity and mode of action of gentian violet. *Biomedical Environmental Science* 1 (4): 406–13.

Dominguez, A., and J.A. Suarez

1963 Studies on the intracardiac autonomic nervous system, myocarditis in Chagas' disease. *Zeitschrift für Tropenmedizin und Parasitologie* 14 (April): 81–85.

Dretske, Fred

1995 *Naturalizing the Mind.* Cambridge, MA: Massachusetts Institute of Technology.

Drèze, Jean, and Amartya Sen

1995 Introduction. In *The Political Economy of Hunger,* ed. Jean Drèze, Amartya Sen, and Athar Hussain, 13–45. Oxford: WIDER, Oxford University Press.

Dujardin, J.P., C. La Fuente, L. Cardozo, and M. Tibayrenc

1988 Dispersing behaviour of *T. infestans:* Evidence from genetical study of field populations in Bolivia. *Memórias Instituto Oswaldo Cruz* 83 (suppl. 1): 435–40.

Duke, James

1985 *Handbook of Medicinal Herbs.* Boca Raton, FL: CRC Press.

Duke, James A., David Aulik, and Timothy Plowman

1975 Nutritional value of coca. *Harvard University Botanical Museum* 24: 113–19.

Ebert, F., and G.A. Schaub

1983 The characterization of Chilean and Bolivian *Tripanosoma cruzi* stocks from *Triatoma infestans* by isoelectrofocusing. *Z. Parasitendk* 69 (3): 283–90.

Edelstein, Ludwig

1967 *Ancient Medicine.* Baltimore: Johns Hopkins.

Edmiston, W.A., T. Yokoyama, J. Kay, M. Bilitch, and F.Y. Lau

1978 Ventricular tachycardia in a young adult with an apical aneurysm. *Western Journal of Medicine* 128:248–53.

Elferink, Jan G.
1983 The narcotic and hallucinogenic use of tobacco in pre-Columbian Central America. *Journal of Ethnopharmacology* 7:111–22.

Faulkner, W.B., Jr.
1940 Objective esophageal changes due to psychic factors. *Journal of Medical Science* 200:796–99.

Feit, A., N. El-Sherif, and S. Korostoff
1983 Chagas' disease masquerading as a coronary artery disease. *Archives of Internal Medicine* 143:144–45.

Fernández-Armesto, Felipe
1995 *Millennium: A History of the Last 1,000 Years.* New York: Scribner.

Ferriolli Filho, Francisco, and Mauro Pereira Barreto
1978 Sistemática é morfología do *Trypanosoma cruzi* (Chagas, 1909). In *Enfermedad de Chagas,* ed. Alfredo Romero Davalos, 47–61. La Paz: Editorial Los Amigos del Libro.

Figueroa, Ciro
1991 *La enfermedad de Chagas.* Tarija, Bolivia: Editorial de la Universidad Juan Misael Saracho.

Filardi, L.S., and Z. Brener
1982 A nitroimidazole-thiadiazole derivative with curative action in experimental *Trypanosoma cruzi* infections. *Annals of Tropical Medicine and Parasitology* 76:293–97.

Flores, B., M. Hernández, M. Contreras, L. Sandoval, A. Rojas, F. Villarroel, O. González, and H. Schenone
1983 Enfermedad de Chagas en Chile. Sectores Rurales. Infestación *Triatomidea domiciliaria* e infección por *Tripanosoma cruzi* del vector, y de mamíferos domésticos de la V Región, 1983. *Boletín Chileno de Parasitología* 39:62–65.

Flores, M.A., A.R. Paredes, and A.Y. Ramos
1966 El método de concentración de Strout en el diagnóstico de la fase aguda de la enfermedad de Chagas. *Boletín Chileno de Parasitología* 21:38–39.

Foege, William H.
1988 Plagues: Perceptions of risk and social responses. *Social Research* 55 (3): 331–42.

Forattini, O.P.
1972 Ecological aspects of American trypanosmiasis. *Revista do Salude Pública* 6 (2): 183–87.

Fornaciari, Gino, Maura Castagna, Paolo Viacava, Adele Tognetti, Generoso Bevilacqua, and Elsa Segura
1992 Chagas' disease in Peruvian Inca mummy. *The Lancet* 339:128–29.

Foster, George
1978 Hippocrates' Latin American legacy: "Hot" and "cold" in contemporary folk medicine. In *Colloquia in Anthropology,* ed. R.K. Wetherington, 3–19. Dallas: Southern Methodist University.
1987 On the origin of humoral medicine in Latin America. *Medical Anthropology Quarterly* 1:355–93.

Fournet, Alain, Alcira Angelo Barrios, Victoria Muñoz, Reynald Hocquemiller, André Cavé, and Jean Bruneton
  1993 2-Substituted quinoline alkaloids as potential antileishmanial drugs. *Antimicrobial Agents and Chemotherapy* 37 (4): 859–63.
Frasch, A.C.C., and M.B. Reyes
  1990 Diagnosis of Chagas disease using recombinant DNA technology. *Parasitology Today* 6 (4): 137–41.
Freire, Paulo
  1970 *Pedagogy of the Oppressed*. New York: Herder and Herder.
  1973 *Education for Critical Consciousness*. New York: The Seabury Press.
Fryer, Michelle L.
  1991 Health education through interactive radio: A child-to-child project in Bolivia. *Health Education Quarterly* 18 (1): 65–77.
Gamboa, J., and L.J. Pérez Ríos
  1965 El rancho venezalano, su influencia en la prevalencia triatomina doméstica. *Archivos Venezolanos de Medicina Tropical y Parasitología Médica* 5:305–28.
Garcilaso de la Vega, Inca
  1963 *Comentarios Reales de Los Incas* vol. 2. In *Biblioteca de Autores Españoles*, vol. 133, ed. P. Carmelo Saenz. Madrid: Ediciones Atlas.
Garrett, Laurie
  1994 *The Coming Plague: Newly Emerging Disease in a World Out of Balance*. New York: Farrar, Straus and Giroux.
Geison, Gerald L.
  1995 *The Private Science of Louis Pasteur*. Princeton: Princeton University Press.
Godoy, R.A., and N. Haddad
  1961 Tempo de transito esofágico em portadores de moléstia de Chagas. Anais I. *Proceedings of the Congreso International Doença de Chagas* 2:591–601.
Goldbaum, M.
  1982 O problema das doencas trópicais e os movimentos migratorios no Brasil: situacao en Sao Paulo. In *Doenças e migração humana*, 33–38. Brasilia: Centro de Documentação do Ministerio de Saude.
Goldstein, Jared Haft
  1989 Darwin, Chagas', mind, and body. *Perspectives in Biology and Medicine* 32 (4): 586–600.
González, J., S. Muñoz, S. Ortiz, D. Anacona, S. Salgado, M. Galleguillos, I. Neira, H. Sagua, and A. Solari
  1995 Biochemical, immunological, and biological characterization of *Trypanosoma cruzi* populations of the Andean north of Chile. *Experimental Parasitology* 81:125–35.
Goudsblom, Orban
  1986 Public health and the civilizing process. *Milbank Quarterly* 641:171.
Grant, I.H., J.W. Gold, and M. Wittner
  1989 Transfusion-associated acute Chagas disease acquired in the United States. *Annals of Internal Medicine* 111:849–51.
Grieder, Terence, Alberto Bueno Mendoza, C. Earle Smith, Jr., and Robert M. Malina
  1988 *La Galgada, Peru: A Preceramic Culture in Transition*. Austin: University of Texas Press.

Grifo, Francesca, and Joshua Rosenthal, eds.
   1997 *Biodiversity and Human Health.* Washington, D.C.: Island Press.
Grollman, Sigmund
   1978 *The Human Body: Its Structure and Physiology* 4th ed. New York: Macmillan Publishing Company.
Guaman Poma de Ayala, Felipe
   1944 *La obra de Felipe Guaman Poma de Ayala "Primer Nueva Corónica y Buen Gobierno,"* ed. Arthur Posnansky. La Paz: Editorial del Instituto "Tihuanacu" de Antropología, Etnografía, y Prehistoria.
Gudeman, Stephan
   1990 *Conversations in Colombia: The Domestic Economy in Life and Text.* New York: Cambridge University Press.
Gugliotta, J.L., H.B. Tanowitz, M. Wittner, R. Soeiro
   1980 *Trypanosoma cruzi:* Inhibition of protein synthesis by nitrofuran SQ 18,506. *Experimental Parasitology* 49: 216–24.
Gürtler, R.E., et al.
   1990 The prevalence of *Trypanosoma cruzi* and the demography of dog populations after insecticidal spraying of houses: A predictive model. *Annals of Tropical Medicine and Parasitology* 84:313–23.
Gutteridge, W.E.
   1982 Chemotherapy of Chagas' disease. In *Perpectives in trypanosomiasis research. Proceedings of the twenty-first Trypanosomiasis seminar, London 1981,* ed. J.R. Baker. London: Research Studies Press.
   1985 Existing chemotherapy and its limitations. *British Medical Bulletin* 41 (2): 162–68.
Guyton, Arthur C.
   1986 *Textbook of Medical Physiology* 7th ed., 754–62. Philadelphia: W.B. Saunders Co.
Hagar, J.M., and S.H. Rahimtoola
   1991 Chagas' heart disease in the United States. *New England Journal of Medicine* 325:763–68.
Hendriksson, J., U. Pettersson, and A. Solari
   1993 *Trypanosoma cruzi;* Correlation between karyotype variability and isoenzyme classification. *Experimental Parasitology* 77:334–48.
Honey, Martha
   1995 Pesticides: Nowhere to hide. *Ms.* 6 (1): 16–18.
Hope, Anne, and Sally Timmel
   1987 *Training for Transformation: A Handbook for Community Workers.* Gweru, Zimbabwe: Mambo Press.
Howard, J.E.
   1962 La enfermedad de Chagas congénita. *Colección de Monografía Biológica,* no. 16. Santiago: Universidad de Chile.
Howard, J., and M. Rubio
   1968 Congenital Chagas disease. I. Clinical and epidemiological study of thirty cases. *Boletín Chileno de Parasitología* 23:107–12.
Hurst, J. Willis
   1986 *The Heart: Arteries and Veins.* New York: McGraw-Hill.

Iosa, Daniel
1994 Chronic chagasic cardioneuropathy: Pathogenesis and and treatment. In *Chagas' Disease and the Nervous System*. Scientific Publication no. 547, 99–148. Washington,D.C.: Pan American Health Organization.

Iñiguez-Montenegro, C.
1961 Transito esofáfico na mólestia de Chagas. Procedimiento de IV Reunion Cientifica Asociación Latinamericana. Ribeirão Preto, Brazil: Ciencia Fisiología.

Jáuregui, L., and C.J. Valdivia
1972 Epidemiología de la enfermedad de Chagas en Bolivia. Simposio internacional sobre enfermedad de Chagas en Bolivia (Buenos Aires), 171–77.

Jáuregui Tapia, Pedro
1987 El xenodiagnóstico y el tratamiento parasiticída en la cardiopatía chagásica crónica. *Proyección médica / Facultad de Medicina, La Paz* (Enero): 50–54.
1991 Interview by J. Bastien, July 22, tape recording.

Jáuregui Tapia, Pedro G., and Alberto Casanovas
1987 Estudio epidemiológico electrocardiográfico en área endémica chagásica. *Cuadernos del Hospital de Clínicas de La Paz* 33 (1): 30–33.

Jensch, H.
1937 Neue chemotherapeutika aus der 4-amino-chinolin-Reihe. *Zeitschrift fur Angewandte Chemie* 50:891–95.

Jorg, M.E., A.G. Bustamante, and Y.A. Peltier
1972 Disfunción cerebral mínima como consecuencia de meningoencefalitis aguda por *Trypanosoma cruzi*. *Prensa Médica Argentina* 59:1658–69.

Jost, L., F. Turín, R. Etchegoyen, A. Lieguarda, L. Torcuato, L. Lotti
1977 Meningoencefalitis chagásica en paciente con tratamiento de inmunosupresión por trasplante renal. *Revista Neurológica Argentina* 3:425–528.

Kalshoven, L.G.E.
1970 Observations on the blood-sucking reduviid *Triatoma rubrofasciata* (De Geer) in Java. *Entomologische Bericten* (Berlin) 30:41.

Katz, Michael, D. Dickson Despommier, and Robert W. Gwadz
1989 *Parasitic Diseases* 2nd ed. New York: Springer-Verlag New York Inc.

Kean, B.H.
1977 Carlos Chagas and Chagas' disease. *American Journal of Tropical Medicine and Hygiene* 26 (5): 1084–86.

Kerner, N., P. Liégeard, M.J. Levin, and M. Hontebeyrie-Joskowicz
1991 *Trypanosoma cruzi:* Antibodies to a MAP-like protein in chronic Chagas' disease cross-react with mammalian cytoskeleton. *Experimental Parasitology* 73 (4): 451–59.

Kete, Katheline
1988 *La Rage* and the bourgeoisie: The cultural context of rabies in the French nineteenth century. *Representations* 22:89–107.

Keynes, R.D.
1988 *Charles Darwin's Beagle Diary.* Cambridge: Cambridge University Press.

Khoo, S.H., E.G.L. Wilkins, I. Fraser, J.L. Stanford
1993 Lack of T cell response to common mycobacterial antigens in HIV-infected

individuals consequence or a co-factor? IX International Conference on AIDS, Berlin, June 6–11, PO-A24-0551 (abstr).

Kierszenbaum, F.

1979 Antibody-dependent killing of bloodstream forms of *Trypanosoma cruzi* by human peripheral blood leukocytes. *American Journal of Tropical Medicine and Hygiene* 28:965–68.

Kierszenbaum, F., S.J. Ackerman, and G.J. Gleich

1981 Destruction of bloodstream forms of *Trypanosoma cruzi* by eosinophil granule major basic protein. *American Journal of Tropical Medicine and Hygiene* 30: 775–79.

Kirchhoff, L.V.

1989 *Trypanosoma cruzi* a new threat to our blood supply? *Annals of Internal Medicine* 111:773–75.

1990 Trypanosoma species (American trypanosomiasis, Chagas' disease): Biology of trypanosomes. In *Principles and Practice of Infectious Diseases,* ed. G.L. Mandell, R.G. Douglas, Jr., J.E. Bennett, 3rd ed., 2077–84. New York: Churchill Livingstone.

1993 American trypanosomiasis (Chagas' disease)—A tropical disease now in the United States. *New England Journal of Medicine* 329 (9): 639–43.

Kirchhoff, L.V., and F.A. Neva

1985 Chagas' disease in Latin American immigrants. *Journal of American Medical Association* 234:3058–60.

Kirchhoff, L.V., A.A. Gam, and F.C. Gillian

1987 American trypanosomiasis (Chagas' disease) in Central American immigrants. *American Journal of Medicine* 82:915–20.

Kobayakawa, T., J. Louis, S. Isui, and P.H. Lambert

1979 Autoimmune response to DNA, red blood cells and thymocyte antigens in association with polyclonal antibody synthesis during experimental African trypanosomiasis. *Journal of Immunology* 122:296–301.

Köberle, Fritz

1956 Über das Neurotoxin des Trypanosoma cruzi. *Zentralblatt für Allgemeine Pathologie und Pathologische Anatomie* 95:468–75.

1957 Patagonia da moléstia de Chagas. *Revista Goiana Medicina* 3:155–80.

1959 El mal de Chagas: La enfermedad del sistema nervioso. *Revista Médica Cordoba* 47:105–33.

1963 Patogenía do megaesofago brasileiro e europeu. *Revista Goiana de Medicina* 9:79–116.

1968 Chagas' disease and chagas' syndromes: The pathology of American trypanosomiasis. In *Advances in Parasitology* vol. 6. ed. Ben Dawes, 63–116. London and New York: Academic Press.

1970 The causation and importance of nervous lesions in American trypanosomiasis. *Bulletin World Health Organization* 4:739.

Kolata, Alan, and Charles Ortloff

1989 Thermoanalysis of Tiwanaku raised field systems in the Lake Titicaca Basin of Bolivia. *Journal of Archaeological Science* 16 (3): 233–63.

Kosofsky, Sedgwick, and Adam Frank, eds.

1995 *Shame and Its Sisters: A Silvan Tomkins Reader.* Durham, NC: Duke University Press.

Köster, Gerrit.

1995 Bevölkerungsstruktur, Migrationsverhalten und Integration der Bewohner von Mittel- und Oberschichtvierten in der lateinamerikanischen Stadt. *Das Beispiel La Paz (Bolivien).* Aachener Geographische Arbeiten, Heft 30. Aachen, Germany: Geographisches Institut der RWTH Aachen im Selbstverig.

Kramer, Jane

1993 Bad blood. *New Yorker* 33 (November 10): 74–95.

Kreutzer, R.D., and O.E. Souza

1981 Biochemical characterization of *Trypanosoma* spp by isozyme electrophoresis. *American Journal of Tropical Medicine and Hygiene* 30:308.

Lainson, R., J.J. Shaw, and R.D. Naiff

1980 Chagas' disease in the Amazon basin: Speculations on transmission per os. *Revista do Instituto de Medicina Tropical de São Paulo* 22:294–97.

Lainson, R., J.J. Shaw, H. Frahia, M.A. Miles, and C.C. Draper

1979 Chagas' disease in the Amazon basin: I. *Trypanosoma cruzi* infections in sylvatic mammals, triatomine bugs and man in the state of Para, north east Brazil. *Transactions of the Royal Society of Tropical Medicine and Hygiene* 73:193–204.

Laranja, F.S., E. Dias, G. Nobrega, and A. Miranda

1956 Chagas' disease, a clinical, epidemiologic and pathologic study. *Circulation* 14:1035–60.

Las Casas, Bartolomé de

1976 *Historia de las Indias.* Madrid: M. Ginesta.

Lederberg, Joshua

1988 Pandemic as a natural evolutionary phenomenon. *Social Research* 55 (3): 343–59.

1994 Speech before the Irvington Institute for Medical Research, Bankers Trust Company, New York, February 8, 1994.

Lehane, M.J., and C.J. Schofield

1981 Field experiments of dispersive flight by *Triatoma infestans. Transactions of the Royal Society of Tropical Medicine and Hygiene* 75:399–400.

Leiguarda, R., A. Roncoroni, A.L. Tartuto, L. Jost, M. Berthier, M. Nogues, and H. Freilij

1990 Acute CNS infection by *Trypanosoma cruzi* (Chagas' disease) in immunosuppressed patients. *Neurology* 40 (May): 850–51.

Lent, H., and P. Wygodzinsky

1979 Revision of the triatominae (Hemiptera, Reduviidae), and their significance as vectors of Chagas' disease. *Bulletin of the American Museum of Natural History* 163:123–520.

Lévi-Strauss, Claude

1979 *Structural Anthropology.* New York: Peregrine Books.

Levin, M.J., E. Mesri, R. Benarous, G. Levitus, A. Schijman, P. Levy-Yeyati, P.A. Chiale, A.M. Ruiz, A. Kahn, H. Torres, M.B. Rosenbaum, and E. Segua

  1989 Identification of major *Trypanosoma cruzi* antigenic determinants in chronic Chagas' heart disease. *American Journal of Tropical Medicine and Hygiene* 41 (5):530–38.

Lewinsohn, Rachel

  1979 Carlos Chagas (1879–1934): The discovery of *Trypanosoma cruzi* and of American trypanosomiasis (foot-notes to the history of Chagas's disease. *Transactions of the Royal Society of Tropical Medicine and Hygiene* 73 (5): 513–23.

  1981 Carlos Chagas and the discovery of Chagas's disease (American trypanosomiasis). *Journal of the Royal Society of Medicine* 74:451–55.

Lewis, Walter H., and Memory P. Elvin-Lewis

  1977 *Medical Botany: Plants Affecting Man's Health*. New York: John Wiley & Sons.

Lieban, Richard W.

  1990 Medical anthropology and the comparative study of medical ethics. In *Social Science Perspectives on Medical Ethics,* ed. George Weisz, 221–39. Philadelphia: University of Pennsylvania Press.

LIS Laboratorio de Investigaciones Sociales-UCV

  1987 *Manual de construcción y mejoramiento de viviendas de bahareque para el control de la enfermedad de Chagas.* OPS-Programa de Enfermedades Tropicales-Organización Panamericana de Salud-OMS. Maracay, Venezuela: Imprenta de Malariología.

Lopez, E.R., and E. Chapadeiro

  1986 Doença de Chagas no Triângulo Mineiro. *Revista Goiana de Medicina* 32:109–13.

Lorenzana, R.

  1967 Chronic Chagas' myocarditis: Report of a case. *American Journal of Clinical Pathology* 48:39–43.

Lucena, D.T. de

  1970 Estudos sobre á doença de Chagas no Nordeste do Brasil. *Revista Brasileira de Malariología de Doenças Tropicals* 22 (3): 3–173.

Luft, Murray

  1983 *Popular Adult Education: The Bolivian Experience!* Toronto: Ontario Institute for Studies in Education.

Lumbreras, Luis G.

  1974 *The Peoples and Cultures of Ancient Peru,* trans. Betty J. Meggers. Washington, D.C.: Smithsonian Institution Press.

Lunt, M.G.

  1980 Stabilised soil blocks for building. *Overseas Building Notes* 184:15.

Macedo, V.

  1973 Influência de exposição a reinfecção na evolução da doença de Chagas. Thesis, Federal University of Bahía, Salvador, Brasil.

  1982 Chagas's disease (American trypanosomiasis). In *Cecil Textbook of Medicine,*

16th edition, ed. B. Wyngaarden and L.H. Smith, 1728–31. Philadelphia: W.B. Saunders.

MacNeish, R.S., A. Nelken-Terner, and A. García Cook

1970 *Second Annual Report of the Ayacucho Archaeological Botanical Project.* Andover, MA: Robert S. Peabody Foundation for Archaeology.

MacSweeney, M., A. Shankar, and N.A. Theodorous

1995 Restorative proctocolectomy for Chagasic megacolon. *Journal of the Royal Society of Medicine* 88:479.

Manson-Bahr, P.E.C., and D.R. Bell

1987 *Manson's Tropical Diseases,* 19th edition. London: Baillè.

Marcondes de Rezende, Joffre, and Alejandro Ostermayer Luquetti

1994 Chagasic megaviseras. In *Chagas' Disease and the Nervous System.* Scientific Publication no. 547, 149–71. Washington, D.C.: Pan American Health Organization.

Marques, A.C.

1979 Controle de vectores de Doenca de Chagas. Experiencia do Ministerio da Saude, Brasil. Abstract T3. International Congress on Chagas' Diasese, Rio de Janeiro, Brazil.

Marsden, P.D.

1967 *Trypanosoma cruzi* infections in CFI mice. II. Infections induced by different routes. *Annals of Tropical Medicine and Parasitology* 61:62–67.

1976 Compendium of symposium on American trypanosomiasis research. In *American Trypanosomiasis Research,* vol. 318, 816–24. Washington, D.C.: Pan American Health Organization.

1983 The transmission of *Trypanosoma cruzi* infection to man and its control. In *Human Ecology and Infectious Diseases,* ed. Neil A.Croll and John H. Cross, 253–89. New York: Academic Press.

Marsden, P.D., and J.W.C. Hagstrom

1968 Experimental *Trypanosoma cruzi* infection in beagle puppies. The effect of variations in the dose and source of infecting trypanosomes and the route of inoculation on the course of the infection. *Transactions of the Royal Society of Tropical Medicine and Hygiene* 62:816–24.

Marsden, P.D., D. Vigens, I. Magalhaes, J. Tavares-Neto, R. Ferreira, C.H. Costa, C.N. Castro, V. Macedo, and A.R. Prata

1982 Ecologigía doméstica do *Triatoma infestans* em Mambai, Goiá, Brasil. *Revista do Instituto de Medicina Tropical de São Paulo* 24:364–73.

Marsden, Philip, and R. Penna

1982 A "vigilance unit" for households subject to triatomine control. *Transactions of the Royal Society of Tropical Medicine and Hygiene* 76 (6): 790–92.

Martin, Richard

1970 The role of coca in the history, religion, and medicine of South American Indians. *Economic Botany* 24:422–37.

Massumi, R.A., and A. Gooch

1965 Chagas' myocarditis. *Archives of Internal Medicine* 116:531–36.

Maurice, John

1992 African trypanosomiasis: Drug effective, but "too costly"? *TDR News* 38 (February): 2–3.

Mayer, H.F., and I.L. Alcaraz

1955 Estudios relacionados con las fuentes alimentarias de *Triatoma infestans* (Hemiptera, Reduviidae). *Anales Instituto de Medicina Regional* 4:195–201.

Mazza, Salvador

1936 Transmissíon del *Schizotrypanum cruzi* al niño por leche de la madre con enfermedad de Chagas. *Investigaciones sobre la enfermedad de Chagas* 28:41–46

1944 Consideraciones sobre la enfermedad de Chagas en Bolivia. In *Misión de estudios de patología regional Argentina Jujuy.* Buenos Aires: Universidad de Buenos Aires.

McGreevy, P.B., and P.D. Marsden

1986 American trypanosomiasis and leishmaniasis. In *Chemotherapy of Parasitic Diseases,* ed. W.C. Campbell and R.S. Rew, 115–28. New York and London: Plenum Press.

McHenry, Paul Graham

1985 *Adobe: Build It Yourself.* Tucson: University of Arizona Press.

Medawar, P.

1964 Darwin's illness. *New Statesman* 67:527–28.

Medina Lopez, M.

1983 Transmissâo materno-infantil da doença de Chagas. Ph.D. diss., Universidade de Brasília.

Medrano-Mercado, N., M.R. Luz, F. Torrico, G. Tapia, F. Van Leuven, and T.C. Araujo-Jorge

1996 Acute-phase proteins and serologic profiles of Chagasic children from an endemic area in Bolivia. *Journal of Tropical Medicine and Hygiene* 54 (2): 154–61.

Mello, D.A., and M.M. Borges

1981 Initial discovery of *Triatoma costalimai* naturally infected with *Tripanosoma cruzi:* Study of the biological aspects of an isolated sample. *Memórias do Instituto Oswaldo Cruz* 76 (1): 61–69.

Méndez Acuña, Johnny

1991 Interview by J. Bastien, Sucre, Bolivia, June 24, tape recording.

Métraux, Alfred

1967 *Religion et Magies Indiennes Amérique du Sud.* Paris: Gallimard.

Milei, J., B. Manter, R. Storino, J.A. Sánchez, and V.J. Ferrans

1992 Does Chagas' disease exist as an undiagnosed form of cardiomyopathy in the United States? *American Heart Journal* 123:1732–35.

Miles, M.A., M.M. Provoa, A. Prata, R.A. Cedillos, A.A. de Souza, and V. Macedo

1981 Do radically dissimilar *Trypanosoma cruzi* strains (Zymodemes) cause Venezuelan and Brazilian forms of Chagas' disease? *The Lancet* 63 (2): 1338–40.

Miles, M.A., M. Provoa, A.A. de Souza, A. Prata, and V. Macedo

1981 Chagas' disease in the Amazonian basin. II: The distribution of *Trypanosoma cruzi* zymodemes 1 and 3 in Para State, North Brazil. *Transactions of the Royal Society of Tropical Medicine and Hygiene* 75:667–74.

Miles, M.A., P.J. Toyé, S.C. Oswald, and D.G. Godfrey

1977 The identification by isoenzyme patterns of two different strain-groups of *Trypanosoma cruzi,* circulating independently in a rural area of Brazil. *Transactions of the Royal Society of Tropical Medicine and Hygiene* 71:217–37.

Minter, D.
1978a Transmisión de la enfermedad de Chagas. *Boletín de la Oficina Sanitaria Panamericana* 84 (4): 332–43.
1978b Triatomine bugs and the household ecology of Chagas' disease. In *Medical Entomology Centenary Symposium, Proceedings*, 85–93. London: Royal Society of Tropical Medicine and Hygiene.

Moffett, George D.
1994 *Critical Masses: The Global Population Challenge*. New York: Viking.

Molyneux, D.H., and R.W. Ashford
1983 *The Biology of Trypanosoma and Leishmania Parasites of Man and Domestic Animals*. New York: International Publications Service, Taylor & Francis, Inc.

Monckeberg, J.G.
1924 Die Erkrangungen des Myokards und des spezifischen Muskelsystem. In *Handbuch Speziellen Pathologischgen Anatomie und Histologie, Band II*, ed. F. Henke and O. Lubarsch, 290–555. Berlin: Verlag von Julius Springer.

Montaño, Sonia, and Ximena Machicao
1992 *Informe de la investigación sobre mitos, habitos, y creencias sobre el chagas y la vinchuca en cuatro comunidades de Tarija*. La Paz: Pro-Habitat.

Moraes-Souza, H., J.O. Bordin, L. Bardossy, D.W. MacPherson, M.A. Blajchman
1995 Prevention of transfusion-associated Chagas' disease: Efficacy of white cell-reduction filters in removing *Trypanosoma cruzi* from infected blood. *Transfusion* 35 (9): 723–26.

Moraes-Souza, H., D.M. Wanderley, Z. Brener, R.D. Nascimento, C.M. Antunes, and J.C. Dias
1994 Hemoterapía e doença de Chagas transfusional no Brasil. *Boletín de la Oficina Sanitaria Panamericana* (AGG) 116 (5): 406–18.

Morales Rojas, G., R.G. Fuenmahyor, G.F. Acevedo, M.A. Capriles, and A.R. Gonzales,
1961 Manifestaciones digestivas en pacientes chagásicos. Archivos Hospitales. *Vargas* 3:179–87.

Morton, J.F.
1981 *Atlas of Medicinal Plants of Middle America*. Springfield, IL: Chas. C. Thomas.

Mosca, W., L. Briceño, and M.I. Hernández
1991 Cell-mediated immunity in Chagas' disease: *Trypanosoma cruzi* antigens induce suppression of the in vitro proliferative response of mononuclear cells. *Memórias do Instituto Oswaldo Cruz* 86:147–52.

Moya, Pedro R.
1977 El hijo de madre chagásica. Ph.D. diss., Universidad Nacional de Córdoba (Córdoba, Argentina).
1994 Chagas' disease in children: Neurological and psychological aspects. In *Chagas' Disease and the Nervous System*, 189-202. Washington, D.C.: Pan American Health Organization.

Moya, P.R., and A.P. Barousse
1984 Enfermedad de Chagas congénita. In *Enfermedad de Chagas. Aportes del Programa Nacional de Investigaciones en Enfermedades Endémicas 1979–1983*, 51–65. Buenos Aires: Ministerio de Educación y Justicia.

MPPSP (Ministerio de Previsión Social y Salud Pública)

1991 *Acción Integral y Sistema para el Logro de una Communidad Antichagásica*. La Paz: Master.

Muñoz, S., M. Lorca, P. Muñoz, and A. Solari

1994 Poblaciones de *Trypanosoma cruzi* altamente homogeneas en una region de baja endemia chagásica: Relevancía en la patogenía de la enfermedad de Chagas. *Revista Médica de Chile* 122:1231–38.

Muñoz Casas del Valle, Patricia

1990 Importancia clínica de la infección por *Trypanosoma cruzi* en niños. Tesis de Magister en Ciencias Médicas, Facultad de Medicina, Universidad de Chile.

Muñoz Casas del Valle, Patricia, and Carlos Acevedo Schwartzmann

1994 Congenital Chagas' disease. In *Chagas' Disease and the Nervous System*, 203–11. Washington, D.C.: Pan American Health Organization.

Muñoz Reyes, Jorge

1977 *Geografía de Bolivia*. La Paz: Editoriales Don Bosco.

Murra, John V.

1972 El "control vertical" de pisos ecológicos en la economía de las sociedades Andinas. In *Visita de Provincia de León de Huánuco en 1562*, ed. J. Murra, vol. 2, 427–76. Huánuco, Peru: Universidad Nacional Hermilio Valdizán.

Murray, P.J., and T.W. Spithill

1991 Variants of a Leishmania surface antigen derived from a multigenic family. *Journal of Biological Chemistry* 266 (36): 24477–84.

Nattan-Larrier, L.

1921 Hérédité des infections expérimentales á *Schizotrypanum cruzi*. *Bulletin de la Société de Pathologie Exotique* 14:232–38.

Neghme, A.

1982 La tripanosomiasis americana. *Creces* 3:23–28.

Nelkin, Dorothy, and Sander L. Gilman

1988 Placing blame for devasting disease. *Social Research* 55 (3): 343–59.

Nery-Guimaraes, F., and H.A.A. Lage

1972 Refractariedade das aves ao *T. cruzi*. *Memórias do Instituto Oswaldo Cruz* 70: 97–107.

Nery-Guimaraes, F., et al.

1968 Um surto epidêmico de Chagas de provável transmissao digestiva, ocorrido em Teutonia (Estrêla-Rio Grande do Sul). *Hospital* (Rio de Janeiro) 73: 1767–1804.

Neu, N., K.W. Beisel, M.D. Traytsman, N.R. Rose, and S.W. Craig

1987 Autoantibodies specific for the cardiac myosin isoform are found in mice susceptible to Coxsackievirus B3-induced mycoarditis. *Journal of Immunology* 138 (8): 2488–92.

Neu, N., N.R. Rose, K.W. Beisel, A. Herskowitz, G. Gurri-Glass, and S.W. Craig

1987 Cardiac myosin induces myocarditis in genetically predisposed mice. *Journal of Immunology* 139 (11): 3630–36.

Neva, Franklin, and Harold Brown

1994 *Basic Clinical Parasitology* 6th ed. Norwalk, CT: Appleton & Lange.

Nickerson, P, P. Orr, M.L. Schroeder, L. Sekla, and J.B. Johnston

1989 Transfusion-associated *Trypanosoma cruzi* infection in a non-endemic area. *Annals of Internal Medicine* 111:851–53.

Nuñez, L.
1982 Temprana emergencia de sedentarismo en el desierto chileno: Proyecto Caserones. *Chungara* 9:80–123.
1983 Paleoindian and archaic cultural periods in the arid and semiarid regions of northern Chile. *Advances in World Archaeology* 2:161–203.

Nussenzweig, V., A. Biancalana, V. Amato Neto, R. Sonntag, J.L.P. Frietas, and J. Kloetzel
1953 Acão da violeta genciana sobre o *T. cruzi* in vitro: Sua importancia na esterilização do sangue destinado a transfusão. *Revista Paulista de Medicina* 42:57–58.

Oblitas-Poblete, Enrique
1968 *La lengua secreta de los Incas*. La Paz: Editorial Los Amigos del Libro.
1969 *Plantas medicinales en Bolivia*. La Paz: Editorial Los Amigos del Libro.
1978 *Cultura Callawaya*. La Paz: Ediciones Populares Camarlinghi.

Oiveira Vieira, G., J. Maguire, A.L. Bittencourt, and J.A. Fontes
1983 Doença de Chagas congénita. Apresentaçáo de um caso com parlisia cerebral. *Revista de Instituto de Medicina Tropical de São Paulo* 25:305–9.

Okabe, K., T.L. Kipnis, V.L. Calish, and W.D. daSilva
1980 Cell-mediated cytotoxicity to *Trypanosoma cruzi*. I. Antibody-dependent cell mediated cytotoxicity to trypomastigote bloodstream forms. *Clinical Immunology and Immunopathology* 16:344–53.

Oliveira Filho, A.M., L.F. Deus, and I.A. Brasil
1987 Slow-release paints, used during house building, as a means of turning huts refractory to infestation by Chagas' disease vectors. *Parasitología, Ciência e Cultura*, Abstract 14-G.1.9.

OPS (Organización Panamericana de Salud)
1982 Enfermedad de Chagas. *Boletín Epidemiológico* 3 (3).
1983 *Estado Actual de la Situación en Relación a la Enfermedad de Chagas en las Americas,* vol. CD29/INF/4. Washington, D.C.: Pan American Health Organization.

PAHO (Pan American Health Organization)
1984 Status of Chagas disease in the region of the Americas. *Epidemiology Bulletin* 5 (2): 5–9.

Patiño, Victor M.
1969 Guayusa, a neglected stimulant from eastern Andean foothills. *Economic Botany* 22:310–16.

Pavlone, I., R. Chuit, A. Pérez, C. Wisnevesky-Colli, and E.L. Segura
1988 Field Research on an epidemiological surveillance alternative of Chagas' disease transmission: The primary health care strategy in rural areas. *Revista Argentina de Microbiología* 20 (suppl.): 103–5.

Pearlman, J.D.
1983 Chagas' disease in northern California: No longer an endemic diagnosis. *American Journal of Medicine* 75 (6): 1057–60.

Peeters, M., W. Janssens, K. Fransen, J. Brandful, L. Heyndrickx, K. Koffi, E. Delaporte, P. Piot, G.M. Gershy-Damet, G. van der Groen
1994 Isolation of simian immunodeficiency viruses from two sooty mangabeys in Cote d'Ivoire: Virological and genetic characterization and relationship to

other HIV type 2 and SIVsm/mac strains. *AIDS Research Human Retrovirus* 10 (10): 1289–94.

Pehrson, P., M. Wahlgren, and E. Bengstsson

1982 Intracraneal calcifications probably due to congenital Chagas' disease. *American Journal of Tropical Medicine and Hygiene* 31:449–51.

Peñalver, L.M., J. Fajardo, and F.J. Aguilar

1953 Aportes al conocimiento de la enfermedad de Chagas en Guatemala. *Revista Colegio de Medicina de Guatemala* 4 (1): 20.

Peñalver, L.M., M.I. Rodríguez, M. Block, and G. Sancho

1965 Tripanosomiasis en El Salvador. *Archivos Colegio Médico de El Salvador* 18:97.

Pereira, P.F., and R.P. Goncalves

1958 Megaesofago chagásico; hipertrofia ou hiperplasia? *Revista Goiana de Medicina* 4:17–28.

Pereira Barreto, M.G.

1984 Characteristics of urban mortality from Chagas disease in Brazil's Federal District. *Bulletin of Pan American Health Organization* 18 (1): 2–9.

1985 Reservorios del *Trypanosoma cruzi* Chagas 1909. *Centro Panamericano de Ecología Humana y Salud* O.M.S. 2:275.

Perlowagora-Szumlewiecz, P.

1969 (T. infestans biology, principal vector of Chagas' disease in Brazil). Estudos sobre Triatoma infestans, o principal vector da Doença Chagas no Brasil (importancia de algumas de suas características biológicas no planejamento de esquemas de combate a esse vetor). *Revista Brasileira de Malariología e Doenças Tropicals* (Rio de Janeiro) 21:117–59.

Petry, K., and H. Eisen

1989 Chagas' disease: A model for the study of autoimmune diseases. *Parasitology Today* 5:11–116.

Phillips, David R.

1990 *Health and Health Care in the Third World.* New York: John Wiley.

Pinchin, R., A.M. Oliveira Filho, C.A. Muller, M.J. Figueiredo, A.P. Szumlewicz, and B. Gilbert

1978 Slow release insecticides for triatomine control: activity and persistence. *Revista Brasileira Malariología e Doenças Tropicals* (Rio de Janeiro) 30:45–55.

Pinchin, R., A.M. Oliveira Filho, C.A.C. Ayala, and B. Gilbert

1978a Slow release insecticides for triatomine control: preliminary field trials. *Revista Brasileira Malariología e Doenças Tropicals* (Rio de Janeiro) 30:57–63.

Pipkin, A.C.

1968 Domiciliary reduviid bugs and epidemiology of Chagas' disease in Panama (Hemiptera: Reduvidae: Triatominae). *Journal of Medical Entomology* 5:107.

1969 The transmission of *Trypanosoma cruzi* by arthropod vectors: Anterior versus posterior route infection. *International Review of Tropical Medicine* (New York) 3:1–47.

Pippin, W.F.

1970 The biology and vector capability of *Triatoma sanguisuga texana* Usinger and *Triatoma gerstaeckeri* (Stal) compared with *Rhodnius prolixus* (Stal) (Hemiptera: Triatominae). *Journal of Medical Entomology* 7:30–45.

Pizarro, Pedro

   1921 *Relation of the Discovery and Conquest of the Kingdoms of Peru.* New York: Cortés Society.

Pless, M., D. Juranek, P. Kozarsky, F. Steurer, G. Tapia, H. Bermúdez

   1992 The epidemiology of Chagas' disease in a hyperendemic area of Cochabamba, Bolivia: A clinical study including electrocardiography, seroreactivity to *Trypanosoma cruzi*, xenodiagnosis, and domiciliary triatomine distribution. *American Journal of Tropical Medicine and Hygiene* 5:539–46.

Ponce, C.

   1984 Prevalencía de la enfermedad de Chagas en Honduras. Paper presented at a meeting concerning Chagas' disease. November.

Ponce, C., and R. Zeledón

   1973 La enfermedad de Chagas en Honduras. *Boletín Oficina Sanitaria Panamericana* 75 (3): 239.

Presencia

   1997 Los millonarios sueldos de los "technócratas." *Presencia,* May 11, p. 12.

Quinteros, Z.T., M.C. Troncoso, N. Arnesi, G. Boggio, and S. Sánchez

   1990 Comportamientos migratorios en donantes de sangre y su relación con infección chagásica. *Cuadernos Médicos Sociedad* 54:3–14.

Rabinovitch, J.E., J.A. Leal, D. Pinero, and D.P. Feliciangeli

   1979 Domiciliary biting frequency and blood ingestion of the Chagas' disease vector *Rhodnius prolixus* Stahl (Hemiptera: Reduviidae) in Venezuela. *Transactions of the Royal Society of Tropical Medicine and Hygiene* 73 (3): 273–83.

Ramírez, L.E., E. Lages-Silva, G.M. Pianetti, R.M. Rabelo, J.O. Bordin, and H. Moraes-Souza

   1995 Prevention of transfusion-associated Chagas' disease by sterilization of *Trypanosoma cruzi*-infected blood with gentian violet, ascorbic acid, and light. *Transfusion* 35 (3): 226–30.

Rassi, A.

   1977 Clínica: Fase aguda. In *Trypanosoma cruzi e Doença de Chagas,* ed. Z. Brener and Z.A. Andrade, 249–361. Rio de Janeiro: Editoria Guanabara Koogan.

   1991 Evoluçâo da cardiopatia chagásica crónica humana no sertâo do estado da Paraíba, Brasil, no período de 4, 5 anos. *Revista do Instituto de Medicina Tropical de São Paulo* 24 (4): 257.

Rassi, A., and J.M. Rezende

   1976 Prevention of transmission of *T. cruzi* by blood transfusion. In *American Trypanosomiasis Research* vol. 318, 273–78. Washington: Pan American Health Organization.

Ratermann, David

   1997 Overview of Bolivian Reality. Cochabamba, Bolivia: Instituto de Idiomas.

Ready, P.D., and M.A. Miles

   1980 Delimitation of *Trypanosoma cruzi zymodemes* by numerical taxonomy. *Transactions of the Royal Society of Tropical Medicine and Hygiene* 74:238–42.

Recacoechea, Mario

1979 A study of 39 cases of acute Chagas disease in Santa Cruz. *Boletín Chileno de Parasitología* 34 (3-4): 53–58.

Recacoechea, Mario, Aimé De Muynck, Hugo Zuna, Aníbal Rivero, Alfredo Romero, Hernán Bermudez, Billy Melgar, and Benjamín Ribera

1979 Estudio Epidemiológico, Clínico y Terapéutico del Chagas Agudo en Santa Cruz, Bolivia. *Boletín Informativo del CENETROP* 5:2–16.

Recacoechea, M., H. Bermúdez, H. Zuna, and C. La Fuente

1980 A propósito de 4 casos de chagas agudo no detectados por los examenes directos de laboratorio. *Boletín Informativo CENETROP* 6:20-24.

Regalsky, Pablo

1997 Interview by J. Bastien, Cochabamba, Bolivia, May 5, tape recording.

Reyes, M.B., G.D. Pollevick, and A.C. Frasch

1994 An unusually small gene encoding a putative mucin-like glycoprotein in *Trypanosoma cruzi*. *Genetics* 140 (1): 139–40.

Reyes Varas, Victor

1988 *El Castellano Popular en Tarija* Segunda edicion. Tarija: n.p.

Reynolds, James E.F.

1986 Nifurtimox. In *Martindale: The Extra Pharmacopoeia*, ed. James E.F. Reynolds, vol. 29, 673. London: Pharmaceutical Press.

1986 Benznidazole. In *Martindale: The Extra Pharmacopoeia*, ed. James E. F. Reynolds, vol. 29, 660. London: Pharmaceutical Press.

Rezende, J.M.

1963 The endemic South-American megaeoesophagus. *Congress International of Gastroenteritis* (Basel, New York) 2:60–74.

Rezende, J.M., and A. Rassi

1958 Comprometimento do esofago na moléstia de Chagas: Megaesofago e cardiopatia. *O Hospital* 53:1–16.

Ribeiro-dos-Santos, R., and L. Hudson

1980 *Trypanosoma cruzi:* Binding of parasite antigens to mammalian cell membranes. *Parasite Immunology* 2:1–10.

Ribeiro-dos-Santos, R., A. Rassi, and A. Köberle

1980 Chagas' disease. *Antibiótica et Chemotherapía* 30:115–34.

Ribeiro-dos-Santos, R., M.A. Rossi, J.L. Laus, J. Silva Santana, W. Savino, and J. Mengel

1992 Anti-CD4 abrogates rejection and reestablishes long-term tolerance to syngeneic newborn hearts grafted in mice chronically infected with *Trypanosoma cruzi*. *Journal of Experimental Medicine* 175:29–39.

Ritvo, Harriet

1987 *The Animal Estate: The English and Other Creatures in the Victorian Age.* Cambridge, MA: Harvard University Press.

Rivas, Daniel, Freddy Martínez, Ariel Sempertegui, Fernando Díaz Romero, and María Del Carmen Camacho

1990 *Evaluación de Medio Termino: Proyecto Control de Chagas en Chuquisaca.* Sucre: Catholic Relief Services and Programa de Coordinación en supervivencia infantil.

Rodríguez Rivas, Julio

1978 Consideraciones sobre enfermedad de Chagas. In *Enfermedad de Chagas,* ed. Alfredo Romero Dávalos, 39–45. La Paz: Editorial Los Amigos del Libro.

Rothhammer, F., M.J.Allison, L. Nuñez, V. Standen, and B. Arriaza

1985 Chagas' disease in Pre-Columbian South America. *American Journal of Physical Anthropology* 68:495–98.

Rowe, John H.

1946 Inca culture at the time of the Spanish Conquest. In *Handbook of South American Indians,* ed. Julian H. Steward, vol. 2, 183–330. Washington, D.C.: Bureau of American Ethnology.

1967 What kind of settlement was Inca Cuzco? Presentation at the 11th Annual Meeting of the Kroeber Anthropological Society, Berkeley, California, April 22, 1967.

Ruiz, R.C., V.L. Rigoni, J. Gonzales, and N. Yoshida

1993 The 35/50 kDa surface antigen of *Trypanosoma cruzi* metacyclic trypomastigotes, an adhesion molecule involved in host cell invasion. *Parasite Immunology* 15 (2): 121–25.

Ryckman, R.E.

1986 Names of the Triatominae of North and Central America and the West Indies: Their histories, derivations and etymology (Hemptera, Reduviidae, Triatominae). *Bulletin of the Society of Vector Ecologists* 11:209–20.

Salomon, Frank, and George Urioste, trans.

1991 *The Huarochirí Manuscript: A Testament of Ancient and Colonial Andean Religion.* Austin: University of Texas Press.

Salvatella, R.

1986 Encuesta de prevalencia serológica de la enfermedad de Chagas en Uruguay. *Revista Médica del Uruguay* 2 (2):119–24.

Schenkman, S., D. Eichinger, M.E.A. Pereira, and V. Nussenzweig

1994 Structural and functional properties of Trypanosoma trans-sialidase. *Annual Review of Microbiology* 48:499–523.

Schenkman, S., M.A.J. Ferguson, N. Heise, M.L. Cardoso de Almeida, R.A. Mortara, and N. Yoshida

1993 Mucin-like glycoproteins linked to the membrane by glycosylphosphatidlylinositol anchor are the major acceptors of sialic acid in a reaction catalyzed by trans-sialidase in metacyclic forms of *Trypanosoma cruzi. Molecular and Biochemical Parasitology* (Amsterdam) 59 (2): 293–303.

Schenone, H., E. Alfaro, H. Reyes, and E. Paucher

1968 Valor del xenodiagnóstico en la infección Chagásica crónica. *Boletín Chileno de Parasitología* 23:149–54.

Schenone, H., J. Contreras, J. Borgoño, A. Rojas, F. Villarroel, J. Valdes

1985 Enfermedad de Chagas en Chile. Sectores rurales y periurbanos del área de endemosootia. Relaciones entre condiciones de la vivienda, infestación triatomidea domiciliaria e infección por *Triposanosoma cruzi* del vector, del humano y de mamíferos domésticos, 1982–1985. *Boletín Chileno de Parasitología* 40: 58–67.

Schmidt, Gerald D., and Larry S. Roberts
  1989 *Foundations of Parasitology*. St. Louis: Times Mirror/Mosby College Publishing.
Schmuñis, G.A.
  1985 Chagas' disease and blood transfusions. *Progress in Clinical and Biological Research* 182:127–45.
  1991 *Trypanosoma cruzi*, the etiologic agent of Chagas' disease: Status in the blood supply in endemic and nonendemic countries. *Transfusion* 31 (6): 547–57.
  1994 American trypanosomiasis as a public health problem. In *Chagas' Disease and the Nervous System*, ed. Pan American Health Organization, 3–29. Washington, D.C.: Pan American Health Organization.
Schofield, C.J.
  1978 A comparison of sampling techniques for domestic populations of Triatominae. *Transactions of the Royal Society of Tropical Medicine and Hygiene* 72: 449–55.
  1982 The problem of Chagas's disease vector control. In *Perspectives in Trypanosomiasis Research*, ed. J.R. Baker, 71–84. Chichester: Research Studies Press.
  1985 Control of Chagas' disease vectors. *British Medical Bulletin* 4:187–94.
Schofield, C.J., and P.D. Marsden
  1982 The effect of wall plaster on a domestic population of *Triatoma infestans*. *Pan American Health Organization Bulletin* 16 (4): 356–60.
Schofield, C.J., W. Apt, and A.M. Miles
  1982 The ecology of Chagas' disease in Chile. *Ecology of Disease* 1 (2-3): 117–29.
Schofield, C.J., R. Briceño-León, N. Kolstrupp, D.T.J. Webb, and G.B. White
  1990 The role of house design in limiting vector-borne disease. In *Appropriate Technology in Vector Control*, ed. C.J. Curtis, 187–212. Boca Raton, FL: CRC Press.
Schultes, Richard E.
  1967 The botanical origins of South American snuffs. In *Ethnopharmacological Search for Psychoactive Drugs*, ed. D. Efron. Washington, D.C: U.S. Government Printing Office.
  1972 *Ilex Guayusa* from A.D. 500 to the present. In *A Medicine-man's Tomb in Highland Bolivia*, ed. Henry Wassén. Etnologiska Studier 32. Göteborg: Etnografiska Museum.
Sensano, Ruth
  1991 Interview by J. Bastien, Sucre, Bolivia, June 16, 17, tape recording.
  1997 Interview by J. Bastien, Sucre, Bolivia, June 13, tape recording.
Sequeda, M., G.A. Villalobos, H. Maekelt, J. Acquatella, J.R. Velasco, J.R. González, G. Anselmi
  1986 Enfermedad de Chagas. VII Congreso Venezolano de Salud Pública (Caracas). February.
Sgambatti de Andrade, Ana Lucia, Fabio Zicker, Renato Mauricio de Oliveira, Ionizetee Garcia da Silva, Simonne Almeida Silva, Soraya Sgambatti de Andrade, and Celina M.T. Martelli
  1995 Evaluation of risk factors for house infestation by *Triatoma infestans* in Brazil. *American Journal of Tropical Medicine and Hygiene* 53 (5): 443–47.

Shafii, A.

1977 Chagas' disease with cardiopathy and hemiplegia. *New York State Journal of Medicine*. 77:418–19.

Silva, L.J.

1985 Disbravamento, agricultura e doenca de Chagas no Estado de São Paulo. *Cadernos de Saude Publica* 2 (2): 124–40.

Silveira, A.C.

1986 Mortalidade por doença de Chagas no Brasil, 1977/1986. *Memórias de Instituto Oswaldo Cruz* 81 (suppl): 70.

Sims, P., and W.E. Gutteridge

1978 Inhibitory action of a 5-nitrofuran drug (SQ 18506) against *Trypanosoma cruzi*. *Biochemical Pharmacology* 27:2815–20.

1979 Mode of action of a 5-nitrofuran (SQ 18506) against nucleic acid synthesis in *Trypanosoma cruzi*. *International Journal of Parasitology* 9:61–67.

Skolnick, A.

1989 Does influx from endemic areas mean more transfusion-associated Chagas' disease? *Journal of American Medical Association* 262:1433.

Smith, S.C., and P.M. Allen

1991 Myosin-induced acute myocarditis is a T cell mediated disease. *Journal of Immunology* 147 (7): 2141–47.

Snary, D.

1985 Receptors and recognition mechanisms of *Trypanosoma cruzi*. *Transactions of Royal Society of Tropical Medicine and Hygiene*. 79 (5): 587–90.

Soares, V.A., and P.D. Marsden

1980 Studies of the persistence of infectivity of *Trypanosoma cruzi*. III. Effect of human sweat. *Revista Brasileira de Pesquisas Médicas & Biológicas* 13:53–55.

Soergel, K.H., F.F. Zobralske, and J.R. Amberg

1964 Presbyesophagus: Esophagus' motility in nonagenarians. *Journal of Clinical Investigation* 43:1472–79.

SOH/CCH (Secretariat of Health and Community and Child Health)

1994 *Chagas' Disease in Bolivia*. La Paz: USAID.

Solari, A., S. Muñoz, J. Venegas, A. Wallace, X Aguilera, W. Apt, S.F. Brénière, and M. Tibayrenc

1992 Characterization of Chilean, Bolivian, and Argentinian *Trypanosoma cruzi* populations by restriction endonuclease and isoenzyme analysis. *Experimental Parasitology* 75:187–95.

Sousa, O.E., and C.M. Johnson

1971 Frequency and distribution of *Trypanosoma cruzi* and *Trypanosoma rangeli* in the Republic of Panama. *American Journal of Tropical Medicine and Hygiene* 20 (3): 405.

Special Programmes for Research and Training in Tropical Diseases

1991 *Tropical Diseases: Progress in Research 1989–1990: Tenth Programme Report of the UNDP-World Bank-WHO Special Programmes for Research and Training in Tropical Diseases (TDR)*. Geneva: WHO.

Spielman, A., M.L. Wilson, J.F. Levitne, et al.

1985 Ecology of *Ixodes dammini*-borne human babesiosis and Lyme disease. *Annual Review of Entomology* 30:439–60.

Stewart, George

1992 Interviews and notes from class on parasitology by J. Bastien, University of Texas at Arlington, tape recordings.

1994 Interviews and notes from class on parasite immunology by J. Bastien, University of Texas at Arlington, tape recordings.

Taber, C.W.

1985 *Taber's Cyclopedic Medical Dictionary* 15th ed. Philadelphia: F.A. Davis Company.

Tait, A.

1983 Sexual processes in the kinetoplastida. *Parasitology* 86 (4): 29–57.

TDRnews

1996 New treatment for Chagas' disease? *TDRnews* 51 (November): 3–8.

Teixeira, A.R.L., E. Jabur, J.C. Cordoba, I.C. Souto Maior, and E. Solorzano

1983 Alteração da resposta imune mediada por celulas durante o tratamento com benzonidazol. *Revista Sociedade Brasileira de Medicina Tropical* 16:11–22.

Teixeira, A.R.L, M.L. Teixeira, and C. Santos-Buch

1975 The immunology of experimental Chagas' disease. IV. Production of lesions in rabbits similar to those of chronic Chagas' disease in man. *American Journal of Pathology* 80:163–80.

Teixeira, M.L., J. Rezende Filho, F. Figueiredo, and A.R.L. Teixeira

1980 Chagas' disease: Selective affinity and cytotoxocity of *Trypanosoma cruzi*-immune lymphocytes to parasympathetic ganglion cells. *Memórias de Instituto Oswaldo Cruz* 75:33–45.

Theis, J.H., M. Tibayrenc, D.T. Mason, and S.K. Ault

1987 Exotic stock of *Trypanosoma cruzi* (Schizotrypanum) capable of development in and transmission by *Triatoma protracta* from California: Public health implications. *American Journal of Tropical Medicine and Hygiene* 36 (3):523–28.

Thiermann, E., P. Muñoz, M. Lorca, and A. Atías

1985 El estudio de las infecciones congénitas por *Toxoplasma gondii* y *Trypanosoma cruzi*. *Revista Chilena Pediatría* 56:143–50.

Tibayrenc M.

1984 La maladie de Chagas en Bolivie: Donnes preliminaires sur les cycles domestiques: Méthodes simplifiées de capture des tritomes. Cahiers CNRS/ORSTOM (Montpellier, France) serie *Entomologie Médecine et Parasitologie* 22 (1): 51–53.

Tibayrenc, M., and S.F. Breniere

1988 *Trypanosoma cruzi:* Major clones rather than principal zymodemes. *Memorias Instituto Oswaldo Cruz* 83 (suppl. 1): 249–55.

Tibayrenc, M., and P. Desjeux

1983 The presence of two distinct zymodemes of *Tripanosoma cruzi,* circulating sympatrically in a domestic transmission cycle. *Transactions of the Royal Society of Tropical Medicine and Hygiene* 77 (1): 73–75.

Tibayrenc, M., L. Echalar, J.P. Dujardin, O. Poch, and P. Desjeux

1984 The microdistribution of isoenzymatic strains of *Tripanosoma cruzi* in southern Bolivia. *Transactions of the Royal Society of Tropical Medicine and Hygiene* 78 (4): 519–25.

Tibayrenc, M., A. Hoffmann, O. Poch, L. Echelar, F. LePont, J.L. Lemesre, P. Desjeux, and F.J. Ayala

1986 Additional data on *Trypanosoma cruzi* isozymic strains encountered in Bolivian domestic transmission cycles. *Transactions of the Royal Society of Tropical Medicine and Hygiene* 80:442–47.

Tibayrenc, M., K. Neubauer, C. Barnabe, F. Guerrini, D. Skarecky, and F.J. Ayala

1993 Genetic characterization of six parasitic protozoa: Parity between random-primer DNA typing and multilocus enzyme electrophoresis. *Proceedings of the National Academy of Science* (USA) 90 (4): 1335–39.

Tibayrenc, M.L., P. Ward, A. Moya, and F.J. Ayala

1986 Natural populations of *Trypanosoma cruzi,* the agent of Chagas' disease, have a complex multiclonal structure. *Proceedings of the National Academy of Science* (USA) 83:115–19.

Tibbetts, R.S., T.S. McCormick, E.C. Rowland, S.D.Miller, and D.M. Engman

1994 Cardiac antigen-specific autoantibody production is associated with cardiomyopathy in *Trypanosoma cruzi*-infected mice. *Journal of Immunology* 152: 1493–99.

Tonn, Robert J.

1985 Problemas e implicaciones del control integrado de la enfermedad de Chagas. *Factores Biológicas y Ecológicas en la Enfermedad de Chagas,* tomo 2, 331–38. Buenos Aires: Centro Panamericano de Ecología y Salud/Servicio Nacional de Chagas.

Torres, C.B.M.

1930 Patogenía de la miocarditis crónica en la enfermedad de Chagas. *Quinta Reunión de la Sociedad Argentina Patología Región Norte* 2:902–16.

Torrico, Rafael Angel

1946 Nuevos reservorios de *Schizotrypanum cruzi. Anales del laboratorio central SCISP* (Cochabamba).

1959 Enfermedad de Chagas en Bolivia. *Revista Goiana de Medicina* 5:375.

Tschudi, J.J.

1918 *Contribuciones a la historía, civilización y lingistica del Peru antiguo* tomo 2. Lima: San Marti.

Tupiza Report

1990 *Resumen informativo: Segundo cuatrisemestre* [Mayo-Agosto]. Tupiza, Bolivia.

Turner, J.

1963 Dwelling resources in South America. *Architectural Design* 33 (8): 360–93.

1968 House priorities, settlement patterns and urban development in modernizing countries. *Journal of the American Institute of Planners* 34:354–63.

1969 Uncontrolled urban settlements: Problems and solutions. In *The City in Developing Countries,* ed. G. Breese, 507–35. Englewood Cliffs, NJ: Prentice Hall.

Uhle, Max

1898 A snuffing tube from Tiahuanaco. *Bulletin of the Museum of Science and Art, University of Pennsylvania* 1 (4): 1–19.

Urbina, Julio A., Gilberto Payares, Judith Molina, Cristina Sanoja, Andreína Liendo, Keyla Lazardi, Marta Piras, Romano Piras, Norma Perez, Patrick Wincker, and John Ryley

1996 Cure of short- and long-term experimental Chagas' disease using D0870. *Science* 273 (16 September): 969–71.

Urroz, C.J.

1972 Estado actual de los conocimientos sobre enfermedad de Chagas en Nicaragua. 3rd Congreso Centroamericano de Microbiología.

Valdivia, J., J. Jáuregui, J. Castedo, R. Jordan, and M. Borda

1977 *Usted y la enfermedad de Chagas.* Santa Cruz: Ateneo de Medicina.

Valdivia, Jaime, and B. Oswaldo Valdivia

1978 Estudio epidemiológico sobre la enfermedad de Chagas en el departamento de Santa Cruz (Bolivia). In *Enfermedad de Chagas,* ed. Alfredo Romero Davalos, 105–14. La Paz: Los Amigos del Libro.

Valencia Tellería, Angel, ed.

1990a *Investigación epidemiologica nacional de la enfermedad de Chagas.* La Paz: Ministerio de Previsión y Salud Pública.

1990b *Estudio de base para control de Chagas, Chaguaya-Provincia Arce, Tarija,* vol. RUC 03879931. La Paz: Valencia & Associates.

Valencia, Angel, Abraham Jemio, and Ana Maria Aguilar

1989 *Memorias: Taller sobre la enfermedad de Chagas en Bolivia, 13 y 14 Septiembre.* La Paz: Ministerio de Previsión Social y Salud Pública.

Van Lindert, Paul, and August Van Westen

1991 Household shelter strategies in comparative perspective: Evidence from low-income groups in Bamako and La Paz. *World Development* 19 (8): 1007–28.

Van Voorhis, W., L. Schlekey, and H. Trong

1991 Molecular mimicry by *Trypanosoma cruzi:* The F1-160 epitope that mimics mammalian nerve cells can be mapped to a 12-amino acid peptide. *Proceedings of the National Academy of Science* (USA) 88:5993–97.

Varas-Reyes, Victor

1988 *El Castellano Popular en Tarija.* Segunda edicion. Tarija: Varas-Reyes.

Vaughan, D., and W. Feindt

1973 Initial settlement and intracity movement of migrants in Monterrey, Mexico. *Journal of the American Institute of Planners* 39:388–401.

Velasco Giacoman, Luis

1994 *Sistemas de construcción en zonas chagasicas y un estudio de mercado de materiales no locales.* La Paz: Pro Habitat.

Vellard, Jehan

1956 Causas biologicas de la desaparición de los Indios Americanos. *Boletín del instituto Riva-Agüero* (Pontifica Universidad Catholica del Perú) 2:77–93.

Vieira, C.B., and R.A. Godoy

1963 Resposta motora do esofago nao ectásico a agentes colinérgicos na moléstia de Chagas. *Revista Goiana de Medicina* 9:21–28.

Villarroel, F., H. Schenone, M. Contrera, A. Rojas, and E. Fernández

1991 Enfermedad de Chagas en el Altiplano Chileno: Aspectos epidemiológicos, parasitológicos y clínicos. *Boletín Chileno Parasitología* 46:61–69.

Voltarelli, J.C., E.A. Donadi, R.P. Falcao

1987 Immunosuppression in human acute Chagas' disease. *Transactions of the Royal Society of Tropical Medicine and Hygiene* 81:169.

Wallace, F.G.
   1979 Biology of the Kinetoplastidae of arthropods. In *Biology of the Kinetoplastidae* vol. 2, ed. W.H.R. Lumsden and D.A. Evans, 213–40. London: Academic Press.

Wassén, S. Henry
   1972 A medicine-man's implements and plants in a Tiahuanacoid tomb in highland Bolivia. *Etnologiska Studier* (Göteborg) 32:8–114.

Wayar, Toro
   1991 Interview by J. Bastien, Sucre, Bolivia, June 20, tape recording.

Webb, D.J.T.
   1985 Low cost housing and parasite vectors. *Parasitology Today* 1 (2): 65–66.

Webb, D.J.T., and A.J. Lockwood
   1987 *Brepak Operator's Manual.* Watford: Building Research Establishment/ Crown.

Weinke, T., K. Ueberreiter, and M. Alexander
   1988 Cardiac morbidity due to Chagas' disease in a rural community in Bolivia. *Epidemiology and Infection* 101:655–60.

Weiss, H.
   1995 Dust to dust: Transforming the American cemetery. *Tikkun* 10:21–25.

Wendel, S., and J.C.P. Diaz
   1992 Transfusion-transmitted Chagas' disease. In *Chagas' Disease (American trypanosomiasis): Its Impact on Transfusion and Clinical Medicine,* ed. S. Wendel, Z. Brenner, M. Camargo, and A. Rassi. Sao Paulo, Brazil: ISBT-Sociedad Brasileira de Hematologia e Hemoterapia.

Wheeler, J., E. Pires-Ferreira, and P. Kailicke
   1976 Preceramic animal utilization in the central Peruvian Andes. *Science* 194:483–90.

Wiesinger, D.
   1956 Die bedeutung der umweltfaktoren für den saugakt von *Triatoma infestans. Acta Tropica* (Amsterdam) 13:97–141.

Wolf, Eric
   1955 Types of Latin American peasantry: A preliminary discussion. *American Anthropologist* 57:452–55.

Wolf, Stewart, and Thomas Almy
   1949 Experimental observations on cardiospasm in man. *Gastroenterology* 13: 400–421.

Wood, S.F.
   1951 Importance of feeding and defecation times of insect vectors in transmission of Chagas' disease. *Journal of Economic Entomology* 44:52–54.

Woodruff, A.W.
   1965 Darwin's health in relation to his voyage to South America. *British Medical Journal* (1) 1: 745–50.

Woody, Norman C., and Hannah B. Woody
   1955 American trypanosomiasis (Chagas' disease): First indigenous case in the United States. *Journal of the American Medical Association* 159 (7): 676–77.

World Bank
1993 *World Development Report 1993—Investing in Health.* New York: Oxford University Press.

World Health Organization (WHO)
1985 Chagas' disease in the region of the Americas. *Weekly Epidemiological Record* 60:37.

1990 Chagas disease, frequency and geographical distribution. *Weekly Epidemiological Record* 65 (34): 257–61.

1991 *Control of Chagas Disease.* WHO Technical Report Series 811. Geneva.

1994 *Workplan of the Task Force on Operational Research on Chagas Disease.* Document TDR/INF/CHA/94.1. Geneva.

1996 Workplan of the task torce on operational research on Chagas disease. *TDRnews* (March).

World Health Organization (WHO) and UNICEF (United Nations Children's Fund.
1978 *Primary Health Care: A Joint Report by the Director-General of the World Health Organization and the Executive Director of the United Nations Children Fund.* Geneva-New York: WHO.

Wren, R.W., ed.
1972 *Potter's New Cylopedia of Medicinal Herbs and Preparations.* New York: Harper and Row.

Yoshida, N., R. Mortara, M.F. Araguth, J. González, and M. Russo
1989 Metacylic neutralizing effects of monoclonal antibody 10D8 directed to the 35- and 50-kilodalton surface glycoconjugates of *Trypanosoma cruzi. Infection and Immunology* 57:1663–67.

Young, D.B, R. Lathigra, and R. Hendrix
1988 Stress proteins are immune targets in leprosy and tuberculosis. *Proceedings of the National Academy of Science* (USA) 85:4267–70.

Zalles A., Jaime
1996 Personal correspondence to Joseph Bastien, February 26.

Zambra, Eduardo R.
1944 *La enfermedad de Chagas. Su historia. Estudio de la enfermedad de chagas en el norte Santafesino (R. Argentina).* Buenos Aires.

Zarate, L.G.
1980 The biology and behavior of *Triatoma barberi.* I. Blood meal source and infection with *Tripanosoma cruzi. Journal of Medical Entomology* 17 (2): 103–16.

Zeballos, J.L., R. Zumaran, and A. Valencia
1978 Investigación epidemiológica de la enfermedad de Chagas en Bolivia. *Revista Médica de la Universidad San Simon* 2 (2): 149–53.

Zeledón, R.R.
1969 The camouflage of *Triatoma dimidiata* and the epidemiology of Chagas disease in Costa Rica. *Boletín Chileno de Parasitología* 24 (1): 106–8.

1974 Epidemiology, modes of transmission and reservoir host of Chagas' disease. In *Trypanosomias and Leishmaniasis with Special Reference to Chagas' Disease,* vol. 20, Ciba Foundation Symposium. Amsterdam: Elsevier.

1983 Vectores de la enfermedad de Chagas y sus características ecofisiológicas. *Interciencia* 8 (6): 834–35.

Zeledón, R.R., and J.E. Rabinovich

1981 Chagas' disease: An ecological appraisal with special emphasis on its insect vectors. *Annual Review of Entomology* 26:101–33.

Zeledón, R., G. Solano, L. Burstin, and J.C. Swarta Walder

1975 Epidemiological pattern of Chagas' disease in an endemic area of Costa Rica. *American Journal of Tropical Medicine and Hygiene* 24 (2): 214.

Zhang, Q., M. Tibayrenc, and F.J. Ayala

1988 Linkage disequilibrium in natural populations of *Trypanosoma cruzi* (flagellate), the agent of Chagas' disease. *Journal of Protozoology* 35 (1): 81–85.

Zippin, C.

1956 An evaluation of the removal method of estimating animal populations. *Biometrics* 12:163–89.

Zuidema, R.T.

1964 *The Ceque System of Cuzco: The Social Organization of the Capital of the Incas.* Leiden: E.J.Brill.

Zuna, Hugo, Mario Recacoechea, Hernán Bermudez, Aimé De Muynck, and Lucila Cardozo

1979 Infección chagasica en trabajadores agricolas temporales y sus familias, Proyecto Abapo-Izozog, Chaco Boliviano. *Boletín Informativo del CENETROP* 5:16–29.

Zuna, H., C. La Fuente, and E. Valdez

1985 Prospective study of transmission of *Trypanosoma cruzi* by blood in Bolivia [English abstract]. *Annales des Sociétés Belges de Médecine Tropicale, de Parasitologie et Mycologie Humaine et Animale* 65 (suppl. 1): 107–13.

Index

Rats, as hosts for *T. cruzi,* 194, 195
Reed, Walter, 8
Regalsky, Pablo, 92, 104, 136, 143, 147, 153, 236n.4, 236n.8
Regenerator (herbal remedy), 39–42, 44
Religion, as motivation in health projects, 110
Repolarization disorders, 204
Reproductive cycle: of *Triatoma infestans,* 174–75; of *Trypanosoma cruzi,* 161
Reservoir hosts: animals and *T. cruzi,* 194–95; vectorial transmission of *T. cruzi* and, 192
Residentes (residents): health education and, 132; housing in urban Bolivia and, 100
Respiratory infections, and ethnomedicine in Bolivia, 68
Restorative proctocolectomy, 74–75
Rheumatic fever, 85
Rhodnius pallescens, 186, 189
Rhodnius prolixus, as vector for *T. cruzi:* defecation rate, 59, 177; feeding activities of, 176; importance of compared to other species of vectors, 186, 188, 189, 191; pheromones in feces of, 174; roof thatching and, 97
Ritual: Kallawaya herbalists and misfortune ritual for Chagas' disease, 30–34; roof thatching in Bolivia and, 91
Rivas, Daniel, 109, 113
Rochagan. *See* Benznidazole
Rodents, as hosts for *T. cruzi,* 194–95
Romaña's Sign, 7, 8, 16, 49, 108, 196–97
Roofs, of houses: alternative low-cost methods, 234n.14; ceramic tile and Chagas' control, 120; thatching as habitat for triatomines, 97; thatching of as ritual in Bolivia, 91
Rotan palm tree, 40
Rothhammer, F., 19
Rural areas, epidemiology of Chagas' disease in Bolivia, 47
Ruta chalapensis, 43

Sajjra wayra (troublesome wind), 69
Samay (breath), 37–38
Sánchez, Daniel O., 168
Sánchez de Lozada, Gonzalo, 103, 104

Sangre de Drago (Croton roborensis), as herbal medicine, 40, 130
Satureja boliviana, 43
Sayaña (house), 92–93, 96, 140
Sayre, as herbal medicine, 37
Schaudinn, F., 1
Schizodemes, and *T. cruzi* strains, 163
Schizotrypanum, 159
Schofield, C. J., 237n.1
Schurria octoarustica, 43
Seasonality, and vectorial transmission of *T. cruzi,* 192–93
Secretariat of Health (SOH, Bolivia), xx, 67, 128, 182, 233n.2, 235n.2, 236n.1
Sensano, Ruth, xviii, 46, 107–23, 135, 148
Serological methods, for diagnosis of Chagas' disease, 219
Serum neutralization, 211
Shamans, and Culture Context Model for Chagas' prevention, 135
Side effects: of benznidazole, 222–23; of gentian violet, 224; of nifurtimox, 221
Sleeping sickness: Chagas' disease compared to, 10–11; discovery of causative agent, 1; discovery of Chagas' disease and, 13
Smallpox, 27
Social factors: economic impact of chronic Chagas' disease, 84, 149–53; spread of Chagas disease in Andes, 22–24. *See also* Class; Culture
Sociology, and interdisciplinary approach to prevention of Chagas' disease, 147
SOH/CCH Chagas Control Pilot Program, 182, 233n.2, 235n.2, 236n.1, 236n.7
Spain, colonialism and *T. infestans,* 26–28
Spartum junceum, 42
Spiders, as predator of *T. infestans,* 43
Spirituality, and Culture Context Model for Chagas' prevention, 140
Spontaneous abortion, and Chagas' disease, 61, 230n.8
Standen, V., 19
Stewart, George, 162, 198, 236–37n.1
Strains, of *T. cruzi:* adaptation in Andes and, 20; classification of and impact on pathology, 163–65; clinical manifestations and, 81; colon pathology and, 22;